D1270950

Gerstäcker's Louisiana

'Gerstäcker's Louisiana

❧ ❧ ❧ ❧ ❧ ❧ ❧ ❧

FICTION AND TRAVEL SKETCHES
FROM ANTEBELLUM TIMES
THROUGH RECONSTRUCTION

Gerstäcker, Friedrich, 1816-1872

❧ ❧ ❧ ❧ ❧ ❧ ❧ ❧

Edited and Translated by Irene S. Di Maio

LOUISIANA STATE UNIVERSITY PRESS BATON ROUGE

Released from
Samford University Library

Samford University Library

Published by Louisiana State University Press
Copyright © 2006 by Louisiana State University Press
All rights reserved
Manufactured in the United States of America
FIRST PRINTING

DESIGNER: Laura Roubique Gleason
TYPEFACE: Minion with Electra LH display
TYPESETTER: The Composing Room of Michigan, Inc.
PRINTER AND BINDER: Edwards Brothers, Inc.

Library of Congress Cataloging-in-Publication Data
Gerstäcker, Friedrich, 1816–1872
Gerstäcker's Louisiana : fiction and travel sketches from antebellum times through Reconstruction /
translated and edited by Irene S. Di Maio.
p. cm.
Includes bibliographical references and index.
ISBN 0-8071-3146-6 (cloth : alk. paper)
1. Louisiana—Description and travel.   2. Louisiana—Social life and customs.   3. Louisiana—
Fiction.   4. Gerstäcker, Friedrich, 1816–1872—Travel—Louisiana.   I. Di Maio, Irene Stocksieker.
II. Title.
F369.G37 2006
917.63'045—dc22
2005035303

Frontispiece: Gerstäcker in his study; drawing by Herbert König from the magazine *Gartenlaube,*
date unknown.

The paper in this book meets the guidelines for permanence and durability of the Committee
on Production Guidelines for Book Longevity of the Council on Library Resources. ∞

F
369
.G37
2006

for

Katherine A. Jensen
Michelle A. Massé
Anna K. Nardo

who gave me words

Contents

Acknowledgments

This project is a source of much joy because it has enabled me to explore the history, literature, and culture of Louisiana, the state that has become my home, and to combine it with my work in German Studies. Many have guided me along the way.

Chance and serendipity play a crucial role in the choice of subject matter that will consume days, months, indeed years, of a scholar's life. Unbeknownst to him, Jeffrey L. Sammons, of Yale University, whose devotion to the writings of some other nineteenth-century German authors I share, first drew my attention to Friedrich Gerstäcker's writing. Learning that Professor Sammons was a member of the Friedrich Gerstäcker Gesellschaft, I wanted to discover what might have piqued his interest in this author with a slightly funny-sounding name who was one of the most widely read German authors in the nineteenth century but has not been embraced by the twentieth-century German literary canon. I soon became fascinated by Gerstäcker's observations on "America" in general and Louisiana in particular. Professor Sammons's scholarship informs this volume, and his support continues to sustain me.

As I began to translate Gerstäcker's Louisiana narratives, my colleagues Katherine A. Jensen, French Studies; Michelle Massé, English; and Anna Nardo, English, all at Louisiana State University, heard me read aloud every single story in this volume. They helped untangle some of the vaguer multiply claused sentences, giving the characters a boost so they could comprehensibly scale a fence to escape or sneak into a cabin on a rescue mission. These colleagues, too, were captivated by Gerstäcker's adventures, appreciating his skill at spinning a suspenseful tale, chuckling at the melodrama, and affirming my conviction that Gerstäcker has much to tell us about Louisiana's history and multicultural society.

A German Academic Exchange Service (Deutscher Akademischer Austauschdienst, DAAD) Short-Term Research Grant and a Publication Grant from the Louisiana Endowment for the Humanities supported my research in the city library and city archives of Braunschweig, Germany, Gerstäcker's final place of residence. I am indebted to Frau Gärtner of the Stadtbibliothek Braunschweig for sending me preliminary materials and arranging for my work in the library.

She and the other librarians cheerfully bent the rules and indulged this American's habit of keeping all the books stacked high on the study table, reassuringly at hand. Manfred R. W. Garzmann, director of the Stadtarchiv Braunschweig, received me with his customary cup of tea at the new city archives. The clear and precise organization of the materials there greatly facilitated my research. Thomas Ostwald, chairman of the Friedrich Gerstäcker Gesellschaft, Gerstäcker enthusiast, biographer, bibliographer, and editor, readily answered questions brought up by my archival explorations. I appreciated the private tour of the Gerstäcker Museum in Braunschweig, where the surviving "exotic" artifacts that Gerstäcker collected on his world travels are displayed.

Of course, Gerstäcker's Louisiana also brought research very much closer to home, to the beautiful Hill Memorial Library. Germain J. Bienvenu, Public Services; Judy Bolton, head of Public Services; and Associate Dean V. Faye Phillips, all of the Louisiana State University Libraries Special Collections, shared their expertise and led me to materials I would need to annotate this volume. Further assistance was provided by the staffs at Middleton Library, Louisiana State University; the Howard Tilton Memorial Library and the Louisiana Collection, Tulane University; and the Williams Research Center, New Orleans.

I am indebted to several scholars for even more than their research cited in this volume. Brian J. Costello, historian of Pointe Coupée, was generous beyond any expectations in reading and commenting on this manuscript, guiding me through the courthouse records in New Roads, and sharing his knowledge about the parish and its people, to whom he is so devoted. Carl A. Brasseaux at the Center for Louisiana Studies, University of Louisiana at Lafayette, promptly provided me with resources I had difficulty locating. Werner Sollors, African and African-American Studies, English, and American Civilization, Harvard University, has, through his Longfellow Project, helped me to place my work in the larger context of the multilingual literature of the United States and encouraged this translation project.

Further, Kazuko Ohta, International Studies, Kyoritsu Women's University, Japan, has taught me much about Louisiana culture. Frank de Caro and Rosan Jordan's *Louisiana Sojourns: Travelers' Tales and Literary Journeys* gave me hope that Gerstäcker's writings would find a new audience. John Lowe, English, Louisiana State University, pointed the way toward antebellum literature of the South. Early on, Christine Smith, then National Park Service coordinator at the German-American Cultural Center in Gretna, Louisiana, invited me to participate in an inaugural lecture series. The audience at the center warmly received excerpts from Gerstäcker's writings, being particularly moved by his treatment of the immigrant experience. I thank Neal Cronin, English, Louisiana State University, for preparing the visuals, and my lovely daughter, Lara, for assisting with them and getting me over that Mississippi River bridge to Gretna. Brigitta Malm, longtime supporter of the study of German culture in Louisiana, presented me with material on Gerstäcker upon every return from her native city of Braunschweig. Robert Chumbley, French Studies, Louisiana State University, reviewed my translations of the French songs, and James L. Griffen, Agronomy, Louisiana State University, gave me a crash lesson on weeds.

My colleague Margaret R. Parker, Spanish, at Louisiana State University graciously arranged a meeting with Maureen Hewitt of LSU Press, who invited me to submit the manuscript. Since then, MaryKatherine Callaway, director, provided insightful advice, and the manuscript came under the care of John Easterly, general editor, and Lee Sioles, managing editor, whom I thank for their pointers and patience. I also appreciate Spencer Wood's assistance in the manuscript's preparation and Elizabeth Gratch's warmth and enthusiasm during the copyediting stage. Finally, I want to thank my anonymous first and second readers. Reader number one captured what Gerstäcker is about, and reader number two, a historian, I presume, nudged this literary scholar into providing more annotations about Louisiana history. The suggestions that both readers provided assisted me in expanding the commentary; any remaining deficiencies are clearly mine.

Gerstäcker's Louisiana

Introduction

When Friedrich Gerstäcker first set foot—and paddle—in Louisiana in March 1838, he was a young man of twenty-one, whose driving, but unfocused, ambition had been simply "to go to America." The journey itself was his purpose. On the final stretch of a trip originating in New York, loneliness prompted him to curtail his journey into Texas and turn back eastward to the Red River. He was just passing through. He navigated his slim canoe through the rapid, log-jammed waters of the clay-colored river, circumvented the Great Raft of logs north of Shreveport on a flatboat wending its way through lakes and bayous, then turned his little vessel into the "mighty Mississippi," and finally, during a lashing storm, boarded a steamer headed for New Orleans. Gerstäcker had accomplished his goal. He did not yet know that what he saw was the embryo of his own literary work. In 1842 he returned to Louisiana and for a year managed the Ferry Hotel in Pointe Coupée, then considered the most beautiful garden and plantation land along the Mississippi. But the institution of slavery sustained the beauty, economy, and development of this area and permeated much of its society. On his final visit to southern Louisiana in 1867, Gerstäcker observed the great destruction and enormous social upheaval caused by the Civil War. Gerstäcker's experiences of Louisiana—its landscape, its people, and its "Peculiar Institution"—during these three brief sojourns became a sustaining resource for his travel books, short stories, and novels.

BIOGRAPHICAL SKETCH

Friedrich Wilhelm Christian Gerstäcker was born on May 18, 1816, in Hamburg. His father, Karl Friedrich Gerstäcker, and his mother, Luise Friederika (née Herz), were both opera singers, and it is to the family's peripatetic life in Gerstäcker's formative years that scholars often attribute his wanderlust and lack of rootedness. In 1820 his father, a prominent tenor of his day, joined the court opera in Dresden, which was under the direction of Carl Maria von Weber. The following year Gerstäcker's father gained even more security for his family by obtaining a life contract with the court theater in Kassel. Unfortunately, Karl Friedrich died of tuberculosis at age thirty-five. Although the elector of Hessia-

Kassel provided Gerstäcker's mother with a small pension, she was not able to support her three children and sent the two older ones—nine-year-old Friedrich and his sister, Molly (1819–93)—to live with their aunt and uncle, an actor, in Braunschweig, while she settled in Leipzig with her younger son, August (1821–1906). When Gerstäcker's aunt died, the children returned to their mother.

Gerstäcker received a secondary education—often exasperating his teachers with his many pranks. Like most boys of that era, he devoured the adventurous tales of James Fenimore Cooper, Walter Scott, and Daniel Defoe. At this stage of his life young Friedrich already wanted to go to America or to study natural sciences at the university in preparation for a career of travel and scientific expeditions. Not being able to afford a university education for her son, but wanting him to get a firm foundation, Gerstäcker's mother sent him to Kassel to study for a commercial career, despite his protestations. Gerstäcker soon left the school, returning to Leipzig on foot, still determined to go to the United States to begin a new life. His mother stalled by insisting that he receive training in agriculture to prepare for such an undertaking. From 1835 to 1837 Gerstäcker was an apprentice on the Haubitz estate in Grimma, Saxony, where he also had the opportunity to practice marksmanship and engage in an ultimately disappointing romantic adventure. In May 1837, barely twenty-one, he sailed from Bremerhaven to New York on the *Constitution*.

At the beginning of his six-year sojourn in North America, Gerstäcker journeyed on foot and by water from New York to Niagara Falls, Cleveland, Cincinnati, Illinois, St. Louis, Little Rock, into the Texas/Louisiana borderlands, then to Shreveport, past Nachitoches, to New Orleans, and, finally, back up the Mississippi River. His temperament was particularly suited for life in the United States, for he was willing to take on all kinds of odd jobs to get by. After his partner in a cigar store in New York City cheated him of his investment, Gerstäcker, on his travels—primarily up and down the Arkansas and Mississippi rivers— chopped wood, made chocolates for an apothecary, served as a silversmith's apprentice, cut cane for pipes, traded his catch for provisions, herded cattle, and was a steamboat cook and stoker. He earned a teaching certificate in Cincinnati but accomplished this more to prove he could than with any serious intent of becoming a teacher, since he had no desire to become a "sedentary philistine."[1]

Gerstäcker spent the major portion of his time in Arkansas. There he briefly attempted to farm with three German partners at the mouth of the Fourche La Fave River, but the enterprise failed because Charles Roetken,[2] the only partner with capital, gained from the sale of his Ferry Hotel in Pointe Coupée, Louisi-

ana, was excessively dominating toward all and even abusive to one of the partners, Korn,[3] who left for Louisiana to make use of his skills as an accountant
there. In Arkansas Gerstäcker lived mostly in the backwoods, subsisting on, indeed almost possessed by, hunting. Gerstäcker had a particular affection for the
independent, honest backwoods people, who lived solitary lives but always
were ready to lend a neighbor a hand in times of need. His descriptions of pioneer life in Arkansas have proved so accurate and important for the history of
that state that in 1957 he was posthumously declared an honorary citizen of
Arkansas. Finally, tired of knocking about and homesick, Gerstäcker took up
Korn's invitation to come to Louisiana. For a year he managed the very same
Ferry Hotel in Pointe Coupée owned by his former partner Roetken to earn
money for his passage home.

Upon his return to Germany, Gerstäcker learned that he was already a published author, for his mother had given the journal entries he sent her regularly
to a family friend. After editing these entries, the friend passed them on to
Robert Heller, who published excerpts in his magazine, *Rosen*.[4] Gerstäcker's
first literary endeavor was the preparation—by considerable expansion—of
the entire journal manuscript for publication as *Adventures and Hunting Expeditions through the United States of North America* (1844).[5]

Gerstäcker then tried his hand at writing dramas, which were never a critical success, but he met his future wife, the actress Anna Aurora Sauer, while
producing his plays in Dresden. Subsequently, Gerstäcker moved to Leipzig to
earn money as a bookseller and translator of English and American fiction. He
labored intensively on the translations and on his own writings as well so that
he would be in a financial position to marry. The couple wed on February 11,
1845, and had two sons and a daughter.

The process of translating tales of immigration and adventure most likely
moved Gerstäcker to try his own hand at recreating his American experiences
and observations in fictional form. The novels and short story collections he
translated early on include Charles Rowcroft's *Tales of the Colonies: The Adventures of an Emigrant*, set in Australia; G. Poulett Cameron's *Travel Adventures in Georgia, Circassia, and Russia;* William Gilmore Simms's *Wigwam and
the Cabin;* Mrs. Seba [Elizabeth Oakes] Smith's *Western Captive: or, Times of
Tecumseh;* and, most famous of all, Herman Melville's *Omoo*. These narratives
appealed to nineteenth-century Europeans because they satisfied both the contemporary taste for exoticism and the readers' desire to learn about various regions of the world during an age of colonialism and expansion. Gerstäcker's
first novel, *The Regulators in Arkansas* (1846),[6] which appeared in New York and

London in two different English translations the following year, is an early German detective story that pits backwoodsmen and an Indian couple against horse thieves and a murderer. This novel, along with *The River Pirates of the Mississippi* (1848),[7] is now included in the canon of German youth classics.

Gerstäcker became involved in the revolution of 1848, joining the Leipzig Literary Association, whose members, like most liberals of the pre-March period (the period before the revolution broke out in Berlin in 1848), wanted a united Germany. The liberals believed that constitutional reform, giving the German citizens a greater voice in government, would only be possible in a nation that was unified rather than governed by thirty-nine different autocratic rulers. Gerstäcker also led a company of Leipzig sharpshooters during the revolution.

Realizing that the public was not much interested in reading travel literature and fiction during these tumultuous times, he thought it would be an opportune moment to travel again and acquire experience and material for future works. Financed by the revolutionary Frankfurt Parliament and the prestigious publisher Cotta, Gerstäcker set out on March 18, 1849, to examine the conditions of the German colonies in Brazil, Argentina, and Chile. Despite warnings that he would perish, he risked his life crossing the Cordilleras from Buenos Aires to Valparaiso in deep winter, accompanied only by two Indian guides, whose trustworthiness he had no way of ascertaining since he did not understand their language. From Valparaiso he sailed to participate in the gold rush in California—having already translated two monographs on the gold rush by J. Tyrwhitt-Brooks—but most of the gold Gerstäcker scraped together there was spent for supplies. He then boarded a whaling ship to the South Sea Islands (Sandwich Islands, Maiao, and Tahiti) and Australia, where he again risked life and limb by making a two-thousand-mile trip up the Murray River in a primitive canoe he had hollowed out of heavy gumwood. His final port of embarkation was Java, from which he returned home on February 2, 1852. This extended trip—as was the case in the past and would be again in the future—provided Gerstäcker with a wealth of material for travel accounts, short stories, and novels. His own works now satisfied the Germans' desire to learn about faraway places, and his short stories about Indians and slavery in Louisiana continue to be reprinted in Germany.[8] Gerstäcker became one of the most popular and respected *Volksschriftsteller,* a writer for the people. Such was his celebrity that a sea captain Gerstäcker met in Murphy's New Diggins during the California gold rush named his schooner after the author,[9] and Gerstäcker and his adventures were the subject of a travel book for juveniles.[10]

In August 1854 Gerstäcker accepted the duke of Saxe-Coburg's invitation and moved his family to the guesthouse of the Rosenau castle near Coburg. He embarked on a second trip to South America in 1860. Although the trip—with its itinerary of Panama, Ecuador, Peru, Chile, Argentina, and Brazil—lasted eighteen months, Gerstäcker curtailed his plans somewhat when he learned of his wife's illness. Sadly, she died before his return. Gerstäcker's response to depression over his wife's death was to work all the more furiously. In the following year he also joined the duke of Coburg-Gotha's excursion to northern Africa (Cairo, Luxor, and Karnak) as a diversion; unfortunately, the duke took full credit for Gerstäcker's account of that trip. Coburg was filled with too many associations with his beloved wife, so Gerstäcker moved to Gotha, where, during the following year, at age forty-seven, he married nineteen-year-old Maria Luise Fischer van Gaasbeek. He had first met Maria Luise when she was seven, while he was a guest of her father, the Dutch assistant resident in Java. They had two daughters. In 1866 Gerstäcker moved his family—and his vast collection of exotica—to Dresden.

Gerstäcker embarked on his final long journey on July 13, 1867. It took him to North America, Mexico, Ecuador, the West Indies, and Venezuela, from which he returned on June 4, 1868. One highlight of the resulting travel account of the North American portion of the journey is his trip out on a train, with Gen. William Tecumseh Sherman, to Council Bluffs, Iowa, where he observed a powwow between the American government and the leaders of various Indian tribes. Another highlight is his observations of the American South during Reconstruction.

In the 1860s Gerstäcker received many honors and honorary memberships in societies. But he did not set much store by, and even satirized, that era's mania for titles. He moved his family for the last time to the more provincial city of Braunschweig, having grown weary of interruptions when visitors arrived unannounced at his doorstep. Indeed, visitors could not even easily reach the doorstep in Braunschweig—they had to be rowed across the Oker River, which flowed gently in front of Gerstäcker's house and dock at the landing, an exotic evocation of the author's many adventures. During the final year of his life Gerstäcker's energies sometimes flagged, and he seemed to grow more irritable. Nevertheless, he did accept the prince of Coburg-Coharry's invitation to join his trip to India, China, and Japan. But he would not make this journey. On May 31, 1872, following an altercation with some boys who had disturbed the nightingale's nest opposite his study window, as well as with the watchman, whom he accused of negligence, Gerstäcker died of a stroke at age fifty-six.

GERSTÄCKER'S NARRATIVES OF LOUISIANA

On his travels Gerstäcker recorded his experiences in copybooks, special note-books made in England that duplicated the writer's entries on an underleaf. During his first sojourn in the United States he periodically sent these copy-books home to his mother; on subsequent journeys he sent the copies to edi-tors and publishers, who printed excerpts from them. Upon every return to Germany he edited the travel journals for publication. Stories, sketches, and even novels based on these experiences soon followed. By the end of his life Gerstäcker had written and published, in addition to four novels set in North America, novels located in Tahiti, Australia, Java, Brazil, Ecuador, Peru, Chile, Venezuela, and Mexico. The general critical consensus, however, is that Ger-stäcker's works of North America have the most authentic ring. This is attrib-utable, in part, to Gerstäcker's having spent more time on the North American continent than anywhere else but mostly to his true affinity with, or at least keen insight into, aspects of the American ethos.

My reading of a typescript copy of the notebooks that became the basis for Gerstäcker's first travel book, *Adventures and Hunting Expeditions in the United States of North America*—and a perusal of these copybooks themselves—reveal that Gerstäcker was initially not interested in writing about Louisiana. He had made only cursory notations about his first trip through Louisiana territory early in 1838,[11] and he concluded his final copybook in July 1842 with a single paragraph concerning his presence in Louisiana:

> I am now in Louisiana while I am writing these lines, and life here is too simple and boring even to consider describing it worthwhile. If I wished to express my views more extensively on the abominable slavery with its un-pleasantries and dangers, that would not at all be in keeping with the in-tention of these pages, which are supposed to be a picture of hunting in the western states. But since hunting in Louisiana is nothing in particular, ex-cept for in the wildest swamps and canebrakes, and I do not have the least desire to see the aforementioned canebrakes and swamps, I want to con-clude these lines. Let a guiding hand protect them and see that they safely reach my precious homeland.
>
> May the great spirit give us all a blue sky and happy dreams.
>
> F. Gerstäcker[12]

I know of only a few other extant records of Gerstäcker's Louisiana so-journs. A brief note to his best friend, Adolph Hermann Schultz, headed "State of Louisiana. New Orleans, April 1, 1838" expressed disappointment that no mail awaited him in that port. While he was bagging bears and panthers in the wilds of Texas and hunting and camping with Indians, he had felt such a great longing to hear from his loved ones.[13] Later that year he reflected on his activities in North America, mentioning that he had gone down to New Orleans twice on the steamer *Chillicothe*, once as a stoker, the second time as a deckhand to earn some wages.[14] In his last letter to his friend, sent from "Bayou Sarah" on December 7, 1842, Gerstäcker again professed homesickness and his intent to return to Germany at least for a while. He claimed he had become a proper gentleman, having exchanged his hunting clothes for a fashionable summer suit of cotton and the pure night air for a stuffy room buzzing with mosquitoes.[15] The letter from Pointe Coupée, Louisiana, dated March 7, 1843, which accompanied the final section of the journal, informed his mother of prospects for a good position in New Orleans (which does not appear to have materialized) and assured her that because he managed to live so frugally, he would soon have enough money saved to return home any time he chose.[16]

The entries in the copybooks are sketchy, in any event, for during the years he spent in North America Gerstäcker did not intend to publish his writing and merely jotted down his experiences as a personal record. Moreover, tramping through virgin forests and keeping afloat on mighty rivers left Gerstäcker precious little time for literary reflection. On subsequent trips he would keep much more detailed journals, using a "Manyfold writer" during time aboard ship in particular to catch up on his entries.[17] Further, the main focus of *Adventures and Hunting Expeditions in the United States of North America* is exactly what the title indicates. The final year spent managing the hotel in Pointe Coupée was not filled with the kind of adventures Gerstäcker enjoyed during his first year in the United States, when he made his way from New York to New Orleans with few resources save wit, flexibility, and good marksmanship. And the relatively docile alligators Gerstäcker found in Louisiana certainly were no match for the bear Gerstäcker encountered on a hunting expedition in Arkansas that left him wounded and killed six dogs and his young English hunting partner.

But Louisiana would prove fertile ground for Gerstäcker's literary imagination. Eventually, he did record his experiences of Louisiana in the first published version of the early sojourn in the United States, and he elaborated on these experiences for the second edition, included in his collected works.[18] His travel book treats three distinct areas of the state: the rough frontier around Shreveport, the rich plantation country along the Mississippi, and cosmopolitan New Orleans. Decades later he augmented these recollections with little sketches and anecdotes. The narratives with a Louisiana setting in Gerstäcker's very first collection of short stories and sketches, *Pictures of the Mississippi: Light and Dark Sides of Transatlantic* (1847–48),[19] take as their central theme precisely the "abominable slavery, with its unpleasantries and dangers" during the antebellum period. The very different topography and culture of northern Louisiana, where woodcutters risk their all to exploit the virgin forest, is the site of the short story "On Red River." New Orleans is one of the nodes along the Mississippi River in the two novels of immigration, *To America! A Book for the People* (1855) and *In America: A Picture of American Life in Recent Times* (1872),[20] in which Gerstäcker's fictitious but exemplary characters meet up and share their experiences. In this port of entry the exaggerated hopes of Gerstäcker's immigrants are first dashed (*To America!*). During Reconstruction, New Orleans becomes the site of racial turmoil as ruined plantation aristocrats reassert themselves through the Ku Klux Klan and liberated blacks insist on their right to public accommodation (*In America*), while German travelers and immigrants try to orient themselves to the scene.

GERSTÄCKER IN THE CONTEXT OF NINETEENTH-CENTURY GERMAN LITERATURE ON LOUISIANA

Travel Books

European explorers and conquerors of the Louisiana Territory laid claims as vast as the area they desired to possess. Early accounts of the region that would become the present state of Louisiana, authored by the Spanish, French, and British colonizers, reveal that the territory these men claimed for the glory of God and country was both enticing and forbidding. From the rich, alluvial soil so desirable for cultivation sprang dense forest and tangled undergrowth that made the terrain impenetrable. Navigators were repulsed and confounded by the ubiquitous waterways, above all the "mighty" Mississippi, that had lured them with the promise of easy access. Whereas some native tribes proffered generous hospitality, many exhibited treacherous hostility. The specter of death in the remote wilderness from illness and disease, accident, the elements, murder from within and attacks from without, hovered tenaciously over every venture to stake a claim. Hernando de Soto's demise at the confluence of the Red and Mississippi rivers in 1543 anticipated many a European's fate.[21]

By the nineteenth century Louisiana was somewhat more settled than it had been in the colonial period, and the steamboat—despite its newfangled threat of exploding engines—brought an increasing number of travelers to Louisiana, including those from German-speaking lands. Nineteenth-century authors writing in German made significant contributions to the literature of and about Louisiana. Yet research on and bibliographies of this literature, unless conducted and compiled by specialists in German studies, focus primarily on literature written in French and English.[22] Thus, a large body of work in German is not generally known to readers interested in the representation of Louisiana's history, society, and culture. Gerstäcker's unique contributions can only be enhanced if the reader is reminded that other Germans visited and wrote about Louisiana, especially during the antebellum period.[23]

While settlers from German lands were present in Louisiana as early as 1719, the earliest published German accounts of Louisiana were written after Louisiana was admitted to the Union as the eighteenth state in 1812. Because their authors came from different backgrounds and had a wide range of reasons for being here, these journals and travel books offer diverse perspectives. J. G. Flügel made brief entries about the challenges of daily life in the journal he kept in English during his final year as a trader on the Mississippi River (1817).[24] In the years 1822–24 the naturalist Friedrich Paul Wilhelm, duke of Würtemberg, undertook an exploratory expedition up the Mississippi, Ohio, and Missouri rivers in search of new species. He enjoyed the hospitality and kindness of fellow Germans and the French in New Orleans before heading up to Pointe Coupée, the base for numerous expeditions to collect specimens of reptiles and birds and the site of a hunt with Tunica Indians and French Creoles, all of which he vividly describes in *Travels in North America, 1822–1824*.[25] The travel book of Bernhard, duke "in" Saxony-Weimar-Eisenach, *Reise Sr. Hohheit des Herzogs Bernhard zu Sachsen-Weimar-Eisenach durch Nordamerika in den Jahren 1825 und 1826*, concentrates on social events and the dynamics between the various races and ethnic groups—especially between the Creoles and the newly arrived Americans—in New Orleans and on the surrounding plantations during his 1825 visit.[26]

Writing extensively on the United States under an alternate pseudonym, C. Sidon, Charles Sealsfield, a monk escaped from a monastery in Moravia, adopts an impersonal style to describe Louisiana's history and geopolitical organization, perhaps to mask his identity,[27] in *Die Vereinigten Staaten von Nordamerika, nach ihrem politischen, religiösen und gesellschaftlichen Verhältnisse betrachtet*.[28] Although Sealsfield does not disclose his whereabouts or activities,[29] he, too, voices decided opinions on the characteristics of the various races and ethnic groups of New Orleans. While most German travelers opposed slavery, albeit remaining vexed about how to dismantle that institution without bringing the plantations to ruin, Sealsfield describes blacks and their demeanor in the most negative terms and has fewer qualms than the other travelers and sojourners about the necessity of slavery for the region's agricultural and economic development. Ida Pfeiffer, in contrast, detested slavery. Recounting her stay in New Orleans and Donaldsonville in June 1854, she notes the requisite landmarks, but the overwhelming portion of her narrative is devoted to the institution of slavery. Having witnessed no brutality herself, she cites instances of vicious mistreatment of slaves from an 1839 book, *American Slavery as It Is*. But even this extensive polemic against slavery contains racist overtones.[30]

Travel and immigration from Germany to Louisiana during the Civil War was drastically curtailed and never regained much momentum during the Reconstruction period for reasons having to do with events in Germany as well as with the turmoil in the South. One of the few German visitors was another aristocrat, Ernst von Hesse-Wartegg, who arrived in the post-Reconstruction period and whose work comments on the Civil War's upheaval of plantation culture and its economy, on race relations, commerce, and Louisiana customs and Creole culture.[31]

Themes that these travel books share—and we will discover in Gerstäcker's travel books, too—are the challenges of the wilderness *and* the beauty of nature; the abundance and variety of the exotic fauna and flora; the centrality of the rivers for transportation and commerce and the struggle to contain them; the seductiveness and cruelties of plantation life; New Orleans as a cosmopolitan hub of trade and site of culture and refinement; the violence erupting from the lawless frontier mentality or from the inhumane enforcement of slavery and the seething resentments this institution engenders; the turmoil of Reconstruction and, again and again, the strikingly multiethnic and multiracial society, with its competing immigrant populations and different races existing in extreme tension yet profound proximity.

Fiction

As it did for Gerstäcker, Louisiana sparked the literary imaginative of other nineteenth-century German authors who dwelled there. During the years 1834–37 Gerstäcker's predecessor Charles Sealsfield published a series of five interconnected plantation novels under the general title *Lebensbilder aus der westlichen Hemisphäre*.[32] The action of these novels occurs primarily along the Red River and in the Opelousas and Attakapas regions, although some main characters reside in New Feliciana.[33] But the focus of these novels is neither the place

nor the psychological motivation of individual characters. Rather, the characters, who represent different groups—the aristocratic Virginian, the refined
French Creole, the crude but boundlessly energetic American/Kentuckian, and
the compliant, childlike slaves (with the exception of a few mutinous brutes)—
serve as pawns in an (inherently flawed) ideological struggle to found the new
frontier, whereby, according to Wynfried Kriegleder, Sealsfield equates plantation society with the United States per se.[34] Jeffrey L. Sammons explains Sealsfield's pro-slavery stance, which is uncharacteristic of German authors, as
stemming from his belief in Manifest Destiny and his commitment to Jack-
sonian democracy: "In the plantation novels, property is an element both of
freedom and of social cohesion," and property in slaves is as inviolable as any
other.[35]

Baron Ludwig von Reizenstein, who resided in New Orleans from 1852 until his death in 1885, serialized his novel *Die Geheimnisse von New Orleans* in the
Louisiana Staats-Zeitung in the years 1854–55. Based on the genre of urban mysteries that had begun with Eugène Sue's *Les mystères de Paris* (1842–43) and was
picked up by German-American authors writing mysteries of Philadelphia,
St. Louis, San Francisco, and Cincinnati, this potboiler scandalized the readers
with its tales of hypocrisies and sexual depravity. It culminates in an apocalyp-
tic scene of a black Messiah avenging the injustice of slavery in the American
South.[36]

Finally, an important nineteenth-century German author, Berthold Auerbach, who never set foot on American soil, transports his characters to Louisiana to fight during the Civil War on the side of the Union for the abolition of
slavery in *Das Landhaus am Rhein*. In this novel about Germany and the United
States the German-Jewish author uses discourse concerning Jewish emancipation and integration to advocate black liberation and a unity that does not ab-
negate difference.[37] As diverse as the ideological, political, and social positions
of these authors are, the issue of slavery is central to all of these works.

The short stories about Louisiana included in Gerstäcker's first collection,
Pictures from the Mississippi, comprise the first plantation fiction written in any
language centered in Pointe Coupée and West Feliciana parishes. Subsequent
writers whose works are in the set in these two parishes that face each other
across the Mississippi but have very different political and social histories, share
a deep appreciation of the region's natural beauty and abundance and a fasci-
nation with the complex relationships among it's multiracial and multiethnic
peoples. Their fiction revolves around plantation life, and the institution of
slavery and its aftermath. Mary France Seibert's novel *Zulma: A Story of the Old*

South (1897),[38] a tale of a loyal slave who is shot to death defending her young mistress from the Yankee invaders, falls into the category of nostalgic "moonlight and magnolia" literature,[39] but it gives an accurate picture of Pointe Coupée Parish's history, ethnic composition, and landscape. In contrast, Maurice Denuzière's more recent *Bagatelle* (1978) is an exoticized, slightly salacious bestseller romance centered on what formerly was one of the wealthiest plantations in the parish during the years 1830–1864.[40] Contemporary readers may be most familiar with Pointe Coupée Parish through the fiction of Ernest J. Gaines. Here, at last, the voices of slaves, former slaves, and their descendants are heard in stories like "Bloodline" and the novel *The Autobiography of Miss Jane Pittman*.[41] Gaines's fiction treats the continuing harsh consequences of a society and economy rooted in slavery for blacks in modern times.

Red Heart, a story of West Feliciana: Dedicated to Sir Arthur Conan Doyle,[42] by Louise Butler, a historian of West Feliciana, is a mystery concerned with the vengeance of the Tunica and Houma Indians who had dwelled in the area. It, too, is haunted by ghosts of previous centuries. A recent novel that alludes to plantation life in West Feliciana parish is Valerie Martin's *Property* (2003), narrated from the bitter, limited, first-person perspective of a plantation owner's wife whose father "was obsessed by the negroes" on his West Feliciana plantation.[43] In the works of Gaines and Martin local color—which can be a romanticizing entrapment of plantation literature—gives way to voice, albeit in very different registers.

GERSTÄCKER ON RACE, SLAVERY, AND RECONSTRUCTION

Like most German liberals of his day, who upheld Enlightenment ideals, Gerstäcker opposed slavery and deplored its dehumanizing effects, finding the separation of families particularly abhorrent. He condemned blacks' lack of autonomy and harshly criticized the controlling devices that kept slaves in bondage: illiteracy and religion. Regarding the latter institution, the secular Continental European differed from Christian American and British abolitionists. Despite his opposition to slavery on humane, enlightened principles and his shock and revulsion at its brutalities, Gerstäcker also harbored racist feelings toward blacks (as he did toward Jews), like most German liberals—indeed, like most white abolitionists in general. He accepted the hierarchy of race that was becoming reified in the name of science during the nineteenth century and sometimes voiced a visceral repugnance toward blacks. In one exceptional instance, however, the anecdote "The Houseboy and the Cow," we hear the true voice of a real slave, the irrepressible maid, Mary, who from her safe position atop a fence rail triumphs over the German houseboy Jacob's tribulations with a recalcitrant cow.

Gerstäcker's notions about blacks were particularly conflicted when he returned to Louisiana during the Reconstruction period. His approbation of the slaves' emancipation was undercut by his alarm at the havoc and destruction he saw all around, especially in the beautiful plantation country where he had dwelled. Believing it just that slavery had been abolished, he nevertheless was alarmed that blacks had been given full suffrage immediately. He found them incapable—because they were untrained—of making legal decisions or of casting an informed vote and ridiculous in their aping of upper-class white society. Their ubiquitous presence seems to have offended him, although he sympathized with their plight and worried about their ability to survive the harsh conditions of the immediate future. He often appears to voice the sentiments of whites with whom he must have discussed these matters. Able to critique the mentalities and institutions of the antebellum South that would make it difficult to rebuild the region, he seems less capable of viewing the current position of blacks in a broader context, particularly with respect to the complex labor negotiations involving black workers, the Freedmen's Bureau, and the planters.[44] Underlying sentiments shared by many whites is the perspective of the immigrant. Gerstäcker objected that blacks were given immediate suffrage, whereas immigrants had to wait five years to vote. In this respect Gerstäcker mirrors the entire debate among abolitionists in the antebellum period about whether Negroes were to enjoy gradual or immediate emancipation.[45] Viewed in a broader context, Gerstäcker's discourse about blacks in the United States often echoes Enlightenment discourse about the status of Jews in Germany. The question was, should Jews be granted suffrage immediately, or would they have to become educated—and assimilated—before earning these rights?

Gerstäcker's imaginative work, while not free of stock characters and stereotypes that are the stuff of plantation fiction and often serve an ideological function—the wicked Yankee overseer and slave trader, the indolent planter, the quadroon as the object of desire—allows the author to transcend his own prejudices. Melodrama and suspense in the short stories set in the antebellum period accentuate the brutality of the institution of slavery in scenes in which those who profit from human beings held as property—slaveholders, their overseers, or slave traders—are depicted in pursuit of escaping slaves.[46] Because the escapees are usually women, they are doubly vulnerable as the objects of violent men's lust, a lust predicated on possession, for when the pursuers are hard pressed, property rights trump sexual desire. Yet Gerstäcker's stories also suggest modes of evasion and resistance that, even when ending tragically, allow blacks some autonomy. When the free quadroon Alfons fails to win his beloved Selinde as she is auctioned off in a game of chance and he is shot to death during his subsequent attempt to rescue her, Selinde defies her purchaser by starving herself to death in the story "The Slave." The slaves in "The Planter" collude with their master in a plot to escape to Texas, preferring to go along with him rather than be separated at auction. In this story the dark threat of the slaves' pent-up resentment is also enacted when the lead slave, Hannibal, avenges his brother's mistreatment at the hands of the patroller Rally by drowning him in the Mississippi.[47] In "Jazede" the eponymous heroine is liberated by the combined forces of free and enslaved blacks, an Indian, and a Spanish river smuggler, who sail swiftly down the Mississippi and slip to the safety of Texas territory. Acting outside of unjust, racist laws, these cohorts outrun, outwit, and outsmart their oppressors.

That the elaboration of the social and political position of blacks in Gerstäcker's fiction can provide a broader and deeper understanding of their condition than Gerstäcker's subjective responses in his journals is especially noticeable when we compare the selections "To Louisiana" and "New Orleans" from New Travels through the United States, Mexico, Ecuador, the West Indies and Venezuela,[48] which close the nonfiction section in this volume, with the chapters "New Orleans" and "The Meeting" from his novel In America, set in the Reconstruction period. In the novel Gerstäcker captures the thoughts and emotions of quite diverse characters, including former slaves, two generations of upper-class planters, and the average inhabitants of the city. The novel helps readers understand the intractability of race prejudice and the arbitrary violence it engenders.

Finally, Gerstäcker's writings on race make it clear that race is not always clearly identifiable. From the "numerous Negroes and mulattoes, mestizos, quadroons, with all imaginable shades from white and yellow to black and brown" observed by Gerstäcker's narrator at the port of New Orleans in the chapter "Ashore" in To America; to the free black, Alfons, who is allowed to buy a chance on Selinde because he is not distinguishable from a French Creole; to the blue-eyed quadroon, Jazede, in whom "not one drop of Ethiopian blood could be detected"; to the bronze-skinned daughter of the forest, Saise, whose slightly frizzy raven-black hair enables her abductors to claim she is a runaway slave; to the blue-eyed blonde octoroon, Hebe, of In America, whom the young German artist who rescues her will ultimately take to Germany as his bride, where there is no prejudice against blacks (and where Germans will not be able to detect Hebe's race through the "telltale fingernails"), these characters are undoubtedly conceived to arouse the white readers' sympathies more readily than might a dark-skinned black, but they also underscore the irrationality of race classification in a society obsessed with race. Gerstäcker most likely shared this obsession because it is difficult to imagine that his exotic tales of the antebellum period, addressed to a German audience, were written with the conscious intent to reform, as were his works on immigration.

GERSTÄCKER ON IMMIGRATION

One of Gerstäcker's life projects was to inform immigrants and potential immigrants to the United States about what to expect in the new homeland. His main goal was to provide immigrants with an accurate picture of life in this rough-and-ready country, to deflate unrealistic expectations, and to suggest the character and constitution required of a person seeking to forge a successful new life. Immigrants must banish the European caste mentality, be willing to work hard at all kinds of tasks, be observant, flexible, and ready to learn new ways of doing things. They must guard against those ever ready to part him from money and possessions, beginning with the immigration agents in Germany. Gerstäcker conveyed these observations in a succinct book, *What Is It Really Like in America? A Brief Description of What the Emigrant Must Do and Can Hope and Expect* (1849);[49] in his first, rather flat, novel of immigration, *The Wanderings and Fortunes of Some German Emigrants* (1847);[50] and in the two novels of emigration and immigration excerpted here, *To America!* and its sequel, *In America*.

On both returns to Germany from the United States, Gerstäcker embarked in New Orleans. New Orleans becomes the port of entry for German immigrants in *To America!* The characters, and the reader, are immediately struck by the diversity of that city's population and culture. Crowding the docks are people of all races and gradations of color, of various nationalities and origins. They speak a variety of languages, often mixing different languages in a single sentence and using both French and English in the courts. The coin of several realms used to trade in goods from all over the world is valid currency. This diversity reminds us once again that the United States was never culturally monolithic, Anglocentric, or even wholly northern European.

Gerstäcker's writings tell us about ethnic and racial diversity, transcultural relations, slavery and its aftermath, and multilingualism—issues that are relevant to contemporary United States politics and society. In a passage from *In America* not included in this volume the narrator surveys the various regions of the country from a bird's-eye view, that is, from an imaginary balloon. He sees the industrious, prosperous, yet bucolic North; the devastated South, where freed slaves struggle against coercion, and all passions are unleashed; and the West, with its battle of wilderness against civilization. Despite these bitter conflicts, Gerstäcker's narrator appears optimistic because a single government with common laws has the potential to protect and transcend radical differences: "And yet it is one great united realm—convulsing here, fermenting there—but also peaceful for thousands of miles. But everyone is governed by one single hand, living under the same laws, with the same protections. Nevertheless there is a jumble of different passions and interests of black, red, and white skin, of languages, which were no less confused in ancient days when workers from all the different neighboring countries were called upon to build the mighty tower of Babel."[51]

Gerstäcker understood the tensions and conflicts in the United States prevailing in his time, many of which still reverberate in ours. Coming from a country that was not yet united, he admired the nation's great potential and appreciated the system of justice and government that he believed would ultimately help the United States cohere and thrive. More specifically, as a sojourner and traveler from abroad, who experienced Louisiana in both the antebellum and Reconstruction periods, Gerstäcker may have been unique. Gerstäcker's writings have much to offer concerning the historical, geographical, social, political, and economic dynamics of Louisiana, a state whose culture is both singular and increasingly representative in its multiethnic and multicultural composition. For this reason I offer my translations of Gerstäcker's Louisiana narratives.

About the Translation

Many of Gerstäcker's works originally appeared in journals and newspapers, as was customary in the nineteenth century. In the introduction to each section of this volume I cite the publication information for the works' first appearance in book form, based on the bibliography prepared by Jeffrey L. Sammons, "Friedrich Gerstäcker (10 May 1816–31 May 1872)," and the *Gerstäcker-Verzeichnis*.[1] My translations, however, are based on the texts found in Gerstäcker's collected works. These are the texts to which I have had constant access, and I believe they would be more readily available to a reader desiring to compare my translations to the German original than might the first editions.

The sole instance in which the choice of edition for purposes of translation has been debated concerns Gerstäcker's first work, *Streif- und Jagdzüge durch die Vereinigten Staaten Nordamerikas*, which I translate as *Adventures and Hunting Expeditions through the United States of North America*. Gerstäcker expanded this travel book considerably when he prepared the second edition for his collected works. As noted earlier, Edna L. Steeves and Harrison R. Steeves provided an introduction and notes to the 1968 reprint of the anonymous translation of 1854, *Wild Sports in the Far West*, which was based on Gerstäcker's first edition. The Steeves' maintain that the earlier version is the more authentic version. While there is merit to this argument as a general principle, I have chosen the expanded second edition for my translation. Were authenticity the sole criterion, then the material devoted to Louisiana in the original copybooks, which is equivalent in length to only three typescript pages, would have to suffice. I wish to provide the reader with all the early experiences of Louisiana Gerstäcker recalls and reconstructs. There may be a few jarring notes in the second edition, such as the occasional comparison between present and past or the recitations on history, fauna, and topography requisite in their day. But the added anecdotes that describe the people of the region more than make up for this. Readers comparing my translation with the anonymous 1854 version should be cautioned that the latter contains some deletions and errors; for example, Gerstäcker's friend from Arkansas and Louisiana is called "Kean" instead of "Korn." In his fine volume *In the Arkansas Backwoods* James William Miller objects to the excessive liberties the 1854 translation takes with the text.[2]

My translations are faithful to Gerstäcker's texts, and I adhere to the tone of nineteenth-century discourse, although the lively dialogue usually does not seem archaic. In the narrative passages I have broken up sentences that would be considered long and overly complex in English and also eliminated indicator particles that are repetitive or unduly pronounced in English. Gerstäcker was at times a hasty writer, and in a few passages I have chosen to vary vocabulary items where there is no stylistic intent behind lexical repetition in a single paragraph. In the rare cases where the meaning of the German text is not clear, I have interpreted it through my translation. This volume includes all narratives set in Louisiana, with the exception of the short novel *The Flatboatman*,[3] in which themes found in earlier stories are reworked. The length of this text was a consideration.

I have made my best effort to identify proper nouns, be they the names of people, ships, or places, and to clarify references to particular events. I was not always successful. Rather than clutter the text with notes to this effect, the reader may assume that the effort was made and be assured that any information that would shed further light on the matter is most welcome.

Gerstäcker's observations on Louisiana in his first travel book, *Adventures and Hunting Expeditions in the United States of North America* (1844), are unusual because he entered Louisiana in 1838 from the northwest part of the state by way of the Red River, carrying out the major portion of his journey through the wilderness solo, in a canoe. Joining a flatboat crew to circumnavigate the Great Raft, he found himself in the company of the roughest of men. Shreveport was a dangerous, violent frontier town, and even the early signs of civilization—rich plantations and prosperous trading towns—were attached to the cruel institution of slavery. Landing, finally, in New Orleans by steamboat, Gerstäcker realized that traveling in isolation had left him unfit for civilized company. He poignantly yearned for human warmth but harbored misanthropic sentiments toward what was, at any rate, unattainable.

Gerstäcker returned to Louisiana in 1842 to work and earn his passage home. He resided on both sides of the Mississippi River in the richest and most beautiful plantation country of the state: West Feliciana and Pointe Coupée parishes. The portion of the travel book devoted to his year in Louisiana treats the area's nature, agriculture, hunting, historical ethnographic differences, and slavery.

Subsequent sketches based on this first Louisiana sojourn appeared in family magazines before being gathered in Gerstäcker's collected works. The sketch "New Orleans" depicts the vibrant, multiracial population of New Orleans but, along with the sketch "In Bayou Sara," demonstrates that the life of the immigrant seeking to better his lot in the city or farther upriver is cheap, the prospect of an unceremonious burial in potter's field being ever present. Yet Gerstäcker's anecdotes usually combine humor with sober reflection, as when he recounts the triumph of the slave housemaid over the lazy German houseboy in "The Houseboy and the Cow"; muses whether the rank and file's insouciant disregard for the excessive number of "officers" at the compulsory military drill near

St. Francisville, which they failed to take seriously, might have contributed to the South's defeat in the Civil War in "A Drill"; remembers his own efforts to keep order in an establishment where the manager was abysmally plagued by alcoholism in "The Ferry Hotel in Pointe Coupée"; or expresses his satisfaction at having collected a long overdue debt in "Mr. Mix."

From *Adventures and Hunting Expeditions in the United States of North America* (1844)

[Gerstäcker first traveled through Louisiana in early 1838.¹ We take up Gerstäcker's account with his description of the Red River as he navigates his canoe toward Shreveport, Louisiana. Gerstäcker has stopped at the cabin of a farmer, who thinks his planned route is dubious.]

The man shook his head in doubt when I told him I intended to pass the Great Raft in my canoe.² I had heard so much about this raft that I asked him for long-awaited information about it. He told me the following:

The Red River is a dreadfully rapid water that washes over and under the banks and sweeps the wood along with it. It often overflows its banks and then washes along whatever fallen logs or branches it finds. During such a flood sometimes half of the river is covered with driftwood—whole trees as well as single branches and trunks—and in earlier times it carried all of that to the Mississippi. But for many years now part of this wood has gotten caught on the sides of the river between the fallen trees; another part has collected on the snags in the middle of the river. More and more wood got caught on it, and the gnarly dam became denser and stronger until finally—because nothing was done to reopen it—it spread out over the entire river and formed a proper tree wall that caught *everything* floating downriver.³ Once the dam had taken hold, it grew with great rapidity. Every year it became higher and deeper. Eventually, this so-called raft, as the neighbors called it, stretched up the river for miles and filled its entire bed. Indeed, sometimes it dammed up the river. Finally, as the raft grew farther and farther upstream, it forced the river to seek a diversion through two lakes on the right bank, Soda Lake and Clear Lake.⁴ Over the years sand, leaves, decaying washed-up animals, earth from the roots, et cetera, collected on the sun-bleached trees rising from the water and formed a new humus cover over which the cottonwood trees spread their feathery seeds and young sprouts shot up cheerfully and greened and blossomed.

The man claimed that the raft was forty miles long already, and even if he were exaggerating, it did fill a long stretch of the river. This interrupted the entire navigation of the wide, deep river, which had been wonderfully favorable to commerce in the interior. So, the enterprising Americans set about *cutting through* this raft. They started to cut and chop and pull with steamboats and saws and axes and over the years really had made a wide canal, which later, however, clogged up again, if not as badly. Recently, the canal had been reopened, and the man told me they expected that a steamboat would soon come through to bring them supplies, if it did not have an accident somewhere along the way. They were in great need of supplies, since a barrel of flour (about 180 pounds) now cost three dollars in the States, whereas they had to pay twenty-two dollars for it here. That sounded worse than it was because the twenty-two dollars were paid in Arkansas banknotes, which at that time were discounted by 40 percent. Nevertheless, flour still cost thirteen dollars and twenty cents a barrel.

The man assured me, moreover, that I could hardly dare to make the trip through the hewn-out canal with a canoe that barely rose higher than the water. The current shot through with such terrible force that the smallest branch I might hit would overturn the slender vessel. Last month a boatman who wanted to try the same thing is said to have perished. Besides, there was a way to circumvent the raft. As he had mentioned earlier, the river itself had forged a path through a bayou into a lake that flowed into the Red River again below the raft, right above the little town of Shreveport. If I entered that *and could find the way,* I could go around the extremely dangerous spot.

That was all well and good, *if I found the way,* but if *not,* I could travel for a month in all the little bays and bayous that usually flow into such lakes and that in places are clogged up with fallen trees. But I did not rack my brains about it for long and decided to leave my future route to chance and a further report about the raft, which, as the old man told me, I could obtain at a house close to the raft, located where the bayou flowed into Soda Lake.

The next morning I was on my way early, and after a warm leave-taking from my host, who adamantly refused to be paid for my lodging, I renewed my old route downstream. The river had risen by several inches during the night. In some spots a mass of driftwood filled the actual current to such an extent that I had to travel alongside it and sometimes even had to cross it in order not to be pushed against the riverbank and be thrown under a tree. Several times I avoided capsizing only with great difficulty. I realized more and more that a trip through such a narrow canal at the present water stage, where the logs drifting down collided everywhere, would be extremely dangerous, perhaps even impossible.

I received confirmation of this in the last house before the raft. But the man there also informed me that a flatboat that had docked at his house for several days and was carrying cotton downriver had just set out that morning. If I hurried, I still could catch up with it before it left the main canal and entered another.

I followed his advice, bought some provisions here so that I would not need to be detained by hunting en route, and confidently steered into the narrow waterway to my right. It soon led me into quite a different landscape, close under overhanging willows and sycamores. Here the current was much weaker, the banks were not as jagged and torn up, and I could see the gray hanging moss, the so-call Spanish moss.[5] It was still new to me then, and it seemed to lend the trees a wonderfully venerable, stately appearance.

I was not preoccupied with nature observations for long because now the most important thing was that I catch sight of the flatboat. That happened sooner than I expected, and I heard it before I even saw it. The crew on board was working with the long, attached oars, the so-called fins, to keep the clumsy boat in the current and avoid the overhanging trees.

Initially, I intended to travel alongside the boat until we had navigated the lakes. But no sooner did the crew hear that I was joining them for a ways than they cordially invited me to come aboard and to hang up my canoe next to theirs. So I did.

On board the flatboat was a "captain," as the owner was called, and a "crew" of four men. The reader is certainly already familiar with this kind of vessel from other writers' descriptions. So, I want to just briefly mention here that flatboats are large, rectangular, clumsy crates built only to go *downriver*. With their far-reaching fins, against which the crew on board presses with their shoulders, they are extremely difficult to steer and propel forward. A rudder similar to the fins is attached in back.[6]

As I soon realized, the crew welcomed my arrival because they had one more *hand,* or, rather, another *shoulder* on board to help them row through the almost still water of the lakes. Because they invited me to share their meals and regarded me as one of them, I did not, of course, think of refusing them my labor.

I now had time to look at the *forest* more closely because the bayou that we followed was hardly twenty feet wide in some places. The forest consisted mainly of cypresses, sycamores, and willows close to the shore and cottonwood trees beyond. Pecan trees dotted the area, and there were some dense groups of swamp oaks. The land here seemed to be completely flat. It was, for the most part, marshland when it was not flooded, as it was now with the high-water stage. With the exception of sassafras bushes and green thornbushes, there was very little underbrush.

The men themselves were a motley crew. In no part of the world does one find such a crazy mixture as in the western part of the United States. The captain seemed to be the overseer of a plantation, or perhaps an overseer's assistant or so-called "slave driver." One of the crewmen on board was a young hunter and trapper from the Rocky Mountains. He was fed up with the wild life there and probably had with him a fistful of dollars for the skins he could not get rid of so quickly and at such a good price in the wilderness. He had intended to go down the Red River in a canoe, as had I, when he met the boat on which he hired out. Thus, he not only found passage but was earning money as well. Two others worked on the flatboat and later drove cattle onto a plantation, where the overseer took them into service. The fourth, who had a wicked, sinister face and most likely had experienced much more than he would care to admit, maintained he was a farmer's son from Louisiana and had come up here with a herd of mules. He kept apart from the rest and remained sullen and withdrawn. The only thing I heard him utter during the days I spent on board were the terrible blasphemies he let fly at the smallest obstacle along the way. At least fifty times a day he cursed the boat itself and wished it to the river bottom.

On the very same evening we ran into Soda Lake. I had had, to be sure, a different idea of this so-called *lake*. It was indeed a water surface about four, five, perhaps six miles wide, but it was full of *trees*. High, stately cypresses were scattered throughout the entire lake, forming groups in only a few spots. Many were dead, some were still alive, and an open canal ran through them like a broad boulevard. The major portion of this lake probably lay dry at the low-water stage, and the open places just indicated the spots where water stood continuously.

That night we tied the flatboat to one of the trees because we could not travel through this wood in the dark. Not far from us a pair of eagles—the bald-headed eagle that is the symbol of the United States—had their nest, an enormous structure of dry branches that lay at the top of a cypress tree. Although the breeding season had not yet begun, we saw the stately birds nearby. Taking little notice of us, they alighted for the night on another cypress about one thousand feet away. When it started to get dark, the hunter from the Rocky Mountains took his rifle and a canoe and tried to paddle within shooting range. But it was not so easy to outwit the clever birds, and they flew away with a slow, heavy beating of wings to find a more secure place for their nocturnal rest.

With the first glimmer of dawn the next morning, we resumed our journey. Never before had I taken such notice of the actual growth pattern of the cypress as here, where it stood singly in the water. Because of its above-ground root system, its slender, splendid trunk only begins eight to ten feet, often even higher, above the ground in which it takes root. A tree trunk that is only one to two feet in diameter at this height measures perhaps twelve feet close to the earth—thus thirty-six feet in circumference. The base forms a regular pointed wooden pyramid, and from its highest point the trunk rises up slender and straight as a reed and does not stretch out its first branches for eighty, or even one hundred or more, feet above the ground. It looked especially strange in shallow spots in the lake. It almost seemed as if the tree, with its broad root base, were swimming on the water and could, at any moment, be knocked over by the slightest breeze. The rest of the roots, instead of quietly continuing to run underground and being content to serve as a support for their trunk, like those of proper trees, make all kinds of wondrous sideward caprices and rise up out of the earth like little fountains then turn back sharply at the top like falling water and take root exactly where they come out. With this they form a so-called *knee*, which actually resembles a human knee, because of the reddish, round bark stretched over the pointed top. In some places, especially in the marshes, hundreds of these "cypress knees," as they are called, stick up three, twelve, or even eighteen inches high out of the ground and make progress endlessly difficult, especially when it is dark. Sometimes the knees shoot up eight to ten feet high, with an average of twelve to eighteen inches below.

Our captain had traveled through these "lakes" a few times before and claimed to have exact knowledge of the water. The eagles' nest was one of his landmarks; a steamboat wreck that lay at the entrance to Clear Lake was another. It seems that in earlier days individual small steamboats had tried to circumnavigate the raft through these lakes. But the very same cypress knees mentioned earlier, as well as other concealed roots and fallen tree trunks, make such a journey quite dangerous, and, as our guide asserted, even for a flatboat it is only advisable to go through here at a very high-water stage.

We ran into Clear Lake as if we were traveling into the middle of the woods. The branches of the overhanging willows hit the boat from both sides, and we could not use the fins at all. But there was a weak current here that helped us move along, if ever so slowly. This lake, with its surface also completely overgrown with cypresses, owed its name to a lower water stage or to an earlier time when the raft did not yet guide the dirty red Red River through here. For even though the water was not as red as in the river, it was still dirty and opaque.

At noon, when we were in the middle of Clear Lake and I was observing various alligator heads that peeked up from the water all around us and looked like swimming pieces of burnt black wood, one of the men quietly and nonchalantly threw off his clothes and prepared to *bathe*. At first I though he had not seen the alligators and quickly jumped up to stop him. But he laughed and said they were quite good and contented fellows who would do no *white* man harm—he had often swum among them.

I must admit I was quite uneasy when I saw the man really jump into the water, quite carefree—it was the hunter from the Rocky Mountains and otherwise a quite splendid fellow. With great trepidation I also observed what I believed to be dangerous animals in his vicinity and feared that at any minute they would swim toward him and attack. He may have noticed this, for he suddenly reversed the situation and himself swam toward the nearest alligator. The others called out to him to stop, but he paid no attention. The alligator seemed somewhat astonished at the bold man-child, for we could see clearly the sharp, pointed head turning toward him. But James, as the young man was called, knew with whom he was dealing, for when he was about five or six feet away, the alligator's head suddenly disappeared underwater. The alligator preferred to avoid the encounter peacefully. James tried the same thing with three or four other alligators, who all submerged and reappeared after a while farther on down. The smartest one yields.

I was emboldened by this as well. The water was not very enticing, so even though the others did not wish to follow our example, I soon swam to James's side, thereby gaining his full respect.

Despite our captain's declared knowledge of the waterway, we had some difficulty that afternoon in finding the right bayou that would lead us back into the Red River. We were forced to tie up the flatboat and go in different directions with two canoes to reconnoiter. Finally, we found the correct spot, which our guide recognized by an old Indian camp. He told us that years ago a Choctaw tribe had camped, fished, and hunted there for a while. Some half-burned tent poles, blackened with smoke, were still standing here and there.

The land was considerably higher here, and through the thinning trees we began to see small, open prairies. Signs of civilization—fences and cultivated land—also became visible. Toward evening we arrived at a large and, it seemed, rather important cotton plantation,[7] with a comfortable residence for the owners, rows of Negro cabins for the slaves, and a so-called cotton gin, or mill, to remove the seeds from the wooly hulls and to clean the cotton. Close by was heaped a twenty- or twenty-five-foot-high mountain of cottonseeds. It was rotting right where it lay and was not even used as fertilizer. Yet these seeds yield an excellent, very pure oil that is especially suitable for artists' paints. One could earn a lot of money if one had a hydraulic press, for wherever there are a considerable number of cotton plantations you can buy the seeds for nothing, or at least for a very low price.

It did me good to set foot on open, sunny land again, and the sight of the charming prairies was a special joy. They had been burned off in the winter, when the high yellow grass was still standing. Now spring brought forth the most wonderful, juicy grass and tiny, lovely flowers. The flowers were barely showing their early buds, and the whole prairie was still one single blanket of splendid green. But there were no mountains.

The plantation owner was one of the richest people in the district and owned several hundred slaves. If everything that the captain told us about him is true, he treated them with terrible harshness, even cruelty. The captain swore to us a few "facts"—and my skin crawled when I thought it possible that human beings are capable of such evil. What he is purported to have done is so awful that I do not even want to tell of it here.

The southern slaveholders, unfortunately, have been granted—even by the laws of the land—far too much power over their slaves, who are, after all, *human beings*. The law, to be sure, protects the slave from too great a tyranny or cruelty. But this must be *proved* in the courts, and how should this happen?—According to the law, a black man cannot bear witness against a white man. Only in very rare cases is a white man a witness, and even then he will not come forward unless he lives independent of these people or is, perhaps, a stranger. Most such cruel deeds are well known, even to the judge, but often no one steps in because there is no plaintiff or because the plaintiff cannot testify.[8]

I know of only one case in Louisiana where a white man really was brought before the court and sentenced to do his penance in jail. He was guilty of such exquisitely atrocious cruelties against different slaves of his, and there was so much talk of it among the neighboring planters, that they simply *could* not overlook it. The same fellow—I have, unfortunately, forgotten his name—had already shot two whites during quarrels; moreover, as was related quite openly, he shot them *from his pocket*. He always carried a loaded Terzerol in his right pants pocket and,[9] while he was quarreling with someone, appeared to keep both hands calmly in his pockets, where he secretly cocked his pistol and took approximate aim, in each case hitting his victim in the body. In this, too, he evaded the law—only God knows how—and when I saw him, he was running around free again under God's sun, thinking up new misdeeds.

Toward evening we finally came into a stronger current and reached the main canal that led into the Red River and into which other bayous flowed. The bank here was about five feet above the present water stage. I was not a little astonished when I saw that the left bank of the bayou, right at the point where it merged with the Red River, was covered with *snow*. Or so it appeared. When we got closer I realized that it was *cotton* that covered almost an acre of land as densely as snow. Our captain told us that several years ago a flatboat loaded with cotton had an accident at the point—at that time the river was *six feet higher*—and when the water subsided the cotton was washed across the land and was ruined.

Right below the mouth of the bayou lay Shreveport, an unattractive little town.[10] The houses were all facade, with large, brightly painted square front sides that concealed tiny little wooden shacks behind. Large letters advertised the various wares and products in the so-called *stores,* but when you entered there was nothing to buy except alcoholic beverages and a card game—in the evenings most likely a knife wound or pistol bullet as well. Things may have changed now, but then its gangs of gamblers and thieves gave it the worst reputation that a young city could possibly wish for.[11]

We landed, and I decided to buy a few supplies and from here to *quickly* continue my journey by myself in the canoe because I had nothing more to fear of the raft behind us. Our flatboat crew also went ashore because the captain had business on the riverbank and also planned to start out in the morning. All the driftwood made travel at night impossible in any case. I allowed myself to be led astray by the crew to visit one of the "groceries." As we entered the building, they were already gambling heavily in one of the back rooms.

I myself am no special friend of strong drink. But after such a long time in which I was not *able* to obtain it, and after all the muddy water I *had* to drink, I thought it would do me good to try something piquant and "get a different taste in my mouth." The cognac they sold was so inferior, made of alcohol and oil of vitriol, that it almost burned my throat. From then on I was content to observe my surroundings without indulging in any further pleasures this place offered. I was most interested in the *gaming room,* a wooden edifice, illuminated, intentionally perhaps, by a single dim oil lamp. Here about twenty or twenty-five people crowded about a round table, seated and standing. The sinister "farmer's son" from the flatboat had already taken his place and seemed far more at home here than with any other kind of work.

The game they were playing was called poker. If I am correct, it is the only game of chance that is still allowed, or is not expressly forbidden, in the United

States. It is similar to our German game of sequence and involves bidding and wagering. Whoever has three knaves, for example, *bids* on that and makes a wager. The other person, with whatever hand he has, may bid higher, that is, he adds more money to the pot. If the one with the three knaves thinks that his cards are better and does not believe that his opponent has three kings, for example, then he bids higher again, until one of them *yields*. Then the other calls in the bid, even if he does not have a suite in his hand; indeed, he does not even have to show his cards. Only if they continue until they are agreed do they show their cards, and whoever has the *best* hand wins. So far this would be a quite honest game, if they played it honestly. But in the United States—and I do not know to what extent this could be said of other countries in which games of chance are played without agreed-upon precautions—almost all games are based on deception. The *cleverest*, as they say, not the *luckiest*, wins. In the Union there are real factories whose sole business is the production of *false cards*. The supposedly random pattern of stars, waves, or dots on the back of these cards follows rules well-known to the players. Thus, for the initiated the back of the card is just as recognizable as the proper side. Besides that, the players resort to all kinds of tricks. Some of them are so crude that I, as a disinterested observer, was astonished by remarkable discoveries. For example, because I kept an especially sharp eye on my farmer's son, whose name was Bob (Robert), I soon noticed that he kept one or two cards on his lap. Therefore, he had better prospects of getting a *full house* than he would have with the customary five cards dealt to him. Moreover, he appeared to carry on quite a lucrative business with his *neighbor,* since the two of them passed back and forth the cards they needed. Once, when he had pulled some such trick again and perhaps did not feel quite safe, he turned his head halfway round and met my firmly fixed gaze. But this did not seem to bother him in the least because he winked at me with his left eye and—continued to cheat.

I had seen enough, and because I did not feel like sleeping in town I returned to the flatboat, where my belongings were stored. I arrived just at the right time for one of the crewmen, who was supposed to stay on board as sentry. Despite the fact that he had been entrusted with guarding the boat—no idle task in *such* a town—he asked me to take his place. He wanted to go ashore a bit and try his "luck" up there. Of course, I told him what I had seen and gave him a well-meant warning, but he laughed and opined that he was just as smart as the others.

I prepared my bed on deck, with my rifle at my side. Not without reason did I believe that I was in far greater danger here than in the middle of the forest or among the alligators. Recently, there had been numerous robberies, and burglary and theft were part of the daily news in Shreveport. Nonetheless, the boat remained undisturbed. Once, in the middle of the night, I heard a shot and loud screaming and cursing from the shore. Then everything was quiet again, and at two o'clock the boat sentry returned. He seemed, by the way, quite meek and finally admitted to me that they had plucked him completely. Of course, his entire fortune had only consisted of eight dollars in Arkansas money.

I asked him about the shot.

"Oh—nonsense!" he grumbled. "They caught one of them cheating, and a miserable Yankee started making a fuss. But they shot the Yankee through the shoulder a bit, and that took care of him."

At daybreak, when the rest of the flatboat crew had not yet returned, I climbed into my canoe, untied it, and steered downstream, turning my back on Shreveport and all its crime.

Here the Red River had a character quite different from that up above the raft. Even though there was still forest along its banks for enormous uncultivated, indeed untouched, stretches, the farms and plantations became more frequent. I only needed to travel for a few miles, at most, before seeing the blue smoke of a cabin shimmering between the dark trees and the white sycamores again.

The farther on down I went, the livelier was the river. Toward evening I even passed another little town, but I did not feel the slightest need to land there. It was turning dark now, and I began to look out for a camping place for the night. In order to be as far away from the *city* as possible, I decided to keep to the opposite bank. As I approached the forest, which was already turning dusky, I saw something that did not appear to be wood floating up ahead in the water. Since I did not need to travel far out of my way to pass it, I paddled toward it. It was light and floated even with the water's surface. It felt soft when I hit it with my paddle, pushing it underwater a bit. As it reemerged, propelled slightly above the surface, I recognized—I had a very eerie feeling—a human corpse. It was drifting forward very slowly and awkwardly, with its back upward and head, arms, and legs hanging down. Now I also saw a wide, ugly gash in the corpse's back. What dark deed had transpired?—Perhaps it was rotten fruit dropped off from the Shreveport I had just left behind.—I lost my desire to land. Because today for the first time the moon poured his friendly light on the river fully, I decided to travel if not through the night, then as long as I could still guide the paddle, in order not to reencounter the corpse floating next to me.

I passed Nachitoches the following day.[12] Here I saw for the first time in a long while fine brick buildings, the bank, for example, as well as several others. A number of steamboats were docked here, among them the *Blackhawk*,[13] which was supposed to make its first trip through the raft. It was loaded with flour, salt, and other products for the farmers and was supposed to bring back cotton in return.

On the third day from here I finally reached the site where the Red River empties into the Mississippi—a wild, wicked-looking place—because the red water welled with dreadful force across the low land of the point, which was covered with willows and cottonwood trees. The water shook and threw the tops of the bushes back and forth, as if it were annoyed that they dared to resist it. Here the Red River is not as wide, but it is just as deep as the "father of waters," the Mississippi. Despite this, the Red River seems to flow into the mighty river as if it were disappearing into the ocean—it has that little effect on the Mississippi. It only gives the yellowish, dirty water a bit redder shade at the site where the waters of the two rivers mix.[14]

I had reached my next goal and had a strange, almost frightened feeling as I dared make my way out onto the immense body of water in my slender, little canoe. That feeling quickly subsided. The wide river was much calmer that the more compressed Red River, even if it flowed just as rapidly. Of good cheer, I steered the little boat swiftly forward with my paddle.

There was a different kind of life here than on the Red River, and I soon recognized the great arteries of the mighty empire. Wherever my eye gazed, I could see the heavily laden flatboats moving with the current. I met a steamboat almost every hour, or one passed me by. Often I encountered three or four together. I had to steer as far away from them as possible, and where that did not work, I even had to flee ashore several times in order not to sink in the high waves they stirred up.

In the case of our European steamships it is established—even through law, I believe—that the paddle boards of their wheels may not be very far apart. Otherwise, they disturb the water too much and damage the riverbanks through the constant waves. In America the law and the boats have blessed little concern about the riverbanks, even if entire acres are torn away. The boats just want to move as rapidly as possible. These enormous boats, which often are capable of loading three or four thousand bales, do indeed have to be able to work hard to stem the current of the mighty Mississippi. Then the boats often hurl the waves eight and ten feet onto the riverbank, and even in the middle of the river, where the waves do not go nearly as high, they have enough height and weight to endanger a canoe.

With the exception of a few plantations here and there I still traveled for a distance between *wooded* riverbanks. More and more, however, cultivated soil pushed back the forest, and soon I ran past the wonderful Pointe Coupée, where the whole land looks like a garden.[15]

I do not intend to depict the Mississippi one more time, which others often have described. My focus here is my trip, and I easily went on my way until the next morning. Around nine o'clock the sky clouded over, and it began to rain. I placed the woolen blanket over my rifle and other baggage and paid it no further mind. I was in the middle of the river when suddenly a storm broke forth that blew off my cap at the start. The storm howled across the water so fiercely that—once I had retrieved my cap—I lay down in the boat to let the storm's first fury play out. Unfortunately, the storm headed up the river, stemmed the water, and not only began to make waves but also prevented my vessel from making the least bit of progress. The storm did not subside. The tips of the strongest waves were already spraying into my canoe, and I had to make for the riverbank—more than a half-mile away. I sat up, grabbed my paddle, and—with the wind at my back—used all my strength to work my way diagonally toward land, going more upstream than down. Twice I had to stop to bail out water, and once I almost capsized. So, I took off my rubber boots, in which I would not have been able to swim, and preparing for the worst, fastened my rifle to the canoe in order to save it. But it went better than I expected, and after an hour of strenuous work I reached a spot that the wind could not penetrate so strongly and where the water, therefore, was much calmer. There, on a lengthy stretch of forest land, stood a little woodcutter's cabin, as the cordwood piled up along the shore indicated. A steamboat headed downriver had just landed to take on its wood supply. I headed toward the house and landed, intending to wait for better weather. The wind got even stronger, and out on the river the waves, white with foam, rolled as if on the open sea.

Standing on the riverbank, I watched the hustle and bustle as the workers and deck passengers of the boat lugged the four-foot-long logs on board. The colossal vessel stood huffing and puffing, as if it were waiting impatiently for the time to depart. The owner of the wood, a genuine American backwoodsman, approached me. He seemed to be in a good mood, for he had just sold twenty-four cords of wood at a rather high price in "cash money."[16] He held the packet of banknotes in his left hand, while with the right he guided a cigar the captain had given him to his mouth and took a few puffs. His son was behind him, with a burning cigar as well. I had to laugh when I saw the little fellow.

He was a boy, three or four years old at best, somewhat pale, like *all* children in the marshes, but otherwise he appeared plump and healthy, indeed almost stout. His outfit, a jacket and trousers of blue material, suited his needs. As is customary with children his age, he wore a little dickey turned backward; nonetheless, he held the burning cigar quite proudly up front. He puffed on it occasionally with a half-anxious, half-determined expression and then took it from his mouth to *blow at* the fire. He was preoccupied with it more than necessary, far more, in any case, than was good for him.

His father addressed me. His first question was where I came from and where I was going. His second was whether I wanted to sell the canoe. The Americans think *everything* in the world is for sale, their family perhaps excepted. Accordingly, they assume that for a decent price other people will also hand over whatever they happen to have. His offer took me quite by surprise, but his remark that I now had the best opportunity to get to New Orleans on the steamboat cast a different light on the situation. I had not even thought of that. The storm was getting more intense, with no sign of subsiding, and in five minutes we came to an agreement. He happened to need a canoe, had received a heap of money, and gave me the same amount I had paid on the Red River— five dollars in Arkansas notes.

I could not hesitate a moment longer—the crew had finished loading wood, the bell was sounded, and I had hardly pulled on my boots and carried my rifle, blanket, and bag on board when the sailors, or deckhands, pulled in the planks behind me. The boat worked its way forward then turned around slowly, its bow facing downriver. As I looked back once more, the woodcutter was standing on the bank waving his hat, and his little offspring stood next to him, still puffing on his cigar.

Despite the fierce wind, which did not subside until around ten o'clock that night, the boat went downriver swiftly. The next day, however, we made a long stop at a sugar plantation, where a number of sugar and syrup barrels and cotton bales were taken on board, so that we did not reach the New Orleans levee until dusk.

It was the first time that I set foot in New Orleans, and after the long, lonely life in the wilderness the large, mighty city made a remarkable impression on me. But first of all I had to stow my things, and when I heard a few young people who passed me by speaking German with one another, I asked them to recommend a German boardinghouse in the vicinity. We were standing near a lantern, and they looked at me somewhat astonished. To them the German language did not seem to fit my wild appearance; they probably had never really been in the woods. Judging by their very elegant dress, they were young merchants. Nonetheless, in a rather friendly manner they described for me the place I had inquired about.

At the boardinghouse my appearance had to pass another examination. When I inquired about lodging, the barkeeper in the pub at the front looked at me from top to bottom—and then from bottom to top again. In the end he did not seem willing to take sole responsibility for giving shelter to *such* a traveler. He called for the innkeeper, who also looked at me rather disdainfully. Only when I became rude did his expression clear. He held the light to my rifle under the pretense of seeing whether it was loaded. But he actually wanted to find out whether it would pay for my meals and lodging should I abscond. He soon realized it was an excellent, richly ornamented, if somewhat beat-up weapon, so he ordered the barkeeper to show me my bed and then, because supper was over, had me served something to eat. I gave him my rifle and bag for safekeeping, and when he had the weapon in his hand he calmed down completely.

After the meal I took a walk through the city, and for me it was an indescribably strange but also pleasant feeling to have *pavement* under my feet again. I was also pleased to see the elegantly decorated and brightly illuminated stores and the bright residence windows hung with curtains. It felt as if I had been removed from civilization for many years, rather than months. The human being is a creature of habit, and he does not easily shake off what was part of his youth. He may even forget it for a while, but at the first opportunity it pulls him back into those familiar circles with even stronger bonds.

Nevertheless, this tumult in the streets left me quite cold, colder perhaps than I myself would have thought. They were nothing but indifferent strangers. Not one of them cared for the other, and I was only comforted somewhat by the fact that they did not pay any attention to me either. Only now did I notice that in my long period of solitude I had almost become misanthropic. In any case I wanted to associate with others as little as possible, and since I did not know anyone in the big city, I could keep to myself undisturbed.

To be sure, when I left New York I had letters of introduction for New Orleans in my wallet. These were used up a long time ago, up in Illinois, as rifle plugs for prairie chickens. What help are letters of introduction in America! At best you get a dinner invitation—which, in my condition, I did not need to fear—and the recipients are happy if they see nothing more of the person introduced.

Strolling slowly with the intention of seeking out my boardinghouse, I had left behind the city center, or at least that section where most of the stores were located, and turned into a residential side street. The houses looked ample and comfortable; in many the windows were brightly illuminated.

It is an odd feeling for a stranger, such as I, to walk through the streets of a city in which he has no home. All around the bright windows show the places where families gather around the evening table in an intimate circle—only *he* belongs nowhere, and if he wished to enter one of these homes now, they would ask him anxiously what he wanted and be relieved when he left again, completely unconcerned about what was to become of him. Happy he, who is no such stranger anywhere on this earth.

As I walked through the quiet street with these not especially cheerful thoughts, because in all of America there were precious few people who were interested in my welfare, I saw a bright light falling onto the sidewalk somewhat farther down, on the right side of the street. I walked toward it and found that it was coming from a wide, ground-floor window. Its shutters were open, and since the window was not very high, I could quite easily survey the room from the outside. It was a very elegant, comfortable chamber with three or four large astral lamps that were almost as bright as daylight. Between them was a large company of dressed-up men and women. Eight or ten young girls and several matrons were sitting or standing in the room, and young people, completely French in appearance, were jumping about laughing and shouting. At any rate, they were playing a parlor game.

Two wondrously pretty girls sat close to the window, their backs toward me.—Their heads almost leaned against the pane at which I stood, and a young man kneeled before them and seemed to claim a forfeit. A strange feeling overcame me. I had been away from home so long that I had almost forgotten the warm family life with all its quiet pleasures and thousands and thousands of charms. Now, when I had just emerged from the middle of the forest, it appeared right before my eyes in all its bright, colorful splendor, as if it had been conjured up by a magician. It was within arm's reach, and yet it was unattainable.

I do not know whether I sighed or whether someone else in the room noticed me, but the two young girls suddenly and quite unexpectedly turned their faces toward me and let out a piercing scream. They fled from the room like frightened deer, followed by the entire bevy of girls.

I looked that terrible? It pierced my heart, but I did not wish to disturb these gay people any longer, turned away, and strode down the street. When I was about one hundred feet away, I heard the shutters being closed behind me.

I spent the night on a hard, unclean bed without any mosquito netting, scourged by countless gnats and other, far worse bed tormentors. There is nothing sorrier and more disagreeable on God's earth than these German boarding-houses in America. Not even the Irish boardinghouses surpass them in filth. In South America I never found anything worse.[17] My "Wilhelm Tell" was no exception, and I would have ten times rather slept in the forest under a tree or in my canoe.

The following morning I got up at daybreak and went to the lower market to observe the hustle and bustle there. I passed by a barber and hairdresser's shop; the same person practices both occupations. The proprietor stood in the doorway, his hands in his pockets, and looked at me as if he wanted to devour me. When I passed, it occurred to me that I might have my hair and beard trimmed, too. This had not been done in the last eight months, and it had been almost as long since I looked into the mirror.

"Well, I thought so," said the hair artist, when I turned around and went into his shop—he was an American. "Bless my soul, sir, where have you been?" I glanced at the large mirror hanging in the room and was no longer surprised that the poor girls had run away in such fright yesterday evening. I looked terrible.

I now looked around for a steamboat to Cincinnati. The *Chillicothe* was leaving from there the next day,[18] at ten o'clock in the morning. I booked my passage for five dollars for fifteen hundred English miles. One cannot travel more cheaply anywhere, almost four hundred German miles for five dollars.[19] Toward evening we left New Orleans.

LOUISIANA SOJOURN AND JOURNEY HOME

[After a failed attempt at farming with Charles Roetken and Korn at the mouth of the Fourche LaFave, where it flows into the Arkansas River in central Arkansas, Gerstäcker spent a period hiking and hunting along the Fourche LaFave and Petit Jean rivers. The farming partnership had broken up because Roetken, the partner with the most capital to invest, became domineering and abusive. Lonely and homesick, Gerstäcker then followed Korn, a bookkeeper, to St. Francisville, Louisiana, so that he might find work and earn some money for his passage home. Gerstäcker landed at Bayou Sara on July 8, 1842, and spent the final year of his first American sojourn in St. Francisville, Bayou Sara, and Pointe Coupée.]

It was about one o'clock when I stepped onto Louisiana soil. My baggage was on land; the little sloop that had transported me from the steamboat to the

shore cast off again and flew back to the smoking colossus as quick as an arrow. The pilot gave the signal to go on, and, snorting and thundering, the
steamboat soon disappeared from my sight. Everything was dark in the town;
not a single light could be seen, and since I did not know a soul there, I calmly
wrapped myself in my blanket and lay down on the riverbank.

The night was warm and most pleasant, but millions of mosquitoes swarmed
around me frantically, and there was no thought of rest. Only when I pulled the
cover over my head so that I could not breathe did they leave me in peace for a
short time. When I stuck out my head to draw in some air, it was the signal for
hordes of them to attack me with renewed fury.

Finally, the first Negro bell—the signal for the blacks to get up—rang on
the opposite shore, and soon afterward the first pale streak appeared in the east.
Now, however, my torturers became totally mad, and it seemed as if all the mosquitoes of Louisiana had gathered just at that spot and intended to drain, dry,
and preserve me. I had to jump up and run around just in order to have a bit
of peace.

Day finally broke, and with it several establishments were opened, among
others that of a German "coffeehouse" proprietor. I deposited my things there
and began to look around the place a bit. After nearly an hour of wandering
about, I thought it was late enough to be able to look up Korn, who was a bookkeeper for the merchant Lf. I soon found him (Bayou Sara is not so big),[20] and
he received me cordially.

First of all, I had to get into some other clothes, for hunting shirts and leggings are advantageous in the woods but are not suitable in a town, in particular under the hot Louisiana sun. Summer clothing was not expensive there,
for a good number of German Jews had settled in that little place and competed
with one another in selling the clothes as cheaply as possible.[21] For a few dollars, therefore, I soon had a quite decent lightweight suit.

Bayou Sara is a little town that got its name from the bayou (little river) that
flows into the Mississippi just above it. At that time the houses were all built of
wood, with the exception of three or four built of brick, and there were about
eight hundred inhabitants, among them many Germans. Now, of course, it has
grown a good deal larger, and the town itself is said to be much improved after
a significant fire.

There are many German Jews there whose business is primarily the sale of
ready-to-wear clothing. They often earn a lot of money. Nothing, therefore, is
more common than to find a Jewish dandy decked out in the most tasteless
fashion. He strolls around grandly with a lorgnette or, coming from one of the

little country towns to buy wares from the Bayou Sara merchants, lies back casually in his one-horse buggy, legs sticking out to one side, and smokes a cigar. They do very well, and I have found similar types only among Berlin firms at the Leipzig fair.[22]

There were quite a few German shoemakers in Bayou Sara. I cannot help mentioning a peculiarity that I have observed in almost all German shoemakers in America and noticed here as well. It is the mania of selling *pepper cake* and *candy* to supplement their business. Since everyone in the United States is at liberty to buy and sell whatever he feels like, one finds—especially among the merchants—all kinds of wares. Even in the smaller towns most apothecaries deal in haberdashery or sell shoes and hardware. Wherever a German shoemaker sets up his little store, it is as if pepper cakes were part of the trade. A few large jars with sundry colored candy canes stand there at the low window, mighty stacks of brown gingerbread (a kind of pepper cake) towering over them. Above them shoes and boots hang on strings, and between them pieces of cobbler's wax and awls dangle picturesquely. I have observed this not only in Bayou Sara and St. Francisville (a town almost the same size situated about a quarter of a mile away on the bluff) but also in all the smaller towns of the United States that I have ever seen, even in several places in the big city of Cincinnati. It is, in any case, an odd fancy.

I had quite a good time in the company of Korn, who was employed by very kind people, until I finally obtained a well-paying position on the opposite bank of the Mississippi, in Pointe Coupée. It was managing the hotel that Roettken once owned and had sold to Mr. Fischer before his departure. Mr. Fischer, however, was always sick and weak, especially at that time. He had to spend the whole time in bed and leave the house in the care of an American who ran it abominably. Fischer's brothers realized that the business would be ruined in no time, and, recommended by Korn, I became the manager.[23]

Although moving in an entirely different sphere from that I had been accustomed to previously, I familiarized myself with my duties and did quite well because I was fully independent and could do what I considered best. With great pleasure I took care of my business and can say that I soon had the whole place running again. I also lived much more pleasantly in Pointe Coupée than in Bayou Sara because here I was mostly in the company of the well-to-do planters of the area and became acquainted with upstanding people among them.[24] In the hotel itself there lived an Irish lawyer who had a thriving practice. In him I found a true friend.

Across from Bayou Sara, somewhat upstream, lies the so-called little town of Pointe Coupée. It consists only of the courthouse, the prison, the Catholic church,[25] the priest's home, and the hotel itself. But since all the land along the Mississippi, especially in Louisiana, is lower than the river during a high-water stage, the settlers had to erect a dam or a so-called *levee* along the entire bank, which is usually only four to five feet but in some places eighteen to twenty feet high. Of course, the maintenance of this dam entails tremendous costs, since the powerful current erodes the banks and tears away entire chunks into its turbulent, dirty stream. Moreover, those living directly on the river have to bear all the costs and the work: they are even *obligated* to maintain this levee, whereas those living in the interior of the land, whose fields are exposed to the Mississippi floods to a far greater extent, do not have to contribute the least bit. During the past few years, however, there have been intense discussions about correcting this inequity.

The main products in Pointe Coupée are cotton, corn, and sugarcane, but all kinds of garden plants also do very well. The gardens themselves are filled with sweet and sour oranges, figs, peaches, and pomegranates, and the mild climate generates an endless quantity of the most beautiful flowers.

But what makes farming difficult (at least in a *part* of Pointe Coupée, for this plague does not exist everywhere) is the so-called coco grass. Similar to our couch grass, it binds together the soil like peat, and its roots penetrate the earth to a depth of twelve to fifteen feet. That can best be seen in spots where the Mississippi tears away pieces of land from the bank. Once the coco grass has taken hold of a piece of land, it is extremely difficult to get rid of it; indeed, it is totally impossible because it grows so quickly that when it is cut down at night, by morning it has shot up an inch. The grass is not especially good for cattle, but the pigs eat with relish its small, pealike nodules, which have a strong, camphor-like odor and taste.[26]

Most of the planters are Creoles,[27] and their main language is French. But since many Americans also live around there, the court sessions are held partly in French, partly in English.[28]

There is also a prison. At that time, however, it had such a pitiful jailor (Fritz Haydt, a German shoemaker)[29] that every prisoner who had the least desire to liberate himself beat up the turnkey and took his leave. In the last few years this occurred several times.

But slavery here makes a disagreeable impression on one not accustomed to it. Although I had dwelled in slave states a long time and had observed the oppressed condition as well as the treatment of the poor blacks, I was never so struck by the horror of slavery as at the first auction I attended, at which the slaves were sold to the highest bidder like cattle. The poor creatures stood there with great trembling and trepidation and followed the bidder with anxious eyes, most likely to determine in advance whether they would find in him a good or a severe master. To be sure, families, especially mother and child, are no longer separated as frequently as in earlier days, at least as long as the child is still young. At larger auctions the court is also humane enough only to sell families together. But the individual person does not bother about the laws that might be *mitigating* in this respect; he also puts slaves on the block singly. How often, then, are the most sacred bonds rent asunder because of a few hundred dollars?

I saw heartbreaking scenes on such occasions. At the same time, the treatment of the blacks is better than it is usually decried, especially by missionaries and abolitionists. It is to the owner's advantage to keep the slave he owns healthy and able to work and at the same time not to exert him too much, since otherwise he will have to feed him in old age. So, the food is probably not any worse than that with which the poor, free man in our dear fatherland must satisfy his gnawing hunger.[30] That there are also exceptions, and that some planters often treat their slaves badly and inhumanely, I will not contest, but on the other hand I saw people who treated their bondmen almost like their own children. In our hotel we ourselves had two blacks, a cook and a maid, who were also slaves, as well as a house servant, but they never, as long as I was there, could have complained about mistreatment.

The black or descendant of blacks may not leave his residence without his master having issued a pass, whereas the free Negro must carry his papers with him in order to be able to legitimate himself in case he is stopped. If a slave has no pass, he is put in jail until his master, after having paid the costs, gets him out.

Frequently, runaway Negroes flee into the woods, and I remember that in Tennessee regular drives were undertaken to get them back. To be sure, African Negroes may no longer be imported—at least there is a severe punishment for breaking this law[31]—but in Pointe Coupée and the vicinity I still saw many blacks who had been transported here directly from their fatherland and were called Guinea Negroes,[32] to distinguish them from those born in America.

It is dreadful that the poor blacks are denied any education, for if they could write and read, they would also write passes for themselves and then perhaps could escape with this aid. Like domestic animals, they are raised for utilization and reproduction—yet these very United States have in their Declaration of Independence the beautiful phrase "that all men are *free* and *equal.*"

In the towns the Methodist preachers take away completely from the poor
blacks the last bit of sense that God left them by instructing them in their ab-
surd faith and making them jump and shout.[33] Jump and shout!—on top of
everything they have to thank God that they are on the earth and are permitted to toil; must, moreover, kiss the rod that thrashes them. Yes, they may sometimes press their lips to the rod, but they leave behind the marks of their teeth,
and after the violent oppression blood flows. For even if they may not rebel
openly against the tyranny of the whites, it takes place in secret, and some of
that hated race silently fall at the hands of those who have been wantonly mistreated. The examples are quite numerous, and even though the punishment
that awaits the Negro who lays hands on a white person is horrible, it does not
hinder him. It just makes the perpetrator more careful.

My *adventures and hunting expeditions* end here, of course, for from now until
my trip back home, which took place in the following year, I did not change my
residence anymore. *Hunting* itself I did not yet give up completely, whenever
my leisure hours somehow permitted, and Pointe Coupée offered me many
new things. To be sure, I had to do without larger game here, alligators excepted,
and be satisfied with smaller game.

That included, for example, duck hunting. The winter there was very mild,
so that on the coldest days only little ponds and pools were covered with ice,
and snow was a rarity. In this season a multitude of ducks flew down from the
North, and I mostly shot them mornings and evenings from the stand—with
the shotgun, of course.

In the spring and the fall I went woodcock hunting all the more eagerly, not
in broad daylight, as is our custom here, or at dawn or sunset, but in pitch-black
night with a pine torch, as I had shot deer in Arkansas. One just had to be careful to put a very weak load in the gun, since by torchlight one gets quite close
to the woodcocks, who run around on the damp meadows in pursuit of their
meal, paying no attention to the light. These animals are so *trusting* that the
Negroes, who are not allowed to carry a gun without their masters' permission,
go there with the torch or pitch-pan and kill the woodcocks—who hardly move
out of the way—with long hacked-off bush branches.

There are two kinds of woodcocks. They are considerably smaller than ours,
but there are enormous qualities of them. In the daytime they lie in the thick
canebrakes and swamps, and in the evening they come into the dewy meadows
and cotton fields, where, if the hunter approaches with the torch, they usually
bow their heads and patiently let themselves be shot. I often felled about twenty

in one evening, that is, in about two hours of walking around. Only when the weather begins to turn warm do they head north. They are delicious and are almost more tender than the German woodcocks. As good as the woodcock tasted to me, all the less can I tell you about woodcocks, for since I always had enough to eat of the former, I did not touch the subject of the latter.[34]

Spring began now, and a spring in Louisiana is truly something enchantingly beautiful. All the grasses and flowers that spring forth from the earth, all the buds and blossoms that burst from the tree branches, fill the viewer with delight. The gray, silver-haired moss is especially beautiful now. Wafting from the trees in long drapes, in winter it makes them look rather sad and barren. But the moss seems all the more lovely in the spring, when, assuming a somewhat livelier color, it is perforated everywhere by the May-green leaves and flower buds and adorns the tree with a silver-gray garb embroidered with green garlands and bouquets. The tall, slender cypresses are the most beautiful when they are draped with the gray veils.

All kinds of birds could now be seen, and the mockingbird, or, as it is also called, "the American nightingale," appeared in large numbers and, especially at night, its song was, if not as melancholy and enchanting as our nightingale's song, still soft and lovely.

In front of the house, as in front of all plantations in Louisiana, stood several chinaberry trees, which are planted everywhere for ornament as well as shade. Among them was an old patriarch, its branches spread out wide. The previous owner had used it as a summer perch. He had stairs built up into it and furnished it with a small round table and several benches. In this tree I had hung my hammock from branch to branch, slung a mosquito net over it, and then slept there among the heliotrope-like tree blossoms, rocked by the gentle night winds, surrounded by fireflies, and lulled by the song of the mockingbird and the rushing sound of the mighty Mississippi that rolled by hardly twenty feet from the tree. Oh, those were heavenly nights!

In May the heat already became oppressive, especially at midday, and the sun seemed to burn straight down. Yet when all the white people had retired for their siesta, I took my rifle and harpoon and went to the swamps somewhat back from the river to shoot alligators that lived in incredible numbers in the warm, stagnant water.

But what frightening stories have already been written about the horror of these very alligators, who are said to lie in wait with a truly ravenous hunger and dreadfully murderous lust for the approach of any human creature and then immediately attack the approacher with great fury. I always found them to be gentle, harmless animals and hunted them with great zeal.

In the enormous Louisiana swamps and in the entire southern part of the United States in general, tremendous numbers of this alligator (*Crocodilus lucius cuv.*) live in the warm waters of the lagoons and rivers. It belongs to the lizard species and has the same shape and constitution of these animals, but, especially in the southern regions of Louisiana and Florida, it often attains a length of twelve to sixteen feet. Its enormous head comprises almost a fourth of the entire animal. Like the shark, the alligator opens its upper jaw instead of the lower jaw, thus displaying a most respectable trap that includes the powerful, rose-red gullet. Its body is covered with a hard, armor-like skin that consists of many angular pieces that run into white, hard scales under the belly. Its nostrils project from the tip of the jaw and lie close together. When on a quiet, sunny day the alligator rests a bit on the water, then only its eyes, with a small portion of the head and the neck, and farther to the front, often sixteen to twenty-two inches away, its nostrils peer out from the water's surface. The eyes themselves are very small and appear wily and feline. The alligator's legs are short and awkward for walking but are all the more suitable for swimming. One of its favorite occupations is to lie in the hot sunshine on the sandy banks of the lakes or rivers and to wait with open jaw for insects that are attracted by the musky odor emanating from some glands under its neck to fly toward it and alight on its broad tongue, until it has enough and snaps closed, dining on them with the greatest relish.

The breeding season is in April and May. The female lays its eggs in a nest that is usually built of mud and reed, and, of 80 to 120 eggs, the sun hatches about 30 eggs. But the young, hatching alligators have very many enemies. Vultures and buzzards, snakes, indeed the male itself, which is said to often devour almost the entire brood, lie in wait. Enough remain, however, to populate to overflowing the numerous lakes and lagoons of the southern states.

During the breeding season the old alligators sometimes fight bloody battles with jaws and tails. The long, armor-hard tail is really its most dangerous weapon, but it is used more to reach rather than to kill the prey, for the alligator catches the intended victim with its tail and throws it forward toward its jaws, which then receive the victim with a most friendly snap.

In one respect the alligator is like Maria Stuart—it is better than its reputation—for the terrible stories that are told about its murderous lust and devastating hatred toward the human race are usually exaggerated.[35] A white man, if he himself does not attack and wound the alligator (and even so only rarely), has very little to fear from it. To be sure, the alligators go after the Negroes. The piquant odor that is unique to this race—which is, frankly, especially on hot summer days, not among the most pleasant—attracts them. They simply love this odor, and who can blame them for it—for some humans chew *asafetida* to cleanse their breath. So, they love the Negroes—at least an occasional arm or leg, and the black sons of Ethiopia are cautious about wading deep into one of these swampy lagoons. In addition, the alligators also cherish a tender passion for young pigs and dogs. A single alligator devours all of the former and only part of the latter, for when a dog is caught, he no sooner gives a cry of pain before the others are attracted by it and move in from all sides and share the spoils. But they avoid the white man—at his arrival they leave the bank where they have been sunning and submerge themselves.[36]

Alligators do harm only to the extent that now and then they snatch a piglet that gets near them, less often pull a young Negro underwater, or catch by the leg a Negro woman who intends to wash at the riverbank. However, since they are of little use to human society and have an ugly, malicious, dangerous appearance, worst of all have a bad reputation (for there is an old English proverb "It is better to hang a dog than to give it a bad name"), they are pursued with bullet and harpoon, often even with big fish hooks, wherever one can apprehend them.

By the way alligators are not entirely useless, for the big, feisty chaps are put into kettles and rendered into fat that is especially suitable for the various machines used to clean cotton. The tails of the smaller ones—up to a maximum of six feet—have a delicate flavor, but the flesh has to be removed from the spine right away, since otherwise it takes on the musky taste characteristic of these animals.

A planter in Pointe Coupée who lived near us had long been after me to undertake a real alligator hunt, since he very much desired to have several gallons of fat from these gentle beasts, and I owned the only good harpoon in the area. When he, therefore, came to me one morning with his son and two pitch-black Negro slaves and said that on the previous evening he had already brought two light skiffs to the lake behind his house, which was connected by small lagoons to five or six others, and intended to embark on a proper hunt, I shouldered my harpoon, stuck my little scalping knife into my belt, and, handing over my rifle to the young Harbour,[37] who knew how to handle it rather well, we strolled slowly down to the lake that was about 1.5 English miles away.

"What are you carrying there, Ben?" I asked one of the Negroes, who was holding under his arm something wrapped up in a coarse piece of cotton that seemed to be alive.

"Can speak for itself—Massa!" said the black, grinning, tearing open his awful mouth from one ear to the other and showing two rows of dazzling white teeth—"can speak for itself," and then with his left elbow he pressed his charge.

"Squeak!" said a little piglet, which now began to kick about with all four legs.

"Hold still, little one," the Negro soothed it—"good little animal—that's right!"

He was carrying the piglet in order to entice the alligators with its squeals and then to shoot them more easily. Finally, we reached a narrow dam that divided the largest lake in half; the boats lay tied at its inlet. Although it was already the end of June, the water was still very high, for the Mississippi, swollen by the snow of the Rocky Mountains, kept the lowland that lay deeper than its banks filled, so that all the interior land was flooded and lay there like an immense lake through which only here and there small strips of land traversed. This wet and spongy dam, where our boats were fastened, also projected barely two inches above the water's surface.

Two printers, who edited, typeset, and printed *The Pointe Coupée Chronicle*,[38] had joined our hunt. All together we were eight, including the piglet. The elder Harbour now set about dividing us up evenly. Into each boat he first put a Negro "to row," then a printer "to observe"—for we did not anticipate they would be of any further use to us—then young Harbour with the rifle into one boat and I with the harpoon into the other "to hunt." I got the piglet, while the elder Harbour stepped into the boat with his son, who now remarked quite cold-bloodedly: the piglet and he (the father) were there to squeal.

The sun blazed fiercely hot, and on the whole wide water surface there was no shade, save that of the occasional lone cypress covered with long, gray moss. Not even a little breeze stirred. No bird chirped. No frog croaked. Everything lay in indolent, limp repose, and even individual alligators, who, with their black heads, drifted on the mirrored water surface like half-burned pieces of wood, looked as if they were sleeping, except when one of the big fellows sometimes opened wide his rose-red jaws, whereupon its upper jawbone stood up for a moment and then snapped shut again with a loud clap.

"Even the alligators are bored here," said Kelly, the printer who was in my boat.[39]

"It will get lively, Massa," laughed the Negro, "when the little one here talks!"

The piglet sighed mournfully in the sack.—

Then we pushed off from the land, kept close together in the beginning, and tried to glide quietly to the alligators. But they were too skittish, and whenever we were almost within shot range, they sank down. I had placed myself at the front of the boat and calmly waited for one of the fellows to appear at a distance of twelve to fifteen feet, but the elder Harbour became impatient and called over to us, "Go ahead and squeeze the piglet, for heaven's sake!"

The printer, however, who had stood upright in order to survey the water surface better and to whom it probably seemed to be too much effort to bend down, stepped on the poor thing's stomach, without changing his expression.

"Squeeeak!" it cried in mortal fear.

"Massa—for God's sake," the startled Negro called out and stopped rowing—"My pig—you'll crush it to death!"

The experiment, nevertheless, had its desired effect. Several of our long companions, who previously had swum away from us, now turned and slowly came toward us—the Negro had to stop rowing and hold very still, and close by, about thirty steps away, moved a powerful old fellow twelve feet in length.— He stopped for a moment and did not quite trust the boats. But the Negro, who had kneeled down to his little pig, made it make a tiny little cry, and enticed by that, the alligator swam toward us.—

"Fire!" old Harbour shouted. The rifle cracked, and almost simultaneously the mortally wounded monster turned around and showed its white, scaly belly. While shooting ahead and flailing, it fortunately came close enough to my skiff for me to throw, and instantly the sharp, three-pronged harpoon struck its side.

The shot that had shattered its skull did not permit the alligator to tear and tug much longer, and we pulled it close to the skiff easily. It would have been impossible, however, to take the mighty animal into the small vessel, and therefore we quickly rowed back to the bank and dragged it under a tree, while it still thrashed about with its tail.

The experiment with the pig was repeated several times, and young Harbour shot four more alligators, of which we only got two, since I could not reach them quickly enough with the harpoon. I harpooned three who had dared come too close to me and realized the danger too late. Two of them were young and juicy, and I immediately cut off their tails for my own table.

Little by little they must have grasped that there was nothing to the pig because they moved around our skiffs in ever greater circles, and we could not entice any more to within shooting range. So, we gave that up, but the Negro who rowed my skiff performed his task so clumsily and created such an abominable spectacle that we could not at all contemplate sneaking up on the alligators with that fellow. Therefore, I replaced him at the rowing bench and handed the harpoon to Kelly, who pleaded with me fervently to be given a chance to harpoon one, claiming to have caught many a large catfish in this fashion back home in Kentucky. Our two skiffs no longer remained together, and I put one oar down, while I took the other out of the oarlock and guided it by hand, since in this way I could glide forward with a minimum of noise.

For a long time I had been trying to get to a rather large alligator, but it continued to evade me, although I had noted precisely where it dove down and at what distance it always resurfaced. Now it was sinking again, and, rowing with all my strength, so that the skiff shot over the water's surface as quick as lightning, I tried to surprise the alligator when it emerged and shouted to Kelly to watch out. I hardly had spoken when the beast's black head became visible, but just as quickly he tried to descend again. It was, however, too close—barely a step away—for Kelly to miss. The iron stuck fast, and the alligator shot forward with a powerful lurch.

Such a harpoon is arranged as follows: the three-pronged, barbed iron is about eighteen inches long and weighs about three or four pounds. To this is attached a light, ten-foot-long pole, which detaches from the iron when it is thrown. Tied well around its center is a strong rope that runs up the pole and is again attached at the top. The rope affords about twelve to sixteen feet of free play, so that the entire length of the throw can amount to about thirteen or fourteen paces. The end of the rope is fastened around the thrower's wrist, so he won't let it glide through his fingers and lose prey and weapon at the same time.

Instructed by experience, I had, of course, warned Kelly to position himself firmly before throwing and not to lose his balance. In the joyous sensation of harpooning an alligator, however, he thought no more of it, and when the wounded animal now raced away with the iron, a sudden jerk pulled the hunter out of the boat. But the Negro, who probably anticipated something like this, threw himself on Kelly. Even though Kelly's body evaded him, he managed to catch a leg, which he held tightly until our united forces succeeded in pulling back into the boat the now inseparable printer and alligator, the first with the pole, the second with the rope.

Young Harbour, in the meantime, had killed a few more small alligators, and, satisfied with our catch, since the heat of the midday sun became too terribly oppressive, we returned slowly to the house. The Negroes brought the kill to the house on handcarts, since a horse won't easily agree to carry an alligator.

Very often I have shot alligators, like deer, at night by the light of a pine torch, and their eyes glow like pieces of red-hot iron. For one such hunt one evening I took my rifle, the pan with pitch pine, and the harpoon and went to the hunting spot. The view of the swamp, when one approached it with the glowing flame, was truly enchanting.

The dark water surface, in which stood immense cypresses with moss that waved back and forth in the night air, the gloomy, dark forest that surrounded it, the hooting of the owl and the melancholy croak of the bullfrog were to me common, all too familiar things. But splashing and jumping disturbed the water's surface, and as the shadow of my head, cast by the torch behind me, fell onto the dark current, hundreds of glowing red eyes that sometimes remained calmly in one place, sometimes swam toward me in a straight, silent line, stared at me from all sides. They were alligators' eyes shining over at me from the water like pieces of red-hot iron.

Since I had only one hand free, I could not use the rifle and the harpoon at the same time. Therefore, with the first I shot one of the nearest alligators in the head, then put my rifle down, grabbed the harpoon, and, throwing it into the body of the alligator that was only six or seven steps away, pulled it with the rope to the shore. I had already secured two alligators in this fashion when I saw a pair of large eyes coming toward me. I aimed, shot, threw down the gun, and, quickly grabbing the harpoon, I took advantage of the moment when the wounded alligator flailed about in the water and showed its white belly and flung the trident into its body. At the moment of throwing, I stood close to the edge of the water, the end of the rope fastened to my right wrist. But the alligator hardly felt the sharp, barbed iron when it shot forward furiously and dove down, and before I could brace myself at all, it pulled me into the water with all its might. The pan fell from my hand, the torch extinguished with a sizzle, and, try as I might, I could not let go, for the rope was fastened well, and twice already the frightened animal's powerful tugs made me go under. Then I felt firm ground—for the swamps there are not very deep—and, bracing myself soundly, I came to a stop. The alligator, meanwhile, was exhausted from loss of blood and exertion. Pulling quietly and carefully, I reached the shore, and only there, when I thought myself to be completely safe, did I begin pulling harder in order to bring the wounded animal to the levee and secure it. Then the beast once again mustered its last strength, and again I flew head over heels after it into the dark current that sprayed up high. But the water there was hardly four feet deep, and, feeling bottom, with only slight effort I now pulled the faintly resisting alligator to dry ground.

Of course, I could not use the big alligator—it was about ten feet long—for anything for it was too old to be edible. But the two I had shot first were about three and four feet long, so I cut off their tails and took them along to eat. Very few Creoles, not even the Negroes, venture to enjoy alligator meat because some are nauseated by it and others believe it is poisonous. Nevertheless, I found it excellent and never felt any bad effects. The meat is white and firm and tastes very similar to fish, actually like lobster, and looks just like it as well. The tail must be separated from the body right away, and the backbone or spine removed; otherwise, it absorbs the musky smell that is especially peculiar to the older animals. Later we always went alligator hunting in pairs, where one shot and the other harpooned, which made the whole affair considerably easier. As much as the alligator flees the white man's presence in fright, all the more maliciously it goes after Negroes and dogs and chases the latter with remarkable rage.

One afternoon, harpoon in hand, I stood waist deep in the water, and, although I saw many alligators swimming, none wanted to get near enough to me. I do not remember how it occurred to me, but in order to entice one, I began barking like a dog. I hardly had repeated the experiment three or four times when I saw about sixteen quite strong fellows coming toward me. That was a bit too much for me! Standing so deep in water, I was not even in full control of my movements, and with mighty steps I worked my way toward the riverbank that was about one hundred feet away. There I resumed barking loudly, but since I stood completely in the open, the beasts were afraid of coming so close and were content to swim around me at a proper distance.

The Catholic religion is the predominant one in Louisiana. Although the worship service is conducted completely in the Roman Catholic tradition, this does not hold true for the organization since the priest is elected by the parish, and the bishop has nothing to say about it.

A short time ago the parish in which I stayed dismissed its priest because the parishioners were no longer satisfied with him. Having been invested by the bishop, he claimed that only the bishop could remove him, hired Mr. Beatty as his lawyer,[40] and sued his penitents.

Mr. Beatty won the case for him at the semiannual court session, but the parishioners, unhappy with that, appealed to the United States federal court in New Orleans. The priest traveled down there, hired another lawyer, and obtained the following ruling: That the citizens of Pointe Coupée Parish, if they were not satisfied with their priest, might send him away, and neither the bishop nor the pope could give orders in the United States. The odd thing about the matter was that my friend Beatty, after having successfully defended the cleric, was hired the second time by the parish itself and likewise won the case for it.[41]

Not until the end of the following year did I finally decide to return to Germany. Korn had been in New Orleans for quite a while already, where he had established a commission business with a Frenchman, Mr. Bourquin,[42] and I began to feel lonely and abandoned in Pointe Coupée. Therefore, I put all my affairs in order and could soon give up my position, since I had prevailed upon a brother of Mr. Fischer, who had been in business with him previously, to take over my position. Everything was running more smoothly and better than before, and the hotel had pretty much regained the good reputation it had enjoyed under Roettken. So, I left Pointe Coupée on July 5 (the same day on which I left Little Rock the year before), and taking leave of all friends and acquaintances there, embarked on the steamer *Eclipse*,[43] and reached New Orleans on the following day.

The banks of the Mississippi in the lower part of Louisiana offer a person hurrying past on a swift boat a wondrously lovely panorama of towns and individual plantations. The plantations are unique and splendid: between dark hedges of orange and pomegranate trees are hidden the masters' houses, against which the slave quarters, which usually consist of nothing but uniform, single-story houses, painted white and laid out in rows, nestle like small villages. In addition, the enormous sugarcane and cotton fields in which gangs of blacks work under the surveillance of a white overseer on horseback, herds of little mustangs or ponies that gallop up and down the bank with raised tails and manes, and small schooners and so-called chicken-thieves that shoot along the shore with swelling sails give the entire scene a lively and friendly aspect. Now, I admit, it did not look so pleasant everywhere. The Mississippi had risen considerably and in several places had broken through the levee so that many sugarcane and cotton fields stood completely underwater. That gave the landscape a desolate, uncanny appearance, but the richness of the land could still not be overlooked, and if one wished to judge according to appearances, then the blue sky here must have spanned a happy countryside—but would the slaves say that, too?

The next morning, around nine o'clock, we approached the depot of the South, the mighty New Orleans, and a great number of sloops, schooners, brigs, and even *barques* lying above the city already testified to the busy activity of the enormous city of commerce.

We had about forty head of cattle on board that were transported down from St. Louis, and we put them ashore in Lafayette, a suburb of New Orleans.[44] That is to say, the boat anchored near the shore, and the oxen and cows were driven overboard, whereby they fell over each other with quite odd capers and somersaults before they landed in the water and then had to swim to shore on their own. That taken care of, the vessel took off again, and, passing ships of all kinds and nations, at ten o'clock we landed among about sixty other steamboats at the levee of New Orleans.

I found Korn right away and went with him to the inn where he lodged in order to deposit my things. Then we strolled around the city a bit, talking about old times. The heat was oppressive, and soon we had to seek shelter in the shade of the house in order to escape the sun's truly searing rays. Toward evening, however, when it became shady and cool, we drove up to Lafayette, where several ships from Bremen were said to be docked, in order to look at them and inquire about their departure dates. We found the *Olbers* and the *Johann Friedrich*, both bound for Bremen. The *Favorite* had just sailed off the previous day. The departure date of both ships, incidentally, did not appear to be precisely determined, and I foresaw that I would have to stay in New Orleans for some weeks.[45]

The city had grown enormously since I had been there and also had improved in appearance. It now extended for seven miles along the bank of the Mississippi, densely bordered by an almost uninterrupted row of the most different kinds of vessels. Otherwise, the city does not offer anything more remarkable than straight, beautiful streets with large, neat houses and shops with tasteful displays. But it is interesting to observe the people who, at every time of day, even in the hottest sun, bustle through the streets, where one can see all gradations of black, brown, and white imaginable.

The lower market, close to the levee, was the most attractive spot to me. There one can buy everything that is available in America, and the stands of the fruit dealers, as well as of the fishmongers with all kinds of fish for sale looked quite inviting. But in the middle of all the noise and spectacle, often amid the maddest throngs, little rest havens are set up everywhere. Here a huge, highly polished brass coffee machine gleams on a little table around which stand several chairs. Cups as well as several plates of pastries are at hand, and pretty young girls tend to the pouring. Hot coffee (at some stands tea and chocolate, too) is available at all times of the day or night. Since I could not bear to sleep in the small, hot rooms where not a breeze penetrated, unless forced to by utter exhaustion, almost every night I strolled around the ever lively streets and drank coffee.[46] At daybreak I then walked around the lower market to observe the life and activity there and to see the multitude of Americans, French, Creoles, English, Germans, Spaniards, Italians, Negroes, mulattoes, mestizos, Indians, et cetera. Then I proceeded home, ate breakfast, whereby, according to Creole custom, one drinks red wine with ice instead of coffee, and then lay down for a few hours. Korn, as far as his business allowed, was excellent company, and we conversed with each other for many a long hour.

Finally, after a three-week wait, on July 22, the *Olbers* was *cleared;* that is, it was all set to put to sea. Our things were on board, leave had been taken—a very heartfelt leave-taking from Korn, of whom I had grown as fond as a brother—and at ten in the evening the tugboat *Porpoise* laid to our side.[47] Here, however, we had company. The *Porpoise* also had a French brig and three schooners in tow, and fastened to the side of the smoking and puffing steamer, we started out down the dark stream like a small flotilla.

Toward noon we reached the mouth of the Mississippi and dropped anchor. But, dear God! what kind of a place is this; everywhere thin green reeds jut out from the water and thus form a land-like contrast to the river, but without banks. Everywhere in between the yellow river pushes through, so that not an inch of solid, secure ground presents itself to the foot or to the eye that darts about almost anxiously. The Mississippi is still a river here, but it no longer has any banks, and yet it still looks as if it were enclosed in its bed. How great was my astonishment when I saw houses jut out from this wilderness of water and reeds and even noticed living beings who seemed to move about between them.[48]

According to our pilot, we could not attempt to cross the sandbank that runs straight across the river here until the following morning, in broad daylight and with the incoming tide. Since we had nothing else to do for the whole afternoon, the captain decided to go over to the row of houses to see whether we could perhaps buy oysters there or something else edible. No sooner said than done! Besides me, Captain Exter took along two passengers—a man from Hamburg, Herr Beuk, and an American—in the longboat, and a half-hour of vigorous rowing brought us to land. To land? No, to boards fastened to piles. I had not yet come across a more dreadful place than this in my life.

This outpost of American bliss rests on piles on which are constructed the houses, under which at high tide the water runs in quite friendly fashion. At ebb tide—and it was ebb tide when we went over—it leaves a thin, sticky mire on which no human being could walk without sinking in and disappearing forever. In order to connect the light wooden houses, piles had been driven or probably only stuck into the mire (I still cannot understand how) and planks fastened to them, so that one could get around only on these. But in the mire below teemed all kinds of disgusting, crawling creatures. Sometime earlier I had heard an American say: the good Lord had not intended for people to live in Louisiana and had created the land solely for mosquitoes, alligators, and bullfrogs. Here now that became quite clear to me, for I still cannot comprehend how it could occur to a rational person to settle down in a place like this.

The inhabitants catch oysters a short distance away, sell part of their catch to the ships, and haul the rest on their little boats up to New Orleans, where they trade them for other provisions, and then return to their families (yes, truly families, for even women and children live there). Almost all the men are pilots. When we arrived, there was not a single oyster in the whole place nor anything else. They told me the entire population was eagerly awaiting a boat with provisions. A glass of "brandy" mixed with vitriol was all that we got there, and, happy to have escaped the frantic mosquitoes in the little settlement, we headed back on board.

At nine o'clock the next morning we weighed the anchor. The steamboat *Porpoise,* which meanwhile had brought several smaller ships across the sandbank, approached and took us in tow. We just barely slid over the sand and could feel distinctly the keel scraping.[49] The *Porpoise* led us for several miles more out into the Gulf and then left us to make our way alone as best we could. . . .

From *Pictures of the Mississippi*
Light and Dark Sides of Transatlantic Life (1847–1848)

NEW ORLEANS

New Orleans, the Queen of the South, the marketplace of countless plantations and farms in all parts of the Union, the crossroads from the cold, northerly climate to the pleasant, mild tropical world, the South America of the Ohio and Mississippi raftsman and flatboatman, the Eldorado and grave of millions. New Orleans, the jousting place of the fashionable world, where the hot-blooded Spanish woman's dazzling white complexion next to the lightly tinged hue of the Creole, with her dark curls, where the lively Frenchwoman next to the serious, doe-eyed American do not permit a man strolling through the Prado to gaze after only *one* beauty because then he would miss seeing three others.[1] New Orleans, the center of all southern trade, the port of thousands of vessels, justly deserves its sobriquet of Queen, if one can at all confer this title on a republican city in a republican realm. But whoever

> Knows the people, names the names
> Of those who hospitably together came.[2]

There is no country in the world that is not represented here. A wild whirl of Spanish, English, French, and German sounds like the ancient Tower of Babel to the newcomer who has not yet become accustomed to all the comings and goings. Only the Irish drayman's cursing and blustering, the working Negro's singing and laughter, the calls of the milk and fruit sellers, and the rolling of countless vehicles, as well as the gasping and groaning of the steamboats that leave and arrive continually, drown out the confusion.

"For how many centuries has this city existed?" the foreign visitor naturally wonders, quickly surveying with astonishment the wealth and splendor spread out before him. "How much time did it take to build up this seven-mile-long sea of houses, these enormous warehouses, these wharfs and levees?"

His astonishment increases when he hears of the fantastic speed with which the city literally arose from the mud and swamp.

In 1718 Bienville, the governor of the French territories at that time,[3] picked out the site for a city to be built on the bank of the Mississippi where New Orleans now lies. He left 50 people there to put up their log cabins. In 1722 New

Orleans, with 200 inhabitants, was declared the capitol of the colonial government. In 1733 the king of France ceded New Orleans, along with all tracts of land that lay west of the Mississippi, to Spain.[4] In 1766 Ulloa came to New Orleans to take possession of all ceded land in the name of the king of Spain.[5] The province at that time had 5,000 whites and 5,000 blacks.

Until 1798 the population grew only slightly. New Orleans did not have more than 5,338 inhabitants. Not until 1803, when Louisiana, according to the Louisiana Purchase treaty signed in Paris, came under the jurisdiction of the North American Republic, did this city's population multiply astonishingly. In 1810 the number of inhabitants amounted to 17,241; in 1820, 27,176; in 1830, 46,310; and now during the busiest time of year, in winter, it is almost 200,000.

Whereas in the healthy winter and spring months the gay crowds of people hurry briskly along the thickly populated streets, in late summer and fall New Orleans becomes dead and barren. The plague-like yellow fever spreads its leaden wings over the city,[6] and its inhabitants flee to the shores of the neighboring lakes or up to the North in order to elude the grim, merciless enemy. Unless there is urgent necessity, no human being can be seen in the open air, which is impregnated with the blight of the nearby swamps.[7] On the brass knobs of the doorbells hang wide bands of black mourning crepe—the death announcements of the plague that is raging within the houses. If one pedestrian encounters another on the empty streets, he avoids him as much as possible and hardly dares to breathe for fear of drawing in death from the passerby. All the stores are closed. Who would go shopping now, anyway? Could one not perhaps carry death to one's own family along with the purchased object? No rattling of wheels is heard—but yes, from that street over there is a noise, and there again, from the other end as well. What could it be? The horses turn around the corner. It is two hearses that cross as they head toward the different cemeteries of the city. And what gigantic corpse is in that large coffin that, shoved straight across an ordinary transport cart driven by a Negro driver, slowly rattles over the pavement with a hollow sound?[8]

Oh, it is not a gigantic corpse that is being transported to its final resting place. It is only a crudely built pine box that contains the corpses of *three* men. Scipio is carrying them out to "Potters Field,"[9] where they can slumber, drifting toward a new life in the damp, marshy soil, just a few inches under the ground.

But away, away, with these pictures of misery and horror. This is not the population of a plague-ridden city rushing toward the bank of the broad, majestic river. Here life and health prevail, here joy and pleasure shine from every eye, and the air from the colder North, blowing fresh impetus and activity through the Orleanians' veins, is as pure as the clear sky vault that spans the charming scene in splendid blue.

There at the landing a steamer from Cincinnati is just docking. It has trouble pushing past the equally stately steamers to get through to the steamboat landing. The sailors run around busily with ropes and hand spokes, first pulling the colossus over toward this side then keeping it away from the neighboring steamboat on the other, so that the steamer doesn't damage and crush its neighbor and, in turn, itself. Finally, the steamboat has reached the spot where a plank can be shoved toward the shore. And now whoever can reach the narrow footbridge from land presses forward to board the newly arrived vessel as quickly as possible to hear what the Buckeyes, Hoosiers, and Corncrackers are doing up North.[10] But we'll just let them keep shoving. We are less interested in the steamboat than in the new city, and from the neighboring boat, with which the steamer lies wheel to wheel, we reach the wooden wharf built out into the river, loaded with vast quantities of all sorts of wares, and at the same time we reach the levee.

Although the name levee is familiar enough in Louisiana, it might require some explanation here.

The word *levee*, which is of French origin, usually means in the American sense the dam or the dike built throughout Louisiana, along the Mississippi and the smaller rivers and bayous emptying into it, that keeps the water out from the lower-lying land when the river has reached its highest stage. With the exception of the area around Baton Rouge, Bayou Sara, and several other little spots, most land throughout Louisiana lies under the so-called high-water mark, and therefore this levee is truly an uncommonly artificial and painstakingly laid-out construction. It is designed to wrest from the water the most splendid, fertile estates and to populate a region that, as the Creoles correctly claim, God really only intended for "alligators, bullfrogs, and mosquitoes." The mosquitoes, then, take quite fierce revenge for these invasions that the human race has permitted itself into their territory and levy a considerable blood tax.

Louisiana's levee is splendid, holding the mighty "father of the waters" in its designated bed and, when there is high water, allowing it to flow to the ocean four to six feet, indeed, at some spots more than ten feet higher than the dwellings of the people who live under the protection of this dam. The New Orleans levee is just as unique and no less surprising.

The "city" with its suburbs stretches for seven English miles along the Mississippi. This entire waterfront, which is, of course, contained by the levee, is covered with thousands of vessels, steamboats, flatboats, keelboats, brigs, *barques,* three-masters, schooners, chicken thieves, and rafts from which there is unceasing lively interaction with the shore. The wares are unloaded and loaded, and there is no end to the riding and driving, the shouting, singing, and charging about.

By the way the most animated section of New Orleans is undisputedly that part of the levee with the steamboat landing that stretches almost to the lower market. At every time of the day and night boats from all the Union's western rivers land—as well as boats from the Gulf, from the eastern and southeastern states, Texas and Mexico. At this point the trade from the icy regions of the North and the hot countries of the tropic zone converge, and all exchange their products here.

In the midst of the valuable goods and wares piled up into mountains, between thousands of coffee sacks, indigo bales, cotton bales, and sugar barrels from the South, lead bars from the North, and the barrels filled with whiskey, flour, tobacco, and salt pork—beautiful mulatto girls with tin milk cans on their heads or flower baskets in their hands; ragged boys with newspapers and novellas; German Jews with notions, pistols, and knives; flatboat people from the North with eggs and cheese merrily jump and climb and scurry about, offering their wares for sale. Even on the river, almost under the wheels of the steamboats, where just a narrow stripe of unoccupied water allows a slender rowboat to slip by, the Mexicans' skiffs glide past with pineapples, coconuts, figs, pomegranates, and oranges.

As soon as the cool evening dusk nears, New Orleans's aristocracy strolls on the Prado. A confluence of beauties of all colors from all corners of the earth surrounds the busy activity of the loading and unloading boats and the shipping and receiving merchants like a magic sash. Meanwhile, guards and watchmen stationed there break up a crowd of ragged Irish and German women who are eagerly boring holes into the sugar barrels with wooden and reed sticks. The guards crack their whips over a similar gang equipped with little handbaskets and pocketknives covertly cutting into the coffee sacks in order to take a few handfuls of coffee as booty.

These are, however, minor interruptions, and only occasionally does the Irish temper manifest itself so far away from home. Then Patrick swings his dray stick at Patrick or, surrounded by a tight ring of crowding spectators, boxes for life and limb with his unfortunate opponent. But these quarrels are relatively rare, considering the enormous mixture that consists of all classes and castes, of all colors and temperaments, from hotheaded Spaniards to cold-blooded Dutchmen. The police in New Orleans are altogether excellent, and the northern visitor who, expecting to be mugged at any moment, wanders through the streets at night armed with daggers and pistols is, to his great surprise, disappointed and finds the city just as safe as the northern cities, even if it is not so peaceful and quiet.

To be sure, there was a time when New Orleans was everything that the most fervent imagination could conjure—robbery and murder, gambling and immorality. Day and night the green tables were spread out on the open street. When the dawning day illuminated the shadowy alleys, blood frequently colored the trampled earth, and corpses with gaping wounds and distorted, often cut-up faces lay rigid on some corner of the main streets. *This* time is now over for New Orleans; an excellent corps of watchmen, armed with clubs, passes through even the most remote, sinister quarters. The sound of their alarms brings help from all directions as quick as a flash, so that once the brawler or criminal is discovered he cannot hope to escape.

The city is divided into three "municipalities."[11] That American and French interests were separated from each other contributed substantially to the improvements that were made later. Each nationality in the municipality in which it not only had the majority but was in general the predominant group put an end to shortcomings and could replace them with more appropriate arrangements. French is closely and intimately intertwined with English. Especially in court the lawyers argue in either one of these two languages and often automatically go from one to the other. In the city itself one hears people speaking in all imaginable tongues. The German peddlers especially have developed the skill of combining broken English, Spanish, French, German, and Italian so dreadfully that only someone familiar with all these languages is able to make out individual words as the peddlers extol the virtues of their wares with excessive volume in this dialect of Babel. The peddlers probably do this so that any passerby, no matter what country he comes from, may hear the sound of his mother tongue and, lured by that, may approach and make a purchase.

But we cannot leave the levee yet; those booths selling oysters, ice cream, and sorbets beckon too enticingly. The most frequented fruit and ice cream tents are near the schooner landing. Here the merchant or planter flees during the heat of the sun and, sipping his glass of lemonade, observes the busy activity on the wharfs or, in the cool evenings, watches the countless strollers.

These places are frequented to an uncommon degree, and a visitor can find no more splendid place to leisurely observe the shore life of the tremendous city than here under the cool tent of the friendly Italian, a cooling refreshment before him, surrounded by all the lively activity that unfolds before his eyes like a grand panorama.

The markets are typical: large halls supported by stone columns with separate sections for the butchers, fishmongers, and greengrocers. Large, shining brass or copper machines filled with hot tea, coffee, or chocolate entice both buyers and sellers to have their breakfast and to render harmless the damp, penetrating fog from the river with a hot brew.

The market, which none in the whole world surpasses in variety, because it combines all products of the South and North, closes around noon. But the coffee stands remain open throughout the night, and the servers, usually young German girls, relieve each other for rest breaks. The harbor is most deserted during the hot afternoon hours. Everyone who is not forced out on the street by urgent business seeks the coolness of the houses. Only the workers on ships and steamboats who are busy loading and unloading cannot take a break and must continue to work in the hot, blazing sun. But when the day draws to a close, these markets acquire a brisker, fresher appearance. The sun has not yet set when some of the sellers arrive in order to be on the spot very early the next morning. They cover their wares for the night with large, cotton cloths, and if they get tired, even sleep wrapped up in the cloths under the protection of the market building.

Aside from the night watchmen, however, they are the only people who are *allowed* to sleep in the open, for if another unfortunate mortal is caught napping by a patrolling watchman, then no protest and resistance will help him. He has to go to the so-called calaboose and spend the rest of the night with drunks and all kinds of riffraff.[12] A poor French dance instructor found himself in this miserable situation. Having just arrived a few weeks ago in New Orleans from Paris, he was not able to sleep in his stuffy room during such a humid May night. Therefore, he went down to the street to cool off a bit, dressed in only a nightshirt. His door opened out onto a rather quiet part of the levee, and, barely 150 feet away, the river rolled by with a dull, mysterious murmur. The son of France, charmed by the nocturnal drama and the refreshing river breeze, sat down on a wooden bench and, feeling completely at peace, looked over toward the towering ships' masts through which single lights shone across from the opposite bank of the town of Algiers.

He had sat there for half an hour when he began to feel too cool in his light clothing and was just about to get up and return to his bed. From around the next corner a figure buttoned up in a large top coat, on his head a lacquered, helmet-like hat on which a number painted on a yellow background could be discerned in the dim glow of the stars. Swinging a heavy hickory stick with his right hand, without further ado he grabbed the surprised visitor by the collar, or for lack of that, by the nightshirt, and in his broad Irish dialect cried with the utmost indignation: "Do you, Arrah, seek to make your bed in front of other people's doors? By Jesus, I'll teach you to break the laws made by his honor, the mayor."[13]

The Frenchman, whose name was not Arrah and who could not understand a single word of what the son of "the Green Isle" had uttered with such volubility,[14] protested in vain, since the other had just as little command of the French language. Finally, the Frenchman tried to pull away forcibly from the watchman's iron grasp to reach the door that was only a few steps away.

Patrick took this completely the wrong way. "What, Sirrah, resisting the higher authority?" he cried in just indignation, "then take *that*, Honey," and thereupon hit the weak little man on the head just lightly with his heavy hickory stick, whereupon he collapsed unconscious.

When the Frenchman came to again, he found himself shivering with cold in the so-called calaboose behind a heavy door with iron bars on a hard plank bed. He was in very mixed company. Fortunately, the man on duty understood French and allowed him to send for his clothes before it got to be full daylight. But the Frenchman was not permitted to leave his cell before the hearing, where he just received a warning to choose his bed more wisely in the future.

The varied and numerous skin colors of the inhabitants of New Orleans make a particular impression on visitors, especially those from Europe. This diversity is probably found in all tropical cities but surely nowhere to such an extent as here. One encounters thirty different people in a row, and there are no two who have the same color face. Their coloring ranges from the darkest black of the native African to the dazzling white of the recently arrived northern European, and countless blends of whites, Negroes, mulattoes, mestizos, Indians, Creoles, Spaniards, et cetera., would drive to despair anyone desiring to inquire more closely and thoroughly about their origins.

Here I must also mention something else about which the foreigner, especially the German, usually is mistaken. He understands the term *Creole* to mean a mixture of the white with the Indian, but that is not at all the case. Everything that is born or produced there is called "Creole." When Europeans come to Louisiana, their children born there are Creoles. This term is even applied to animals and inanimate objects. The little horses native to Louisiana or bred there are called "Creole ponies," and in the year 1843, after an unusually cold night, a New Orleans paper reported as a curiosity that in the Exchange Hotel people had drunk mint juleps with *Creole ice*.[15]

New Orleans has another peculiarity in its cemeteries, where the graves are not under but above the ground. One can only dig a few feet before striking water, which is also the reason why no house has a cellar, and only here and there cemented cisterns serve this function.

New Orleans has five churchyards, and three of these, one Catholic and two Protestant, are constructed similarly. They are surrounded by a strong brick wall about twelve to fourteen feet high and ten feet wide, and this mass of stone contains the graves that, not unlike baking ovens, are built just big enough to take up a coffin.

When the dead person has moved into his narrow house, the narrow space is closed again, and the outer part of the grave is indistinguishable from the entire red, uniform surface. Only small black or white marble tablets announce whose bones rest in this quiet place. But it is a sad business to read the inscriptions on the various graves. A cold shudder involuntarily runs through the stroller's bone and marrow, and, trembling, he muses, "When will your hour toll? Everyone here—everyone—died in the prime of life, and most victims were young men and maidens." The yellow fever, the plague that returns annually, snatches up thousands and thousands, but more rush in and fill the deceaseds' places, for a while in life, then perhaps in their very same graves.[16] The open space enclosed by these walls of graves is in turn divided into square plots on which, at almost the same height as the walls, similar layers of graves are constructed. This lends the cemetery the appearance of a small city, an uncanny comparison if one thinks of its inhabitants.

I was told that after a period of ten years these "ovens," if they are not private property, are opened again, cleared of the remains of the persons previously buried there, and prepared to take up new corpses.

They do not, however, bury all the dead in such an expensive, space-consuming manner. Many thousands die in the hospitals as foreigners, without a friend. Many in the city die without leaving enough money for even the cheapest burial. These people are taken to "potter's field" outside of the city, where the bodies are put into a shallow grave. But the swollen marshy earth does not always tolerate them in its lap, the waters rise, and often enough they push the coffin with its contents back up to the surface of the spongy ground, where the body must decay in the open air, for even the vultures finally turn away in disgust from this repulsive meal.

At New Orleans the Mississippi is between one and a quarter and one and a half English miles wide and is said to be two hundred feet deep. This must certainly be true, considering its current, for the river has about the same width at St. Louis, and from that point on, in addition to countless smaller rivers, it takes in the mighty Ohio, Arkansas, Red, and White rivers.

To add a concluding remark, New Orleans lies on the east bank, or, looking down from above, on the left bank of the river. Strangely enough, all visitors presume that the city is on the opposite side. Even while standing on the spot, they learn only with great difficulty and puzzlement that the city is on the east bank, since the river here, instead of following its main direction from north to south, appears to flow back and runs almost entirely to the north.

From *From My Diary*

Collected Stories (1863)

IN BAYOU SARA

Bayou Sara is a small town at the mouth of the Bayou (or the little swamp water) Sara, which lies opposite Pointe Coupée on the Mississippi. It is not distinct from the thousand other places of similar size scattered throughout the Union. I do not intend to tell the reader about anything extraordinary or unusual here but only about something that has happened in the Union countless times already and, unfortunately, is still happening.

In Bayou Sara there lived a German tailor whose name in Germany probably was Schadwig, or something like that, because the Americans, who ruin *all* names, called him "Chadwick." He was a quiet, harmless, and diligent man. His shop was right next to our boardinghouse, where he took his meals and had a very plain room on the second floor. He did not charge very much, and we Germans gave him almost all of our business. He lived modestly, had no debts, and was liked by all.

I had lived in Bayou Sara for several months before moving to St. Francisville, which was about a half-hour away on the next hill. In the beginning I still went down occasionally to the town on the river. But since my only friend there soon moved to New Orleans, I no longer had a reason to go, and so I did not hear much about what was going on down there.

After quite some time had passed, I finally heard that Chadwick, as he generally was called, had been very ill but was feeling better. I decided to go down and visit him in the next few days. That evening, however, a German came up from Bayou Sara, and I inquired about our poor tailor. He told me that Chadwick had had a relapse the day before and was worse than ever.

The next morning I went down and, without first sticking my head into the pub, headed straight up the stairs to his room. To my surprise it was empty and aired out; the floor was freshly scrubbed; and there was no bed nor table nor chair. I could not imagine what had happened to the sick man and asked below where he might have been transported.

"Oh," said the innkeeper, a genuine, "Americanized" German,[1] "we just moved him one flight higher, for if he had died in our best room, we never could have let it again."

"And who is up there with him?"

"Now—I really don't know," was the answer. "My wife was up there this morning, but she said he looked bad."

I rushed upstairs, for I knew quite well that right under the uninsulated roof there was only a dark attic room, which was burning hot when the sun's rays beat down on it. While I was still on the stairs, I heard moans and groans. Stumbling up the last few steps, I was immediately at the bedside of the poor man, who was lying, alone and forsaken, in his battle with death.

"Water!" the poor devil moaned, when he heard the sound of my footsteps, and before even saying a word to him I hurried downstairs in order to fetch what he wanted. When I returned with it, he no longer needed water. With eyes staring straight upward, he lay stretched out on his hard bed. He was foaming at the mouth, and his lips were blue and ghastly.

"Poor Chadwick," I called to him, "how are you? Here is some water!"—He did not reply. I held the glass to his lips and tried to pour a little water into his mouth, but he pressed his lips firmly together. He shuddered, and then he lay quiet and peaceful and stirred no more.—He was dead.

I went downstairs to inform the innkeeper.

"So?" he said calmly. "Well, I almost expected that! It is better for him than if he had suffered here for a long time."

The doctor was summoned to determine whether Chadwick had truly departed, and the burial was set for the next morning. I remained in Bayou Sara for the day and heard that quarrels over his estate had begun. The innkeeper claimed that he was owed board and lodging for I don't know how many months, but it was well known that Chadwick paid promptly each week. The innkeeper also demanded compensation for caring for the patient. Others also showed up with this and that demand, and the inheritance—six to eight different garments and pieces of cloth—was almost divided before the body had turned cold.

The burial took place on the following morning because bodies can not be left above ground for long in the warm climate. It was executed as simply as the poor devil had died.

An acquaintance of his owned a dray, a two-wheeled, horse-drawn transport wagon, with which he earned his livelihood. He loaded the pine board coffin onto the dray and drove it up to the cemetery situated on high ground near St. Francisville. It was just we four Germans who followed the coffin to pay the deceased our "last respects." There was need of us as well to lift the heavy coffin from the wagon and let it down into its quiet grave. There was no minister—after twenty-four hours there was not enough left over from the estate to *pay* for one, and no one felt compelled to provide the "foreigner" such a service for free.—There was also no need for one. We, his last friends, said a silent prayer over his corpse and then released the body to rest in peace. A few minutes later the grave was filled, and the wagon rattled back into town to await the next steamer and not miss out on earning the daily wages.

THE HOUSEBOY AND THE COW

Upstairs I was leaning on the windowsill, looking out onto the little fenced-in pasture, in which Mary, the housemaid, had already been trying for half an hour to tame and milk a new cow that had just been brought in that morning.

Mary was a robust young Negro girl with a wild, exuberant sense of humor. She was bold and confident, difficult to restrain, and black as a raven besides. But the cow was all that, too, and as stubborn a rogue as had ever been concealed in a black hide. The cow allowed the girl to approach and pet her, but as soon as the maid quietly and carefully bent down and began to milk, the cow knocked the milk pail aside with one kick, turned its sharp horns around, and the girl had to hurry to get out of the way.

In the hotel there—it was the Ferry Hotel of the French settlement of Pointe Coupée on the Mississippi—we also had a "white" houseboy, a German. We must mention that he was white because in the slave states there rarely are servants who are not colored. He was, by the way, a white man only by descent, since the Louisiana sun had burned his skin color so that he looked like a proper mulatto.

Now Jacob, a fat, easygoing fellow, who could get by with doing very little work and also enjoyed good food and drink, was standing below in the enclosure. He was busy, or at least acting as if he were busy, splitting and cutting up one of the logs washed up by the Mississippi. A low thicket of Ricinus shrubs, the so-called wonder tree[2]—whose shoots, adorned with charming leaves and blossoms, sprang up everywhere in the meadow—separated him from the cow and the girl.

As long as these attempts at milking lasted, Jacob did not lift a finger. Only when the girl retreated timidly from the cow's threatening horns did he say in his broken and odd-sounding English, "Don't be afraid, you dumbbell; *she won't butt!*"

At first the girl, annoyed at the stubborn animal, did not pay any attention to what he was saying and tried again and again to approach the cow, who rebuffed each renewed assault just as firmly. The cow's eyes became ever more threatening, and from several similar, bitter experiences with such beasts I realized that it soon would lose its patience and in the end could become dangerous. In such cases women, with their long skirts, are not able to get out of the way quickly enough. Therefore, I called to the girl from above to leave the cow alone and not bother her anymore; she did not *want* to be milked. Perhaps she would be in a better mood that afternoon.

"Oh, nonsense," Jacob opined, "the silly goose doesn't know how to handle it. Every time she pulls back, the cow gets wilder. Just take hold of her boldly, Mary, she won't butt!"

"Yes—she won't butt!" cried the girl, who now got annoyed at him, too. "You can talk from behind your bushes there. If *you* are so smart, then come over here and milk her. Anyone can say that she won't butt!"

Jacob stood for a few seconds and thought it over, for he appeared to have no intention of doing anything at all. But when I called from the window: "Leave him alone, Mary. He's afraid of her, too!" it roused his sense of pride, and rolling up his sleeves decisively, Jacob worked his way through the bushes and said, "Well now, give *me* the pail—clumsy girl can't even milk an old cow like this!" He picked up the pail confidently and approached the cow, caressed her back with his right hand, and said, "Come on, old girl, be smart—you can't get out of this!" With that he hunkered down next to the cow and reached for her udder.

Meanwhile, the cow stood quietly, without making a move, and patiently allowed Jacob to approach. But Mary did not like either the way the cow turned toward Jacob, holding her head low, nor the color of the cow's eyes. She took a few steps back.

"So, Mitzie," Jacob said, "that's a good girl—oh! ouch!—oooh!" he cried and jumped up as the angry cow suddenly lunged toward him and tried to reach him with her horns.

"She won't butt, Jacob!" Mary called out, laughing. Jacob seemed to have developed a completely different opinion, for he quickly jumped sideways and had barely enough time to evade the cow's attack. "She won't butt!" Mary rejoiced. "That's a good cow!" Whether the girl's loud laughter irritated the cow or whether the prior attempts to approach had already made her impatient, the cow again turned toward Jacob, lowered her head in a rage, and tried to grab him with her horns.

"Satan's beast!" Jacob cried, taking a forward leap that would have made a pole-vaulter proud. He threw the milk pail away, perhaps as a decoy for the an-

gry cow's advances. But neither this clumsy maneuver nor the stout little fellow's leaps back and forth distracted the cow. With a short, low bawl she rushed
after him. As his last possible escape route, Jacob took a death-defying run
through the thick Ricinus bushes in order to detain his pursuer.—Mary was
bent over with laughter, and the only words that she uttered, rejoicing and
shouting, were: "She won't butt, Jacob—oh Jacob, she won't butt!"

The Ricinus bushes, to be sure, held up the cow somewhat, since she got
stuck by the horns a few times but never long enough to give poor, frightened,
and agitated Jacob time to reach the nearest fence and hurl his imperiled limbs
over it into safety. Each time, just as he was about to reach the fence and climb
up, the cow was fast at his heels, and he had to take off again in fear, under the
burning sun.

Mary, meanwhile, who had reached the fence and climbed up onto it right
after the angry cow's first leaps, sat there, still shouting for joy, "Don't run, Jacob, she truly won't butt!" Jacob, already completely out of breath, desperately
looked around for help. Had the cow reached him, he would have been badly
off because she had wicked pointed horns and clearly intended to use them.
Now she was barely two feet away from Jacob—she would have caught up with
him in the next two bounds. I blamed myself because I was at least partly responsible for his approaching the cow. From the window I shouted loudly at
the cow in hope of distracting her from her victim. But Jacob trusted no such
futile tricks and in blind desperation fled into a last refuge.

In the middle of the narrow pasture there was a water hole, perhaps four or
five feet deep and about twelve feet wide, into which the dirt from the yard was
also swept. Recent heavy rains had almost filled up the hole, and as anxiously
as Jacob had avoided it in his flight up to now, he now sought it out just as
hastily. The cow was almost touching him with her horns when he flew sideways with one diagonal jump and in the next moment was up to his neck in the
mud and water. If the cow followed him there as well, he would be lost. I raised
my rifle, which I kept at the ready, into the air, firmly resolved to shoot the cow
dead before I would allow the man to be hurt.

But this jump freed Jacob from his tormenter without my needing to shoot,
for when the dirty brown water closed over his head and sprayed far and wide,
the cow stopped, stunned, looked down at him first, and then ran around the
hole bawling.

"She won't butt, Jacob, she won't butt!" Mary rejoiced, quite beside herself
with amusement over this new turn. But when I saw that Jacob was out of danger at least for the moment, I myself jumped down to try to lend him a hand.

An Irish lawyer who lived in the hotel had also heard the noise and came out.[3] Grabbing two poles, both of us finally succeeded in driving the cow back into the opposite corner of the fence. Jacob needed no invitation to leave his refuge and get out of the enclosure as fast as he could. It was up to us to deal with the cow.

The next morning Mary made a new, very cautious attempt to milk the cow. Again, the cow would not let her get near and could not be restrained until we tied her horns to a tree and tied up one hind leg; then the cow stood still because she simply *could* not move.

But for many, many months afterward Jacob had to hear the phrase "She won't butt!"

From "Louisiana Sketches,"
Wild World (1865–1867)

A DRILL

The last American war commanded not only Germany's attention but the attention of the entire known world,[1] as far as news could penetrate—and we saw there not *one* battle, no, three, four different battles being waged simultaneously in states scattered across the map. Each individual battle produced such a loss of human life that one would have believed it *must* lead to a decisive victory for one side or the other—but always for naught. Human lives were, to be sure, the cheapest thing in the Union from way back, and therefore they gambled with human lives to their heart's content.

The common and, unfortunately, all too well-founded complaint in the American army concerned the lack of competent leaders—of men who not only possessed enough personal courage to be at the head of a battalion and throw themselves into a bayonet attack but also of the sort that understood how to master the wild, agitated game of war in its *entirety*. Hundreds of thousands had to be slaughtered because of this lack of leaders who could direct a battle.

American education, however, was not at all based on training such people, for up to the moment when this war began, they knew nothing about a "standing army" and made do with a small number of mercenary troops who sufficed to protect the borders against the Indians and keep them in line. Even the Mexican war was not fought with a regular military but almost solely by volunteers.—California was conquered by just a small troop of volunteers as well, and even in *Washington's* day the officers complained that their soldiers were excellent when on the battlefield and active, but they were good for nothing when it was a matter of remaining in camp for a while and patiently waiting for the time to attack. In that case the officers could do nothing with them, and even the harshest punishment did not stop them from deserting.

Of course, in the United States it was the law—which was also enforced—that *every citizen,* indeed every foreigner who had submitted his declaration of intention, that is, who had declared before the court that he wanted to become a citizen, was liable for military duty and had to participate in the monthly drills—but what kind of drills they were!

First of all, the officers, right up to the major, were not chosen for their military experience—oh, God forbid, they naively assumed this—but only for be-ing "esteemed people," and there were different ways of becoming "esteemed."

If someone had distinguished himself in a boxing match; if a man was a skillful hunter—especially in the West—who perhaps had slain a panther with his knife in a fair fight; indeed, even if someone owned a good hotel and knew how to approach the right people at the right time, then he had a definite claim to the rank of captain, even to the rank of major. From this militia came the countless men who ran around calling themselves generals, "curnels" (colo-nels), and captains in America then and probably even more so now. There one hears people use the title of general and major just as often as one uses the ti-tle of doctor in Leipzig.

These "superior officers" had the duty to undertake the required monthly drill, the so-called muster—usually on the first Monday or Saturday of every month. Announcements were made ahead of time in every town and settle-ment and were posted in every inn.

The men's *appearance* at the drill, from which only a physician's statement could dispense them, was the sole *constraint* that one had over these people. *How* they wished to appear and with what weapons did not matter at all. To be sure, the order stated "with arms," but, dear Lord, not everyone *had* a gun, and if he had *none,* how could he manage to borrow one precisely on that day when all rifles were needed by their owners themselves?

In the West, indeed, in the backwoods, there is, of course, no farmer who does not have his long rifle hanging on two pegs over the door, and he could march out with that easily. But in the "old states," especially east of the Missis-sippi, in Alabama, yes, even in Louisiana, what did the people need rifles for, since there was no longer anything to shoot in that area? Just for the drill?— Any old stick would serve the same purpose, and, moreover, in warm weather it even had the not-to-be-underestimated advantage of not being as *heavy* as one of those old muskets that some dutifully brought along.

A uniform was not even required. Everyone came dressed as he pleased, ac-cording to taste and season, and it would be best if I described for the readers one such drill. That way they can get some idea of how it was conducted.

It was the first Saturday in August—a fiercely hot day, with not one little cloud in the sky that could promise even momentary shade—when we were called or ordered to appear, very agreeably "after dinner"—after the noon meal—at three o'clock. At that time I was living in St. Francisville, a little town in Louisiana that was about a quarter of an hour away from the eastern bank of the Mississippi, on the first of the bluffs that rise there.

The drill took place about an hour away from the town, where a small prairie lay, which was used as a pasture and was excellently suited for a drill. The troops were proceeding to show up "according to their means" or to how near or far they lived from that spot: some on horseback, some in the customary little cabriolets that were open in back (so-called gigs), and most, of course, on foot.

I myself, fortunately, was mounted, for the march in the hot sun stretched out for a frightfully long time. Furthermore, the riders would amuse themselves excellently by galloping past a troop of choking and sweating comrades and enveloping them in a cloud of dust—while from behind the comrades cursed at these riders—to rein in by acquaintances and chat with them for a while.

"Let me sit behind you for a little bit!" those on foot often demanded, and here and there two long-legged young rascals clung to one old nag, which kept trying to jog along but could not get its feet off the ground.

How lively things appeared on the little prairie, which lay right in the middle of a proper forest of splendidly blooming magnolias. Whole swarms of young fellows were already camping there. Sensibly, they had used the cool of the morning for their march and had spent the day here in jolly fashion. They were encamped about the prairie wherever they could make use of the leafy shade. Little fires were lit, kettles boiled on them, and everywhere coffeepots were at hand.

What picturesque groups were among them as they lay in this prairie, their guns strewn about in disorderly fashion. Here one man was stretched out, facing the treetops; there two leaned back to back; a third stretched his legs up against a tree. The men told one another stories and anecdotes and shook with laughter. There was no lack of whiskey and other strong drink, since Major *Riley* himself owned a pub in St. Francisville and had sent out his barkeeper today with barrels and bottles and baked goods and candy as well, in such large quantities that he could have supplied *three* such drills.[2] Nevertheless, the liquid wares sold rapidly for the day, as noted, was frightfully hot, and along the way the people had become correspondingly thirsty. The barkeeper had hardly enough hands to serve them all.

Rather punctually at three o'clock the general staff burst onto the site: General X, the editor of a newspaper in the neighboring Bayou Sara and also the owner of an apothecary and its attached dry goods store; Major *Riley,* the innkeeper of the St. Francisville Hotel; and a number of "curnels" and captains, with not a lieutenant among them—all on horseback. Only one of the curnels, a little, fat fellow, sweating terribly, followed on foot about a quarter of an hour

later. His battle steed had thrown him en route and afterward stubbornly refused to be caught again.

The appearance of the general staff, however, even if the gentlemen wore
their feathered hats, swords, and epaulettes, did not make the least impression
on the troops. They remained in the same places and positions, grouped as they
were, perhaps only turning their heads toward the pattering of the horses'
hooves so that afterward they could share their humorous remarks about the
"big bugs" and laugh. They were not impressed, and the men waited calmly for
the signal to begin.

But stragglers were still arriving from all directions. They, of course, all
wanted to have something to drink first. The major, who was supposed to give
the signal, hesitated a while with the command—he couldn't cut off his own
customers—until the general became impatient. It was not any fun to stand in
the sun in the middle of the field, and, in any case, he did not want the whole
affair to detain him for long.

"Fall in!" the command now thundered over the resting men, for the major
had a strong bass and a powerful voice—"Rank and file to the front!"

And how slowly the fellows got up to obey the order. No one was in a hurry.
Indeed, some remained in their places without moving and seemed to think
the matter over, while others poured themselves coffee, which, perhaps, was just
freshly brewed, in order to enjoy it before the drill.

The general himself rode up to the bar, ordered a glass of brandy and water, and complained that the barkeeper had not brought any ice.

The major still did not hurry his people—what was there for anyone to
miss—and it took a good quarter of an hour until all the troops were at least
on their feet. Meanwhile, they had hitched the horses under the magnolias as
well as they could so that they stood in the shade as long as the roll call lasted.

Finally, the men, with the captain's friendly encouragement, stood facing
each other in two sets of double rows, and their names were read aloud. The
monotone reading and the varied responses: here—all right—on the spot!—
aye, aye—yes, Sir! et cetera, just as it pleased each person, continued until it was
the name Michael's turn. "Michael! Michael!" the sergeant shouted.

"Just pouring out a tumbler of whiskey toddy to the captain, Sir!" remarked
one of the men, with his hand to his cap.

"Here!" Michael, the barkeeper, called from his stand at the same moment,
still going about his business.

"Why isn't the fellow standing in rank and file?" asked the general, who
came riding up again.—He should have known.

"Beg pardon, General," said the major, turning his horse toward his superior. "There's no one else at home who can fill his position, and in *this* heat—"

"Continue!" said the general with dignity.

Whoever was missing was noted, and if he had not submitted an excuse and could not justify his absence at that time, he had to pay the legal fine later.

The exercises now began in unbelievable confusion, for certainly a third of the men had never stood in rank and file, since everyone tried his best to avoid this drill.

And what a colorful line it was! Men in dark denim coats and white jackets, some with tall felt top hats, others with straw hats, with light and dark trousers, with muskets, rifles, sticks, tree branches, even thick cornstalks, which were the lightest and easiest of all.—And how they marched! "Left foot forward!"—yes, most managed to do this, but within two minutes they were out of step again, the one stepping on the other's heels.—And then counting off the columns— left and right they turned, and the poor officers broke into a sweat trying to put the unruly mass into some kind of order. The restoration of the broken lines was out of the question, unless each individual was pushed back one by one into the position where he belonged.

Marching straight ahead went the best. A small musical chorus, which had been joined by a violin player—although that was out of place in the military procession—helped them keep step. They seemed to just catch on to "right and left flank forward" when a break was ordered, so that the troops could imbibe some refreshments—in that heat. The major, also the bar owner, had personally requested that the general call a break.

The break lasted about a half-hour, perhaps somewhat longer, for the barkeeper could not serve the many thirsty men so quickly. Moreover, he was slowed down by having to change dollar bills—there was no credit out here. But then the rigorous drilling started up again, and before five o'clock the major had yelled himself so hoarse that he could not utter another loud word.

But why drag on with the description of the exercise. The reader could not picture this chaos anyway. The general finally put an end to the disgrace, threatening that if the men did not perform better the next time, he would call for a drill every eight days.

The order "dismissed" had no sooner been given when the troop let out a shout of joy and jubilation that would have done honor to a swarm of Indians. Like lightning, everything turned into confusion, and in an instant there was a race to see who could make it to the bar first.

Half the fellows were already tipsy, and many were simply putting on the finishing touch—in order, as they put it, to have a very jolly return home—and so it was.

If *two* occasionally had sat on one horse on the way out, now three climbed onto many an animal that looked as if it could carry them. They hacked at the unfortunate creature with their heels for so long until they got it going for a short stretch at least. Of course, it could not carry the burden for long and either threw its riders or itself onto the ground. The bystanders greeted this with a roar of true exultation.

One pair particularly distinguished itself. In the saddle sat a young, rather tipsy and sleepy fellow, who no longer could hold his head up. During the final part of the drill, which he considered beyond the call of duty, he had lain under a tree and slept. Another, an ex-sailor, who now had settled on terra firma, was also more than two sheets to the wind and had jumped on behind him the wrong way, so that he sat back to back with his comrade.

"Hello, John!" he called out. "Full sail ahead and let her rip, the old nag! We have a splendid wind, and *I'm* steering." With that he pulled up the rather good-natured animal's tail and held it tightly. John kicked the horse with his heels to show that he wanted to go home. But even though this animal put up with a lot in daily life, *this* treatment was beyond the pale. It began to go sideways and pressed toward a fence that bordered the road.

"Whoa—whoa!" the sailor cried and tried to turn his makeshift rudder in the other direction, as he would have done on board in order to steer the bow to the right—. "Damn the old vessel, it won't steer anymore—a bit more steam, John, a bit more steam. We're not making any progress and are dead in the water."

Only semiconscious, John again kicked both heels against the horse's flanks, and the helmsman turned more sharply. But now it became too much for the tortured animal, and it kicked backward.

"Whoa! Whoa! Stop her!" the sailor shouted and tried to keep his balance by holding onto the tail. But that was the straw that broke the camel's back. The horse became really angry, kicked backward a few times despite its double burden, pressed its head between its front legs, and the two fellows hit the ground with a thud.

"Yippee!" a pair of riders galloping past shrilly screamed out their hunting call. "Go it ye cripples."[3]—The first rider flew over the one fallen man with his horse and enveloped the whole scene in a cloud of dust. Now the rest of the cavalcade rattled forward—the commanding officers had left the place right after the first dismissal—the thrown men hardly had time to stagger out of the way. Like a wild hunt, during which one tried to get ahead of the other, the mad ride headed toward the town.

Those on foot, of course, followed more slowly. Along the way many turned off here and there toward their own homes. The majority, however, continued as far as St. Francisville—since the day had been "interrupted" anyway, they might as well add an "evening" to it.

Thus *this* drill ended—thus did every drill end. The whole affair was just a *formality* that had to be observed because of the law. All the men knew just as little about drills and maneuvers when they went home as they had known in the morning when they marched out.

THE FERRY HOTEL IN POINTE COUPÉE

I had already lived in Louisiana for a half-year, partly in Bayou Sara, partly in St. Francisville, and had become acquainted with a merchant there who had a store farther up on the Mississippi,[4] at the mouth of the Atchafalaya. One day he suggested that I take over the Ferry Hotel that lay directly across Bayou Sara on the west bank of the river, or, rather, that I manage it for his brother in exchange for a certain wage. He explained right away that his brother was a dear good soul but was so taken by drink that the business there was ruined. On top of this, a good-for-nothing barkeeper—also a German—had exploited the brother's almost always unreliable condition and cheated him shamefully. If this continued, the essentially profitable place would have to be sold in order to pay the accumulating debts.

Now the offer came a bit unexpectedly. I had barely returned from the western forests, where for many years I had sustained myself by hunting. Only on exceptional occasions, when I went to Little Rock, had I even *slept* in a hotel. I had a very incomplete concept of how to manage such a place.

Nevertheless, after thinking it over, I accepted the offer. You simply have to try everything in this world and never know ahead of time what you really can do. I did take the precaution of asking the merchant how I should act toward his brother if he really were in a drunken craze. The merchant—an elderly, very calm gentleman—asked me to treat his brother like a child in such a case and even to *use force* if necessary. The next morning he himself would thank me.

That was, to be sure, a peculiar contract. But it suited me to manage this business accordingly because I could not have easily made my way into a well-run establishment. So, the next morning I packed my few possessions and boarded the little steam ferry that ran between Bayou Sara and the Ferry Hotel to introduce myself to my new employer.

The steam ferry, a little steamer like one now finds on the Mississippi in great quantities, had just been established the year before by an enterprising Yankee and did very good business. It handled the considerable traffic between the two riverbanks, and the Yankee, not satisfied with that, had also installed a small mill on board with which he transformed corn and other grains into flour en route and then sold it for a good price.[5]

At about ten o'clock in the morning I entered the hotel where I would reside for a year for the first time. *Charles F.,*[6] who had already been informed of my arrival, received me most cordially and told me he hoped we would get along together very well. *Should* he ever get a bit *cross*—for sometimes he was not quite well—then I should not be offended by what he said—he really meant no harm and later usually did not even remember the incident.

Charles F., or *Charley,* as the servants (two female slaves and a German houseboy) usually called him, was a small, frail man—dear God, he has been lying in his grave for a long time now—with blond hair, blue eyes, and a somewhat puffy, reddish face. He insisted that we drink a "welcome" together, and at the bar he poured me a half-beer glass of Madeira and then pushed the bottle toward me. We clinked glasses and drank. Then I went around the house to look at the inventory and to make a few notes about the supplies that needed to be ordered. There was a paltry enough inventory, for money seemed to be in short supply. In the cash box, at least, there was nothing with which one could even have made change for a dollar.

Crawling around had made me warm, and when I returned to the bar at noon to drink a sip of wine Charley was gone, and the bottle he had just opened that morning was *empty.* So, Charley had started in again. His brother had already told me that he often did not touch a drop for days and was quite sensible then. But *if* he enjoyed even one glass in the morning, then he was not able to stop until he passed out.

No guests happened to be there—since the hotel mostly was frequented by the local planters—with the sole exception of the hotel's permanent resident, an Irish lawyer, a quite splendid human being of whom I soon became very fond. We sat down to eat—still rather taciturn, since we were strangers to each other—and after the meal each one went about his business.

Around four o'clock Charley's bedroom door opened suddenly, and the hotel's owner stumbled out with all the signs of complete drunkenness and swayed toward the bar. There he grabbed another bottle—Madeira again—took a glass, and was about to pour himself a drink.

"Allow me to help you, Mr. Charley," I said and took the bottle from his hand.

"Please do," he mumbled and leaned against the nearest pillar. He looked at me in astonishment when I pushed back the bottle and glass, locked the bar, put the key into my pocket, and said calmly, "Be so kind as to go back to bed."

Charley seemed so astounded by this treatment that at first he could not utter a word, but finally, with eyes blazing, he spouted: "Hey—you there—what is your name? I don't even know your name—please—will you—will you be so kind to leave my house immediately?"

"May I beseech you to go to bed?"

"No—such impudence—never—never happened to me before—my—my own bar?—here"—and with that he looked for and finally found his right pants pocket, reached in, and pulled out a whole handful of dollars—that had to be the cash box—"here now—there you have your money—I don't owe you anything more—so, now vamoose! Did you understand me?"

I calmly took the money from him, put it into *my* pocket, and replied then, "May I ask you *now* to go to bed?"

He looked at me fixedly, closed his eyes, opened them again, as if he took me for a ghost, then turned sharply on his heels, went into his room and two minutes later was snoring so loudly that I could hear it outside.

The lawyer had watched the little scene from *his* door. Now he nodded at me, said "bravo" with a laugh, and went back into his room.

The next day Charley appeared somewhat late, and he must have remembered yesterday's scene, for at first he tiptoed around me very bashfully. But I acted as if not the least thing had happened and only said, "Mr. Charley, yesterday afternoon you were kind enough to give me eleven dollars. I put the money in the cash box and made a note of it. You do wish that the necessary purchases be made?"

"Yes, indeed—yes, indeed—thank you," he said, turning beet red. He then went out onto the veranda to take his usual walk there.

From that day on he did not drink a drop for three weeks, until one morning, when I was supposed to ride over to False River on business, he broke out again and carried on so much that afternoon that I forcibly carried him into his room and locked him in. Inside, he took to his bed, lay down on his back, and kicked out all the windows with his boots. I let him have his way until he fell asleep.

After this day—I had gotten to know him better—I tried to make him comprehend his drinking, but it did not help. As long as he was sober, he agreed with everything and promised never to touch a drop again. But it never took long before these scenes were repeated ever more frequently.

When he became crazed again, he had the idiosyncrasy of only drinking *one kind* of liquor, and then always from *one* certain bottle. If he had first drunk cognac in the morning, he stayed with it the whole day—it was the same with Madeira, sherry, rum, or port. That made another experiment easier for me. Namely, I noted the bottle from which he was drinking and poured into it enormous quantities of tartar emetic that I had acquired for this purpose. That helped him get over drinking for almost four months. I never let him get really drunk anymore, but the medicine had such a strong effect that he was miserable for a whole day. Finally, he caught on, and even when he was extremely intoxicated, he changed bottles. I experienced such scenes with him; it would be impossible to describe them all.

Meanwhile, business really improved, for the Ferry Hotel enjoyed an extraordinarily favorable location and was, in fact, the only place in the entire widespread settlement where the planters could assemble in decent fashion.

On this side of the Mississippi lay the largest cotton plantations and even sugar plantations, since the low, warm land favors the cultivation of these plants.

The banks of the Mississippi are, in general, remarkable. A brief description of them is appropriate here, insofar as the terrain itself also explains the kind of war that was waged in this part of the country and why the Union troops only tried to take possession of the *east* banks of the Mississippi.

Along the entire Mississippi, from the mouth of the Ohio downward, the high land extends directly to the river only on the east bank. In some places the high land overlooks the river in rows of hills, as at Vicksburg, and in others in steep bluffs, as at Memphis and Natchez. The bluffs begin in Kentucky with the iron bluffs (*bluff* means "steep decline"), or iron banks—then there is low land on both sides until the Chickasaw bluffs, and down below on the Tennessee bank the second, third, and fourth bluff, below which the capital Memphis along with old Fort Pickering lies. With the exception of a few completely insignificant elevations, the entire state of Mississippi has low, marshy banks at the Mississippi River until the Walnut Hills, with Fort M. Henry, which lie right above Vicksburg. The fort is joined on high banks by Vicksburg itself.

From that point on there is low land until the city of Natchez, which is built on a high bluff, although a rather extensive suburb has formed down along the river.

The Ellis Cliffs come below Natchez. Even farther down, on the border of Louisiana, are the Loftus Heights with the old Fort Adams. After this the land first rises again behind Bayou Sara, which lies directly opposite Pointe Coupée, rather close to the river itself.

After this Baton Rouge sits on raised land—still on the same bank—and, as far as I can remember, Red Church as well. From that point on the complete lowland begins.[7] It extends down to the silent, reedy marshes of the false banks of the mouths of the Mississippi.

The right, or western, bank of the Mississippi is, is contrast, marshland—or lowland. There are only a few places where the flooding of the rivers discharging there raised the ground and soil to the extent that there is no need to fear flooding, which otherwise occurs right and left over the banks and for miles into the interior.

For that reason high dams (the so-called levees) had to be cast up on both banks in order to be able to cultivate the almost incredibly fertile, indeed inexhaustible, land of the lower Mississippi, which, with the exception of these bluffs, consists solely of alluvial deposits. When such a dam breaks, the entire interior land is flooded at once.

That happened a while ago in New Orleans itself, which lies about twelve or sixteen feet below flood level, and put the whole city underwater.

For this reason these banks cannot be protected from an enemy coming down the river. It is too extensive to be garrisoned everywhere. So, during the month of June the enemy always has it in his power to send the Mississippi's torrent over hostile soil.

Those high points on the eastern bank reign over the river completely. Almost everywhere on the bank opposite the bluffs lie sandbanks that must be avoided and that force vessels over into the deep water.

Pointe Coupée lies on the western bank and is a colony founded by the French and protected by the levee. It extends along the Mississippi in a broad, fertile, low-lying strip. Behind it again lies a sorry swamp, overgrown with cypresses and inhabited by alligators, bullfrogs, and mosquitoes.

On the higher land opposite all kinds of people had settled in such a mixed population as one really only finds in these small American towns: peddlers, craftsmen, merchants, lawyers, doctors, newspaper editors, barkeepers, et cetera. They were the wildest mixture of Americans, Germans, Frenchmen, Englishmen, and even Italians, whereas the west bank completely maintained its aristocratic character. To be sure, a doctor lived there, but he, too, owned a substantial cotton plantation, and only two lawyers, our Irishman and a Frenchman, resided there as *garçons*⁸—but nonetheless as gentlemen.

These people mainly, indeed almost exclusively, frequented the hotel. But they had almost stopped coming because when they came in the evening or wanted to spend the night there, they found Charley in the condition that, at that time, was almost habitual for him. He asked what they wanted, and if they told him they wanted to eat, drink, and sleep in his place, he attacked them and screamed that they should clear out and go home. Decent people and heads of families belonged at home and should not spend nights in taverns and at card tables. After that he usually slammed the door in their faces. Laughing and cursing, they had to do what he said.

Notwithstanding this sad war with Charley, my stay at the Ferry Hotel was very pleasant. During the appropriate season I also went on a torchlight hunt every evening for alligators and snipe, yes even for wild ducks, which settle there by the thousands during the migratory period. But I have described this rather thoroughly elsewhere, and it is actually out of place here.

Charley, meanwhile, behaved with moderation and once remained sober for six whole weeks in a row. He himself seemed pleased that his hotel was frequented more often again, sat up in the evening until eleven or twelve o'clock, and watched the cardplayers without touching a drop—in a word, his behavior was exemplary. Then one day I had to go over to Bayou Sara on a legal matter that detained me until four in the afternoon, and when I returned I found the Ferry Hotel deserted.

No human creature was to be seen, since the Irish lawyer just happened to have a court session over on False River—not even the slaves. I myself had dismissed the houseboy eight days previously. Even Charley had disappeared, and everything stood empty and free and open. Broken windows and bottles, however, clearly indicated *who* had turned everything upside down. Charley's bed was lying in the yard, the chairs stood on the long dining table, the woolen blankets had been dragged from the bedrooms throughout the whole house, the tap of the of the cistern was turned on, the bowls with the still untouched noon meal stood under the beds. In short, it was as if a band of robbers in great high spirits had wreaked havoc everywhere.

I finally found the two black girls in the courthouse and parish jail next door, where they had fled from Charley, who had chased after them with my rifle—which fortunately was not loaded—and threatened to shoot them dead. He had also been looking for me in order to do the same to me.

First of all, I assigned the girls to put the house back in order, for it looked terrible, and then I started out to look for Charley. Just before nightfall I found him *behind* the property fast asleep in a castor bean thicket under a pecan tree. My efforts to rouse him and get him into the house were futile. I could not wake him, did not want to carry him in, and since the nights were warm and pleasant and there were no more mosquitoes *outside* than in the rooms, I let him lie there for the night to sleep off his monstrous drunkenness.

From then on he carried on worse than before. Every week there was a new attack, and I finally thanked my God when a younger brother of his arrived from Europe to take over the hotel together with Charley.

A week later, just as Charley had landed behind the bottle of Madeira again, I myself set off for home and embarked on a steamer to New Orleans. For Charley, being only halfway inebriated, the leave-taking was moving. In true bliss that he was finally getting rid of me, he wanted to give me everything he had in the house. He pulled out everything and embraced and kissed me to boot. When I laughingly pushed the things back, he did not stop until I at least had a bottle of Madeira under each arm. With that I left Pointe Coupée.

From *Hustle and Bustle* (1870)

MR. MIX

I have led an exciting life—that cannot be denied—and sometimes when I sink into old memories, quite peculiar things come to light.

"I am Mr. Mix"—I have to laugh every time I hear that name. Here is what happened:

As the reader of my *Adventures and Hunting Expeditions* perhaps remembers, I once kept a hotel down on the Mississippi, in the French colony of Pointe Coupée. That is, I was supposed to put the business back in order, since its owner, who was always drunk, threatened to plunge head over heels into bankruptcy.

First and foremost, of course, I tended to the books, in which numerous debtors were noted. I made up the bills and collected many of the debts. But numerous bad, or, rather, mysterious, debtors were in the ledger, for Charles Fischer, as the owner was called, had kept it in a most eccentric fashion.

Tipsy most of the time himself, he had dealings with a lot of people with whom he was not acquainted, indeed whose names he often did not even know. In such cases the page headings of those designated as *debtors* sounded quite comical. Among others there were: "The Man with the Red Nose" and "The Man with the Wart on His Chin."—"The Man with the Torn Vest" owed six dollars for lodgings and two bottles of Madeira.—"The Redhead" was down for some twenty dollars in the book, and Fischer claimed that if he saw him, he would recognize him immediately. But he did not show up again, and I never could find out who the man was.

In other cases the names were cited without any indication of the place where the men resided and could be found—an extremely difficult matter, since the establishment had many clients not only from all the plantations but also on the right bank in Pointe Coupée, False River, and the little town of Waterloo below and across the river in both Bayou Sara and St. Francisville.

Nevertheless, I had to make the *attempt* to find out where these debtors resided, so I covered the different areas thoroughly on horseback. Since I carried a list of the names in question, through tenacious and tireless inquiry I succeeded at least in bringing the majority to light and to gradually tracking them down. Despite this, not everyone paid up, alleging that Charles Fischer had received the money from him on the spot. The small, constantly inebriated man was not able to attest to the contrary, for in his condition it may or may not have happened.

Of all the persons noted by name there was only *one* I could *not* find out, despite all my efforts. He was simply entered as Mr. Mix, and he owed five dollars. The amount was, of course, not large enough to be worth a great deal of effort, especially because of the uncertainty of the debt. Nevertheless, I had inquired about him everywhere, without success, and still carried his bill in my pocket along with the rest, out of habit, whenever I combed through the various neighborhoods.

Thus one day I had been in St. Francisville for this purpose for the third time and was on my way down to Bayou Sara when I encountered a rider on a splendid little horse. He appeared to be extraordinarily friendly and was singing to himself loudly. I was not acquainted with the man and was about to ride past him with a brief greeting, as was customary on the open road, when he abruptly turned his little animal around and rode up to me, his hand outstretched.

"Sir," I said, shaking his hand, "you have the advantage; you seem to know *me*."

"Yes," the cheerful man laughed. "I have a very extraordinary memory—you live in St. Francisville."

"No, not anymore—I'm living in Pointe Coupée now."

"Aha—but you used to live there?"

"To be sure."

"Well, you see, we met there. I am *Mr. Mix*."

"Oh, my dear Mr. Mix," I responded, putting my right hand into my pocket and pulling out his bill, "it is *indeed* a pleasure to meet you here. But where do you live?"

"I?" said Mr. Mix with a mistrustful glance at the paper. "In Portland, about twenty miles behind Francisville."[1]

"*Might* I then request that you settle this account—it is only five dollars that you have owed Mr. Fischer in the Ferry Hotel for many years? Be so kind, I will give you a receipt right away."

The man was so dumbfounded that he took the bill and automatically reached into his pocket. I did not give him much time to think it over. I always carried pen and ink with me, and without dismounting I had quickly finished my preparations.

"Hmm, yes," said Mr. Mix, embarrassed. "I had indeed completely forgotten it; please, allow me to take the bill."

"You're not asking me to ride twenty miles to Portland behind St. Francisville again to collect the five dollars you have owed for five years?" I asked.

As I spoke, I had prepared the receipt.

"Here, Mr. Mix—if you would be so kind."

Mr. Mix had a gold piece in his hand. He cast a parting glance at it and then handed it to me.

"Good morning, Mr. Mix." I gave him a friendly nod.

"Good morning," said Mr. Mix and rode up the street. But I had spoiled his morning, and he no longer was singing.

THE ANTEBELLUM PERIOD
Fiction

Gerstäcker shaped his first experiences of Louisiana's natural environs, people, plantations, river towns, and cosmopolitan New Orleans, which he describes in his travel book and sketches, into short stories as well as into chapters in the immigration novel *To America! A Book for the People*. While Gerstäcker does paint a seductive picture of Louisiana's natural and man-made beauty, his stories are primarily about the people who dwell in the plantation country. The tales are populated with people of all races—black, white, American Indian, and, often, a blend of races. The characters extend beyond the customary plantation owner, slave, overseer, and slave trader of plantation literature to include the shopkeeper, the sheriff, the lawyer, the judge, and the woodchopper of the desolate north.

Gerstäcker mixes real people he knew or may have heard of with invented characters. Using the devices of melodrama and suspense—characters are pursuing and being pursued, escaping or coming to the rescue—Gerstäcker exposes the injustices of slavery. Lacking autonomy, the slaves are subject to others' whims and to the vagaries of fortune. But the fiction also provides the oppressed, or those who are merely unlucky, the chance to resist, exact revenge, and renew and reinvent themselves.

The antebellum fiction section concludes with an excerpt from *To America!* The author intends this novel to be a cautionary tale, a prophylaxis against the immigrants' unrealistic expectations and exaggerated hopes. As the ship enters the mouth of the Mississippi, the passengers' palpable excitement turns slowly to misapprehension and melancholy, reverting once again to unbounded joy as they approach the port of New Orleans. But on deck the steerage passengers are no more than a nuisance to the sailors preparing to moor, and, having been set ashore, the new immigrants sit on the levee in a new world that is utterly indifferent to their fate.

From *Pictures of the Mississippi*

Light and Dark Sides of Transatlantic Life (1847–1848)

THE SLAVE

The mail boat had just arrived from New Orleans. Across the plank that had been shoved to the shore, an unbroken stream of almost all the businesspeople and idlers of the little town of Bayou Sara came aboard. In part they wanted to receive their letters and packages that had arrived; in part they wanted to satisfy their curiosity and sip a glass of brandy or ice water at the ornately decorated bar.

The captain of the mail boat, a small Frenchman with a gray coat, a black felt hat, and boots with an extraordinarily high polish, seemed to be everywhere. As large drops of perspiration shone on his reddened forehead, he grumbled in terribly broken English about God and the world but primarily about the postmaster, who, hardly had the captain turned his back, had in his all too great zeal carried off a packet of letters from his office and taken it up to the post office.

"God damn him!" thundered the little man, banging his fist on the desk covered in green baize so that the ink sprayed up high, "what business does the plaster smearer (the postmaster also had a pharmacy and a small shop and liked to be called 'doctor') have in my office? Hauls up letters, aye? Then thinks he's done miracles; but just wait—I'll get you."

"Captain! Letters arrived for me?" a slim young man asked, tapping the aggravated man on the shoulder with a laugh.

"Go to hell or up to that quack!" the captain continued cursing, without even going to the trouble of looking to see who addressed him.

"Hello! What's up this time?" the young planter laughed. "Are the boilers about to burst? There's enough steam to blow three ordinary boats up into the air! You're still the same! You Frenchmen are queer fellows, fired up right away, like Dupont's gunpowder!"

"The postmaster has taken up the letters," answered the bookkeeper, instead of the captain.

"Damn him!" cried the captain, and slammed the glass door behind him so that the panes rattled.

"Never mind," said the planter, "he wants to get his quarter dollar for it—

all for the good of Uncle Sam;[1] I know him well. Whoever picks up a letter must buy a little something in the store or take along a box of medicine. But I'll go up and see whether something has come for me."

With that he stepped out on to the gangway, went down the cabin steps, and had just jumped over the plank to the shore when he felt a hand on his shoulder and a friendly, familiar voice addressed him. "Whoa, Ned, where to in such a hurry? You look as if you'd just come from an election and were bringing the most important news!"

"Guston! By all the devils and angels of the four elements," he cried out in joyful astonishment. "Guston! For heaven's sake, how did you get here? I thought you had settled down respectably and permanently in Connecticut. Are you already fed up with the eastern states?"

"Completely, old boy, completely," Guston responded. "The devil take the free states. A planter just cannot exist where there is no slave trade. In the beginning I had all kinds of fantastic ideas about people's freedom and equality," he continued, as he took the young man's arm and strolled up the bank with him. "I thought it was a sin to exploit and torment my 'black brother,' as the Methodists say. So, I asked my old man for travel money and went to New York. From there I wrote to you that I was inclined to buy an estate in the north of the state or in Connecticut and settle among the genial Pennsylvanians who had moved there. At that time it was my intention, and had I done it, we would not be standing here on Louisiana ground now. But just then I became acquainted with a young man whom I joined and became intimate friends with. Since he had to go to Europe on business, I went along and sailed over to the 'old country' with the *Great Western*."[2]

"So, you've been in Europe meanwhile?" the young planter interrupted him in astonishment.

"For sure," nodded Guston, "in England, Ireland, and Germany. I accompanied my newfound friend through the first two countries until he suddenly fell so madly in love with an Irish girl that the wedding took place in four weeks. At present he is chasing foxes and steeples with all kinds of old squires and young gentlemen, is jumping over all the hedges, ditches, and walls that can be found, and if he has not broken his neck in the meantime, he is doing quite well. I myself soon grew tired of the place, returned to England, and from there sailed to Germany. There I had the opportunity to become familiar with the lower classes of people, with the life of the *poor*. Ned, from that time on, I no longer felt sorry for our slaves. It must be tough to lose one's freedom and to be at the mercy of a master who is often too harsh. But the misery that I saw there, the poor unfortunate people's *lack of food*—their own children starve and perish before their eyes. Moreover, the cold in winter, when the father, the sole breadwinner, *is imprisoned* after he no longer could stand to look at the misery at home and went to the woods to break off a few branches to at least warm his family, even if he could not satisfy their hunger. The nobility's vain, downright insane pride vis-à-vis the unfortunate poor—and, furthermore, a 'legal' arbitrariness that with greedy hands and the full pomp and circumstance of the law takes away from the unfortunate man the *last thing he owns* and seems to mock the ruined man by showing him the splendor and luxury of the powerful—that which he must do without, not even being able to feed his children as well as the great feed their *dogs*. That, Ned, filled me with loathing and disgust, and I must admit to you, I was happy when I had put the 'old country' behind me. It might appeal to those who call it their *homeland*—the Eskimo likes his icebergs and blubber, of course—but it is a sad abode for whomever is not under this spell—I would not like to live there. After a short stay in Germany I returned to New Orleans via Hamburg and, as you see, came up with the mail boat to reach my father's plantations overland from here."

"You truly did not need to go to Europe to learn that," Ned laughed. "Every child knows that our Negroes have it better than the poor people in Ireland or Germany, the devil take them, yet the miserable rascals still grumble." But tonight you'll stay at my place, and tomorrow morning you'll take my horse. Your old man has not seen you for such a long time that one day will not make a difference."

"Agreed!" cried Guston. "But let us seek the shade; the heat here on the bank is unbearable. You, by the way, will have to lead me because I do not recognize Bayou Sara any more. There were hardly ten houses when I left, and now there's a proper town."

"Well, the mulatto Nelly is still alive," laughed Willis, "and sells just as good brandy as before. We'll go by there first. Perhaps you'll find some old acquaintances."

With these words he took his newfound friend's arm in his again and strolled with him toward the nearby coffeehouse, from which loud laughter and rejoicing resounded.

They entered a rather small room that opened toward the street. A long bar filled out the back. The actual bar consisted of a somewhat high top finished with grained wood on which were laid white marble slabs so that the liquids spilled on it could be easily wiped up. On a large tray covered with white cloth stood several dozen clean glasses; on another very close to it sparkled a large glass bowl with a silver-plated lid containing grated sugar. Next to it there were two little bottles, tightly corked shut and equipped with a quill running through the cork that served to drip the liquids contained in the bottles (Staunton bitters and peppermint) into the drinks, giving them a piquant taste. Behind the bar were long rows of all kinds of drinks, wines and liqueurs, in ornamental, colorful, and finely polished bottles and carafes. Between them were stacks of oranges and lemons, lending the whole affair a fresh, cheerful look. Under the bar stood a large basin of ice; pieces of it were thrown into the glasses to cool the drinks. A young man in a white linen jacket and wide trousers of the same material was busily serving drinks to the thirsty guests, who had turned up in considerable number because of the excessive heat. A tall doctor from the other bank of the Mississippi, from Pointe Coupée, seemed especially busy at emptying his glass again and again. Everyone else had to help him with this because he swore that he did not want to drink *alone*. Over and over he had his own glass as well everyone else's refilled, although he could hardly stand on his feet. To be sure, one person or another tried to slip away from the doctor, but with eagle eyes he discovered and caught the deserter, and a fresh glass was the punishment that awaited him. Several men, unable to drink another drop, were sitting in the corner when our two friends sidled up to the bar to fortify themselves and immediately were received by the doctor with open arms.

"Willis—aye?" he addressed him. "Thirsty? Always thirsty?"

"Doctor, this is a friend of mine, a certain—"

"A friend of yours? He must drink with me. Sir, shake hands—so—I am Doctor Seal,[3] from Pointe Coupée. You must have heard of me. What do you want to drink? Here, bartender, quickly, here is a man who is thirsty—that's right, glasses and ice in them—no ice for me, though; I want to have it hot, hot as lava, want to cure heat with heat. What the deuce! Whose long face is staring in through the window there? Come in, sir; what do you want to drink?"

"Thanks, thanks," said the new arrival, stepping through the doorway quickly and letting his glass be filled without any further ado.

He was a man of unusual height who surpassed the exceedingly tall doctor by several inches. One could recognize that he was a Yankee by his prominent cheekbones and gray, sharp eyes that glanced about shrewdly. His blue tailcoat was buttoned shut despite the hot, muggy weather, and a high, white felt hat that he wore pushed back somewhat on his head only served to make the tall figure even taller. His boots were worked in the most modern fashion and were quite new. But they probably pinched him because on both boots he had made a cross-cut with a knife just over the toes. In general he seemed to love what was comfortable, for he immediately sat down at the bar with the greatest ease, whereby his elongation proved very useful, and emptied the glass filled with gin and water that had been handed to him.

"Gentlemen," the Yankee began, after he had answered several of the doctor's queries with just as many other questions, "I think we can do business together."

"For heaven's sake, you don't have any wall clocks to sell?" asked the doctor in comic horror.

"No," replied the Yankee with a laugh, "I don't deal in that."

"You gentlemen don't seem to tie yourselves to anything definite, otherwise," objected Guston, approaching the tall man more closely.

"But this time to the contrary," the Yankee answered. "I have taken up the trade in human flesh, and this does not combine well with another, with the exception of cattle- and horse-trading. But I sold my last mustangs in Baton Rouge and only have left a Negro girl about fifteen years old whom I want to auction off in a lottery this afternoon at four o'clock.[4] Then I can go back to New Orleans with the mail boat on Wednesday and from there return to my homeland."

"And how much does a chance cost?" asked Willis.

"Five dollars—we will throw the dice for her!" was the reply. "She's a splendid girl, healthy and strong, and the most beautiful Negro girl you have ever seen."

"But where is the wench hiding?" the doctor interrupted. "Bring her here, and if she looks good, then I'll take three or four chances."

"She is only a few steps away from here," said the Yankee, getting up from his seat. "Wait a moment, and I'll bring her over; some other gentlemen here also wanted to have a look at her." With these words he left the barroom and soon returned with a beautiful, young Negro girl.

Her short, wooly hair was black as a raven. Her nose, true to her Ethiopian descent, was pressed flat, but it was small and delicate. Her cherry red lips were slightly parted. Between them, when she spoke, two sparkling white rows of teeth became visible and stood out all the more against her velvety black skin and her dark, glowing eyes. She was not tall but was slender and uncommonly graceful, so that even the doctor, who was hardly in control of his faculties, let out a curse and swore she was a devilishly pretty little witch.

Several planters from the area had just joined the group, and almost all bought chances. The Yankee led the girl away up to St. Francisville in order to find even more participants in the dice game, in which a human being was the prize.

When her master led the girl into the barroom to put her on display, a young, pale, but very decently dressed man entered directly behind her. He listened to the entire dealings with eager attentiveness and, finally, when everyone bought a chance, also pulled out his ready money. There was no question that he intended to buy two chances, for he counted his money several times. But it apparently was not enough, for with a sigh he shoved several dollar bills back into his slim, heavily worn wallet and for five singles bought only one single chance.

Soon thereafter, when the doctor looked for him again and swore by everything that lived in heaven and on earth that he had to drink with him or else fight with him, he had disappeared.

Meanwhile, the fourth hour of the afternoon approached, and a great number of people had gathered in front of the aforementioned coffeehouse, where they impatiently awaited the Yankee. Finally, he came—the Negro girl walked at his side and not far from her, but somewhat behind, the pale young man.

Noisy jubilation greeted the new arrivals, and the doctor was the most exuberant and merry of all. The billiard table in the large barroom was quickly converted to a dice table, the list of gamers read aloud once more, and the innkeeper posted himself at the billiard board with a piece of chalk in order to write down the name of the person who would make the highest throw and to note the number of the thrown dice. The girl stood in a corner on a platform raised for this purpose so that all could see her. Two large, bright tears hung on her dark, lowered lashes.

One heart only, amid all the pushing and shoving, felt and shared her pain. It was the pale young man, who, leaning against a window only a few steps away from her, with lips pressed together and cheeks momentarily reddened by a feverish heat, his arms folded tightly, stood there and stared down at the floor. Only once in a while did he raise his dark eyes to her quickly, with a glance that betrayed the greatest fear. But when the signal to begin was given and all attention was turned toward the billiard table, when even the victim looked up for a moment shyly and trembling, their glances met. In a second he was at her side and, brushing past her closely, whispered, "Have courage, Selinde, have courage—you shall be mine, even if I must steal you from their midst!"

A faint smile momentarily crossed the poor child's face, damp with tears.

Soon, however, it disappeared again, and she sank her little head sadly and wept silently.

Meanwhile, the game had begun. The participants crowded closely around the billiard table, watching the rolling dice with anxious attentiveness in order to count quickly how many had been thrown.

"Forty-five!" cried Willis, when his third lot had been cast—trump that, doctor, if you can."

"Well, I have five chances and can just watch for a while," the doctor responded. "But now I want to try once, too."

He took the three dice in the cup, shook them, and threw three ones.

"That is a good start," he cried out, vexed, when loud laughter greeted him from all sides. "But let it be, I am not going to throw anymore for this first chance. At best I could only get thirty-nine—meanwhile, I want a drink."

He stepped back from the billiard table, others pushed forward, and for a while a tense, anxious silence prevailed that was only interrupted by the rattling of the ivory. The pale young man, whom no one in the room seemed to know, now approached and called in a soft but firm voice, "Give me the dice!"

The volume with which these words were spoken was faint, but they coursed through the young girl's body like lightning. She shot up and, holding her breath, lips parted, listened attentively for the slightest sound.

The player cast one glance at the figure leaning forward, another at the ceiling, as if pleading for help, and then the fateful dice rattled onto the green cloth—two sixes and a four. "Sixteen!" the scorekeeper counted in a monotone, "Once more!" Again, the same numbers lay there. The third time the player threw the dice into the cup, shook it, and—three twos rolled out. "Thirty-eight!—bad!" cried the caller, and the unlucky man stepped back from the table, pale as a ghost. Another took his place, and, shuddering, the Negro girl could hardly hold up her trembling body. But after a few moments she pulled herself together and asked a white man standing nearby for a glass of water.

"Damn you—fetch it yourself; do you think I am your nigger!"[5] he cried, turning away from her churlishly. Without any reply she reeled over to the bar, took a glass from there, filled it with the cooling ice water, and emptied it. Thus fortified, she walked back to her place with a light, almost elastic gait, and, leaning against the wall, hid her face in her hands. She clearly paid no further attention to her fate, and only sometimes, when a gamer's crude, joyful outcry penetrated her ear, a sudden fear seemed to agitate her inwardly, and a slight shudder passed swiftly over her limbs.

The game continued without interruption for about a half-hour and was coming to a close when the pale man, who had disappeared for a short while and for whom the possession of the young girl seemed so important, suddenly approached the slave trader again and in a low, suppressed, but trembling voice asked him for another chance.

"Fine, sir, I have just two more. Wanted to throw them myself, but as a favor to you, here is one," he answered courteously. "However," he continued, bowing politely, "you understand that I will not give up the opportunity of winning my property back for nothing—I can only give you the chance for ten dollars."

"Mister," the poor man rose up, grabbing the Yankee's shoulder in desperation, "I have sold everything that I had with me to get together the paltry sum of five dollars, and now you want ten. I don't have it. My entire fortune consists of six dollars."

"Hardly enough to begin dealing," the Yankee said, regretfully, "but I remember that my brother Isaiah once—"

"Here is a ring, too," the other suddenly interrupted him, pulling a simple golden band from his finger. "Take it and give me another chance. It is worth twice as much," he continued impatiently, when he saw that the Yankee looked at it and weighed it in his hand distrustfully and guardedly, but no further assurance was necessary. The slave trader knew the gold's value all too well not to be quickly convinced that the young man was speaking the truth. He handed him one of his chances, while he himself stepped to the billiard table and made his three throws. He was not lucky, and calmly waiting for the game's result, he retired to a corner of the room.

Now the doctor had made his last throw and shouted triumphantly, "Forty-six—the girl is mine!"

"Forty-six! Best throw!" the scorekeeper repeated in a monotone.

"Stop! I have one more chance!" the young stranger cried and pushed his way to the table.

"Why didn't you throw a long time ago?" responded the annoyed doctor.

"Did I not have just as much right as you to wait until the end?" he asked him, touchily.

"It's all the same to me," the doctor laughed. "You're not going to throw a forty-six anyway and might as well have saved your five dollars. But wait!" he cried out and grabbed the arm of the young man, who was just about to throw. "I like the wench. She has a damned pretty face. I'll give you fifty dollars if you give up your turn."

"May the dice decide," the young stranger cried, freeing himself from the doctor's hand. For a moment the blood rushed to his temples so that his veins threatened to explode; in the same minute it returned to his heart and left not one drop in his cheeks. The dice rattled, and in a monotone the innkeeper counted the eyes.

"Seventeen!"

"By heavens, a good throw!" cried everyone standing around the green table in anxious anticipation.

Once again the fateful pieces of ivory rattled in the leather cup. Dead silence prevailed, and all eyes were on the thrower's hand, while the poor frightened girl had sunk to her knees in prayer and kept her face covered with her hands. Her restrained sobbing was the only thing that broke the grave-like silence. The dice had been cast.

"Seventeen! Again!"

"Damn," growled the doctor.

"The third throw, the third throw!" everyone cried impatiently when they saw the stranger stop for a moment in anxious reflection. Almost convulsively, he seized the cup two times, each time shuddering as he faced the deciding throw. But he could wait no longer—the half-drunk crowd was getting impatient—and again the cup rattled. Leaning forward, everyone crowded around the billiard table, the dice fell—and it was only eleven.

"Hurray!" the doctor rejoiced, throwing himself on the billiard table with revolting pleasure. "I won! Who wants a drink? I'll treat everyone in the house. Müller, hey! Whoa! Over here! Fill up the glasses. Give everyone as much as he wants to drink—I'll pay for everything!" Then, sitting down on the billiard table, he cried out, "Bring the girl here—I want to look at her!"

When Selinde heard the doctor's jubilant triumphal cry, she almost lost her senses, and she would have sunk, had not the stranger supported her. But now she collected herself with amazing strength and before obeying her new master whispered softly to her protector, "Flee Alfons, flee, before they discover you!" and then walked up to her master with a firm and steady step to receive his orders.

"She is a pretty girl!" he mumbled drunkenly, interrupted by violent hiccups, leaning against the edge of the billiard table with his left elbow and looking up at her with glassy eyes. "Fine, fine—my wife will look cross-eyed when I bring the nigger into the house for her, but—"

He could not finish. The alcoholic beverages he had consumed on this day finally got the upper hand through the last bit of excitement. He sank back unconscious onto the billiard table. From there he was carried away and put on a bed to sleep it off.

The innkeeper took the Negro girl in his care and locked her in a room so that he could turn her over to her master when he awakened.

Meanwhile, some young people, Willis among them, had whispered eagerly to each other and cast probing glances at the pale young man the Negro girl had called "Alfons," who was leaning passively in a corner. His kinky, raven-black hair hung down over his forehead in long curls; his lips were pale and his eyes reddened. Suddenly one of the young people approached him, placed his hand on his shoulder, and called in a curt tone, "Alfons!"

As if bitten by a snake, the unfortunate man jumped up at the sound of this name. He looked around wildly at the circle of strange, unfamiliar faces surrounding him until his frantic glances fixed on the man standing opposite him, who observed him with a firm and penetrating look. When the man's features became clearer and more distinct to him, Alfons hit his forehead with a clenched fist, let out a deep sigh, and sank back in his chair in defeat. On the other hand, the young man who had caused such a change in Alfons's entire being turned triumphantly to his comrades and cried, "I knew the fellow, and you may call me a scoundrel if it is not a miserable nigger."

"What, a Negro?" they all cried, crowding around the man sitting there motionless, "a Negro? Mingling with us whites?"[6]

"Out with him! Beat him into the ground! Throw the dog out the window!" These were the cries that succeeded one another as quick as lightning. Shouts alone did not suffice, for at the same time the poor man was seized by powerful hands, thrown to the ground, pulled up again, dragged to the window, and, a few seconds later, was thrown out onto the street. The fall was barely seven feet, and he was injured only slightly when he hit the ground. But he already heard his pursuers' cry of revenge in the hallway. They were not about to let him get off so cheaply.

He jumped up and turned his bloody face toward his enemies. The expression with which he awaited his tormenters showed not the fear of death but, rather, cold defiance and disdain for the worst he might encounter. Selinde's voice rang out from one of the upper windows. Foreseeing her beloved's demise, she called to him in deathly fear, "Flee, Alfons, flee—for my sake!"

He cast one glance up at the poor girl's slender figure leaning halfway out of the window, one glance full of love, fear, and defiance. But then, as if a new thought were flashing through him, and before the storming pack could reach him, he ran up the street as quick as the wind and soon disappeared, hidden in the copses that surrounded the town.

Reeling and cursing, a few of the soberest followed him for a short distance, but they soon stopped trying to catch up with the swift-footed refugee and returned to the tavern. They swore that whenever they caught sight of that damned Negro, they would tie his hands and feet and throw him into the bayou.

Guston had taken no part in the whole incident and, leaning in a window, had calmly watched the scene. Once, to be sure, just as the pack was tossing the poor man out onto the street, he cringed as if he were about to come to his aid. But whether that only seemed to be the case, or whether he thought better of it, he resumed his casual attitude and throughout the whole affair seemed to be an uninvolved, almost indifferent observer. Only after everyone had calmed down and the noisy bunch had returned to the bar to resume drinking, he left quietly—even Willis did not notice him—and deep in thought went up the street toward St. Francisville.

Meanwhile, the sun had set, and deep twilight spread over the valley when Guston reached the foot of the hill on which the little neighboring town is built. To his left he saw a dim light shining through the cracks of a small log cabin in which, as he remembered from before, dwelled two mulatto women, mother and daughter. The thought occurred to him that the pursued man could have fled there. Although he had no clear purpose in mind, he quickly went up the gentle slope of the hill and soon was standing at the door that was latched from the inside and heard voices whispering softly.

Guston placed his ear against one of the cracks and could distinguish the girl's consoling voice, encouraging someone to take heart but now and then letting out quite a deep, deep sigh herself. Guston was convinced that the unfortunate man had found shelter here. He was still undecided how he would be able to gain entry into the home, since its residents could not possibly realize that he was well disposed toward them, when he heard the old woman's voice, as she approached the door, telling her daughter, "I just have to take in the wash hanging outside; otherwise, there will be precious little of it left tomorrow morning. You put the kettle on the fire—the poor man needs nourishment and rest." At the same time the large, heavy, iron latch was pushed back, and the old woman stepped into the doorway, caught sight of the young man at that moment, and, recoiling, was about to slam the door shut again when Guston jumped forward quickly and prevented her from locking the door.

The women cried out in fear, and Alfons, who had thrown himself onto the bed weak and exhausted, jumped up in fright and pulled out a concealed knife from his belt. Guston, however, signaled with his hand that they should be silent, helped lock the door himself, and then, pulling a chair up to the table, sat down with such calm and sangfroid as if not the least thing had happened.

"Mr. Guston," the old mulatto, who had not recognized him until now, cried out in astonishment. "Mr. Guston! For heaven's sake, how did you get back to Louisiana and to our cabin—you don't want to—?"

"Don't be afraid, old woman," the young planter interrupted. "I have no evil intentions. I have come solely out of curiosity and can even be of help to the poor man. But how could you dare to be so cheeky," he now turned to the quadroon,[7] who was staring ahead mute and motionless—"as to mingle with the whites and gamble and drink with them?"

"I did not drink with them," answered Alfons in a monotone.

"All the same," responded Guston, "you must have known the danger to which you were exposing yourself, and that without gaining any benefit or use from it. For if you had really won the girl, under these circumstances you would not have been allowed to keep her."

Alfons let out a deep sigh.

"But tell me, where are you from? You are as white as any of us. I myself would never have suspected that you are descended from black blood. What is your relationship with this Negro woman? For you must have had a secret reason; otherwise, you would not have undertaken something so foolhardy."

"And what use would it be to me and you if I told you the story of my suffering?" said Alfons sadly. "It is the story of thousands of my brothers, and you will find the same in all the southern states of this free, blessed land! Oh, it is a free country!" he continued, pressing both hands against his temples in pain.

"You yourself are not a slave?" asked the planter, rising from his chair quickly.

"Not I," the poor man mumbled, shaking his head sadly. "But convince yourself," he continued, pulling out several papers from his pocket. "Convince yourself. My father gave me my freedom. Oh, oh, at that time I thought it was a beautiful gift. I was not raised like a young mustang foal with the other Negro children. I was allowed to read and to learn to write, and, deceived by the complexion of my skin, thought I was as free and happy as the Americans. It was a brief but beautiful youthful dream. They knew me everywhere, knew that my mother was a mulatto, and the 'damned Negro' could not be seen anyplace where there were whites without experiencing the most painful insults and humiliation."

"I would have left the land of my birth with a light heart, had not a slave of my father—the same young girl over whom they were gambling today—held my heart and my soul captive on that plantation," he continued in a low, trembling voice. "Selinde returned my love, and we were supposed to be united by a priest, for my father had promised me he would set her free and give her to me. Then death suddenly tore away from me the only person who had still protected me, since my mother had died a year before. Strangers seized the property that, as I was told, had been mortgaged and sold because of reckless speculations. I was thrown out into the world with only a few dollars. Because the new owner had brought along his own fifty slaves from Georgia, Selinde was sold along with other male and female slaves to a slave trader. This trader left Alabama and headed for New Orleans to sell the slaves he had purchased cheaply for a higher price. He succeeded in selling all the slaves, with the exception of Selinde, whom he wanted to keep for himself, until he came here to Bayou Sara with her, and it occurred to him to sell her off in a dice game."

"I followed them from my birthplace and often risked my life to see the girl of whom I was so fond. Then this morning, having just arrived, I learned of the planned dice game. New hope revived me. I believed no one here knew me. Trusting my white skin color, I dared go to the inn and used my last penny, as well as a ring my mother had given me on her deathbed, to buy two chances. You know the rest. The young man who recognized me is my father's nephew—my own cousin."

Alfons became silent, but the two women sat in the corner and sobbed. Even Guston was moved.

"But how did you avoid being noticed by the slave trader?" he finally asked, after a pause. "He must have seen you on one of your father's plantations."

"Often enough," Alfons continued. "But since I slept in the master's house and the slaves always addressed me as 'Mr. Alfons,' he did not suspect in the least that I myself could belong to that despised race."

"And what do you intend to do now?" Guston inquired sympathetically, handing back the papers he had skimmed quickly.

"What *can* I do?" the quadroon exhaled softly.

"Be back at this house tomorrow evening," said Guston, standing up. "I want to speak with the doctor tomorrow morning. Perhaps I can help you."

Alfons shook his head, smiling bitterly.

"We cannot hope for anything more today," Guston continued, talking more to himself than to Alfons. "At ten o'clock the doctor is going to Pointe Coupée on the steamboat ferry, so for this—"

"Tonight at ten o'clock?" Alfons asked, listening up.

"With this low-water level the steamboat ferry certainly won't go so late at night?" asked the old mulatto woman, drying her eyes.

"I have just heard that women from Taylor's plantation are on this side of the river,[8] and they demand to be taken over," Guston replied. "They want to let the doctor sleep it off, and then they will take him along. By then he'll be sober and can pay attention to his slave girl. But enough for this evening," he interrupted himself. "Perhaps I have done wrong in lending you such a sympathetic ear. For according to the laws of the state in which we are living, you deserve punishment rather than compassion. But we'll offer no opinion on this subject for now. So, farewell, by tomorrow evening I want to see what can be done for you. Stay hidden, so that your *cousin* does not see you; he doesn't seem to like this relationship very much.—That's all right," he said, stepping back somewhat and averting with a gesture Alfons's attempt to grasp his hand. "That's all right. You don't owe me any thanks, except for not divulging your presence, and I do not have the least desire to do that. So, good night, old woman; good night, Anna," and pushing back the latch again, he jumped down from the high door sill and soon disappeared into the darkness.

He had scarcely reached the wide street leading to Bayou Sara and continued along it for a few steps, when two dark figures jumped out from the thick growth on both sides of the road and seized him. He had already grabbed his knife and, expecting no good, tried to get past them when he recognized Willis's voice. Letting him loose, Willis exclaimed, laughing, but with a hushed tone, "What the deuce, we've caught one of our runaways, but not the right one. For God's sake, where are you coming from?"

"I intended to go to St. Francisville, but then I changed my mind," Guston said. "But what in the name of reason are you doing here like highwaymen on the open road? At first I truly believed I had fallen into the hands of some runaway Negroes and was about to begin to slash my way through with my knife when, fortunately, I recognized your voice. Who are these people, and what are you all doing here?" he continued, looking around in astonishment as he saw a lot of men approaching. They were at his side in a few seconds, and he recognized all the gamblers. The tall slave trader and the plaintiff and cousin of the runaway appeared to be in the lead.

"Quiet," said Willis. "We know that the impudent scoundrel who insinuated himself into our company in such a disgraceful manner is sitting in this street in Mother Hoyer's house to the left. We want to encircle the house and catch the fellow. He needs to learn how whip lashes feel in Louisiana."

"Why look for the poor devil again?" Guston interjected good-naturedly. "You've punished him once; let him run. He won't dare mingle with white men so soon again."

"Silence, man, the European in you is speaking," Willis responded dryly. "No Negro will get away with such light punishment if I can help it."

"I am just sorry that we did not tie him up and throw him into the river right away," the unfortunate man's cousin interjected with an annoyed but suppressed tone. "I never could stand the boy. But come along, we're losing time, and the light is shining over there."

Guston turned his back on the heartless man with disdain and headed for the town, while the crowd quietly crept up to the little log cabin. Suddenly, however, as if seized by another thought, he turned around quickly and followed his friends, softly muttering to himself, "At all events they shouldn't kill him!"

He had only gone a few steps back toward the cabin when it seemed to him that a dark figure was crossing the road. He stood still and called to it in a low voice, but there was no answer. Soon he reached the little cabin that the men had surrounded without making a noise, while its inhabitants, who did not suspect anything bad was about to happen, sat talking by the dim lamplight. Now and again a soft sob pierced the still night. Willis stepped forward, and, pounding at the door with the large end of an enormous leather Negro whip that he had brought along, he demanded to be let in. For a moment deathly silence prevailed. Only when he repeated his demand could one hear the voice of the old woman, who calmly told him to move on—it was nighttime and she would not open the door for any stranger because only two single women were inside.

"We know better, you cursed witch!" Willis called out loudly now, beating at the door with all his might. "Open up immediately, or we'll tear down your rotten roof over your head."

The rest also had approached from all directions and, tightly encircling the house, appeared to be about to carry out this threat literally when the latch was pushed back. Without waiting for the door to open, Willis sprang against it with full force and, pushing it open, threw himself at the mulatto's head so violently that the poor woman, dazed by the blow, reeled back unconscious and fell. With a loud scream, the girl threw herself over her mother's body. Paying little attention to her, some of the pursuers stormed into the room as quickly as the narrow entranceway allowed in order to catch their victim.

In vain they looked about the room for their prey. In vain they shone a light into every corner, behind every box. In vain they even overturned the poor women's beds to find the man who might be hidden under them. He had disappeared without a trace. Willis turned menacingly to the poor old woman who, still stunned and spent by the blow, was leaning on her daughter's shoulder.

"Where is the fellow who was here just a few minutes ago? Speak, old woman, or I'll wring your neck."

"Leave my mother alone, sir!" cried the girl, repulsing the enraged Willis's arm, which was already stretched out toward her. "Leave her alone—you have already almost killed her."

"Nigger!" he cried, rising up angrily. "Are you telling me what I should or should not do?" Hauling back his whip, he was about to strike down the fearless girl standing opposite him when he felt Guston grab and hold fast his arm. Guston whispered to him softly, "You will *not* strike the girl, or you will have to deal with me!"

"Why the deuce are you interfering in my affairs?" said Willis, furiously turning toward his friend. But meeting Guston's serious gaze, he dropped his arm and said, half-laughing, half-annoyed, "Why is that stupid girl so defiant? I did not mean to harm her. She just has to tell me where the fellow who was still here a few minutes ago is now!"

The young girl cast an anxious glance at Guston to find out whether he had betrayed her. But soon she seemed to let go of this fear, for she shook her head lightly and whispered, "I did not see anyone."

"Lies!" several voices from the pack called. "He was here; we know it. When did he leave?"

"I did not see anyone," the trembling girl repeated softly.

"Gentlemen!" Guston said now, turning to the men crowding around him. "You see, the man is gone. *Where* he's gone should not be a matter of concern for the moment, for how could we pursue an individual in the pitch-black night? Come back to town with me, and we shall drink together for half an hour; it's on me. Tomorrow, perhaps, we'll have more luck finding the fellow. Who's going with me?"

"Well, I think," said the slave trader, cutting off an enormous piece of chewing tobacco from a wide bar with the greatest equanimity and shoving it into his mouth, "we're all going."

"Yes, let's go; to hell with the nigger!" they all cried and crowded out the door again in order to resume their carousing at the inn. Guston was the last to leave the house, and the girl followed him with a teary-eyed, grateful gaze. She saw in him her mother's savior.

Laughing and shouting, the men ambled toward the town and soon reached the inn, where Guston, keeping his promise, treated them all to as many drinks as they wanted. The conversation was very loud, and the slave trader in particular scolded and cursed the escapee, whom, he assured, he had seen more than twenty times but had always taken for a white man. Suddenly, bending and stretching, the doctor appeared in the doorway with a pale, sleepy face. He was greeted with general rejoicing and then, astonished by the nigger's unheard-of impudence, learned what had transpired while he was sleeping.

"The *nigger!*" he finally cried out with indignation. "I myself thought he was one of those dark-skinned Creoles whom one often can hardly distinguish from mulattoes, much less from quadroons. But surely you tied him up and punished him right away or at least have locked him up?" Now Willis told him somewhat sheepishly that he got away from them, but they would undertake a serious search the next morning. "I have an excellent Negro dog," he continued his argument, "and if we set him on his tracks—"

"Bah," the doctor cried, annoyed. "Do you think he will hang around here in the bushes and the swamps when so many *boats* lie on the riverbank? He will steal one tonight, if he has not already done so, and by tomorrow morning he will have left few traces—I guarantee that. Well," he said in a consoling tone, "perhaps he'll come within our field again another time, and I know the fellow now. But do you think I'm a powder magazine, the way you're all crowding around me and keeping me so dry, as if a drop of spirits would spoil me? Hey, innkeeper! Something to drink! You've kept my girl safe, haven't you?"

"Everything is secure," the innkeeper replied, pushing a glass and a bottle toward the doctor. "But, doctor, the ferrymen are just about to go over for the last time. Mr. Taylor intends to be on the riverbank at ten o'clock sharp."

"Mr. Taylor," said the doctor, filling up his glass halfway and emptying it, "can go to—pasture! But it's better that I ride along. Bring the girl down and get her ready."

"Her bundle is in the kitchen," said the Yankee. "She doesn't have much, but—"

"Right—you Yankees would let a slave take a lot of stuff along!" the doctor interrupted him, laughing. "To believe that, one could not know you. Well, if she is hardworking and neat, I'll buy her a few new rags."

Leaning against the billiard table, Guston stared straight ahead for a while

and listened to the conversation. But when he heard that the girl had been led
to the door and the doctor was preparing to ferry across the river, he went up
to the doctor and asked to accompany him for a moment, for he had something
to tell him. The doctor followed him, and soon both were standing on the open,
empty street in the bright, starry night. They were not far from the unfortunate
girl, who was tied with her hands behind her back to a post that actually served
to hitch horses. Leaning against it, the girl in her thin white dress looked up
sadly to the golden stars.

"Well, what do you want from me, sir?" the doctor finally asked, standing
only a few steps away from the slave.

"I would like to buy this girl from you," Guston answered firmly and calmly.

"The devil you will!" cried the astonished doctor. "What can you be thinking of?"

"I like her," responded the young planter in an indifferent tone of voice.

"I do too," said the doctor, laughing. "And I will not sell her again. No, for a
long time my wife has been wanting to have a housegirl, and *this one* seems to
be made for that: light, nimble, pretty, and strong."

"Doctor, a few dollars more do not matter to me. But I would like to have
the girl, and if you do not ask too horrendous a price for her, then—"

"No, no," the doctor interrupted him, "nothing will come of these deliberations. If I needed the money, then yes, it might be different. But just yesterday
I received a bill of exchange, as good as silver, so I will not sell the girl. Inquire
again at Christmas and—I won't guarantee the money will last that long—perhaps even earlier. But for the moment nothing will come of your offer."

In the beginning the girl had listened in fright, since she heard that the conversation concerned her. For a while she tried in vain to penetrate the darkness
with her sharp eyes in order to study the features of the person who wished to
buy her. But finding that impossible she fell into her dreamy state, not paying
much attention to the continuation of the conversation and the consequences
it had for her. She was used to being regarded and traded as a commodity. It
did not matter to her which of the two would become her new master, since she
had lost Alfons irredeemably. Two big tears welled up in her dark eyes and, followed by others, found their way down her velvety soft cheeks.—She could not
dry them; her hands were tied.

Now the rest of the planters and merchants came out of the inn and walked
together toward the nearby riverbank to accompany the doctor to the boat.
Guston turned away and silently walked alongside Willis, who told him a thou-

sand tales and jokes and did not care whether his companion was listening to him or not. Guston was going to the little town of St. Francisville to spend the night there and then arrive at his father's plantation the following morning.

Since Guston had lived away from the slave states for a long time, the fate of the two unfortunate people really pained him, and several well-meaning plans for their future were running through his head when he tried to buy the girl from the doctor. But since the doctor did not agree, he believed he had done his part and soon forgot the misfortune of people whom he could not help anyway. He had not yet reached the top of the hill and the first houses of the little town, when he chimed in with Willis's mood and told him about his travels and wanderings.

Meanwhile, the passengers who still wanted to go over to Pointe Coupée had embarked the ferry, and Selinde also was brought on board. When the boat pushed off from the land, she was untied, and she stood in front at the bowsprit of the small, wide vessel, looking over the low railing down into the dark, ripping current, lost in gloomy, sad thoughts.

In the cabin, meanwhile, the doctor, along with two other planters, had joined Taylor's family and told them about the day's events, while the boat ran slowly up along the riverbank and was just about to pass the little bayou from which the small town got its name.

"Isn't the gentleman who is still standing on the bank coming along?" the helmsman, a German, suddenly called out to the boat's master, who was leaning against the railing, not far from the slave.

"No, has his own boat," was the laconic answer, and the engineer, who also filled the position of fireman, gave the boat full steam in order to complete the night trip as quickly as possible.

The boat now arrived at the approximate point from which they could hope to reach the opposite landing. The helmsman let the bow veer toward the backboard side, and soon the loud noise at the bowsprit indicated that the boat had gotten into a stronger current. Slowly the boat moved toward the sandbank, which in the summer months projects out from a little island in the middle of the river and extends about two miles. To get to the customary landing place in Pointe Coupée, the boat had to go around this sandbank. The boat was hardly three hundred feet from the woodsy shore when the call of a loon sounded three times from the middle of the river across the smooth water surface.[9] The master seemed to pay little attention to the oft-heard sounds. But at the second call Selinde stood upright, as if seized by sudden fright, and listened to the third with bated breath. For a few minutes everything was silent, and then the same three melancholy cries of the shy waterfowl called over to her. Leaning forward with wide open eyes, she tried to penetrate the darkness, as if trying to discover the source of these sounds.

"The loon sounds quite doleful this evening!" cried the helmsman.

"Yes, it's going to rain," said the master, casting a searching glance at the sky. But the sky did not seem to verify his weather forecast, for not even one little cloud covered the myriad of stars that shone down from the dark blue firmament in blazing splendor.

Approaching the vicinity of the sandbank, and therefore somewhat calmer water, the boat now cut through the current with greater speed. The loon called out at two more short intervals but fell silent as soon as the ferry approached.

"Stay upstream!" the master now called to the helmsman. "You're getting too close to the sand. There—that's enough!"

From there they ran quite quickly up along the sandbank in totally dead water and were getting nearer and nearer to the point, when the helmsman called out that he saw something black up ahead on the water that resembled a skiff.

"I can't make out anything," cried the master, straining his eyes and bending forward.

"Come over here. It must be a boat that's gotten loose and been driven onto the sand over there. If we had our dinghy, we could catch it."

"Disgraceful!" cried the aggravated master. "The fellows coming behind us in the rowboat will find it now. But we can't go any closer; otherwise, we'll get stuck."

Meanwhile, they had reached the same elevation as the dark object, which did indeed turn out to be a skiff. However, it was not empty. A lone man sat in it and was rowing toward the ferryboat as if he intended to go past it closely. At the same moment one could hear the call of the loon, very near and extremely soft.

"Be careful! You're going under the ferry!" cried the master from the deck to the lone rower, who was only a skiff-length away. But he paid no attention to the warning, and—"Selinde!" the stranger called softly. At that moment his skiff touched the steam ferry, and with one leap the girl lay against her beloved's breast. Knowing well, however, that he needed his arms for more than an embrace, she slid nimbly to the boat's stern and pushed the boat off with a short oar that lay there. Before the ferrymen could recover from their surprise, the little boat quickly got into the steamer's wake.

"Stop! Damn you! Help! Stop them!" The master and the helmsman cried simultaneously. Disregarding the danger to his limbs, the former took one leap from the helm to the deck below to prevent the boat from getting away. But it was too late. It had already disappeared into the darkness, and they could hear clearly the boat shooting over the river's surface, propelled by strong, regular strokes of the oar.

"Why are you all yelling as if you were stuck on a spit?" cried the doctor, coming out from the cabin with the other men. "You're making a hell of a racket."

"The Negro girl is gone!" the master cried.

"She's *what?*" the doctor screamed. With a few steps he was at the side of the master, who was scared to death himself. The master quickly called to his helmsman to turn the boat around and to follow the escapee downstream, and then, in a few words, he told the doctor what had happened. Cursing and raging, the doctor jumped to the helm, offered the helmsman ten dollars if he caught up with the fugitive, and spent his time going back and forth on the deck contemplating how he would punish the two of them when he had caught them.

The master, meanwhile, had also approached him and, interrupting the doctor's fervent gesticulations, told him to be quiet for a moment, for he thought he heard oar strokes. They listened with anxious attention and could hear clearly the oars hitting the water with regularity. But it could not be the escapees, for the sound was coming from Bayou Sara, and the helmsman finally broke the silence by affirming it was the sailboat.

"Good," cried the master. "We'll call them to help with our search. It will be bad if we don't catch the little couple before they can reach Waterloo."[10] Holding his hands to his mouth like a funnel, he loudly yelled his "Boat a hoy-y" across the calm surface of the water.

His second call was answered, and soon a satisfying "Aye—aye" responded to his slow, clear call, "Come over."

The steam ferry, meanwhile, shot toward the sandbank with considerable speed, always keeping a distance of about one hundred and fifty feet away from it in order not to run aground. The men attentively observed the strip of water between the ferry and the sandbank because they presumed with good reason that the fugitive would sooner try to escape under cover of the night than rely on his own strength and head for the middle of the river, where, were he discovered, he would not have the least bit of hope of getting away.

They were only a few hundred feet from the little island when the master suddenly grabbed the doctor's arm and, pointing directly opposite him to the sandbank that jutted out about three feet above the water's surface, called out, "There they are, as true as I am a Christian. Do you see over there?"

"Where? Where?" called the doctor, who had been looking only for the dark boat.

"There, the white spot," cried the master, "the girl's dress!" Without waiting for a further answer, he jumped to the helm with one leap and, turning the boat upstream again, steered it toward the white spot. The fugitive had landed here hoping to lie undetected behind the steep sandbank, which was several feet high, and, when the ferry had passed by, to quickly reach the middle of the river and then, going downstream, to escape imminent pursuit.

Pulling somewhat closer, the master cried out, "Now we've got them!" when he was really convinced that it was the escapees. "The water is deep here, and I would be quite mistaken if we couldn't land close to the fellow. We'll try in any case."

The poor fugitives were in quite a miserable position, for the ferry, which did not go into water very deeply, could indeed have landed exactly at this point. At this critical moment, however, the man, who had been steeled by the school of misfortune, did not lose the necessary presence of mind. With rapid strokes of the oar he flew about fifty feet directly toward his pursuers. They were already loudly rejoicing in the expectation they would soon have him in their power, and the doctor was even getting a rope ready to tie up "*the damned nigger*," as he called him. Suddenly, using a narrow strip of shallow water between two long spits of sand, Alfons shot away from the ferry to the right. Misled by the skiff that went only a few inches deep, the ferry got into too shallow water and ran aground. In the next moment the escapees had disappeared into the all-enveloping darkness.

Suddenly, a clear, nearby "Hello!" echoed over, and a few moments later the sailboat coming from Bayou Sara lay at the side of the ferry, which was stuck in the sand.

"Hello!" the Creole, who was stretched out comfortably in the stern, called once more. "Why are you cursing so blasphemously here in the still of the night? That's the doctor, isn't it?"

"Beauvais!" he cried. "Heaven has sent you."

"Softened by your prayers?" laughed Beauvais.

"Come here, quickly. Take us aboard. My Negro girl has been stolen from the boat by the white nigger. They got away barely three minutes ago. We must catch up with them."

"Get in then, quickly!" cried the Creole, steering his boat to the ferry. "If my four boys don't have the pale scoundrel in ten minutes, then I won't touch any more gumbo for the rest of my life,[11] and, doctor," he continued with a laugh, "that would make me as cross as you would be if you had to give up brandy."

With incredible speed the sailboat, which had taken aboard the doctor, the master, and the other planter, left the stranded ferry and flew toward the middle of the river to catch up with the fugitives.

"I hear the oar!" cried the master, who had been listening with his hands cupped behind his ears. "I hear the oar clearly, just under that bright star. There—a bit more to the right!" he called, as Beauvais quickly changed his course accordingly. "There—now we're on the right track. Now, my boys, take big strokes!"

The boat hardly touched the water's surface, and the white foam sprayed up high at the bowsprit.

Meanwhile, Alfons had not been idle. Large drops of sweat pearled down his brow, heated by the overexertion of rowing. For a long time the two lovers did not exchange a word. Now Selinde broke the silence and whispered in a soft, trembling voice: "I gave you away, Alfons. My white dress revealed our hiding place to our pursuers. Oh, how unhappy I am!"

"My poor girl," Alfons comforted her, without slowing down for a moment. "Stay calm. I'll elude them anyway. If only the sailboat weren't there. But I heard them calling it, and I fear we will have to land and hide in the swamp. I would not like to fall into their hands on the water."

"But they must hear us, Alfons," the girl sighed. "The awful oars are creaking so. It's resounding far across the water. I also hear the boat behind us."

"I don't have anything to wrap around the oars. Every moment I hesitate brings us closer to certain ruin," Alfons said softly.

"My dress betrayed us; may my dress save us," smiled the girl under her tears. She tore the thin material into strips and placed it under the oars. Without making a sound, the boat now glided over the calm surface of the water, and, praying softly, the poor girl's slim figure sank down into the stern of the little boat.

"Damn the dogs!" cried the doctor when the Negroes rested a moment, and all listened attentively, but in vain, for the sound of the fugitives' stroke of the oar. "Nothing is moving anymore."

"Down below is a flatboat,"[12] cried the master. "Perhaps its crew has seen something of the fugitives."

Hearing no further sound, they steered quickly toward the clumsy vessel.

They soon reached it, and the doctor cried out to them without further ado, "Have you seen a boat?"

"Someone rowed past about a hundred feet away from us."

"What direction?"

"Closer to the land."

"Who was in it?"

"Don't know," called the flatboatman. "Are you looking for a runaway slave?"

"Yes, indeed, friend," Beauvais answered. "How do you know that?"

"Good, I think you're on the right track. The fellow going down here had wrapped up the oars. It seemed suspicious to me right away."

"That's them!" the doctor screamed. "Now boldly, my boys. Strike out!"

"You said they were keeping close to the land?" the master called back once more, as the sailboat shot away from the flatboat.

"Yes," was the answer. The pursuers raced toward the dark shore, still using the current somewhat, in pursuit of the unfortunate Alfons, who had, indeed, headed toward land in order to be able to reach the protective darkness of the woods in an emergency.

The sailboat had literally been leaping across the river's surface for a few minutes when the master, who was crouching up front, looking attentively over the expanse of water, jumped up, and exclaimed: "There they are. I see the boat!"

"Hurray! Boys, row faster!" yelled the doctor. "And you, master, give me your knife. I want to show the pale nigger what it means to steal a Negro in Louisiana."

Without saying a word, the addressee reached under his vest, pulled out his long hunting knife, and handed it to the doctor, who tore it from its sheath and waved it jubilantly.

Alfons had steered the course with superhuman strength. But when he heard his pursuers' oar strokes coming closer and closer and realized that he would be able to keep up the rowing that taxed his strength for only a short time longer, he turned closer to the shore. Once he reached the woods, then all pursuit would be impossible in the dark and without dogs. As Alfons used his last strength to complete the task, as he saw that his pursuers were already close behind him—his right oar broke and his boat spun around.

Beauvais and the master recognized immediately that the fugitive was in their hands and let out a cry of joy. Beauvais turned to the doctor and warned him, "Do not kill him!" as his boat shot over to the other boat and the doctor jumped across jubilantly, the knife raised high.

But he was not to enjoy his triumph for long. Alfons, knowing full well that he had lost all hope and firmly resolved not to fall into his tormenters' hands alive, had jumped up onto the seat and was swinging the broken end of the oar around high over his head. Hit by a heavy blow, the doctor plunged backward into the boat. The knife fell from his hand and sank into the river.

Beauvais was about to follow the doctor and would have shared the same fate had not the master, careful not to get within the dangerous range of the oar, pulled out a pistol and quickly and deliberately fired at Alfons, who was standing clear.

At the crack of the gun the mortally wounded man convulsed. The raised oar fell from his hand, and for a moment he stood upright, staring fixedly at the sky. Then he groaned, "Selinde!" and sank backward into the current.

"Alfons!" cried the girl with a heartrending scream and followed the sinking man like a flash. But Beauvais, noticing this just in time, jumped into the little boat and, grabbing her fluttering white slip before it disappeared, pulled the unconscious girl back on board with the help of his crew.

Fourteen days had passed when the doctor rode over to Bayou Sara, behaved in moderation, took care of his business quickly, and was about to go back over to Pointe Coupée. He looked very pale, and a wide, not yet healed scar extended across his forehead.

As he strode toward the riverbank to get to the ferryboat that was just landing, he heard someone call his name. Turning around, he recognized Guston, who waved to him and was soon at his side.

"Well, doctor, how are you? he inquired, shaking his hand. "How is your forehead? That must have been a hellish blow!"

"It was, Guston, it was. Threw me down like a piece of wood. But the dog got his payback."

"He is said to have fallen overboard and drowned?" asked Guston, fixing the doctor with a sideward glance.

"I'll be damned if I know how he got away. The last time I saw him he was still standing on the seat of the rowboat firmly enough to knock me to the ground with the sharp-edged piece of wood. But the good master—you are coming with me to Pointe Coupée, aren't you?" he suddenly interrupted himself.

"The master is supposed to have shot him—as I was told," Guston continued, ignoring the interjection.

"The Negroes know nothing and cannot be witnesses in court. I wish, by
the way, I had accepted your suggestion that evening and let you have the girl.
I wish I had done that!"

"Well, aren't you satisfied with her? I will not take back my offer even now—
even if it is not for the same reason as before."

"Unfortunately," the doctor blurted out, "I had her buried this morning."

"*Buried?*" Guston asked, taking a step backward in astonishment. "Buried?
That strong young girl?"

"I would be glad if I had never set eyes on either her or that good-for-
nothing tall Yankee. The wench cost me a considerable sum, and then the little
she-devil lies down and gets sick. First I thought she was just trying to make a
fool of me, and, taking my wife's advice, I had her thrashed. But she did not
complain and finally fainted. Then I sent her to an infirmary and had an old
woman take care of her. I did not want to lose her; she was worth at least the
five hundred dollars. Then the black scamp gets it into her head that she will
not eat anything anymore, lies down, and does not move. In vain I went to her
myself and tried everything to bring her to her senses. All for nothing I threatened her with the most horrible punishments and actually had her whipped a
few times, just to show her that I was serious. It was all in vain. She let everything be done to her. Yesterday afternoon, when I went to her to see if more severe threats might perhaps make a bigger impression on her, she suddenly sat
up in bed, babbled all kinds of nonsense about Alfons, father, and mother and
keeled over—she was dead."[13]

"I do wish you had let me have her at that time," Guston said crossly, looking down in thought. Then he turned away hastily from the doctor and slowly
strode back to Bayou Sara.

THE PURCHASED HANGMAN

Far to the east a pale streak in the overcast firmament proclaimed the approaching day, when a lone rider on a foaming steed stopped at the garden door
of the Ferry Hotel in Pointe Coupée, Louisiana, and tried to wake up the sleepy
inhabitants with loud shouts and thunderous knocking.—Finally, the green
house door leading to the gallery opened, and the innkeeper stuck out his head.

"Who's making so much noise up front, as if it were broad daylight?" he called. "Do you think that people who go to bed at two usually get up again at four?"

"Is that you, Roettken?" the rider asked, swinging down from the saddle and tying the reins of his panting horse to a little branch sticking through the lattices. "Open up, quickly—I am in a hurry and have to leave right away."

"Hang it all! Who the devil are you, anyway?" Roettken asked again, without opening the door any farther, for a cold, harsh wind was blowing down from the Northwest. "Do you think I know everyone in the settlement by their voices?"

"Well," the man outside laughed. "You've almost hit the nail on the head. The hangman and I belong together. My visit this morning does concern the hangman. I came here because of him—I am the constable."

"Oh, Bedford, it's you," the German cried.—"Wait now. I'll open up in a moment; I just have to throw on some clothes."

With that he retreated for a short time but soon reappeared at the door and opened the two interior latches.

"Good morning, Roettken!" the man said, entering, shaking Roettken's extended hand. "Good morning! But first off you've got to open your bar for me. The harsh morning wind has dried me out remarkably."

"What in the world brings you here before daybreak?" Roettken asked in astonishment, leading the way into the house and lighting a lamp.

"You will soon find out," the constable responded. "But first give me something to drink. Then send your houseboy down to the ferry and the boats to stand guard right now, and don't let him step one foot away unless someone relieves him."

"Hello—whom are you after again?" he asked in surprise, while opening the door that led into the bar and fetching bottles and glasses.

"A terrible murder took place yesterday," Bedford continued.—Banizet, up in Pointe Coupée, just above Morgan's plantation[14]—you know the place— killed his pretty young wife with an axe and has fled."[15]

"The devil and damnation!" cried Roettken, looking up at him in surprise.

"Fortunately," the constable continued, "one of the Creoles living there was riding by late in the evening, and the screams and moans of the children that he could hear from the street—although the house lies two hundred feet back—caught his attention. He hung his horse's reins over the fence, went through the little cotton field between the low cabin and the road, and opened the door.—You know Luizot; he is a big, strong man. But he swore to me that he sank to his knees in horror at the sight he saw. The fire in the fireplace was burning brightly, and next to it, illuminated by the red flickering glow, stood the murderer, his face pale, his black, curly hair streaming wildly at his temples—still holding in his hand the axe with which he had wielded the death-blow. At his feet lay his wife. Her pale, beautiful face was marred by bloodstains; her long, raven curls were soaked with the red life stream; and her forehead had a wide-open gash. Deathly afraid, the children had fled into a corner and filled the little room with their wailing."

"Banizet did not hear his friend enter; he did not even see him. His eyes were fixed on his murdered wife's lifeless figure, and a ghostly smile stole across his face. Then Luizot called his name, and, as if hit by a bullet, he jumped up. The axe fell from his hand, his gaze turned toward the open door and the man's figure, and at that moment the full horror of his deed as well as his predicament seemed to strike him."

"'Murder, murder!' Banizet screamed, so that even the children, frightened by the unearthly sounds, were silent for a moment. Then with one bound he fled into the next room and from there into the open. Luizot tried to follow him, perhaps more with the intention of comforting than catching him, but it was useless. In the cotton fields he was able to keep sight of him for only a short distance, until Banizet reached the fence surrounding Morgan's sugar plantation,[16] where he immediately disappeared into the thick cane. Luizot then went back to the house and took the children away from the scene of horror and brought them to his own home. Along the way, however, he woke up the neighbors in several places, told them what had happened, and exhorted them to help.—Help? The poor woman no longer needs help, but the men want revenge, and most of them are now combing the fields and the swamps in all directions, while one has raced down to the judge and called upon all the planters along the way to guard their boats at the riverbank. A messenger has been sent up to Fischer's store for this purpose, and I am going down as far as Waterloo. So, watch your boats, since it is quite likely that the fellow has fled this far through the fields and plans to use either your or one of Taylor's boats down here."

"Well, don't worry," Roettken assured him.—"My houseboy will stand guard at the river bank with his double-barreled rifle, but he'll be careful not to hurt the dog's neck so that you can still hang him properly."

"That's settled, then," the constable responded, and emptied his second glass of brandy. "But now I must go. By the way, one of your men might arm himself a bit, for we need many people to ferret out Banizet, since he can't have left the marshes or fields yet. I hear Morgan and Beauvais want to call up all their slaves, and perhaps I can persuade Taylor down here to do so as well—if the damned stingy fellow can be persuaded at all. Then we can organize a proper hunt. So, adieu, do your job well, and watch out." With that he stepped out the door, swung himself up into the saddle of his little mustang, and galloped down the wide road, which ran along the river between the fenced-in fields and the Mississippi toward old Taylor's plantation, which lay about a mile farther down.

Roettken, meanwhile, followed the orders that had been given, and the houseboy, a native Alsatian, who, to be sure, had never before held a rifle but was considered to be reliable enough to serve as a sentinel, was just stepping through the doorway in order to go down to the boats when one of the Negroes, who worked in the house, too, sidled up to the innkeeper and whispered, "Massa—Massa—there—across street—man crawling—white trousers!"

"The devil, too!" Roettken cried. "Do you know for sure, Scipio?"[17]

"I sure!" he said.—"Right there at corner."

"To your post, Gottlieb, quickly!" Roettken cried, grabbing his rifle. "If it's the scoundrel, he'll not get away alive. But there come the Creoles already.— Good, now we have him for sure!—You, Scipio, sneak down to the levee.[18] Here, take the old sword and hit the fellow in his legs if you can get close enough. And you, Gottlieb, stay down here behind the little bush or behind the old tree trunk over there, where you can shoot at the boats—you've shot a rifle before, haven't you?"

Gottlieb grunted, "Of course I can shoot!"

"Fine. If he comes to the boat, then order him to halt, and if he does not do it—fire! But at his legs—spare the scoundrel's neck. "Meanwhile, I'll walk down the open street and whistle as if I knew nothing about it until I cut off his path. So, let's get going!"

Scipio had already crept away like a cat, with a mighty old cavalry sword in his hand, and Gottlieb, too, had assumed his position. But the Creoles stopped for a moment next to the church, at the home of one of their acquaintances, most likely in order to request his assistance.

Banizet—the figure whom the Negro's sharp eye had seen slipping down the street—meanwhile, was creeping close to the edge of the water, protected by some tree trunks that had washed up there. He was headed toward the boats, which, as he knew, never were locked up, in order to try to reach the opposite bank of the river and at least avoid the imminent danger of being captured.

Banizet knew that the boats' owner had been warned, for he had heard the constable's horse gallop down the road. He hoped, however, to find him not yet prepared and quickly approached the boats attached to the ferry, keeping close watch on both the riverbank and the pier projecting sharply out over him. Then he saw something moving behind one of the tree trunks.—It was Gottlieb, who was sliding around in his ambush in order to get more comfortable and was holding the rifle up high so that it wouldn't shoot off by itself.—At the same time Banizet heard the German whistling on the street and knew he would be discovered at any moment. Only a quick decision could save him, and presuming correctly that all of his pursuers were below the boats, he continued crawling swiftly and silently along his path, and hidden by an old tree root, he slipped into the water and slowly moved toward the boats. Of course, he understood that under these circumstances it would be impossible to get away with one of the boats, so he waded behind them up to the ferry, passed to its end, then crawled straight over it onto land. Now his only salvation was to reach the fields that had concealed him before and the marsh behind them, since he was, for the moment, cut off from flight across the river. So, he crouched down behind a half-cord of wood that had been set out onto the bank, wiped the water from his hair and clothes with his hands, and even took off his boots in order to get rid of the water that had collected in them, too, and would hinder him on his flight. He had just finished with all his preparations when he heard the beating of hooves as the Creoles galloped toward him. He knew they were his pursuers, and now he had to take the most extreme risk or be caught. With a mighty leap he went over a tree trunk lying there and ran up the steep riverbank. Gottlieb, rifle in hand, had been keeping watch but had no idea that the fugitive was on this side. He was so startled by Banizet's sudden appearance that his hand automatically pressed the trigger and the shot went into the air.

At the same moment Banizet reached the ridge of the low levee and saw seven or eight riders barely one hundred feet away. Spurred on to the wildest haste by the shot, they burst toward him in a headlong career. Gottlieb was closing in on him from the opposite side. In order to make up for his mistake, Gottlieb came rushing up with the butt-end of the gun raised, unmindful of the second, still loaded barrel. Threatened on both sides, Banizet had no choice but to scramble over the ten-foot-high fence that ran along the other side of the road. Without hesitation he crossed the road in just a few steps and scrambled up the horizontal rails as fast as a cat. Meanwhile, the Creoles were also forging ahead, and Scipio, with his sword, was only two steps in front of him when Banizet swung up on the uppermost rail. The rotten wood collapsed beneath him, and he hurtled into the interior of the enclosure and immediately fled through one hundred feet of meadow. At the other end the same kind of fence separated the meadow from the fields lying behind it. Several pistols were shot at the fugitive as he ran through the open space, but he reached the second fence and had already climbed it when a second shot was fired. He let out a wild cry of pain. It had been Roettken's rifle. Roettken, who had just arrived at the scene of the battle as Banizet was bounding across the enclosed space, could not shoot until Banizet held still for a moment while climbing the steep fence. Roettken's bullet met its mark. Nevertheless, the wounded man escaped into the field on the other side and in a few moments disappeared between the cotton plants.

Day began to dawn, and a thin, damp fog lay down on the low land of the settlement until it became ever thicker and soon rested on the river's surface in heavy, opaque masses. Isolated bursts of wind did not break it up but seemed to push it forward like a continuous whole body.

The Creoles had all jumped down from their horses, tied them to the fence, and were just about to follow the fugitive when a large, yellow hunting dog, tracking the scent, jumped over the fence below the house, howling. The dog ran to the water's edge, followed the scent up to the point where Banizet had crawled back to the shore, stood at the woodpile for a moment and then found his master's scent again. Everyone recognized him as Banizet's dog. Unable to jump over this fence, the dog had squeezed halfway through, when Scipio threw himself upon him. The animal struggled with all its might and was biting wildly about himself, but Scipio, with the help of a few other men, who quickly guessed his intentions, succeeded in holding the dog and then tied a leash that Roettken had fetched from the house around his neck.

"Yeah—yeah—yeah," the Negro laughed to himself, when the dog finally quieted down a bit. "No danger anymore—own dog best finds own master—Massa, hold dog—Scipio put fence down." With that he hurried to take apart the individual fence boards to make an opening, while several Creoles were busy with the dog, which still tried his best to escape them and follow his master's scent. The fence was soon dismantled, and the men quickly crossed the enclosure. Here the faithful dog almost dragged the man holding his leash in a run behind him and again had to be held down by two men at the second fence. Now the dog nosed out the spot where his master had jumped down. It was moistened with his blood. The dog stood still—sniffed at the fence and then the ground—after that at the grasses and leaves sprinkled with blood—raised his head in the air and let out such a wild, mournful howl that even the Creoles looked at each other with a shudder, and no one dared utter a word.

But the faithful animal's outburst of pain did not last long. With relentless haste he now followed the fugitive's scent as quickly as the leash allowed. The dog went through the long cotton field up to the point where it was bordered by the swamp. Here, too, the dog continued to wade forward, now and then picking up the scent he lost in the water on the fallen branches and the tree trunks strewn about, until, finally, he came to deeper places (one of the countless natural lagoons, which make up the largest portion of that area and often extend into small lakes). He did not want to swim through them. In vain he searched up and down the shore with great zeal, often stopping and briefly howling and barking, and appeared to invite his master to answer him. But he always returned to the spot where his master had stepped into the deeper water and made his way through. All efforts to get the dog to swim through this body of water, however, failed. He sniffed out his mortal enemy, the alligator, and his instincts told him that he would be irretrievably lost as soon as he delivered himself up to him.

"*Diable!*" one of the Creoles swore (he was the murdered woman's brother). "Should we let such narrow strips of water stop us and allow our certain booty to escape? Hell and the devil, no! I've got to see the scoundrel hang, even if I have to wade around between all the alligators of Louisiana for a whole year. I'll carry the dog through the water. Who will follow me?"

All the Creoles and even Roettken were willing, but Gottlieb and Scipio preferred to remain on the shore, and the latter opined quite calmly: "Alligator—smart animal—doesn't like white man—nigger and young piglet his favorite food!"

Gottlieb was quite content that the black man kept him company, for, as he openly admitted, he would have felt quite uncomfortable to stay alone among all the long, black "beasties." But the Creole picked up the dog, who knew him, and, followed by the rest, made his way through the waist-deep water.

To be sure, masses of greedy alligators were swimming about in the warm, stagnant water of the swamp, but they shyly retreated from the approaching white men. Only once, as the dog yelped when the man carrying him squeezed too tightly, did several of the boldest and largest alligators turn and follow the men. Soon, however, the men reached the shore. There they put the dog back down on the ground, and in a few seconds he found his master's scent again and followed it, barking and tugging at the leash.

The men no longer had to look very far. Barely two hundred feet away from the water, the unfortunate man sat on a fallen tree trunk, leaning against a cypress tree, half-concealed by the gray, waving moss that hung down from the adjacent trees, and calmly awaited his pursuers.

They had barely caught sight of him when they let the dog loose. Rejoicing, he ran toward his master and jumped up on him. The poor creature could not know that through his loyalty he had actually betrayed his master. Meager thanks and greeting awaited him here. Banizet, who quickly realized how his enemies had succeeded in catching up with him, grabbed the dog, who was licking him fondly, with his left arm, and with his right hand thrust his short knife into the dog's heart three times. Poor Pluto sank into his master's arm with a whimper, once more licked the hand that had wielded the deathblow and, when his master let him go, fell to the ground lifeless and heavy.

Once again the knife flashed in the Creole's hand, and he raised it to aim it at his own heart.—But a cowardly fear of death made him drop the knife, and, without resisting, he let his former friends, now his bitterest enemies, seize and bind him.

Roettken's bullet had gone through Banizet's left thigh. Exhausted by the loss of blood, he was not able to go any farther. But he had hoped to deceive his pursuers by going through the marshy, wet ground, leaving only occasional traces. God's hand, however, lay on him, and his most faithful friend had become the means that delivered him into the hands of justice.

Now the murdered woman's brother was in favor of hanging Banizet right there on the spot, so they would not have to bother with him anymore. But the others would not allow that. Roettken, especially, appeared to feel sorry for the poor man, bound up his wounds and gave him courage. Offering no resistance, Banizet let them do with him as they wished. Only when they had lifted him up to carry him away did he ask the men to let him see his dog one more time.—These were the first words that he spoke. Even when his brother-in-law had suggested hanging him on the spot, he did not utter a single syllable but only stared down in front of him. There was something so serious and almost eerie about this request that everyone immediately obeyed in silence and let him slip back to the tree trunk where he just had been sitting.

Rigid and mute, for several minutes he viewed the beautiful animal that lay stretched out at his feet, covered with blood. Then he bent down—way down over him, until his mouth touched the dog's shoulder, pressed a long kiss on the corpse grown cold, and whispered softly, "You were my *last* friend!" Two tears shone in his big, black eyes, but suddenly he seemed ashamed of his weakness, stood upright at the tree, looked at everyone in the circle, and said, "Messieurs, I am ready!"

The men took turns carrying Banizet, first through the lagoon and then, aided by Scipio and Gottlieb, over dry land toward the Mississippi. Banizet was unconscious, for the extreme excitement and exertion, as well as the painful wound, had stupefied him. Finally, they delivered him into the hands of the jailer and deputy sheriff, a German by the name of Fritz Haydt.[19] They enjoined Haydt to secure him better than he had his prior prisoners, whom he had regularly allowed to escape. But the men had no need to fear that Banizet would flee; his wounds alone would have prevented that. Therefore, his jailer did not chain him to the wall but merely guarded the heavy oak door that led to his barred cell.

The day of judgment was two months away, and the prisoner had to await his fate patiently. When the decisive day finally arrived, little spoke in his favor at the hearing.

According to his testimony, it was jealousy that had driven him to commit that terrible crime. It was unfounded jealousy, but in his blind passion he *wanted* her to be guilty, and on that fatal evening, returning from the inn that was only a few miles away, he believed he saw a dark figure climbing over the fence. Inflamed by wine, he stormed into the house, took his wife's fright caused by his raging entry to be a confession of guilt, and knocked her to the ground with the axe that, unfortunately, was leaning against the wall.

The jury unanimously declared him "guilty" and sentenced him "to be hanged by the neck until he was dead, dead, dead!"

Throughout the entire United States of North America the sheriff has the sole charge of carrying out the sentence, unless he has a vice or deputy sheriff, as was the case here, who then takes over the business of hanging. But Fritz Haydt had been raised in the old European belief that to take a human life by force and by order of the authorities dishonored the person who carried out that order. He saw the third day approaching with dread, and several people claimed that he had already made plans to let the prisoner, whose wound had now healed completely, get away for the sole reason of not having to carry out the sentence. Then a peddler came down from the Atchafalaya settlements driving his green-lacquered, two-horse wagon and stopped in front of the Ferry Hotel to spend the night as well as to ply his wares on the many guests who had gathered there because of the hanging that would take place on the following day. His name was Wolf.

Since he had known Fritz Haydt for many years, even before supper he went over to his residence, the courthouse, which lay barely three hundred feet away from the hotel, to pay him a call and chat with him a bit. But he found Haydt very depressed and soon learned the cause of his distress.

"I would pay fifty piastres,"[20] said the deputy sheriff and slammed his fist on the table, "fifty hard piastres, if I could find someone who would relieve me of *that* duty."[21]

"Paid in advance?" Wolf asked and looked at him skeptically.

"Paid in advance!—here on the spot," cried Haydt, in whom these words awakened renewed hope. "Wolf—Gold-Wolfie[22]—do you want to earn fifty hard piastres with one single knot?"

"Will they let me?" asked Wolf, doubting. "Then anyone could come along to do the deputy sheriff's duty."

"Anyone *could!*" the little vice sheriff interrupted him with impatient haste. "Anyone could come. And if the devil himself came and wanted to amuse himself by hanging the man, the court would not have anything against it. Wolfie! He's just supposed to be hanged—it doesn't matter *who* hangs him!"

"But I don't know," Wolf continued, thinking the matter over. "It's a very strange feeling when you're supposed to kill a human being!"

"But *you* aren't going to kill him, Wolfie!" Fritz Haydt continued to implore. "The court will kill him, and the court has already killed him, solely by the judgment.—You'll merely stand on the ladder and make a noose. If the hallowed law sticks a human being's head into the noose, it's not *your* fault!"

"Yes, that might still be all right," said Wolf. "But to pull out the support afterward—so that the trap falls down—I don't know, I think that's too horrible."

"You don't have to lay a hand on it," Haydt encouraged him. "You can do that with your foot, and—it's just like with the noose, my dear Wolf. You didn't put the criminal up there. That always goes back to the judge!"

"Well, all right," Wolf finally cried. "If one washes oneself afterward, it will be fine again."

"Then you've agreed?" Haydt asked.

"Here is my hand," said Wolf.

"Agreed!" the little man shouted and ran right to his suitcase, took out fifty dollars from it, and handed it to the peddler.

"But my rather lengthy stay here in Pointe Coupée," Wolf objected—"the big bill at the inn—"

"I'll pay it," Haydt interrupted. "That shouldn't be any hindrance. In the meantime, you perhaps still can do some good business with your trade. All the inhabitants of Bayou Sara and St. Francisville over there, all the planters from False River and Waterloo as well as from the Pointe Coupée colony and the Atchafalaya settlements will be here tomorrow."[23]

"Fine, *our* deal is concluded," Wolf responded, shook Haydt's hand once again, and afterward helped him empty a few bottles of red wine that Haydt pulled out from a little crate under his bed.

After supper they continued their drinking bout. But the deputy sheriff had to give the peddler his word that he would not tell anyone about their agreement, except for the sheriff.

The next day dawned bright and clear. An enormous crowd from the entire vicinity had gathered in and around the hotel in order to attend the execution. They observed the gallows, which stood about fifty feet from the courthouse, not far from a solid little building, which had been used as a powder magazine in earlier times, when the Spaniards still inhabited that region.

Finally, the time came—it was eleven o'clock—and two slaves led the condemned man down from the jail toward the gallows. Close behind him walked the sheriff and the deputy sheriff, followed by the constable and several other members of the court. A murmur of surprise ran through the crowd when they saw the peddler between them; no one as yet suspected the agreement. The procession reached the foot of the gallows, and the condemned man, supported by the Catholic priest who had joined him, said his final prayer. Just as he was about to step up the ladder, he saw the peddler close behind him and stopped in astonishment.

"What do you want?" he asked him in a low voice but with a clear, firm tone.

Wolf hesitated in embarrassment for a few seconds, his face turned bright red, and he stammered a few senseless phrases. But at this moment Fritz Haydt stepped up and explained that Monsieur Wolf was charged with filling the deputy sheriff's office for today and that the sheriff had given his permission. Then Wolf pulled the fatal noose he had ready in his pocket, as Banizet's face turned deathly pale, and he followed Banizet, who slowly climbed up the ladder ahead of him, to carry out the execution.

But why dwell on this horrible picture? The sentence was carried out, and after an hour the corpse was taken down and buried. Having completed his task well, Wolf went along into the deputy sheriff's room to drown with drink all the unpleasant feelings that might overcome him.

The observers—for the most part Creoles or Americans and Frenchmen from the little town of Bayou Sara across the river[24]—did not take the matter so lightly. All were outraged that a human being would volunteer to kill another, even *if* he was condemned by the law, for money—for a miserable fifty dollars (for the matter was made known by the sheriff as well as by Fritz Haydt himself). At first they gathered together and scolded and cursed the mercenary scoundrel. Gradually, they talked themselves into increasing agitation, until one of them suggested they punish the venal hangman.

"Damn him!" a Creole cried in his broken English.—"If it is a man's job— if a man is charged by the court to put rope around another human being, I don't dispute that—but *damn him*—scoundrel takes money—deserves hard blows!"

"Blows?" a man from Bayou Sara interrupted. "Blows? If that had taken place on *our* side, the scoundrel would be hanging already, although not on the same gallows—for he did not commit a crime—but on the nearest tree limb, and I think the large pecan tree over there would be strong enough to hold a dozen such cursed peddlers' souls. Do with him as we recently did with the Negro who hit his master—he was hoisted up right down in the lowland where we caught him—*damn him*—he is *still* hanging, and as long as the wind does not change direction he can remain hanging."

"We want to take a vote!" cried a tall doctor from Pointe Coupée.

"What for?" everyone screamed. "Is there anyone here who is against hanging the mercenary scoundrel?"

Everyone was silent.

"Well, then—away with him!" the crowd raged.—"We have enough deceitful peddlers here in Louisiana. Away to the tree with the scoundrel—let him wriggle a bit first, and then he can lie down next to the one on whom he earned his blood money!"

"To the gallows with him!" another group outshouted them.—"Banizet was a brave, hardworking fellow before he committed that shameful murder—he did not defile the crossbeam!"

"No, to the tree!" the others cried.

All agreed to *hang* the peddler; the point of debate remained *where*.

And where was the main character keeping himself during all these deliberations? Where was the good "Monsieur Wolf," as Fritz Haydt had called him? Not suspecting what storm was gathering over his unfortunate head, he had just emptied the second bottle with the little deputy sheriff and was dancing merrily across the so-called pasture toward the hotel. In front of the hotel door, close to the bank of the Mississippi, his death sentence was being as good as signed by more than two hundred people. Roettken met him at the back door and, since every soul had streamed to the front of the house to participate in the meeting, pulled him into his wife's room and closed the door behind him.

"But, Mr. Roettken—for God's sake—what are you doing with me? Why are you locking me in?" he mumbled with a quite heavy tongue. "Just give me something to drink, I'm remarkably thirsty."

"And do you know the danger you're in?" Roettken asked, bending down over him closely. "Do you know what that crowd of people you see through the window—don't get too close, or they'll see you—what that crowd of people has decided about you?"

"Well?" Wolf asked, and his chin sank considerably.

"To hang you by the neck until you are dead, dead, dead—they just haven't quite decided whether on the gallows or on the pecan tree! Which would you prefer?"

"Mr. Roettken," Wolf stammered, scared to death. The execution of such a deed did not seem at all improbable, for acts of violence like that had taken place rather frequently, especially in recent times.—"You're joking? Oh, don't look so serious—Madame Roettken—God—if it really were true! But—you will—you will not hand me over to them? Oh, for God's sake, can't you send for the constable?"

"From what I know about the courts," Roettken said, shaking his head— "the judge as well as the constable are a good ways away from here and are spending the night God knows where, just so they won't have to hear about a matter that they can't easily stop, perhaps don't even want to stop—for, the devil take you, Wolf, it was a miserable deed on your part to act the hangman for a few paltry dollars; I myself really feel like—"

"Oh, my dear Mr. Roettken," the now quite sober peddler pleaded, deathly afraid—"they are coming—save me—speak ill of me, beat me, step on me— I deserve it—but don't hand me over to those men," and with that he got down on his knees and buried his face in the covers hanging down from the wide bed.

He had heard correctly. The deliberations had ended, and the mob thronged through the house and around the buildings. Raging and shouting, they called for Roettken and the peddler.

"Save me for Jesus Christ's sake," the Israelite, sensing the peril, pleaded on his knees and tried to grasp Roettken's hand.—"Save me if you care about your own salvation—oh, Madame Roettken, you don't want to see me murdered here in cold blood?"

"Where is the peddler? Hand over the peddler!" the crowd raged.

"Save me," the unfortunate soul whispered in a subdued, trembling voice. "Don't forsake me, if God is not to forsake you in your final hours."

"Roettken—father—save the man!" the wife pleaded. "You won't allow them to drag him out of your parlor?"

"Where is the peddler? Hand over the dog!" the mob shouted under the windows.

"Put him into the bed, Emilie," the German whispered to his wife quickly— "put him away well—take the narrow mattress from the single bed there and lay it on ours. He can lie down behind it and press himself against it—they won't suspect that he is there. Meanwhile, I'll try to set the bloodhounds on a false scent."

"Angel—savior!" the peddler mumbled and tried to grasp his hand—but Roettken pushed it away.—"Away!" he insisted in a hushed tone. "Save your thanks—I don't do it gladly, for—God forgive my sin—but—I think I would like to see you hanged myself!"

With that he stepped out in front of the door in order not to arouse any further suspicion and to calm the raging men, who now were racing around the house like a surging tide and demanding the Israelite.

"Where is he?—Roettken—hand him over—damn it—you yourself will be in trouble if you are in cahoots with him—turn him over, or we will search your entire place and set it on fire if we find the scoundrel."

"Go to the devil," called Roettken, who knew these people well—"go ahead and set it on fire, if you dare. But I'll shoot a bullet into the head of the first person to approach with a torch—what the deuce do I know about the peddler? You all saw that he went over to the deputy sheriff's right after the execution— you'll probably find him there. Fritz has good wine, and I wouldn't be at all surprised if—"

"Over to the courthouse,"[25] the mob clamored—over to Fritz—hurrah— hurrah!" And they streamed over in an uncontrollable flood to exercise an act of justice, as they called it, and to make the man whom they considered guilty atone for his sacrilege.

Roettken hurried to the water now to see whether the boats were free. But guards had been posted as a precaution to prevent the man ordained for death from making any attempt to flee. Indeed, some sentries were even dispersed along all the fences that surrounded the hotel and the neighboring courthouse, thus encircling the place entirely. Every prospect of flight was cut off, for it could be foreseen that the excited mob would not even spare Roettken's rooms if they did not find the peddler elsewhere. Thus, Roettken returned to his wife rather disheartened and shared his fears with her.

"You may not stay here," he finally turned to the peddler, who climbed out of the bed, staring and pale as a corpse. "It wouldn't help you anyway. In the beginning, I believed they only planned to scare you rather than to hang you.

But now that all these measures have been taken there is no longer any doubt that they intend to take your life. A fox could not sneak past anymore—and, I fear, we have no way out but to appeal to the mob's *mercy*."

"Mercy?" the peddler screamed in horror.—"Mercy? If you had seen their delight when they hanged the Negro over there, how they rejoiced and danced. If you had seen, as I did, how these same Americans burned a mulatto in St. Louis a year ago; if you had been present in Tennessee, as was I, when they tied a horse thief to a tree and used him as a target for their bullets: you would not speak of mercy, would not think of mercy.—The panther who has fasted for fourteen days and catches a lamb would sooner show mercy; sooner the half-starved wolf who attacks a herd.—Mr. Roettken—save me—you know another way out! You must know another way out—it is not possible that I should die in such a miserable, terrible way!"—

He covered his face with his hands and sobbed loudly.

"Roettken," his wife asked, "can't you hide him in the cistern?"

The peddler listened most attentively.

"Yes, by God," the innkeeper cried, "I did not think of that! It is unlikely that they will look for you there. But it is half-filled with water.—Wolf, can you swim?"

"I never tried it in my life," he replied, trembling.

"Well, a pole is leaning inside it. You can hold onto that," Roettken said.— "The water is eight feet deep. I just measured it this morning. After a while we will water the horses, and I think I can let out three feet without arousing suspicion. But quickly, the 'hurrah' shouts over there announce their return. Quickly, before it is too late, and just hang onto the pole; it will keep you above water. When it turns dark, I'll let you out again."

"How can I ever thank you!" the peddler sobbed.

"Away, away, no more talk. Into the water, and don't let go of the pole."

"But if it is too deep?" Wolf asked anxiously.

"You know the old proverb," Roettken replied, "what is supposed to hang will not drown. That might comfort you."

With that he stepped to the door first to make sure that no unwelcome witness could detect the fugitive. But he saw no one except the guards posted around the hotel, and a newly planted peach grove prevented them from seeing the spot where the cistern stood.

The cistern was a large, round, high container that was fashioned like a water barrel. It was eight feet in diameter at the top and bottom, about sixteen feet high, and half-filled with water. It was not buried in the earth but, rather, was freestanding in the garden, close to the house. Girded by strong iron hoops, with a faucet at the bottom to let out the water easily, it was loosely covered with a few boards, so that the water would not lose oxygen and spoil.

Since the house stood higher than the cistern, Roettken could, by bending over the gallery railing, just reach one of these boards with his hand and lift it up. Wolf slipped down under it, and, gripping with both hands the pole about which his savior had spoken and sliding down it, he let himself into the warm water until it was up to his neck. It was high time, for Roettken had barely locked his parlor door behind himself when the mob stormed it and, without first asking permission, swarmed through the house from top to bottom in order to find the fugitive. No fireplace, no chimney, was forgotten. They crawled in all directions under the house built on four-foot-high brick pillars. The stables, the kitchen, the storehouse, the Negro cabins, everything, everything, was searched most thoroughly. Even the beds in Roettken's quarters, as he had predicted correctly, did not escape the general visitation. But they searched in vain. The peddler remained hidden, for no one thought of the cistern filled with water.

"The devil take you, Roettken," said a saddler from St. Francisville, whom the others called "Captain." "You must have hidden him well, or he is able to make himself invisible. I'll be damned if I know how he got away. He's not hiding in Fritz's quarters either; I'd swear to that. We searched every corner. Fritz even had to open up the jail cells. But one thing is for certain: he'll turn up again because we won't leave the place until he is here!"

"Well," said Roettken, "then be prepared to wait a long time. I don't believe that *he* will ever grace Louisiana, or at least the Feliciana and Pointe Coupée parishes, with his presence again. It didn't agree with him—but—"

"Hello—what's that?" cried the Captain, taking notice. "Isn't something splashing in the cistern? The dog wouldn't—"

"I'm keeping a young alligator in it," Roettken responded quickly.

"An alligator?" the Captain said, scrutinizing the German. "Roettken, Roettken, if the scoundrel is hiding in the cistern—"

"Are you stupid?" the innkeeper responded, feigning annoyance. "It's got eight feet of water in it!"

"Give me a pole," cried the saddler, "any piece of cane or lattice!"

"Yes, a lattice, a pole, one of the fence poles over there," screamed several in the mob, who had crowded around the men discussing the matter.—"We want to look into the cistern."

"Well, you really don't believe that a man can survive underwater!" cried the

German, now seriously concerned that they might discover the unfortunate man's hiding place. "Give *me* the pole. I'll show you how deep the water is"— and with that he climbed onto the windowsill under which the others crowded. "Don't climb up, Captain; everything is decayed and rotten up here," he called to the saddler, who was about to follow him to the edge of the water container. "You could break your neck!"

"Don't worry about *my* neck," the saddler laughed. "First I want to see whether there's a neck in there that we need out here."

"Well, then, come and be damned!" Roettken cursed and lifted up the board under which the peddler had climbed into the cistern. The Captain reached the edge of the cistern at the same time as he, and they looked down—but a deathly silence reigned below. They could not see the least thing on the smooth surface of the water, and only the pole was leaning in the container as before. Roettken looked at the American in mute horror.

"Your alligator appears to be lying on the bottom," the Captain said, looking down at the murky water.

"Yes!" breathed Roettken and barely maintained enough strength to hold on tightly to the top of the cistern, when the Captain noticed his sudden pallor and jumped down just in time to keep him from sinking.

"What the devil," he called to him, "what's the matter with you? You're turning as pale as a ghost. Hey, Wilkins—Long—George[26]—help me—by all that is holy, Roettken is fainting!"

"Let it be!" he pleaded. "I'm feeling better already. I haven't felt quite well all day; it was just momentary.—But come—come, let's have a drink—I'm thirsty—come along now!"

Although the men accompanied him to the bar and drank with him, they did not want to abandon their posts. Their blood, however, had cooled a bit. Content to curse and scold the peddler, whose disappearance remained a mystery to them, they broke into his wagon and scattered about and destroyed most of his wares. But then they headed for home—quite late, to be sure—making their way toward Bayou Sara on the ferry or riding on their little mustangs up or down along the river.

The sound of the last hoofbeat had long faded, and the splashing of the retreating oars had died down. Deathly silence rested on the quiet colony, and only the monotonous call of the loon echoed like a soft lament from the island on the opposite side of the river. But Roettken still sat at the front of his house on the gallery that overlooked the river and with a corpse-like expression stared dully at the broad, muddy waters of the Mississippi.

One and a half hours passed thus; his wife implored him several times to come into the house—he didn't move and did not respond to any of her pleas. Finally, he heard the hollow thud of the oar being thrown into the boat. The ferrymen had returned and, carrying the sail pole and oars, came through the garden gate. When Roettken saw them, he stood up, waved to them, and said darkly, "Come, we are going to bury a corpse!"

In a few words he informed the men of the poor man's terrible fate and with their help pulled his lifeless body from the cistern. Wolf's hands were clenched tightly—he must have been seized by a cramp or had a stroke. Quietly and without attracting any attention, they carried him through the cotton field back into the marsh and lowered him into a hastily prepared grave.

"Fifty dollars in, too?" Scipio asked, when they had laid out the corpse.

"Do you want that blood money?" Roettken turned toward him.

"I—Massa—no, by golly," cried the black man, "I not touch it, even if it be five thousand."

The grave was finished quickly, heavy tree trunks and branches were then rolled on top of it, and soon only the solitary owl circled over that barren, deserted place.

Afterward guests coming to the inn often asked Roettken whether he had ever seen the peddler again. But he never answered this question, and for a long time after that incident he remained quiet and withdrawn.

The day after Wolf's death, the boiler of a steamboat headed for New Orleans exploded. Because Wolf was never seen again—indeed, did not even demand through a third party that his wagon and horses be returned to him—the general consensus was that he had fled onto the boat, where he met his fate.

The wagon stood there unused, and the horses ran freely about on the pastures until the following year, when another peddler, whose name also was Wolf—or at least he pretended that was his name—announced himself to be the rightful heir. Since no one contradicted him or even bothered about the matter, he took both wagon and horses into his possession.

THE PLANTER

It was October 1840. The sun rose up from the dark shadow of the lowlands that form the eastern bank of the Mississippi. The mockingbird swayed in the tulip trees of the garden, and swarms of silktails were intoxicated by the enticing fruit of the chinaberry tree. Huge, snow-white herons, slowly waving their wings, sailed close across the river's surface or stood in solemn observation on a tree trunk lying in the water, waiting for a little fish to appear. Nature was celebrating the Sabbath—but the humans were not.

On the road that runs along the Mississippi between the high protective wall and the plantations, coming down from the Atchafalaya settlements, a gang of Negro slaves—men, women, and children—walked in double rows, followed by an ox-drawn wagon that carried the blacks' baggage. They were not in chains; they were not even tied to each other with ropes. But on each side of the procession rode two overseers armed with loaded double-barreled shotguns, and the caravan's leader carried not only a rifle and a knife but also two powerful holster pistols in his belt.—The Negroes seemed to pay little attention to their serious predicament. Laughing and singing, they walked next to each other and passed the time with stories and jokes.

Whether it was indifference to what they *knew* awaited them, whether it was the easy disposition peculiar to this race that made them seize the happy, idle moment, what did they care about the future—they were *slaves*. No plan that they could devise themselves, no goal that they could strive to attain, was of any use to them. But the *moment* was theirs, and that could not pass without being exploited and enjoyed—it would never return, and tomorrow, perhaps, they would again bend under the cruel overseer's whip.

Meanwhile, the higher the sun rose, the more lively the road became, and the Negroes frequently were overtaken by Creoles and American settlers on their fiery little mustangs.[27] The passersby exchanged a few words with the driver, briefly sized up the slaves that they let file past, and then, following the course of the river, sprang at full gallop toward the courthouse of Pointe Coupée. Most of the planters of the entire parish had gathered there to attend the auction of the "movable and immovable" property of a Frenchman at the "great bend,"[28] who had recently died, and midst the usual formalities the sale began with the plantation, the buildings, and the uncultivated land of the deceased. In the meantime the slaves, too, arrived at their destination and were put on display by the overseers, some individually, some in families.

The Negroes' careless mirth had now disappeared. The grave import of the next hour, which would decide their fate, seemed to press upon them. Only now and then was a low whisper heard among the unfortunates. With anxious timidity their glances flew from one buyer who was inspecting them to the other in order to read in advance from their expressions what lot awaited them should this or that buyer purchase them.

Finally, the sheriff gave the signal to begin, and a powerful Negro with broad, good-natured features and truly herculean arms was led out first. He was followed by a young, sickly looking woman with hollow eyes and sunken cheeks, who led one child by the hand and carried an infant on her arm.

"*Nero,*" the judge read out from the auction catalogue. "*Nero,* male slave, thirty-five years old, with a sturdy build and a healthy constitution, a smithy by trade, can also wield an axe especially well. *Maria,* his wife, eighteen years old, particularly useful in the cotton field; *Scipio,* their child, three years old—and a female infant."

"Won't you sell the man alone, judge?" called a planter from Feliciana Parish. "The woman looks damned thin!"—The poor woman clutched her child to her breast and looked around the circle with an anxious expression, and her husband reached for her hand, as if he feared being torn from her.

"No," replied the judge. "The families will not be separated." The poor woman's heart was relieved by a sigh that came from the depth of her soul.

"Six hundred dollars!" said a Creole from False River.[29]

"Seven hundred!"

"Eight hundred!"

"A thousand!" called a little, round man with a genial countenance, who had just now ridden into the courtyard and had not yet dismounted from his horse but who knew the slave under the hammer.

"A thousand dollars!" the sheriff repeated, when a momentary pause ensued. "Gentlemen, a thousand dollars—the man by himself is worth twelve hundred!"

"A thousand and fifty!" bid a lanky man in a blue coat and nankeen trousers.

The Negro cast a pleading glance at the little fat man, who seemed to understand it, for he nodded to the sheriff and called, "Fifty more!"

"Master Turnbull,"[30] the lanky man said softly, stepping over to him— "don't outbid me anymore, and afterward we will make a deal on the man."

"So? Do you think?" Turnbull asked, viewing him from the side. "You want to separate the people, aye? Probably are a slave trader?"

"That's my trade," answered the lanky man. "So, let me bid, and when they are knocked down to me, then, as I said, we will come to an agreement on the smithy."

"Twenty more!" he called out now, raising his voice and walking away from Turnbull.

"A hundred more!" called Turnbull, and the eyes of the two slaves shone for joy.

"Go to the devil!" the slave trader muttered and walked to the other side in order to inspect the next Negroes to be auctioned.

"Twelve hundred and twenty!" cried the sheriff. Twelve hundred and twenty going once, going twice, and—three times!" he repeated, and with the last word he struck his hammer against the railing. "Mr. Turnbull, they are yours."

Both Negroes had awaited the auctioneer's hammer with anxious anticipation. But now they raced toward their new master in joyous haste, for Turnbull was known to be the most kindhearted man in the whole parish. They took his hands, kissed and squeezed them, and acted like children who have received a new toy.

"I was afraid Massa wouldn't come," said Nero, while he grabbed his new master's hand again and then petted the fiery little animal he was riding.

"Away with you, away," cried Turnbull, pretending to be annoyed. "Clear out! The devil take you! You've well near torn my clothes off! But, Nero, take your wife to the inn next door and have them give you something to eat. Just tell them it's for Turnbull." Then he turned back to the auction that had resumed, and the slaves, happy to have gotten such a good "master," hurried to obey his orders.

The auction now proceeded apace. Turnbull bought another boy twelve years of age and a seventeen-year-old girl whose parents had died recently— the boy for four, the girl for six hundred dollars. The slave trader bought two whole families, saying he wanted to take them to Kentucky. Among them was a sixteen-year-old, almost white girl, the daughter of a mulatto woman, for whom several planters offered him a considerable sum. But he claimed he would be able to get a much better price for the beautiful southerner in the North, and, handing the auctioned-off slaves to his overseers, he turned to the ferry that had just arrived to ride over to Bayou Sara and from there to travel up the Mississippi by steamboat.

"Why does Hawthorn look so morose,[31] Turnbull?" a young planter from the area asked him. "He didn't bid at all, and I heard him sigh deeply a few times."

"On the first Monday in November his property is supposed to be auctioned off, too," replied Turnbull sympathetically. "So, he probably feels strange when he thinks that he's got the same thing ahead of him. He got into too many speculations and cannot pay his debts. I feel sorry for him and for his splendid slaves, too—about fifty-two head. They'll be separated."

"That's not what's eating at him," an approaching Creole interrupted. "He just confided in me that *cholera* has broken out on his plantation.[32] According to him, from yesterday noon until early this morning, when he left home, seventeen have already died."

"The devil!" cried the men, terrified.

"Yes, yes, it's no joke," affirmed the Creole. "He shouldn't really circulate among other people. The devil knows, he might be infected, too."

"Well, that's all we need in these hard times," said Turnbull, shaking his head. "A bit of cholera among the Negroes to help us get rid of our property in a hurry. Then we can go to Texas with the volunteers—surely we'll have a rifle and a horse left. But here comes Hawthorn. He should tell us whether he thinks we're in danger."

The man they spoke of had a slim, almost delicate build, with quite prominent cheekbones and lively gray eyes that did not fix on one spot for five seconds but flew in a constant circle from one of the men gathered there to the other. Heavy burdens seemed to weigh on his heart, and his face was pale; his hair and his whole suit were disheveled. With a casual greeting, he was about to pass the men when Turnbull, who had dismounted and was leading his horse by the reins, stepped into his path.

"Hey, Hawthorn, what's happened to you since I last spoke with you? You don't look your usual self. Bless my soul, man! You mustn't take a contrary wind so to heart. Who knows, tomorrow it might blow from a better direction."

"Turnbull," responded the planter, taking his friendly consoler's hand, "a man can bear much misfortune, even the most terrible. If it hits us with its full horror, it can't easily throw the strong man to the ground. But if it come gradually—drop by drop, wounding the same spot again and again—then it no longer just bends the mind; it destroys the elasticity of the soul, and the heart collapses, faint and withered."

"Courage, Hawthorn, courage!" Turnbull exclaimed. "We live in a land where rapid changes of fortune are not uncommon. One single good speculation can make you as rich as before, even richer."

"I'm finished!" said the American, shaking his head. Misfortune has been pursuing me for five years now. It first began with a bad cotton crop. Fine, all of you weren't any better off. In the next year, however, my cotton gin burned down— a Negro probably set fire to it—and almost half my crop along with it. In 1837 the foot-and-mouth disease robbed me of half my herd. In the following year I speculated in Texas, bought three hundred mules there, was, as you know, attacked and robbed by the Comanches, and only a miracle saved my scalp. Last year I got talked into putting my money into the Consolidated Bank, which went bankrupt right after that.[33] Not bowed down by all of this, I hoped at least to be able to satisfy my creditors by selling my slaves and to stand as an honest man. Then the epidemic—my son, the doctor, even fears it is cholera—breaks out among them, and God knows whether in a week I won't be—a beggar."

He was silent, and Turnbull looked at him sympathetically. "What if you moved your healthy slaves to another parish so they could escape the epidemic?"

"Am I allowed to?" Hawthorn responded. "They, like all my property, are up for sale, and you know yourself that I no longer have any right to dispose of them."

"I want to ride over with you," said Turnbull after a painful pause of silence. "I want to take a look at things myself."

"What use will that be?" Hawthorn responded. "You can't help and—will put yourself in danger of catching something."

"I'm going to accompany you anyway, even if it's just to see whether the neighboring settlements are in danger.—But whom are they bringing in there? The sale doesn't appear to be over."

His exclamation was aimed at a Negro who, one could say, was enveloped in chains and was being brought up by the deputy sheriff. He was a captured mulatto whose owner could not be determined. He himself claimed to be free but had no kind of identification. In the name of the state he was now to be sold to the highest bidder. He had been put in chains because, despite all precautions, he had already escaped from three prisons and had almost beaten the turnkey to death the last time. Everyone was afraid of buying him, and for a long while the sheriff tried in vain to auction him off for the low price of two hundred dollars. A planter from the New Orleans area, who was there by chance, finally decided to take him and use him on his sugar plantation. He bought him for two hundred and one dollars.

"No one can escape from my place," he laughed, "unless he swims across the lake, and there my alligators keep watch—splendid beasts in this respect. They've already chewed up three of my slaves, who just barely got away, one without a leg and two without an arm. But it was a warning to the rest. No one would go waist deep into the water now, even to save his own father's life.— But how will I get the fellow to Waterloo?"

"There's your chance right now," one man said. "Here comes the little Frenchman who is going back with his bread cart. You can put him in that."

"That's a good idea!" cried the planter from New Orleans, and holding the slave by one end of the chain, he led him to the cart, which was just rattling past, hitched to a single scrawny pony.

"Hello!—you in the cart there."

"Monsieur?"

"Can you take along my slave to Waterloo and drop him off there at G. Pleuvier?"

"*Impossible,*" cried the driver. "The cart is crammed full, and there isn't even room for a dog, much less for a full-grown Negro and a hundred and fifty pounds of chains!"

"How would it be if we tied him up behind?" suggested the planter. "He doesn't need to ride, but you'll deliver him properly, won't you?"

"*Certainement!*" laughed the Creole—lock him fast in back, then he can help push. But if he is accustomed to a slow pace, then I am sorry that I won't be able to accommodate him. I'm in a hurry, and so he'll have to run a bit."

"How far is it, then?" the planter asked.

"Only twelve miles; I can travel that in one and a half hours."

"Oh, if it's not any farther," the other opined. "That will limber up his legs a bit."—Without any further ado the unfortunate slave was led to the cart and, with the aid of two large padlocks, fastened to the back of the light cart covered with blue canvas. In a sharp trot, then, the Creole rode down along the riverbank with his poor charge in tow. The chained slave had to keep pace to avoid being dragged along, relieved only by the fact that most of his chains were lying on the cart itself.

Turnbull and Hawthorn, meanwhile, had been ferried across the river and rode through Bayou Sara and St. Francisville, both thriving little towns, toward Hawthorn's plantation, which was still six miles away.

But there it was a bleak and sorry sight. All work had ceased, the hedges were torn down, the windows of the living quarters were open, as if the inhabitants had moved out. The horses were grazing in the garden, treading down the flowers and gnawing on the fruit trees. The usually so lovely plantation looked more like a place that had been attacked and plundered by robbers than a peaceful dwelling of a Louisiana planter. Here and there the Negroes stood together in groups talking with one another. They did not even seem to notice their master's arrival; only one separated himself from the others, came toward both riders, and stopped in front of Hawthorn's horse.

"Well, Hannibal," he asked, "how are things? Are the sick any better?"

"In the last three hours four have died, and William and Celeste are drawing their last breaths," replied the old slave in a monotone and in deep pain. "I myself am not well," he continued after a short pause. "Hannibal's turn will come soon!"

"Dreadful!" cried Turnbull. Hawthorn did not answer and with dry eyes stared darkly and wildly at the ground.

The door of a little dwelling that lay at the center of the Negro cabins opened, and twelve Negroes carried two wide coffins down the steps. The Negroes standing around joined the procession, and, with the exception of Hannibal, who remained at his master's side, everyone soon disappeared into a small magnolia grove that bordered one side of the plantation.

"And why only two coffins?" Hawthorn inquired after a pause, in which Turnbull stared at the coffins in uneasy terror.

"The time is too short, Massa, to build a coffin for each person. They are dying too quickly. The seven carpenters we have left—two are already lying in that mound—had to work hard enough in the last two days. It's happening too quickly; they can't keep up."

"Fine, fine," Hawthorn shouted and waved his hand impatiently. "Do what you want; it's all right with me—if only I were at rest! Don't you want to come along into my hospital?" he turned to Turnbull. "It's worth taking a look at. It could not look worse if I had the sick people of a whole town in my care. I cleared out my overseer's house for it and took him into my quarters."

"Thanks, thanks!" Turnbull said, anxiously taking a step back. "One shouldn't put oneself in danger unnecessarily. The illness is contagious, and I would not like to carry it home. But who comes riding there?"

"It's one of my Negroes," Hawthorn answered. "My overseer was supposed to send him over to the neighboring plantation this morning to fetch food. I see he's returning with the baskets."

The slave rode up to his master and threw the empty baskets down from his horse.

"What's that, Scipio?" he asked in astonishment. "Why aren't you bringing back what I ordered?"

"Wouldn't let nigger onto any plantation!" the addressee said in an angry voice—"Was at every one—at Lobkins, Whartons,[34] Heckmann, Saier, whatever their names are. Said nigger should go to the devil, he carried the plague!"

"I thought so!" sighed Hawthorn. "I'll ride back with you again, Turnbull," turning suddenly toward him. "I must have distraction. If I remained among my own for a day, I would go mad!"

"Come, then!" replied Turnbull, who did not mind avoiding the dangerous proximity of the sick slaves. "Perhaps there are still ways and means to help you. An upright man should not despair as long as he has a horse he can ride and a head with which he can speculate. Come along to my place. You can rest a bit there, and perhaps in the meantime the epidemic will have run its course. In any case you yourself will avoid the danger."

The two men turned their horses back toward the road in silence, leaving the place to its ghastly emptiness and solitude. But before they left the clearing and entered the forest they heard the Negroes' wild dirges as they lowered their friends and relatives into the grave.

A peculiar feeling overcomes even the boldest, most fearless person when he approaches an area where a contagious illness is raging, where death maliciously bursts from his ambush and seizes his victim before he even suspects the terror is near. Many a man will throw himself at a row of bristling bayonets with a defiant heart and unflagging spirit, but his foot hesitates when he is to enter the land where the plague is reaping its grim harvest. With fresh courage he would attack the enemy into whose eyes he could gaze—but here, where he must presume death is in every friendly handshake, in every breath, he turns and flees the cursed place. So it was with the inhabitants of West Feliciana Parish. No one set foot on the plantation of the unfortunate Hawthorn, and when the death reports became ever more frightening, when news came that corpses were lying on their beds with no burial, a true cordon was drawn.

Four weeks later, at the end of October, several men had gathered at the landing of Bayou Sara to await the arrival of the mail boat from New Orleans, when a young planter from the area galloped up and handed the reins of his horse to a Negro standing there. He was Hawthorn's nearest neighbor, and all crowded around him with questions about the so sorely tested man's fate.

"He has passed away!" he said, looking around the circle in sorrow.

"What? Dead?" they all cried, as if with one voice.

"Dead!" the planter repeated. "I've just come from the place where one of the female slaves who was still healthy fetched food every morning—every morning less—and I heard the horrifying news. The day before yesterday the last of his male slaves died, his faithful Hannibal, who, constantly tending to the sick, kept on going for an unbelievably long time. Hawthorn, whose son up to that point had also escaped the pestilence, could not survive the loss of his faithful servant, and, as the girl told me, shot a bullet through his head this morning!"

"Dreadful!" they all cried.

"His son, the Negro woman told me, is near despair and reproaches himself most bitterly for not calling for another doctor."

"The fellow should be hanged!" cried Turnbull, who had just joined them. "For a long time I've been telling the old man that the fellow knows nothing. No, he had to keep on practicing quackery on the niggers until he had them all happily underground. If I were one of the creditors, he should not escape his fate. What do they plan to do now? How do things stand with the sale next Monday?"

"God knows!" replied a merchant from Bayou Sara. "Since the plague has been raging there, no one has thought anymore about the sale. I am among the creditors, but we stopped guarding the place about fourteen days ago. At first we kept close watch on the plantation because we had good cause to suspect that Hawthorn wanted to bring himself and the Negroes to safety in Texas or some other place.[35] We don't have to fear that anymore, and even though I will lose a lot of money, I still feel sorry for the poor devil."

"And where is his son, the doctor?" asked Turnbull.

"They say," replied the planter, "that after his father's suicide he mounted his horse and bounded away; no one knows where."

"In any case we have to go out there tomorrow!" cried Turnbull, after a moment's reflection. "This can't go on. We won't be able to answer to God and the world if we leave the few people who are still there without rescue and aid. The illness must have run its course."

"I will not go along," insisted the planter. "This morning, as the wind was blowing over from there, I could smell the corpses—I shudder just to think of it!"

"I will not go, either," said the merchant. "I've lost enough with this whole business. I don't want to risk my life on top of it."

Everyone had an excuse or said outright that they were afraid of catching the plague, and Turnbull had to abandon his benevolent plan because he would not be able to accomplish anything by himself.

Meanwhile, what did things look like on the plantation that, avoided by everyone, seemed to have succumbed to the evil spirit? Desolate stillness reigned there. The vultures closely circled around one of the low Negro cabins and flew into the nearby trees, from there to observe with greedy eyes the spot where a splendid meal would have awaited them were it not for the battens that obstructed the entrances.—Now the sun sank behind the tops of the magnolias into her green bed. But it turned darker and more sinister on the forlorn settlement. Here and there a faint star twinkled down from the blue sky dome—when, quickly but cautiously, five Negroes wrapped up in dark blankets appeared on the place and approached Hawthorn's dwelling. Having arrived at the back door, one of them struck his knife on an old tin coffeepot that appeared to have been tossed out there carelessly and repeated the signal five times before the door opened and Hawthorn, dressed in the outfit of the western backwoodsman, with a leather hunting shirt, leggings, moccasins, rifle, and knife, stepped out and, standing at the threshold for a moment, looked around sharply.

"All safe, Hannibal?" he asked then, turning to one of them who had just arrived.

"Yes, Massa," the faithful slave replied, "There's no need to worry anymore.

In the dark no one will dare set foot on this infamous place. But it's time to get going!"

"And did you secure boats? Is the path through the magnolia ravine clear? Did you take the proper precautions, in case we encounter someone?"

"All taken care of, Massa!" Hannibal replied with great satisfaction. "The young gentleman is waiting at the boats with William and Scipio and six others, and the rest of us are enough to carry all our baggage. What we carried down to the marsh on the bank of the Mississippi last night is secure, and we can load it when we row past."

"So, let's hurry, my fellow!" said Hawthorn with a smile, affably slapping the old slave on the back. "It will not be to your detriment, Hannibal, that you have served me so faithfully and eagerly—not to any of yours. But now, let's go! The minutes are precious; we have a long way ahead of us."

At his signal Hannibal hurried back to the abandoned house, unlocked the door, and called. The seemingly empty rooms turned lively, a confused riot of voices resounded, and a number of Negroes—men, women, and children—jubilantly crowded into the open.

"Stop!" cried Hawthorn, laughing, raising his arm to halt them. "The dead can't create such a spectacle, lest the living be hurt. Hush, children, until we are in Texas! Then you can jump and rejoice. But now be quiet. Hannibal and Nelson will show you the things that must be carried to the boat. Stay right in the middle of the hard-trodden footpath so that no tracks are visible at the edge!"

The blacks went to work with brisk zeal, and in a short time each one had lifted his burden. The signal was given, and the procession got under way.

Close to the western boundary of Hawthorn's plantation was a small thicket of evergreen palmettos and splendid magnolias that extended for about three miles along a deep ravine. A little brook flowed through here toward the low valley land and the Mississippi itself. In this ravine and through the dense canebrakes a narrow footpath led to a small log cabin that had not been lived in for a long time. A murder had once been committed there; therefore, its occupants had abandoned it. The prudent Hannibal had the wares that were brought to the river the night before stored here, and now he quietly crept along the path, followed by the porters, who walked behind him quickly and silently. It was a splendid night for such an undertaking. Thick, moist fog concealed the stars like a heavy veil. Only rarely did a star break a path through the moist vapors, and rolling thunder in the distance signaled an approaching storm.

At first Hawthorn followed the troop with his rifle on his shoulder, but then he pressed through the bushes and passed the Negroes, who were slowly marching forward. He wanted to make a few more arrangements with Hannibal, who was at the head of the group, when Hannibal suddenly stopped and pointed to something white in the thicket.

"There!" he whispered in a barely audible voice. "Shoot, Massa, shoot at the white spot. It does not belong here in the forest!"

"Who's there?" the American called and, aiming at the bushes with his cocked rifle, took one step forward. "Who's there? Answer, or I'll shoot."

For a moment the figure still seemed undecided about what he should do, but the danger was too imminent to hesitate long. With firm steps he walked up to Hawthorn and stood facing him.

"Rally!" Hawthorn cried in surprise. "What brings *you* here?"

"The suspicion that not everything stood with *you* as rumor had it!" the young man replied. "Hawthorn, Hawthorn, you have played a vile game, and God has sent me here to punish you!"

"Hell and the devil!" cried Hawthorn, gnashing his teeth. "Your cohort, the fine Morris, probably devised the plan to spy on me here? How much is he paying you?"

"It's true I used to be in Morris's service," Rally answered, straightening up. "But now he knows nothing of my doings; I came over here on my own. I suspected this dishonorable deed. Don't think, however, that you will escape just punishment. You will harvest the curse that you have sown!"

"Do you think so?" said Hawthorn with suppressed anger, as Rally turned away from him. "Do you really think that I am fool enough to let you go now so that you can broadcast the news to the whole world? A pox! You must hold me for a damned fool."

"Dare to come near me!" the young man cried and tore a pistol from his belt. At the same moment, however, Hannibal grabbed his arm from behind with an iron grasp, and despite his fierce flailing and cries for help, the outfoxed man was bound and gagged in just a few minutes.

"You can blame that on your foolishness and impudence," said Hawthorn, as he turned from him in order to step to the head of the procession. "Now you must go along with us at least as far as the Texas border, and then perhaps you will wise up."

"Doubt it," said Hannibal, with a mischievous glance toward the young Creole.

"Doubt what?" asked Hawthorn, turning around sharply.

"That—that he will wise up," answered the black hesitantly. He handed over the bound Rally to two of his trustees and hurried after Hawthorn.

Now they reached the swamp. But the hot summer sun had dried it up, with the exception of a few deep spots that were connected to each other through narrow arms like small lakes. Without any significant interruption they continued on their way until they reached the willows hanging over the riverbank. The low-sounding hoot of an owl echoed toward them from there. Hannibal responded with the deceptive call of the whippoorwill, and soon thereafter young Dr. Hawthorn stepped out from the thicket and greeted the arrivers cordially.

"Everything in order?" his father asked, looking around at the boats.

"Everything," the doctor replied. "It went splendidly. Not a soul noticed us or even suspects that we are still walking on the earth."

"*One* does," said his father. "But we'll take him along with a gag in his mouth."

"Do you know him?" cried the doctor.

"Certainly! It is Rally, the young Creole."

"Hell and the devil! The spy! His cursed vigilance is solely to blame for our not being able to leave the state two weeks ago—Morris's creation! And what do you plan to do with him?"

"Take him along to the Texas border," said the elder Hawthorn.

"Or at least a piece of the way," Hannibal mumbled to himself. "Should I be entrusted with guarding the scoundrel?" he asked louder.

"Do what you want," replied Hawthorn, going down to the boats. "But hold him so that he can't betray us."

"Aye, aye!" laughed the Negro, and in response to his signal some of the blacks carried the captive, who resisted with all his might, down to the smallest boat.

"Tie his feet together, so!" said Hannibal. "Now let's embark. We must be safely on the other side of the river before daybreak and have to row at least fifteen miles upstream. So, make haste, my boys, make haste!"

With brisk zeal four young blacks set to the oars, and soon thereafter they were lying in the shadow of several mighty cottonwood trees, below the feared little house. At the given signal Hawthorn's overseer, who had stood watch by their belongings, stepped to the riverbank, and after a brief exchange of words, the men began loading the boats. Then, favored by a fresh south wind, they hoisted the sails and glided up the Mississippi as closely along the riverbank as possible in order to avoid the stronger currents.

Along with the four Negroes he had selected, Hannibal had taken the smallest boat and in it put the captive, who, bound tightly and gagged, could not move. Hannibal could have been well ahead of the others because of the speed of his vessel, but he intentionally let the wide, short sail flutter, remained a rope's length behind the rest, and stayed somewhat farther out in the river. The strong splashing against the bow soon revealed that the little boat was now working against the whole body of water. After he had drawn the sail taut to catch every breeze that blew up from the Gulf of Mexico, Hannibal tapped the shoulder of his prisoner, who seemed to lie passively on the floor of the vessel.

"Massa Rally!" said the slave, and a devilish smile passed across his face—"Massa Rally, do you remember that last spring in Bayou Sara you had Hannibal tied up and beaten because he did not want to stand guard while you paid your friend's wife a call? To be sure, you had another pretext then: the 'damned nigger' had been impudent, was even supposed to have *threatened* you, and that required punishment. My master was not there, and you knew the law was on your side."

The white man clenched his teeth fiercely and raised his eyes in gloomy query to the dark figure bending over him. For a moment it seemed as if he wanted to speak, but then he sank back. The Negro, who had observed him keenly, continued: "Do you still remember how four weeks later you shot at my brother with buckshot just because he had come over without a pass, even though every child in Bayou Sara knows him, and he tried to avoid a twenty-four-hour detention by fleeing back to his plantation? Once again, you had the *law* on your side. What did you care that the poor devil had to stay in bed for months because of the pain? Do you remember all that?"

The captive looked up with a fearful, wild glance at the dark figure, who bent over him with an ever more threatening expression, but he did not move.

"Good," Hannibal continued in a suppressed tone, "you certainly have not forgotten that, and blessed be the day on which I can avenge my poor brother.—Commend your soul to God, for you will not live a quarter of an hour longer."

With his heart pounding ever more anxiously, the gagged man heard the Negro's threatening words that pronounced disaster, but he still believed that the Negro was just using his momentary power to vent his anger and hatred. Now, however, when the horror loomed before him and a terrifying premonition of his fate dawned on him, he used the strength that only desperation provides to break his bonds and free himself. But Hannibal had anticipated this, and the ropes were strong. After a few minutes of futile exertion the unfortunate man sank back again, a cold death sweat on his brow.

"All in vain!" Hannibal laughed, shoving a fresh piece of chewing tobacco into his mouth. "Get going, fellows, away with him! We have to get back to calmer water; otherwise, we'll lose the others. I have lost sight of their sails already. Help him overboard!"

The Negroes followed his order quickly and, it seemed, with joyous zeal. The unfortunate man was lifted up, despite his resistance. For a moment he swayed over the water, held by their strong fists. Then, accompanied by the leader's loud "ahoy," he flew into a current that sprayed up high and then closed over him.

Meanwhile, Hannibal had untied the sail so that it flapped in the wind. The boat stopped running, and the Negroes watched attentively as the drowning man bobbed up again, sank, and, once again, rose up. But when the murky current closed over him this time, Hannibal grabbed the rudder without saying a word, and with swollen sail the light boat, driven by a sharp south wind, flew toward the riverbank and glided along it swiftly and silently.

The day was already dawning when the fugitives stopped at the mouth of a small river that empties into the Mississippi below Tunica.

"Here is the place," said Hannibal, who had sailed up to his master's *barque* again. "If we wish to lay by during the day, not a soul can find our hiding place in this thicket. Tomorrow night we can reach the Atchafalaya, unload, and continue the trip over land, before the fearful Creoles have dared to set foot on the 'pest hole,' as they recently baptized our plantation. How surprised they will be when they find the dead cows in the cabin!"

"Good," replied Hawthorn. "We will take your advice but won't forget the sentries.—Do you have the captive secured?"

"*For sure!*" replied Hannibal, who was the first to glide into the mouth of the river with his little *barque*.

Five weeks after this incident Turnbull received the following letter from Texas:
Texas, 4 December 1840.

My dear Sir!—Since you are the only man in Louisiana whose opinion means something to me, I feel compelled to give you a brief explanation of my apparently unlawful conduct. It will, in part, justify me in your eyes or at least mitigate the sentence that you have already given me in your heart.

You know how desperate my situation was, that I was about to lose at public auction everything that was necessary for my life and future existence. I saw myself standing at the edge of an abyss, from which my own efforts could never again have pulled me up. I had to keep the means to be productive, to be active, and I was about to lose them through the greed of my creditors, especially Morris. Surrounded by their spies, I had no other way out but to think up a way to frighten both friend and foe away from my plantation. That could only be done by an illness that appeared to cause terrible devastation among my slaves, while the doctors' own fear of the epidemic helped me leave it to my own son to cure the supposed plague.

It was easy for me to persuade my faithful Negroes to stand by me. For if the plan succeeded, they could all stay in my possession. I had always treated them justly and kindly, indeed in a fatherly manner. In contrast, their fate was quite uncertain at a public auction, and they, who were for the most part related, would, no matter what, be torn apart. Hannibal was most useful to me in this matter. His cleverness guided the entire conspiracy. Empty coffins were kept ready, and as soon as a stranger appeared on the plantation, they were buried—in the beginning with ceremonious pomp, later in a somber silence that proclaimed disaster, while the women wept their dirges. Soon we achieved our purpose. The neighbors drew a cordon to ward off contagion, and from then on we lived in relative safety. But to strengthen the suspicion, we killed a few cows and kept the vultures away from them so that anyone who approached the place would smell the stench of decay and think it was the unburied corpses of those who had died in such rapid succession.

Our plan succeeded. We embarked, sailed up the Mississippi, lay in a cane-brake during the first day, which concealed us and our boats, reached the Atchafalaya on the second night, and traveled down it without any further fear of being discovered. Near the Mexican Gulf we were supposed to find mules, which we planned to use to help us continue our journey over land. We waited in vain for one whole long day, however, for the beasts of burden promised us. They did not come but, rather, a steamboat that carried us to the shore of the promised land in a much easier and swifter fashion.

Arriving in Houston, we journeyed into the interior, full of hope, and now one can hear the blows of my Negroes' axes and the crashing of the conquered tree trunks.[36]—Texas is still a young, strong land, and with the means that presently are at my disposal, I have the best hopes of becoming a prosperous man again and of being able to pay off my debts gradually, without becoming a beggar myself.—Just remember your own words, dear Sir, 'A real man must not despair as long as he still has a horse on which he can ride and a head to speculate with.'

I won't tell you yet where I am located, although I am not worried about seeing one of my creditors here. First I want to have a solid accomplishment. Then you will hear from old Hawthorn, and I hope that in the future—be it in

Texas or in Louisiana—we will drink many a glass of brandy together and exchange many a friendly word.

> In sincere friendship
> Your
> died and arisen
> William Hawthorn

JAZEDE

It was springtime—springtime in Louisiana. The May-green leaf clusters burst
out from the pecans and cypresses through the low-hanging, gray, waving Spanish moss so that the mighty trees looked like silver-haired old men adorned with
green foliage. From the south diverse lovely, colorful songbirds drew near, and
countless chains of wild geese and ducks were heading toward the far North to
build their nests, not to return to the beautiful South with their young brood
until the fall. Meanwhile, on the bank of the Mississippi the great white heron
sat warily on a tree trunk that jutted out into the river and was looking most
seriously and attentively into the rushing stream below. Now and then the heron
swiftly and surely dipped into the water with its long beak, resulting every time
in the capture and death of one of the happy little denizens of the river. The
heron thereupon stretched out its long neck smugly and self-satisfied, snapped
its beak a few times as if to say, "No matter how clever you are, I still will catch
you," and then resumed its motionless position. The mockingbird whistled in
the blossoming tulip trees.[37] The loon rocked in the highest branches of the immense trunks that grew from the fertile, marshy ground and let its piercing cry
echo through the still forest.[38] Out of the bushy chinaberry trees from which
last year's fruit was just now falling, the turtledove enticed with melancholy,
sweet tones the unfaithful male, who was billing and cooing with another,
strange female on the wide, shingled roof of the plantation building, weighted
with blooms and blossoms and surrounded by a hedge of oranges.

The treetops of the untouched, primeval forest that still stood here and
there swayed and dipped eerily. The mighty river of the West, the majestic Mississippi, foaming and roiling within, rolled its muddy stream toward the Gulf
of Mexico, which, with its crystal-clear water, draws back at first and does not
want to acknowledge, to receive, the dirty, slimy intruder. But he forces his way
into the saline flood with his long-accustomed and proven strength, seizes the
resister with his seven arms, and embraces her in triumphant rapture. He does

not defile the immaculate one but, rather, purified and cleansed himself, his wild raving disperses in the gentle waves of the beautiful sea, and, freed of all impurity, as crystal-clear as in the place whence he sprang from the cold waters of the North and bubbled down through rocky cliffs and fertile valleys into the flat land, he mingles with her waters.

The sun, not covered by a single cloud, was just rising above the dense sea of foliage that enveloped the broad plantations. In the fields gangs of Negroes were working with hoe and plow, guarded by several overseers on horseback. The overseers' heavy whips, often raised at them in a threatening manner, warned the idlers of the danger of being struck by the weighty instrument of punishment. On the levee an old Negro woman—she was seventy-two years old and no longer useful for any other work—was driving a herd of sheep to graze off the rank grass. The bleating of the lively animals joined in with the soft, melodic sounds of a bell from the neighboring chapel, the call to prayer. Huffing and puffing, one of the colossal steamboats gasped downstream toward New Orleans, the queen of the South. With sails billowing, numerous smaller sloops and schooners—in particular, a kind of sailboat the planters there call a "chicken thief"—shot down the river, which was ruffled slightly by a fresh northeasterly wind.

We are approaching one of these chicken thieves to become better acquainted with its crew. Somewhat larger than the usual boats of this class, an extraordinary amount of care had been given to readying and fitting it out. Its slender mast, bowing under the snow-white, billowing sails, was decorated with colorful, fluttering pennants. The narrow deck was scrubbed dazzlingly clean. The trim on the cabin as well as on the low sidewall had been freshly painted a bright green, and the blue, red, and white stripe that ran around the entire boat had been executed on the black ground with special care.

The crew's exterior matched the boat's pleasing appearance. At the helm leaned a young Negro, about eighteen, dressed in bright white shirt and pants. On a woolen blanket spread out before the mast camped two white men, or rather Creoles, for even though they were of European descent, their olive complexion and raven-black, shining hair were evidence that the two were the children of a more southern region.

One of them seemed to be the boat's master, and his demeanor, as he intermittently called out commands to the blacks, showed he was quite accustomed to giving orders. Like the Negro, he had divested himself of all unnecessary articles of clothing. He was, however, wearing shoes and stockings; a colorful silk scarf held together his shirt collar; a red sash was wrapped around his hips; and a broad-brimmed Panama hat shaded his dark eyes, which peered out from under it searchingly and seemed to be reconnoitering an object on the shore.

"Port! Bill, port! You're running straight onto a sandbank!" he cried to the black man, who obeyed the order with a loud "Aye, aye, sir." "So—that's enough," he continued, as the little vessel turned away from the perilous land— "that's enough—but I would like to know where the dead pecan trees are standing. We certainly cannot be past them!"

"What the deuce," the other grumbled. "Today you are unbearably impatient. I have told you ten times already that they are farther down. It was three o'clock when we passed Baton Rouge, and they are thirty miles from there. A steamboat could hardly have reached them by now."

"Hello, Massa," the black man called. "What that down there? Directly across from steamboat?"

"Hah, indeed," rejoiced the young man with the sash, quickly jumping to his feet. "That's the spot; do you see the smoke there? Quapas is expecting us— stop over there, Titus—stop over there. Now we can't be too far from Duvont's plantation."

"Another five miles," replied Titus. "But we must put round; the wind is far too adverse!"

The sails were soon turned, and the slender boat now hastened along easily, getting nearer and nearer to the designated spot. Three tall but dead trees, surrounded only by gray Spanish moss that hung like mourning veils, stretched their jagged, barren arms out wide. Thin blue smoke rose straight up from this group of trees, and a figure dressed in blue summer clothing stood on the levee and waved a red cap as a sign of recognition. Soon thereafter the chicken thief, whose cabin bore the name *Jazede* in newly painted letters, slid close to the shore. But the plank that one Creole had grabbed in order to shove it to shore was useless, for with one daring leap the one waiting there, a young dark-skinned man, who was barely sixteen, jumped aboard from a slightly protruding tree trunk, laughing out loud at his successful leap. He grabbed the slender mast with his left hand for support, and with his right, in which he still was holding the bright red cap, greeted the boat's owner.

"Be careful, Quapas," the owner called with concern, "you are going to break your neck with those wild leaps, blasted boy, and that, in any case, would be twenty-four hours too early."

"Afterward I'll be dispensable, won't I!" laughed the Indian, for the new arrival was a member of the Quapaw tribe,[39] and the Creoles called him by the name of his entire nation. "Yes, yes," he continued, pushing his long, shining hair from his face and setting his cap back on, "that is the fate of our people, why should I be an exception? But—"[40] He was about to say more when he met the friendly gaze of the young Spaniard, who held out his hand to him affectionately, and shaking it with a laugh, the Indian called out, "Wouldn't it be childish to pay attention to the words of a man who is weary of his own life? Señor Laniera, you must think that no one here on the shore knows you, since you're standing big and tall on the deck in your bright shawl. Keep more to the middle of the river and remember that almost every plantation owner here has a telescope."

"So what!" replied Laniera defiantly, but he did turn his back to the land and signaled the black man to follow the suggestion he'd heard. Then, seizing the Indian's hand, he called out, "The letter, Quapas. I hope you have not come without the letter?"

"No, not this time, Señor. But first take in your sails because the boat is running too swiftly. We are quite close to our meeting place, and I am not inclined to dock there any longer than is absolutely necessary."

Hastily, the Spaniard tore the letter from his hand and broke the seal. The Indian, as if he had done and said enough, lay down on the deck and, with a pleased expression, looked up at the bright, fluttering pennants that played in the morning wind.

—But now we would like to cast a brief glance at our travelers' circumstances and plans.

Señor Laniera, as the Indian called him, was the captain of a smuggler's schooner and under no circumstances could appear openly in this area of the Mississippi because during his last landing on the coast he had gotten into a quarrel with one of the planters and shot him in a duel.[41] Only through Quapas's cunning did he evade his pursuers then, and with good reason Quapas had warned him to be careful, since the victim's brother had sworn bloody revenge on the murderer.

The men were now embarking on a much more dangerous mission, for they were about to abduct a girl, a *slave*, from the middle of a well-guarded plantation, as if from the interior of a densely populated country. The penalty for this crime was *death*. But Laniera was not the man to pay attention to dangers or even to fear them, and, trusting in his courage as well as his cunning, he faced this adventure as lightheartedly as if it were only an excursion on the Gulf with his beloved. It was, of course, a matter of his entire future happiness. Why should he not risk his life, for it would be of no further value if he did not achieve his goal.

During his earlier trips, when he mainly visited the banks of the Mississippi, he had become acquainted with a young girl on the plantation of an enormously wealthy Frenchman. She was the planter's daughter as well as his slave. Conceived with a light-skinned mulatto, not one drop of Ethiopian blood could be detected in her, and no one who looked at her light-brown flowing hair, her dark-blue eyes, and her dazzling white complexion would have thought Jazede descended from that despised race. She had been kept in her father's house like his own child but without freedom, constantly exposed to the danger, should the old man suddenly die, of being sold to the highest bidder as part of his estate.[42]

Laniera, scorning the prejudice of his people, who see dishonor in a white man's marital union with a descendant of the despised nation but in every other respect do not shy away from the most intimate intercourse with this very race, even with its basest members, had grown to love the girl, an angel in heart and soul, and had asked her father for her hand. The old Frenchman, happily surprised by the young Spaniard's unexpected offer, gladly granted him his daughter's hand, and in a few days the lovers were to be united forever. Meanwhile, Laniera lived in the planter's house but suffered only with impatience and suppressed wrath the taunts of several American neighbors, who sneered at his union with a slave.

One Creole was especially malicious in expressing his opinion about this. He once even felt free to use the word *nigger* in speaking of the Spaniard's fiancée, and in the next moment he lay on the floor bleeding, struck by Laniera's heavy fist. His friends joined in, and on that very same evening the enemies exchanged bullets.

The Creole fell. Laniera fled and narrowly escaped on his ship. How great then was his horror when after several days of restless cruising, the faithful Indian, whom he had sent to discuss a meeting place with the old planter, returned and reported to him that the planter had died suddenly—without having drawn up the letter setting Jazede free. Expedited by Laniera's enemies, the public auction of the deceased's estate, including Laniera's fiancée, would be held as early as the third day after his death. The brother-in-law of the man who had been shot in the duel, an American who also was the parish sheriff, had sworn he would purchase the girl, even if it cost him five thousand piastres. What awaited the unfortunate girl if she fell into the hands of the wicked Yankee could be foreseen, and poor Laniera learned of his beloved's fate with a shudder.

Now it was a matter of acting swiftly and decisively. He knew he could expect no mercy, no pity, from his enemies. He quickly resolved to free his beloved, and if trickery did not work, then he would use force, for his schooner, which had loaded provisions in Natchez for the southern market, was following him a short distance away. The Indian had been sent to obtain a secret parlay with Jazede and to discuss with her a plan to escape.

The letter contained her answer. Laniera skimmed over it with shining eyes—it was his beloved's handwriting. But ever more gloomily, ever more ominously, did his brow furrow, and, while he read, several times his hand reached convulsively for the ivory-embellished knife in his sash.

"A pox!" he finally called out. "The blackguards think I am in Havana or far enough away not to spoil their fun. Just wait—if they have not miscalculated this time, they may call me a Yankee.—But port!—Titus—port!—hard to port with the rudder and down with the rags—steer the little boat toward the island that you see over there, and then take the telescope and watch the schooner— you do have the rockets to signal?"

"Everything's in order, Massa—everything's in order," the obedient black cried, and ten minutes later the pretty vessel glided under the overhanging willows to a small, pleasant island and soon thereafter lay tied to one of those willows secure and motionless. The men sprang ashore, where Laniera familiarized them with the plan.

As long as it was still light, he himself, of course, could not be seen on the shore among his enemies. Quapas, on the other hand, who had lived there since childhood and for the most part had been raised in the old planter's house, aroused no suspicion. Even if the inhabitants there surmised that he had a friendly relationship with the escaped Spaniard, they believed the latter was in the Gulf of Mexico to elude their wrath. They had no idea that he could have learned about the old man's death.

Quapas, therefore, was supposed to be with the chicken thief, which Laniera had purchased in Natchez for this purpose, while the Spaniard would wait in the vessel for the dark of night to go ashore, bring his beloved onto the little boat, and then reach nearby New Orleans with her on the same night. There lay the steamship *Cuba*,[43] which was leaving for Texas at six o'clock the following morning. Once they were aboard it, any pursuit was impossible, for in New Orleans there existed no faster-sailing vessel that could catch up with the *Cuba*. When they landed in Texas, he would only have to go a few miles into the interior in order to make his enemies give up any possible pursuit.

The chief boatswain, Boyuka, as well as the rest of the schooner crew were not to participate in the kidnapping, if at all possible, for now Jazede was considered to be a slave, and the residents of the slave states would regard her abduction to be more than theft. The provoked people could easily recognize one of the crew and confiscate the vessel and cargo. Boyuka was just to remain in the vicinity. If things came to the worst, if he knew his captain to be in danger or if he heard the alarm signal, then there would be no holding back. Twelve well-armed, daring Havanans comprised the crew, and, led by Boyuka, they would become formidable foes for the planters, who did not expect such numbers and thus were not prepared for that.

The sun was already setting in the west when Titus reported to the men, who were holding their siesta quietly, that the schooner was visible at the next spit of land and had already answered the signal. Now life came into these figures, who, up to now, lay about almost indifferently. Once again Laniera repeated the instructions exactly for his friend and made him promise to follow them faithfully. Then he slipped down into the small cabin of the chicken thief, where he had prepared a hiding place. The Negro hoisted the sails and took the helm again, and Quapas stretched out on the foredeck, leisurely smoking a cigar, while the slender, tightly built vessel, propelled by a fresh breeze, shot down the river toward the eastern shore of the Mississippi. Meanwhile, Boyuka waited for the approaching schooner, went aboard in a longboat that had been sent out for him, and slowly followed the chicken thief, which raced ahead, its pennants just disappearing behind a bend in the river.

The chicken thief easily cut through the turbid current of the mighty river, and the sun had not yet set behind the green treetops of the primeval forest when it approached the plantation of the recently deceased planter. The sail rolled down, the rope flew onto the shore, and, following it quickly, young Quapas jumped onto land and slung the rope around the burnt-black tree trunk of a dried-up cypress that had lost its branches.

"Hello, Indian," a bass voice called down from the levee. Looking up, the young Indian saw the parish constable staring down at him in amazement. "By thunder, where did you get that charming boat?—Didn't find it on the river, I hope."

"With the Negro on it, no?" laughed the Indian, quickly climbing up the riverbank and shaking the constable's extended hand. "Well, what do you think about my purchase?" he continued with a grin, pointing to the charming little vessel.

"*Your* purchase? Confound it, boy, where did you get the money? Listen, listen, I fear that on the very same day that you die, somewhere a rope will be stretched out considerably. What do you intend to do with it? Where did you get it, and where have you been these last few days?"

"Stop—stop—stop—for heaven's sake!" shouted Quapas. "Consider, the sun is setting, and I won't have time to answer even half of so many questions. But first I must tell you that I want to become a proper merchant and *marry*."

"Nonsense!" said the constable.

"You don't believe it? All the better. Now listen, I intend to buy the dried peaches that are supposed to be auctioned off with the other things here tomorrow. I know that there are more than two such boats can hold, and they will be hammered down cheaply enough. I will run up to St. Louis with them and bring back otter and beaver skins.—I have relatives among the Osage, as you must know, and then—"[44]

"Nonsense!" the lawman interrupted him again, shaking his head disgruntledly. "But whom does the Negro belong to?"

"Mine!"

"Yours?—And where are the papers?"

"Here!" said Quapas, who fortunately was prepared for this and carried in his pocket the papers concerning Titus's purchase that had been issued to Boyuka and signed over to him.

"Hmm—amazing!" mumbled the old man. "Listen, Indian," he then continued, turning to him, "your quick wealth still seems a bit suspicious to me—tomorrow we intend to look into the matter further."

"Then *today* you will drink a bottle of Lisbon wine with me," the Indian countered cheerfully, slapping the constable, who responded to the invitation with an affable grin, on the back. "Hey, Titus, bring up the bottle that's lying on top of the basket—and two glasses as well. But what are you doing here this evening already?" he asked the constable, while the black man followed his order.

"Heston has invited us to a supper, and after that we are supposed to sleep at his house so that we can be here early tomorrow morning. The auction will begin at six o'clock."

"And Jazede?" inquired the Indian.

"What's Jazede to you?"

"Hey, no one can stop me from asking! You can imagine that I am still interested in the nigger."

"Well, she's going to be auctioned off, too—Heston is hot for her, like the devil for a poor soul. But he won't get her for under two thousand piastres."

"Do you think that he would let someone else have her for a higher price?"

"Don't even think of it; he swore not for five thousand—but there comes the wine. My dear boy, tomorrow you will have to account for how you suddenly got to be a rich man—and—so help you God, if I catch you up to no good!"

Nonetheless, the constable drank down the fiery Portuguese wine with apparent pleasure. Meanwhile, several more of the neighboring planters, on whom Quapas had not counted, had gathered at the landing, and a good number of them even boarded the tiny little boat and climbed down into the cabin, among them Heston himself, the brother-in-law of the planter Laniera had shot, who hardly suspected that he was so near to his enemy.

"A plague on you, you redskin, how dare you name your vessel *Jazede?*" he asked half-vexed, half-laughing, after he had inspected the entire boat from top to bottom and now discovered the name on it. "You intend to bid tomorrow, too?"

No, sir!" the Indian replied, shrugging his shoulders. "I would have to be engaged in the slave trade as long as you to be able to pay *that* price. By the way, the name is a coincidence; it was on the boat when I bought it!"

"What will you take for it, as it is?" asked Heston.

Quapas looked up at him quickly, for he almost feared the planter had divined the Spaniard's hiding place, but he convinced himself to the contrary and responded with a laugh, "I'm not ready to sell it yet. I have to make at least *one* trip in it in order to know how a 'shipowner' feels—after that we can discuss it."

"Fine," said Heston, "let me know if you feel like making a deal—I like the vessel."

The Indian was happy when the men went ashore again, for poor Laniera must have been sweating blood in his narrow hiding place. But finally they left the vessel's deck and climbed up the levee, whereupon Heston invited Quapas to come to the house this evening. Where so many people were eating, there was sure to be something left over for him.

"Just wait, you arrogant scoundrel," the red son of the forest muttered through his teeth, when he was alone again. "Left over? You think you are too good to eat from the same platter with an Indian? Just wait for the Indian to spoil your meal completely."

Quickly, he went down to his master in the cabin, where the three men— the Negro was included in the deliberations—agreed upon the plan to get Jazede on the vessel and then reach New Orleans and the steamer headed for Texas before daybreak.

As the Indian had learned from the constable in their brief, confidential conversation, Jazede was being kept in a secure log cabin that used to serve as a prison and was being treated like a common slave. Heston had also put two of his own Negroes, whom he believed he could trust, to stand guard at the cabin. The abduction would not be nearly as easy as Laniera had originally thought, and it seemed almost impossible to attain their goal through a ruse.

"Now, then," he finally said, decisively, "if it is not through cunning, then it will be by force. She must be mine before the day dawns, even if I have to go among these scoundrels' knives by myself to fetch her. But it is not that dangerous yet. All together we are sixteen, for in this matter I can consider Quapas to be a *man,* and if worse comes to worst, let those who have driven me to it be accountable for the blood that I spill. For now, however, we shall see what can be accomplished through cunning. You, Quapas, are invited to supper tonight—"

"Yes, to eat scraps with the Negroes—and the dogs," the Indian muttered bitterly.

"That will give you the opportunity to scout around the plantation," Laniera continued, ignoring the remark. "See whether you can gain admittance to Jazede through trickery or bribery—here is gold—or, wait, it's better to take silver—the rogues aren't familiar with gold. In any case try to give her this note, and if that does not work, then whisper to her somehow to keep in readiness until *one* o'clock. We have to leave by that time, for if the wind subsides and we are forced to row, then it will hardly be possible to reach New Orleans before five or six o'clock. When the time comes, fetch your mandolin—you know how much the Creoles like to hear it. Play a lively song for them—they like to hear their native songs best—play for them what you will; just keep them captive near you."

"And the guards?" asked Quapas.

"The pox on them!" said the Spaniard angrily, stamping his foot. "We will have to resort to using force in the end—I'd not like that. But wait—sit near the door, so that they can see you from outside, or at least hear you, and I'll bet my life that the black rascals won't remain at their post. Where there is music, the devil himself can't hold them back. Above all, try to speak with Jazede and check out her prison closely, whether—"

"I know it from top to bottom," laughed the Indian. "Do you think that I would be in one place for years and not know every board of its houses?"[45]

"And is there a way to rescue her?" Laniera asked quickly. "Is there a window, a weak spot in the roof?"

"The latter might be possible, although it will hardly be of use to us," the

Indian mumbled to himself, reflectively. "I once slept in that house for three nights in a row—"

"Locked in?" smiled Laniera.

"No—it was a speculation of sorts—a—well, I can tell you. I had brought a few barrels of whiskey to the plantation and sold it to the Negroes. Had old man Duvont caught me, it would have been the end of me, as much as he liked me otherwise. But the trade went splendidly. The Negroes stole whatever they could get their hands on in the vicinity, and a Yankee, with whom I was in partnership—that is, he bought the whiskey, and I served it—and who remained with his boat on the opposite bank for three days, got such a load of geese, turkeys, pigs, chickens, ducks, eggs, corn, and sacks of cotton that he could not have bartered twelve barrels full of whiskey for in the largest city of the world. The pigs are, by the way, the most restless guests during a theft. The rascals squeal loud enough to be heard three plantations away—"

"You were going to tell me about the roof."

"Yes, well then, my warehouse was in that old house, for its back wall butts right against the fence separating the cane field from the plantation grounds. I also slept in it in order not to arouse suspicion through my comings and goings. I remember that it rained down into the left corner up toward the river. I had to sleep in the other; it could be that the boards there were rotten, but they seemed to be nailed down damned tightly. The best plan, in any case, is to go through the door honestly and properly. Climbing over the fence would take time, after all, and from the cane field one would have to go around the entire plantation to get back to the riverbank. But—just leave it up to me, Señor—I intend to play so well that the angels themselves will come down from heaven— all the Negro songs I know. But wait—how will I get on board when we've succeeded? If I remained behind, Heston would show me poor thanks."

"Can you get hold of a horse?"

"Two, if I have to. Whatever can be obtained through the Negroes stands at my disposal. The black rascals are waiting for a new supply of whiskey, and the promise of a single bottle will make them walk on coals for me."

"Fine, then, tie the horse up somewhere outside, perhaps in the shade of the orange hedge over there. When the alarm has sounded, gallop down to the second spit of land. You must get there before us, since we are forced to avoid the sandbank.—Titus will wait for you there with a little boat. I will give the signal to the schooner—two lights on the chicken thief's side facing the river. Then Boyuka will send one of his men over to me with the little sloop. He can stay on board, while Titus rows downstream."

"But that way we will have one less man up here," said Quapas.

"Not exactly. One would have to remain on board in any case, for I do not trust that fellow Heston. He is cunning and malicious, and if he did not believe me to be in the Gulf of Mexico for certain, as that boatman assured him, he would have had this vessel searched from top to bottom. As a precaution, however, I have ordered half of the schooner's crew to be over here at twelve o'clock. As soon as it is dark, they will row up the other bank, cross over, and then let their boat drift quietly downstream until they reach that pecan tree. They will lie in wait there for my orders or for the alarm—a shot."

"But if they recognize you and capture you on the plantation?"

"The first would be possible, but the second will be difficult for them and would cost warm blood. But go now—go—do your job well, Quapas—remember that from now on we will live a splendid, free life in free Texas. Think of the hunting grounds there and be clever and daring—but also cautious. Don't spoil anything through haste."

"Don't worry about me, Señor," laughed the descendant of that old, strong tribe. "Quapas has sometimes duped them more in fun than in earnest. His usual good luck won't desert him today."

"You are forgetting your instrument!"

"No, one of the guards should fetch it. Perhaps you will have a better opportunity then to carry out the plan with the roof. But first of all I am going to tend to the horse and tie it up farther down. In the worst case I'd rather depend on my legs to go a few hundred steps. If the alarm sounded, and I could not get out in time, then one of the scurrilous Creoles would mount the pony, and what should be my salvation would be your ruin. So, adieu! To a happy reunion on board the chicken thief here, but let's hope not in this spot!"

The slender figure of the Indian sprang easily onto land, made a detour around the plantation, exchanged a few words with a Negro working on the levee, and jumped over the fence nimbly, hurrying toward the little log cabin that, as he knew, held Jazede captive and was guarded by two sturdy Negroes, who leaned against the door lazily, almost motionless.

"How are you, Sam? What are you doing, Scipio?" he called to the Negroes on arrival. "The hangman take the rogues. Their mouths are gaping as if they had not gotten an hour's sleep in eight nights."

"Oh, Massa Quapas!" called Scipio, while both took off their old straw hats and greeted him in a friendly manner. "How are you, Massa Quapas? Hey, Massa—you've something in the little boat, hey." The Negro made a quick, furtive gesture that signified drinking.

"Do I!" the Indian whispered. "This evening you may fetch the samples—but—don't bring me such large bottles this time. Live and let live. Remember that even the largest barrel has a bottom!"

"Never mind, Massa!" grinned Sam. "I'll bring big turkey—big goose. Much money in New Orleans—many blows here. Last time they caught Sambo, Lord 'a mercy what blows."[46]

"You see," laughed Quapas, "that will make you smarter the next time. What are you both doing at the door here, as if there were no more cotton fields on earth? You must have an extraordinarily good-natured overseer."

"Yes, very good!" said Scipio, looking around cautiously. "Brings poor Negroes something every time—last time big, fat whip from New Orleans. There it is called 'nigger whip'; here they've named it 'Scipio.'"[47]

"Aha, you've broken it in—but what do you have in here?"

"Stop, Massa—no one gets in—the white nigger is in there—Jazede—you know that."

"What? Jazede still here? I was told Mr. Heston had already taken her to his plantation."

The Negroes silently shook their heads.

"Now, you really aren't going to bar my admission to an old friend?"

"Stop, Massa—by jingo it won't work—Massa Heston will beat us to death."

"The devil take you and your nonsense. Massa Heston will let you live, and Massa Quapas," he continued, speaking more softly, "has the whole boatful of whiskey that he will give you today and tomorrow, as much as you can drink."

"But, Massa Heston—" Scipio said hesitantly.

"Knows me," the young Indian interrupted him. "Here, boys, is a half-dollar, and I have brought along a whole packet of the kerchiefs you liked so much. I want to see to it that I can send you down to the boat under some pretext. Titus, the black man on board, can give it to you—but do not let the others see."

Making these various promises, Quapas pushed aside the two, who offered only faint resistance, opened the door, and slipped inside.

It was a small, crude cabin built of uncommonly thick logs, with a somewhat raised entryway—under which Quapas used to store his whiskey—with no window other than two firing hole—like openings, hardly six inches in diameter, through which the setting sun was just casting its last glowing red rays, illuminating the little room for a short while. There were no household utensils—nothing but a bed of boards, on which lay gray moss freshly torn from the tree that the prisoner had obtained through the kindness of her two guards. A half-gourd contained somewhat murky-looking water, just as it was drawn from the Mississippi, and a piece of cornbread that had been bitten into lay next to it, covered with ants. Leaning forward on the bed, her head propped up in her hands, sat the prisoner. Her long, light-brown curls welled through her fingers in unrestrained abundance and beauty. Single large, bright teardrops trickled down her fingers and hung like pearls from the coarse, threadbare dress wrapped around her slender, delicate figure. The poor girl was crying quite bitterly and did not hear the Indian enter quickly and silently, until he gently laid his hand on her head, and she jumped up with a start.

"Jazede!" said the Indian sadly, holding out his hand, which she grasped in a friendly manner. "Jazede, you're crying?"

"Have you seen him?" the maiden now asked hastily, wiping the clear drops from her large blue eyes. "Have you seen him? Does he know my fate?"

"Here, take this letter—quickly—be ready to escape tonight at one o'clock —Laniera still does not know how it will be possible, whether by deception or force. But he is here. His boat lies out by the riverbank, and at one o'clock—"

"Ha!" breathed Jazede.

"And at one o'clock?" asked a hoarse voice at the door.

Oh, it's you, Mr. Heston?" said the Indian, turning and quickly composing himself.

"And at one o'clock?" asked the planter, observing him keenly.

"We passed Nolton's plantation. I was just telling Jazede about the dance that the Negroes had there on the bank; it must have been a celebration. But I could not anchor because the wind was favorable, and I did not want to lose that good time."

"When was that?" asked Heston.

"Today about one o'clock. It could, by the way, have been a bit earlier. Time has passed slowly enough for me."

"And don't you know that I had given strict orders not to let anyone in to see the slave? Didn't the wooly-headed rascals outside tell you that, eh?"

"Certainly!" laughed the Indian good-naturedly. "I really did not believe that the ban applied to me."

"And why not to you, Quapas?" asked the American darkly. "But you are right in a way. You know too well the danger to which you would be exposed if you were deceitful. Go on now; the game is over. Tomorrow Jazede will be mine, and I'll take care of guarding her until then."

"Quapas turned to leave, shook the beautiful girl's hand quite naturally, and said, "Farewell, Jazede, may things with your new master go as well for you as you deserve."

"Your prophecy, or rather your wish, will come true, Indian," laughed Heston. "She will get what she deserves, and that is a nigger's share. We'll see if the hoe in the sugar and cotton fields will agree with her tender hands."

Laughing bitterly, he flung the door shut and, taking Quapas by the arm, whispered to him in a serious and threatening tone, "If you set one foot near this hut before tomorrow morning, it is at your own risk. You know me!"

The Indian replied to the fierce warning with a loud laugh and asked the American, who was somewhat disconcerted by this, why he thought it was necessary to take such terrible precautionary measures against him, the poor savage. "Don't be foolish, Mr. Heston," he continued, "we two have been good friends long enough not to quarrel because of a girl who really is nothing to me and whom I perhaps never will see again in my life. I intend to start out on my pilgrimage, probably even before the auction starts, and return a rich man. If you still wish to purchase the chicken thief then, and we can come to an agreement, we can make a deal."

"And you two scoundrels," the planter now turned to the two Negro slaves who stood there meekly, "if you let another living soul enter this door, you will each receive fifty lashes with the new whip. You, Scipio, know how it hurts and can tell Sam about it. So, take care—you know I seldom jest."

The American, followed by the Indian, went slowly toward the house, which was about two hundred steps away. There a good number of neighbors from both sides of the river had gathered to take advantage of Heston's cordially extended hospitality and to be present at the auction that would begin early.

"What will come first, Heston?" asked a tanned Creole with black curls, whose dark, fiery eyes glowed deep in their sockets as he mixed a glass of grog from the bottle of rum standing there and emptied its contents with one gulp.

"Well, the plantation, of course!" replied the addressee. "It's always the first thing, as you know."

"And then?" the Creole continued to query, leering and smiling faintly over the glass at his host. "And then?" he repeated, when Heston seemed to overhear his question.

"Well, then, I thought we would take the slaves, at least some of them, then the horses and the rest of the animals—for the cotton and last year's cane sugar is gone—and finally the movables, the wagons and boats, the farm implements and tools, et cetera. Are you satisfied with that?"

"Oh, why not?" grinned a rich planter from the opposite bank of the river. "I had a damned mind to buy the quadroon girl, but Heston probably has an eye on her, and I wouldn't like to pay too high a price for her."

"Gentlemen, dinner is ready," called Heston, for whom the conversation was starting to become unpleasant. "The claret will get warm if we do not make haste." The call was quickly obeyed, and the Indian, whom no one asked to be seated, leaned his shoulder against the doorpost and, humming, seemed to be avidly engaged in observing the stars. His heart, however, was beating fearfully and fiercely, for the illumination of the house had been the signal for Laniera to begin his bold plan. Bending forward, he listened for the slightest noise that the evening breeze blew toward him and with every moment hoped more and more to see the signal of success, the rocket from the boat, rising. But everything remained deadly calm, and only the raucous gaiety of the drinkers resounded from the brightly lit hall, while from the dark edge of the forest the owl answered their jubilant shouts with its hoarse plaintive tones.

It was time to clear the table.

"Hey, Quapas!" Heston called to him. "You haven't eaten yet, lad. Come, sit down here. There's plenty left, and enjoy the claret."

"Thank you, Señor," the Indian replied. "I don't feel well. I'd rather stay in the fresh air."

"God's wrath! You don't want to leave the house hungry after I've invited you to come to the table? Why are you peering out there so anxiously?"

"Looking anxiously up at the stars?" Quapas asked calmly. "Really don't know, unless I was waiting for one to come down and make me rich. But—I'd best take your advice and eat something, at least drink a glass of wine. Perhaps that will make me feel better."

"How about playing a little game of cards?" asked one of the sugar planters from the other side of the river. He was lying in the hammock stretched out in the gallery, picking his teeth.

"Yes, indeed; yes, indeed," many cried. "A game of loo or euchre?"[48]

"Who will be the banker for a game of poker?"

"I will!" said a Creole, "if no one else wants to."

"Oh, the devil take your game!" cried a third. "Here is Quapas. Surely he must have his instrument with him. He should sing us a song!"

"Yes, for sure," others chimed in. "It's too late for a game. It must be past midnight."

"Fine, then, let him sing a song for you," laughed the Creole, "and we'll play cards as well. Both are easily done together. So, Quapas, get out your lute or zither, or whatever you call that thing, and sing one of your Indian battle songs. I like to hear them here in the room, but I'll be damned if they sounded as good when we fought against the Creeks and Seminoles and expected that at any minute we'd have a piece too much of iron and a piece too little of skin on our head."[49]

Quapas silently got up from the table, stepped to the door, and called over to Jazede's cabin, "Hey, Scipio, go down to the boat and fetch my mandolin, but hurry!"

"Why the devil are you sending Scipio away from his post, Quapas? Eh? Didn't I order you to leave those fellows alone?" asked Heston, stepping up quickly. "Hey, Scipio, you stay there!" he continued, calling out the door. "You stay there, you hear? Scipio!—Scipio!"

"Went down to the boat, Massa," Sam answered for him.

"Hell and damnation!" the planter cried, vexed. "He's obeying this fellow's order with fantastic speed. Just wait, you scoundrel, you'll pay with your hide tomorrow."

"Don't be angry, Señor," Quapas bade. "I didn't want to send someone from the house here because I thought they were busy."

"And why didn't you go yourself?"

"I thought I was your guest!" said the Indian, straightening up proudly and looking right into the planter's eyes with a cold but serious expression, so that he turned away and muttered a curse into his beard but gave no further response. The Negro was gone for a while but then crept up and handed the instrument to the Indian, who had been waiting for him in the doorway. Without paying any further attention to Scipio's signals, he sat down with it. He struck a few chords and then began to strum the strings with a practiced hand.

The cardplayers, meanwhile, had gathered around a table and hardly paid attention as the young savage enticed melancholy tunes from the instrument for a while then suddenly switched from the soft minor chords of the Spanish songs to one of the shrill war dances of his tribe, which was followed immediately by the quick tempo of a comical Negro song.—That had its intended effect. Circumspectly, he watched the white-clad figure of one of the Negroes sneak up. He had been crouching in the shadow of a big fig tree that stood between the planter's home and the outer buildings.

Almost unconsciously, Quapas played the chords ever more lively and enticingly. He himself did not hear what he was playing. His ear was glued to the faraway rustling of the chinaberry and pecan trees that shaded Jazede's cabin. His heart beat loudly and violently, and he could feel his pulse beat feverishly in his temples. But everything still remained calm and undisturbed. Even the mockingbird that was sitting on one of the trees hanging over the little building had not yet stopped singing. Suddenly, it was silent, as if something had disturbed it; almost instinctively, the Indian's fingers rested motionless on the strings. Bent halfway forward, he forgot everything surrounding him.

"Well, Quapas, why are you stopping in the middle of the song? You were just playing quite well. What is the matter?" a Creole asked.

"I—I can't remember the rest!" the Indian answered distractedly.

"Can't remember the rest?" the Creole laughed good-naturedly. "God bless us, he's been playing the tune ever faster and livelier for the seventh time now, and suddenly he can't remember the rest, ha, ha, ha!"

"You must be sick of hearing the same tune over and over again!" said Quapas, with presence of mind and composure. "But now you will hear your favorite song. You'll like it better." With nimble fingers he began to play the song from Normandy, "Quand tout renaît à l'espérance,"[50] which most of those present joined in humming.

"Bravo, Quapas!" the oft-mentioned Creole cried. "Bravo! But whom are you looking for here?"

"Where is Heston? He was still here a few minutes ago," the Indian asked, looking around anxiously. "Wasn't he playing in the game?"

"He's probably gone out for some fresh air," the other answered. "It's close and muggy in the room. But come, play the second verse. What's Heston to us!"

"Oh, I just inquired about him because he likes this song so much. Here, then, is the second verse: J'ai vu les champs de[51]—but wait. I know a merrier song—the hangman take all the gloomy, melancholy tunes. The wine doesn't even taste good with such jeremiads. My tribe hates the laments. Here's a happy song for you:

> Jeune fille aux yeux noirs,
> Tu règnes sur mon âme,
> Tiens, voilá des anneaux,
> Des croix d'or[52]—

Then a string broke.

"You're tearing into it as if you wanted to break them all. That comes from being dry, par Dieu! You've only drunk one single glass. Come on, help yourself—then it will be better!"

Quapas stood up to moisten his feverishly hot lips. But just as he was about to put the glass to his mouth, the first sounds from the distant cabin echoed toward him. Now someone was laughing. He could understand it clearly.

"To what we love!" he said, lifting the glass and emptying it with one gulp. "To what we love!" several of the players chimed in.

"Ha—don't you hear anything?" one of the Creoles cried. "That was a cry for help! Where is Heston?"

A momentary silence followed, and once again the cry *Help!* sounded from the nearby Negro cabin.

Now, however, we must move to another site of our story, back to the dear, unfortunate quadroon girl who was being held captive by the sheriff in such a cruel way.

Raised by her father, the rich Duvont, in all the luxury and comfort of the southern planter's life, Jazede had never thought that she might ever be put on the same footing as the despised race from which her mother descended. She did not know that her father had not issued a letter of manumission for her, or perhaps she did not consider it necessary, for who would have dared offer the rich Duvont's child for sale? But the planters in the neighborhood knew her background, and even if the planters' sons hung around the beautiful girl and babbled to her about love and hot passion, they were careful not to appear to have serious intentions. For the thought of entering a union with a "nigger" would have been unheard of.

Then Laniera landed on the coast with his schooner and saw and loved the charming girl. But Jazede maintained a cold and proud reserve, although her heart was not indifferent to the handsome stranger. "If he learns what race you are from," she thought to herself, sadly, "then he will act like the others. He will despise and—forget you." Laniera, however, thought otherwise. He had observed the lovely girl's activities and entire demeanor in her quiet domesticity and had sworn to himself to call her his own, if he could win her heart.

It had been a mild autumn evening when he first confessed his love to her and asked her to requite it. Blushing, then turning pale, the poor trembling girl responded to the man who had already become so dear to her by saying that he could not think of a union with her because she was of Ethiopian descent.

For a moment it is true—for a moment he was startled when he heard her own mouth confirm what up until now he had taken for slander from the lips of others. But his better instincts soon prevailed, and he repeated his earlier proposal with many even more heartfelt words. Oh, with what bliss did the dear child lean on the beloved man's breast, the first who had approached her with true, open love! Her father was glad to give them his blessing, for he knew that his daughter was thus assured a white man's respect, which would not be granted her in any other case. Then the previously mentioned fight with the

Creole broke out. Laniera killed his opponent and had to flee. Immediately thereafter, old Duvont died suddenly and unexpectedly. Some even mumbled that he had been poisoned, and Heston, the deceased's neighbor and also the chief sheriff of the parish, seized the departed's property and hastily arranged for its sale. As we have seen, he had his own special designs.

He had already made disrespectful propositions to Jazede, since he did not seem to hold her in higher esteem than any other "nigger." She rejected him, however, with great disdain. Indeed, the last time she even threatened to see the insult avenged, so that he now was hot for vengeance. He did whatever he could to make the poor unfortunate young woman's situation worse. He treated her as horribly and hard-heartedly as he could, and a criminal would have deserved a better bed, a tastier meal. How much more so the poor girl, who could be accused of no other fault than that her grandmother had been a Negro.

God knows what the scoundrel intended to do with her when she became his slave and he had full power over her, but many of the neighboring planters must have feared the worst and therefore gave him serious warnings. But he rebuffed them with a laugh, adding with a terribly menacing look in his face that he knew what he had to do and knew the laws of Louisiana exactly.

Woe to the poor slave whose master, in anger, went as far as the laws allowed.

The house in which she was kept separate from the other slaves, which had served not only as a prison but also was once used as a powder magazine, was very solid and built to last. The roof was constructed with thick one-and-a-half-foot-wide doubled-up boards. The strong cypress logs were laid over each other and fastened once more at the corners with iron clamps. The door fashioned from oak planks could only be opened from the outside with a heavy iron hook, and as the sun began to set, Heston had even put a big lock on it and carried the keys in his pocket. Moreover, the two stocky Negroes, Scipio and Sam, armed with heavy clubs, were encamped at the door, and Scipio, mindful of his master's warning, walked around the house several times.

At the stroke of midnight Laniera had sneaked out and was crouching under the adjoining fence to wait for the auspicious moment. But he had not dared to take one step forward until he heard Quapas's call to Scipio to fetch his instrument from the boat. The black, hoping to obtain the whiskey the Indian had promised him, quickly obeyed the order, and now Laniera climbed up the cabin's corner beam as agilely as a cat and examined the roof.

Here, however, he found out that, despite a few rotten patches on the roof, it would not be possible to force entry by this route without making a considerable racket. Teeth clenched, he climbed down again, determined to conquer force with force, to call his men, and to shoot everyone down rather than give up his plan and leave his beloved in the hands of the enemy.

Meanwhile, Scipio had hurried to the boat and saw that Titus was just about to untie the skiff in order to wait for the Indian several miles downstream as had been agreed upon. Two sailors from the schooner replaced him on board the chicken thief. Leaping down the riverbank, Scipio called out to the faithful Titus quickly but in a suppressed tone, "Stop, Massa Nigger! Old fellow, where is the whiskey that Massa Indian promised me? I be the one who is supposed to fetch music."

"Are you one of the guards?" Titus asked. A new plan suddenly occurred to him.

"Yes, I Scipio, guard of Jazede," the Negro assured him, in order to dispel any doubt about his share of the drink that was promised him.

"Fine, then, go downstairs but don't fall; the bottle is on the table."

Without wasting any further words, Scipio obeyed, and quick as a flash Titus leaped over to the two men from the schooner and called to them to grab the Negro. At the next moment Scipio lay tied up in the cabin of the little vessel, a pistol pointed at him, ashen with fear and fright.

"Now hand over your clothes, boy," Titus cried, laughing. "I want to see whether I can't find another honorable good-for-nothing like you. Who's standing guard with you?"

"Sam," the captive whimpered, as he took off his jacket with the help of the one sailor and handed it over to Titus, along with his straw hat.

"So," the latter grinned, "I am wearing white pants myself. Now I want to see what can be done with Sam. And you, sir," he turned to one of the Spaniards, "know that I am familiar with every square foot of this shore. Row down to the second spit of land, where the three boats lie tied up at Bonier's plantation, and wait there for Quapas. You won't have to wait long. What are you going to do with the drill?"

"Blockhead," laughed the Spaniard. "Didn't you say that the three boats are there? Wouldn't it be better to make good use of the time and put them out of action rather than having them pursue us later with full sail?"

"Good, for sure!" rejoiced the Negro. "We can do the same thing with the two boats that are lying here. But go on now—they are waiting for the instrument. Above all, send the sailors up to the fence. We've got to go now—a lost moment can ruin everything."

Titus leaped up the bank and soon reached the open door of the dwelling, where Quapas was waiting for him impatiently. He tried to signal to the Indian, but Quapas, who had no inkling that the faithful Negro was so close, quickly turned away and took a few steps into the light, where the false guard did not dare follow. It was difficult now to find his master without arousing Sam's suspicions. But Titus relied on good luck and—his long double-edged blade. He slipped back to the door in haste and, without replying to the guard's query, stepped behind the house softly and silently at the same moment as Laniera climbed down from the roof and was about to call to the schooner's crew for help. Laniera's feet had hardly touched the ground when the figure of the Negro, whom he took for one of the guards, stood before him. Quick as a flash, his knife was out of its sheath, and he was just about to attack his presumed enemy when the latter hissed softly, as had previously been agreed upon. It was like the threatening sound of a snake, and Laniera, blade raised high, stood fixed.

"Psst, Massa!" the faithful black whispered. "Quick now, gag Sam or—" he made a signifying gesture. "Or perhaps," he continued, "promise freedom, and Sam will help."

No further words were necessary. Just as the first notes of the mandolin resounded from the open door of the house, Titus again approached the guard, who, of course, took him for his comrade returning from patrol.

"Oh *damn it*, Scipio," Sam grumbled, "don't run around the house all night. We can hear someone breaking into the back from here. Listen to Massa Quapas, instead, but—did you bring whiskey?"

"Ahem!" Titus nodded, bowing his head a bit so that the straw hat covered his face. He held the knife handle in a way that made Sam believe he was carrying the concealed bottle. But no sooner had he gotten close to the unsuspecting slave leaning there than he aimed the sharp steel at his chest and threatened him with instant death should he make the least noise. At the same time Laniera's dark figure slipped to his side. He, too, had a sharp weapon, and the frightened slave fell to his knees in deathly fear and lifted his hands imploringly.

"Do you want to help us and be free?" Laniera whispered to him quickly and softly.

"Free?" asked the slave, pricking up his ears.

"Free as a bird in the air," the Spaniard assured him. "Stand by me now, and I'll take you along as far as Texas."

"And there?" the black whispered cautiously.

"I will write you your letter of manumission and give you travel money to Boston or Canada."

"And what do I have to do?"

"Help me abduct Jazede. Think it over quickly—you yourself know we have no time to lose."

"But Mr. Heston—"

"Have no fear. We will protect you from him."

"Even if the rescue fails?"

"You will go with us!"

Without a further word, the black shook the Spaniard's hand but then asked softly, "Who are you?"

Laniera took off the little half-mask and revealed his familiar face to the astonished Negro.

"Oh, Massa Laniera—"

"Hush, fool!" Laniera whispered, pressing his hand over Sam's mouth. "Do you want to give me away?"

"No, no, Massa, not on my life. I will go with Massa and Missus Jazede."

"Titus, creep under that fig tree and if danger nears, signal with a loud hiss or, even better, with the call of a nighthawk that you can imitate so well. If our escape is successful, the rocket will rise up from the boat, but you follow as soon as you hear it hiss. Let's get going. Sam and I will pry the lock open easily enough."

Titus obeyed the order and waited as anxiously as Quapas for the signal announcing success.

Meanwhile, the two men had some difficulty in breaking open the lock because they had to take care not to make any noise. Fortunately, Sam remembered a heavy hook used to *roll* the cotton bales that hung somewhere in the cabin. He looked for and found it, and they were finally able to pry open the lock. The door moved on its hinges without a sound; from the inside the cautious girl had poured water from her pitcher on it. The door had only opened halfway when she flew into her beloved's arms, and, forgetting everything around him in his bliss, he almost let out a loud cry as he embraced her. But she anxiously pressed her delicate fingers to his lips and pleaded, "Oh, away from here, away from this horrible place, away with you, even it be to the grave!"

"That could happen!" a deep, threatening voice nearby said angrily. Instantly, a powerful blow of the fist smashed the unsuspecting Spaniard to the floor. Seized by fear, the poor girl moaned, "Heston!" and fainted.

"Ha, ha, ha!" the American laughed triumphantly. "I thought so—and you scoundrels—stop, what do you want? Help! Help!"

"That's right," cried Titus, who had pulled him down from behind, "and now take him away; the rope will hold and the gag, too. Ha, there they are, the

brave fellows, it was high time. Here, men, carry these two—they're unconscious. The two of us will follow with this fellow who is still kicking, and the
rest of you cover our backs." At the same moment a row of dark figures, having crept up to the fence, jumped over it, and several picked up their captain,
while others made a stand against Heston's guests, who came flocking.

"Stop!" cried Laniera as his men helped him up. "Where is Jazede?"

"Here! But we must get away. There come the scoundrels from the house.
Hurry now! Hold the sharp blades to them and the double-barreled rifles, and
shoot the dogs down!" Titus rejoiced.

"No killing!" ordered Laniera, who had quickly recovered from his momentary stupor. "No killing, if we can help it. Only a barbarian shoots at unarmed people—they have no weapons." And, taking Jazede into his arms with
these words, he ran toward the entrance, covered by the sailors, while Sam and
Titus dragged the heavier Heston after him.

As soon as the Creoles heard Heston's cry for help, they bounded out of the
room and flew toward the scene of the battle. No sooner were they close enough
to recognize that their host was held captive by what they believed to be his own
Negroes and were about to throw themselves on them than a bunch of dark figures jumped down from the adjoining fence. Before they could decide what to
do, the defenseless planters found themselves staring at shiny weapons and
ominous rifle barrels.

"Mutiny!" cried those in front, jumping backward, for they thought the Negroes had rebelled and feared the worst.[53] Then Heston's overseer, who had
been attracted by the noise, called, "Into the house, into the house. There are
weapons for everyone up there. The rifles are loaded. Hurry, the scoundrels
must not escape us. Ha, I want to put the noose around this one's neck myself."
With a wild leap he threw himself upon the nearest man. But he misjudged his
opponent, for, without using the knife that he held in his hand, the latter hurled
the overseer back with such force that he fell to the floor half-unconscious.

"Oh, Lord," Sam whispered to Titus, as he saw his overseer fall, "if I could
get as close to Massa overseer with such a long knife this evening—gracious!—
how deep I'd drive it into his body—damned scoundrel!"

Although the Creoles followed the felled overseer's orders quickly, they discovered that Quapas had stolen a march on them. No sooner was he standing
alone in the doorway, for the planters paid him little heed as they stormed out,
than he slammed the door shut, locked it from the inside, and jumped through
one of the low windows into the garden. The whole business transpired much
more rapidly than the time it takes to recount it, and the last of those rushing

up saw the slim figure of the Indian reach the garden wall, swing up onto it, and disappear.

To be sure, the crowd—on whose strength Quapas had counted—stormed the door with all their might and broke it down. But at least it had detained the pursuers somewhat, and when the planters bounded up the levee with the weapons they'd found in hand, they just caught a glimpse of the chicken thief gliding out into the river with full sails and a man racing down the road in wild haste.

"Aha—they've left him behind," an American rejoiced. "I've got him for sure, for my horse is still tied up here. The Negro rascals forgot to bring it in. A pox on them! Now, redskin, you're going to have to make fast tracks if I am not to catch up with you before you reach the nearest boats."

Meanwhile, he had swung up onto his horse and, spurring it on, flew after the Indian as fast as the horse could go. The Indian became alarmed when he heard the thundering hoofs on the hard road.

The American was getting nearer and nearer to the fugitive, and in the faint starlight he could already see him looking back at him anxiously. Then Quapas sprang momentarily into the dark shadow of an orange hedge that was swaying over high palisades. Before the jubilant pursuer, believing the fugitive intended to evade his gaze in the dark there and lead him away from his tracks, could reach that spot, Quapas sprang out on a small, fiery pony and flew down the road quick as a flash.

The American soon saw that his horse was no match for the Indian's. Racing wildly, both men arrived at the plantation where a boat was supposed to await the Indian. The agile son of the forests jumped from his steed, which continued to storm on. Quapas was down in the boat in a few bounds and in the next minute out of range of the two Terzeroles, which the American, raging with dashed hopes, shot at him.

The Creoles, too, had fired their double-barreled shotguns at the chicken thief, which flew by in the favorable wind, but without success. They could not even get the better of the second, clumsier schooner, which, as soon as all the guns were unloaded, glided by under the protective darkness of the riverbank and sailed out into the wide river. In vain they looked around for the skiffs that usually were tied up there but could find not a one. Mounting their horses, they galloped down along the levee toward the next small town so that they could pursue the escapees from there with reinforcements and good sailboats.

Meanwhile, the storm was blowing from the Northwest with such raging force that the small, weak vessel tilted to the side, and the foam and the waves sprayed high onto the bow. The sail even had to be lowered. But with almost miraculous speed the little chicken thief, *Jazede,* flew down stream, so that plantation after plantation was left behind, and the increasing activity on the river indicated that great seaport, New Orleans, was near.

"What should we do with Heston and Scipio?" Titus asked now. "The river is getting ever more lively, the plantations ever denser, and we can't take them along with us to New Orleans."

"No, that's true!" Laniera murmured. "But wait—I've thought of something. Can you swim, Scipio?"

"Oh, take me with you, take me with you!" Scipio pleaded. "Massa would beat me to death if he had me at home."

"Dare, dare to steal the slaves!" Heston gnashed his teeth. "Dare it at your own peril. But remember that I will risk my life to see you hang!"

"All right!" Laniera laughed. "Untie him, Titus, so—now, sir, hear my final words: I know you hate me, would kill me if I were in your hands, as you are now in mine. But I want to act more nobly—I don't have a taste for your blood. I am not stealing the slaves because they can go along with me of their own free will. As soon as we have stepped onto Texas soil, all three Negroes will be free men; I will make them that. As far as Jazede is concerned, she is my wife—gnash your teeth—you will never see her again—but enough of you. I know that you can swim—the river is rising, and vast quantities of tree trunks are floating by. Jump overboard and hold onto one; the wind will lead you to one of the banks.—Get ready and don't expect any further mercy from me. If you reach the land, then you may pursue me as you wish; I will laugh in your—but," he added with flashing eyes and a low, fierce voice, "don't ever come close enough to me that I can reach you with a knife. Now adieu!—There's some driftwood!"

"A pox and death upon you, scoundrel!" the planter cried, raising himself up high. "But wait! The vengeance of the law will overtake you, or my hatred will, must, do it.—For now, however, take *that* and go to hell!"

With these words he tore out a knife hidden in his belt, hurled it at the Spaniard, and jumped overboard with wild, scornful laughter. He had aimed surely and well, but, fortunately, the sharp steel ricocheted off the butt of the pistol that Laniera carried in his belt. Quickly, Titus reached for one of the muskets lying on the deck to shatter the skull bobbing up out of the water, but Laniera grabbed his arm.

"Let the good-for-nothing go. He will not escape his punishment," he said, waving Titus off. "I am too happy now to want to shed human blood. Look— he's grabbed the trunk. When daylight comes, he can reach one of the plantations and sound the alarm. But if the wind stays this strong, I won't fear him or his whole gang anymore."

"And what will happen to the schooner?"

"Don't worry about it," laughed the sailor who had rowed Quapas on board. "Don't you see it shooting past all the sails? It may reach New Orleans sooner than we do ourselves. There's no way that it will remain behind for long."

Laniera, who had remained on deck as long as his presence was needed, now went down into the cabin, where Quapas was sitting at Jazede's feet, telling her all kinds of foolish tales and jokes, so that the dear girl had to smile at the half-civilized savage's cheerful mood, despite all her fears and cares. With a joyful shout she flew toward her beloved fiancé when he opened the door of the small room. Close to his heart, she forgot everything that might still have frightened or saddened her.

"And are we sure, Laniera? Can't they catch you anymore? Will we be able to live together in joy and happiness in a faraway country?"

"Be of good spirits, my girl," the Spaniard answered cheerfully. "The blessed Virgin and the dear saints are in league with us. The wind is blowing as if it wanted to carry our boat away on its wings. Up to now I was almost afraid we'd arrive too late. Now, I think, we're out of all danger. To be sure, the day is already dawning, but we only have a little ways till New Orleans, and once we are under way on board the *Cuba,* we will be safe from any pursuit."

The sun was rising now, and the wind still drove the little chicken thief forward with unabated speed. They had already reached the first houses of Lafayette—above New Orleans, now a section of the city—and ship lay by ship in a vast row along the shore, when Titus stuck his wooly head through the door and asked the captain to come up to the deck. Laniera quickly obeyed the call, and on deck he found the little boat's entire crew busily gazing up the river with rapt attention.

"What's going on? What's the matter?" Laniera asked hastily. "The schooner is sailing over there."

"Yes," murmured Titus. "That is not the only sail that we see.—Massa, I think we are being followed—there's something wrong about the boat back there."

"Fetch me the telescope!" The Negro sprang below and, followed by Quapas, brought it immediately to his master. Laniera took a long, hard look through it but could not make out anything.

"Let me have a look!" said the Indian. I know many of the vessels, perhaps the one back there as well."

With these words he took the telescope, and no sooner had he cast a sharp glance at the little sail that just was becoming visible as it turned around a spit of land than he loudly uttered "Ha!" straightened up, wiped his right eye, and peered through the glass once again, even more attentively than before.

"Who is it? Do you recognize it?"

"Do I recognize it!" Quapas muttered to himself. "It's Merville's fast-sailer, and the Creoles are aboard. If we don't reach our destination soon, we'll be caught."

"Not yet," laughed Laniera. "New Orleans is big. We can easily reach Lake Pontchartrain without being noticed, and I also have a schooner there lying at the entrance to the New Orleans canal.[54] But—there is the *Cuba,* and, for sure—it's ready to put to sea. Unfurl the sails, Titus—spread out every rag— now it's a matter of death or freedom—do you hear the bell—by God—its wheels are already turning—quickly now, my slender *Jazede,* save the dear creature, whose name you bear—it is the last trip we're taking together."

The little boat shot like an arrow over the water's lightly ruffled surface. Laniera, however, stood on deck, clenching the helm, and his eyes darted feverishly from the mighty colossus that was slowly getting ready to begin its journey over to the gull-like boat that sailed past like a gigantic white bird. Ever nearer it approached. Had the steamboat lain just a few hundred feet farther down, the pursuing sailboat would have caught up with them. But the puffing *Cuba* lay right in front of them, hurling high waves out from behind, and slowly it began to move.—They were just a stone's throw away from it—with a bold turn they flew past its monstrous bow.

"We're coming aboard, we're coming aboard!" Titus rejoiced. But Massa— for God's sake—where are you going?—ashore—Jesus Maria, now we're lost!"

By all means he had cause to be afraid because, instead of heading toward the rope ladder hanging down from the *Cuba,* the bow of their own little vessel suddenly veered away from it, and the steamboat, which had just got under way, shot past them.

"It's too late!" cried Laniera, while Quapas, with wide-open eyes and a deathly pale face, looked over toward the Spaniard, who appeared to have thrown their last anchor of hope overboard. But Laniera had calculated the magnitude of the danger correctly. Just as he flew around the mighty steamer, instead of latching on to the *Cuba*'s deck, he used the slight wind to run between several boats along the shore that resembled his.

"Down with the sails!" he shouted with a stentorian tone. "Down with the sails and pennant!" Frightened by the unusual vehemence of the man who otherwise was so calm, all rushed to lend a helping hand, so that in a few seconds the vessel, with bare booms, lay motionless among ten or twelve similar boats at the shore.

Meanwhile, the steamer had completed its turns, and the engineer's little bell was signaling to give full steam, when the sailboat came within shouting distance. Shots and waved cloths called the captain's attention to the new passengers' tremendous haste, and, as Laniera had correctly foreseen, the steamboat came to a standstill.

The boat's crew, who had to believe that all the fugitives were on board, because they had lost sight of them behind the *Cuba,* and who did not suspect that the Spaniard would dare to land when he was being pursued so closely, climbed in wild haste up the steep sidewalls of the mighty colossus. In the next minute the steamer puffed down the river with tremendous speed, while the sailboat that had been left behind, manned only by two Negroes, swayed wildly on the mighty waves the *Cuba* left in its wake.

But on the chicken thief sat Scipio, holding his sides and laughing until his big, rolling eyes threatened to pop out of their sockets. The boat people sunning themselves on the shore looked up, startled, and then joined in with the black's exuberant mirth, even though they hardly could know what had triggered the broad-shouldered Negro's wild hilarity.

Laniera's glance, however, soon tempered his gaiety. Even if they had escaped the immediate danger and did not need to fear that the *Cuba,* once under way, would stop, much less turn back, in order to put the pursuers on the right track, they still were in Louisiana. In no way must anyone suspect that they were about to aid fugitive Negroes, or they would be subjected to the harshest, most merciless laws. Therefore, above all, they had to avoid any delay in New Orleans, which could too easily be their downfall, and as quickly as possible reach the Gulf via the lake lying behind the city.

Titus, meanwhile, obeyed his master's brisk order, for the schooner was just gliding past them with full sail, probably fearing the worst for the crew's friends. Two shots fired off in rapid succession, and a rocket thrown toward them made them aware of the captain's vicinity.

Right after that it ran ashore at the schooner landing about five hundred feet below. The blacks carried the lovers' baggage through the city toward a canal boat that was about to head toward Lake Ponchartrain. Laniera gave a few more orders to the helmsman of the schooner, who had rushed up to him. Then

Laniera jumped on board the canal boat, which was under way in the next moment, and only now, as with each second he left the city farther behind, only then, when he had the blue water of the Gulf under him, did he feel that he was free, that he was saved. Blissfully pulling his beloved to his heart, he whispered into the dear, blushing girl's ear, "My wife—my sweet wife!"

From *From Two Parts of the World* (1854)

THE DAUGHTER OF THE RICCAREES:
A PORTRAIT FROM LOUISIANA

A glowing September sun shot its nearly horizontal rays on the wide cotton and sugarcane fields, on the extensive marshes and prairies of Louisiana. All of nature was resting, or rather seemed to lie spent and weak, languishing and exhausted. With feverish pores it yearned for the night dew that was supposed to nurse the earth's parched lips and return to the trees their color and to the flowers their scent. A glowing September sun drove the soft planter back into the interior of his cool home. Behind closed jalousies, he lay dreaming in his wicker rocking chair, the claret-filled crystal beaker next to him. He passed the time by pushing around with a long silver spoon the ice that sparkled like rubies in the wine, until the ice melted.

But outside on the field, exposed to the searing heat that burned down on their bare shoulders, stood the Negro slaves in long rows—men, women, and children—with large, light baskets tethered to them in which they collected the cotton tufts from the woody pods. In the shade of a nearby pecan tree, a large, leather whip in his hand, leaned the *overseer*.[1] With a yawn he surveyed the panting horde, now and then casting just a fleeting glance at the nearby piazza of the residence, where a more charming, more lovely, picture captivated his eye.

Ten steps led up to the gallery of the master's house, which was shaded by tall chinaberry trees and two fragrant magnolias. White climbing roses crept up the fantastically carved columns until they reached the wild grapes above, which, extending along the low sheltering sunroof, sank their blue, full grapes in between the tender rosebuds, as if they wanted to draw the perfume from them and, in exchange, bestow on them the cool juice of their berries. Rare tropical and northern plants were set up all around the interior of the leafy space, mixing their sweet scents with those of the vines that proliferated around them.

Not only bloom and blossom, however, adorned the entrance to the house of the rich Beaufort, who was known and respected as one of the wealthiest planters on the entire Fausse Rivière.[2] Not solely bloom and blossom swayed and waved in the barely perceptible west wind that blew over from the "false river's" wide surface of water. Hung between the posts, crowded with buds and fruit, there rocked a brightly colored, wonderfully woven hammock, kept in motion by the hand of a little Negro child. In it, leaning her petite head, which billowed with raven curls, on her full, white arm, while her dainty little foot was barely visible under the wide, pleated dress, lay the planter's dear child, the most charming Creole woman of Louisiana. Half-pensively, half-dreamily, she looked up at the blooming splendor, around which fluttered and stole colorful butterflies and hummingbirds that sparkled like diamonds.

Around her lay scattered some freshly broken off flowers, some large, velvety magnolia petals on whose snowy surface she had drawn figures and names with a needle. French books and journals were scattered across the hammock and the little table standing next to it—a sign that Mademoiselle had tried *everything,* even the last resort, to banish the boredom.

And was the sunburned, sinister overseer of the blacks sending his glances, glowing with passion, toward this dear blossom? Did he dare lift his eyes to the most beautiful and richest heiress of the land? No—he knew well that she hated and despised him. He knew well the abyss that gaped between him and the maiden in every respect. No, he did not want to bill and coo; he wanted to *enjoy,* and his lascivious gaze had chosen a creature other than Gabriele Beaufort.

Next to her mistress, holding a wide, folded peacock fan with which she not only fanned cooling for the beautiful girl but also banished the swarming insects, leaned on a soft seat another child who was almost as charming, if quite different from the first. She was an Indian. The dark bronze color of her skin, her lively, sparkling eyes, her snow-white teeth, and the girl's whole nature, her entire bearing, announced the daughter of the forests. Only her slightly frizzy, raven-black hair, which otherwise was long and pulled back, seemed to resemble that bluish coloration that gives the quadroon girls, the cross between the whites and the mulattoes, their unique charm.

Her slender figure was clothed in a soft, airy garment, fashioned in the style of her tribe. A colorfully embroidered bead belt held it together over her hips and, with two identical strings of coral beads, one wound around her velvety soft neck, the other around her temple, comprised the dear girl's only adornment. Only the moccasins made from softly tanned hides, into which slipped her small, dainty feet, still carried the marks of the skillful hand of Nedaunis-Ais (the little daughter), or Saise, as Gabriele called her for short.

As wonderfully lovely and charming as was the picture of the two maidens surrounded by a world of flowers, such sad, melancholy feelings seemed to raise

Saise's bosom, and once—alas, she turned her head away, so that her mistress would not notice—with her slender finger she even wiped away a pearly drop from her long, silken lashes, and a soft, soft sigh escaped the poor child's breast.

But what was it that here, surrounded by splendor and plenitude, constrained her heart? Was she thinking of the fate of her tribe?—her entire people who, driven from the land they once had owned, almost destroyed by the whites' steel and firewater, now had to dwell in the far West, far from the graves of their loved ones, while one of their daughters was serving the descendant of that proud, defiant race, when she herself was actually the mistress of this land according to birth and law? Alas! She would have had good cause to mourn about that, and the two dear creatures provided a true, but therefore all the more melancholy, portrait of the two nations, the victor and the vanquished. But it was not that, also not the feeling of servitude—for Gabriele did not treat her like a servant but, rather, like a friend—no, it was probably the separation from her beloved parents, from whom she had been abducted through a devilish ruse. The thought of those mourning her back home filled her lashes anew, and this time the tear dropped full and heavy down onto her lap.

Gabriele took notice.

"Saise, my dearest Saise, what is the matter? Why are you always so sad and do not want to make me the confidante of your sorrow?" asked the young Creole woman sympathetically. "Am I not your friend, and have I not revealed to you all my little cares and plans and asked for your advice and help?"

Saise pressed her mistress's hand and, smiling sadly, for a few seconds looked into her clear, trusting eyes. But then her gaze fell on the little Negro girl rocking the hammock, and Gabriele, understanding the gesture, said: "Go down, pickaninny,[3] and count the little chicks that are running around in the yard. But don't come back until you can tell me exactly how many there are."

The round little child gave a friendly smile with her wide mouth and sprang quickly through the narrow entrance down the stairs in order to carry out her "Missus's" order. Smiling, Gabriele watched her for a moment, but then, turning with interest to her companion, she said sincerely: "You see—the child is gone. Now tell me frankly what is bothering you—certainly I can help you."

"You will hear everything," whispered Saise—"perhaps it is even better that *you* know, for if—" She was silent suddenly and with a shudder buried her face in her hands.

"But what is the matter with you, by all the saints?" asked Gabriele. "I have never seen you like this."

"Then listen," said the Indian, collecting herself. "I can confide everything to you in a few words. Even if I am still young, I have suffered terrible things. I am the only daughter of a Riccaree chieftain, and a small portion of our tribe—your brothers eradicated almost our entire nation from the earth—had settled close to the Osage, between these and the Cherokees.[4] My father was a friend of the whites—he saw that the game was dwindling and felt that the pale faces were superior to us in cleverness and skills. But he also believed that the sole security for the sparse remainder of his people could be found only by adopting the customs and ways of their victors, cultivating the field, and uniting with them as *one* people.[5] Therefore, every white person was welcome in our hut, and he was friendly to everyone. Only once did the old, almost extinct warrior spirit awaken in him when a white, a rough, unfriendly man, whom we received cordially, became fresh and forward toward me and finally maintained that I ought not act so modest because I was only, as my hair clearly demonstrated, a little—nigger."

"Had an arrow struck my father, he would not have sprung up from his seat faster. He had been one of the best warriors of his tribe, and my mother was the daughter of a Sioux chieftain, whom he once had abducted during an attack, grown to love, and taken as his wife. All the more terribly, therefore, did this word wound his pride, and, driven by rage and fury, he tore his tomahawk from his belt and flung it at the head of the—*guest*."[6]

"The white man fell down unconscious. Immediately, my father was seized by distressing pain at the thought that he had violated the law of hospitality. He sprang toward the fallen man, studied the wound, and tended to and nursed him like a son until he had recovered and could leave our settlement.—But that man was a devil—the blow he received filled him with rage and revenge. While he was still recuperating in our home, he was on the lookout in the house and surroundings for an opportunity, and after only three days he returned secretly and treacherously with his henchmen. They attacked our hut without making a sound, struck down my old father, who tried to throw himself against the abductors, tied and gagged me, lifted me onto a horse, and, in wild and impetuous haste, dragged me toward the great river."[7]

"As I came to from a long faint, deep night surrounded me, and I could only feel that we were bursting at full gallop on a hard, narrow path under low trees and bushes, for the pounding of the hooves echoed far into the still wilderness, and now and again little branches scraped my cheeks. Whatever my abductors planned to do with me, they probably feared pursuit or knew they really were being pursued already, for ceaselessly, inexorably, they raced on and did not stop before they had reached a place that surely had been agreed upon before-hand and here found their vile companions."

"Only God knows what later became of my dear old father. I did not see him again. Instead, a strange, sinister man, who, in my presence, while I still lay tied up on the floor, concluded a deal over me, received from my abductor a docu-ment—a *bill of sale,* as the latter called it—and then carried your poor Saise into a canoe and paddled off with her."

"Helpless—abandoned—lost, I lay on the floor of the pitching canoe. Ev-erything that threatened me rose before my inner soul in terrible images. I felt utterly, defenselessly, subject to the tyranny of this man, who firmly fastened his covetous gaze on me. I knew that I, sold as a slave, could no longer hope for mercy from the whites, and for the first time the thought of suicide quivered through my feverishly beating pulse."

"Poor Saise," said Gabriele.

"The canoe was one of the ordinary boats roughly chopped out of wood, narrow and with a round bottom. Whenever I moved just a bit, I felt it sway and saw the anxious movement of the rower, who tried to keep it balanced. A jolt—a sudden thrust by me—would capsize it, and I—would be free. No sooner did I get this idea than a cold shudder coursed frostily through my veins—and, fixed and horrified, I looked up at the white man. But he, who most likely ascribed my anxious expression to fear, sneered and said, 'Don't fret, my little doll. If you are pretty and good, you will become my little squaw,'[8] and then he laughed so loudly and satanically that at that moment he truly seemed to me to be an evil creature who ascended from the abyss. That only reinforced my decision—I wanted to die. Only now and then, when the canoe swayed to the right or left side a bit, could I recognize the riverbank and now saw that we were not far from a long island, which, it seemed to me, lay directly in front of us. I can swim like a fish, but the bonds that tied my hands together prevented any movement. I could hope for no other salvation than that which death would bring."

"Poor Saise!"

"Once again I sent up my prayer to the Manitou of my people[9]—Once again I glanced up at the friendly sunlight that greeted bright and streaming across the far woodland, alas, for me for the *last* time. Once again with a long, long breath I sucked in the balsamic air of the beautiful world—then closed my eyes and with a sudden vault, exerting all my strength, I threw myself against the side wall of the narrow vessel."

"'Stop! We're sinking!' my abductor screamed horrified and tried to regain balance on the other side. But I quickly followed his movement, and at the next moment I felt the cool flood close over me. The canoe had capsized."

"I did not know whether that white man could swim. If so, he would have been capable of pulling me to the nearby bank, for my hands were still tied. But he would not touch me again alive. I dove down, in fact, with the firm resolve never to return to the surface.—God wanted it otherwise. Lifted by the welling flood, I rose up again to the light but suddenly felt my head hit against a hard object. In the first moment I believed it was the canoe, the next, however, convinced me that I had landed under driftwood and, indeed, at a place where I touched ground with my feet. Wildly jammed-up logs had formed a little hollow into which I could stick my head and—breathe. I was, for the moment, saved. But wouldn't the powerful pressure of the current that, rushing and foaming, was breaking against the trunks and branches only a short distance away from me compress this fragile defense and push me back into the depths inch by inch and destroy me? With unfailing courage I had looked a *speedy* death in the eye but perhaps to die here slowly, slowly—oh! it was dreadful."

Saise, seized by the thought and shuddering, buried her face in her hands again.

"You unfortunate child," whispered Gabriele, sheltering the beautiful girl's brow in her bosom. "You poor—dear—bad child, why have you kept all this from me so long? Was that right of you? But how did you escape that frightful danger?"

"For hours," Saise continued, "for hours I waited before attempting to save myself, for even more terrible than death was for me the thought of seeing the light of day and along with it the face of that sinister man again. Even then, however, it was still difficult and dangerous to carry it out, for, of course, I had lost my bearings in the water and was afraid that I, continuing to swim underwater, would land deeper in the driftwood. But God above had protected me up to now, and I trusted him. Since, moreover, I could no longer bear it in the water and my limbs were shivering with cold, I once more listened carefully to determine from which direction the crashing of the current sounded then quickly calculated on which side of the island I must be and now tried to get rid of the bonds that still held my hands tied. And see there—I succeeded. They were straps made of deer hide, and the water had stretched them. My hands slipped through and—I was free."

"Now I feared nothing anymore. That man must have long taken me for drowned and left the site.—I dove down—took powerful strokes, and after a few seconds, in which my heart stopped, I saw the dear, splendid light of day again. But I did not dare to stand up for a long time, for I did not know how close that white man was. I just crept quietly and carefully along the flat bank warmed by the sun, and with a fervent prayer and a soothing stream of tears assuaged my so grievously distressed heart.—You know all the rest; your father found me in the forest five days later—I was homeless.—I did not dare to appear back home again; they had struck down my own father before my eyes, and could the poor remainder of my tribe protect me from the white men's pursuit? You took me in, Gabriele, and at your heart I have found peace and protection."

"But why then this constant sorrow, you dear child?" cajoled the maiden. "Be happy like me. You are among friends who will let nothing harm you—or is another pain afflicting you?"

"Did you see today?" asked Saise, looking around anxiously, "did you see how they handed over the poor creature to her master from whom she—he said so—had fled?"

"But that was a slave and he her master, dear child."

"And how do you know that he was her master? Did she not swear she had never seen him before in her life?"

"He had, you see, the bill of sale in which her entire person was described," smiled Gabriele. "You foolish child, why are you torturing yourself with such dismal, fearful scenes; why does this concern you?"

"He had the *bill of sale* in which her whole person was described, and the people here—great God—they handed her over to him—" cried the Indian, jumping up from her seat.

"Help, heavens!—Saise!" called Gabriele apprehensively, for she feared for the unfortunate girl's sanity. "What is the matter? What is it?"

"He led her away in shackles," the girl continued in dreadful agitation—"in shackles! And for me, too—for *me,* too, they have issued such a bill of sale. *My* person, too, *my* appearance—my hair—my eyes—even the mole on my shoulder are described.—Oh, merciful God!"—She collapsed, sobbing, and buried her face in the pillow of the chair next to her.

Alarmed, Gabriele jumped from the hammock and bent down quietly to the unhappy girl. With consoling words she wanted to assuage her troubles. But alas! She herself knew only too well the danger that threatened the poor pursued girl under such circumstances, if she really were to be discovered by that rascal.

"Come," she then said suddenly to the Indian, whose fear had dissolved in a soothing flood of tears, "come, take heart, I still know a way to help you. You know our friend," she continued, as the girl looked up to her with her large, dark, moist eyes. "You know the young Creole, St. Clyde—he is well disposed toward us—both—toward you as well as me, and has even lived for a long time on the southwest border of Missouri, between the Cherokees and the Osage. He will find a way. Either he can hurry there and fetch witnesses, or he will send a messenger to accomplish that. In any case you yourself must bring suit against the criminal; that is the only way to counter his attack.—Celeste—Celeste," she then called her little Negro girl, who still was keenly busy below counting the little chicks running around. "Celeste, come up here quickly and first send Endymion to me!"

The little girl obeyed the order and appeared at the top of the stairs right away. But her large, dark eyes were filled with tears, and her face had a terribly mournful and seriocomic expression.

"What is the matter, Celeste?" asked Gabriele in a friendly tone.

"Oh, Missus"—sobbed the child, whose pain broke out at these friendly words, "oh Missus—I—I can—I cannot count—count—the chicks—little chicks—they run, boo hoo—they run so fast."

"Funny child," laughed Gabriele. "Go—call Endymion quickly and leave the chickens alone!"

Endymion, however, no longer needed to be called. He emerged from behind his playmate and said quietly, "Missus wants Dymion—here he is."

"Endymion," Gabriele called quickly—"you know where Mr. St. Clyde lives—don't you?"

"Massa Clyde—yes," nodded the black boy—"but Missus—a strange gentleman is below—"

"Very well—send him to Father," the Creole girl continued impatiently. "You will ride to Mr. Clyde and ask him to come over here as quickly as possible, this evening if he can—do you understand me, Endymion? This evening, I—we—we have something important to discuss with him."

"But the stranger, Missus," Endymion interrupted her somewhat anxiously—"the stranger—Massa is sleeping, and poor Dymion would get many blows if he waked him—"

"Then have him step into the hall below. There are books there, and he may pass the time as well as he can. But you, Endymion, hurry and also feed my riding horse; it could be that we will need it quickly for a hasty ride. Go on, Endymion, and come back soon!"

The boy's full, round face disappeared suddenly under the steep staircase. By the sound of the hooves a few minutes later one could hear him flying on a speedy runner along the Fausse Rivière toward the Mississippi.

Saise, meanwhile, had comforted herself with the new hope of soon being spared from all danger. She knew—at least she had to admit to herself with a slight blush—St. Clyde would do everything in his power to free her from every care and danger. If she herself could appear as the plaintiff, then that man, were he really to show up, would first have to clear himself of all suspicion, and by then she would be able to provide the proof of her pure descent. She grabbed her friend's hand, lifted it lightly to her lips, and whispered, "You are good— you are as good as an angel and with your friendly words have poured comfort and peace into my heart."

The girls embraced each other tightly, and Gabriele first held the face of the dear daughter of the woodlands between her gentle hands for a long time, looked into her large, dark eyes in a sincere and loving manner, and then pressed a hot, fervent kiss on her brow.

The overseer noticed from his tree the stranger's arrival and strolled slowly toward the house.

"Why the devil are the two girls gossiping so earnestly today," he muttered to himself. "The devil take me, if I didn't wish the little red thing were mine— a damned shame that one can not buy red skin just as easily as black.—Who could the stranger be?—Probably a cotton speculator from New Orleans.— Well, it's high time that he came—probably nosed out that our cotton has not yet been loaded—now must take the gleanings with him, too."

Muttering these remarks to himself in a low voice, he walked slowly past the Negroes' cabins constructed in regular rows toward the master's house, climbed the wooden steps leading up to it, and at the next moment stood next to the man who had just arrived.

"By thunder!" he exclaimed—"Pitwell—where the devil are *you* coming from?"

"Duxon?—by all that is blue—here in Louisiana?" replied the man thus addressed, cordially holding out his hand to the overseer.—"See, old friends do always come together again after many years. Where did we see each other last?"

"The less we say about that, the better," laughed Duxon.—"I for my part, at least, never bragged about that story."

"Oh—now I remember," smiled Pitwell. "Yes, yes, had forgotten the trifle. But, nonsense, the statue of limitations has run out and the man long—" He was suddenly silent and threw a quick, mistrusting glance at his companion. "But what are you doing now?" he led into another topic. "Are you staying here for fun, as the loafers in the calaboose say?"[10]

"I am overseer on the plantation."

"Good business, that?"

"Pretty good—puts food on the table."

"The owner?"

"Mr. Beaufort."

"How many bales?"[11]

"Hundred eighty."

"Damnation!" cried Pitwell in astonishment—"Can't one do business with the man? He must have money like Spanish moss—"

"If you had Negroes—we need a few good workers and a maid in the house. But somethin' pretty—the old man can't stand the ugly faces."

"Negroes? I could perhaps get some. By when do you need them?"

"As soon as possible."

"Are the prices good?"

"That depends. Do you have some?"

"Hmm—yes—but apropos—who are the two ladies up there on the gallery? Probably the mistress and daughter of the house, eh?"

"*Two* ladies! There's only *one* lady in the house," said the overseer contemptuously. "The other is an Indian who wangled her way in here, God knows how, and on top of that acts remarkably proud and prim—the stupid creature!"

"So? Can't one even get to see this Mr. Beaufort? I would like to know what kind of man he is before I make a deal with him—it is easier to bargain."

"You can't conceal the Yankee in you, laughed Duxon, "but I hear him coming down the steps. Just between us, flatter him a bit about his charming plantation—you know what I mean."

"Thanks—thanks!" the stranger said in a friendly tone—"won't fail."

Mr. Beaufort stepped into the room now, greeted the guest, and welcomed him warmly to his home. Soon the planter had him engaged in a very interesting conversation, and he invited him, since the evening was approaching, to spend the night at his home, which the stranger gladly accepted.

Beaufort, a man in his forties and, as mentioned already, the richest planter on False River, or Fausse Rivière, was among those southern money aristocrats who divide the human race into only three species: namely, in *planters*, in *non-*

planters, and in *Negroes*. The first were again divided into two subcategories, that is, those who cultivated more than and those who cultivated less than fifty bales. He chose his associates from the first group. The second species—the non-planters—he regarded merely as having been created to supply the planter with his various necessities, and the third—the Negroes—he despised as a true Creole. Even the most remote mixtures, mestizos and quadroons, were an abomination to him, and he only suffered them around him to the extent that he needed them to serve him. This disdain for the Ethiopian race went so far that once in New Orleans he threw his knife at a poor devil of a mestizo whom in the darkness he had taken to be a Creole acquaintance and had gone down several blocks with arm in arm. The sharp blade, however, only hit the poor frightened fellow in the thigh, without causing any further harm.—This to characterize Beaufort. His guest, on the other hand, stood in sharp contrast to the planter both in appearance and behavior, in no way to his advantage. The planter was portly, had a healthy complexion, and, notwithstanding his pride, had very good-natured qualities. The stranger, however, looked pale, with gray, penetrating, but lively eyes, a high brow, and a somewhat hooked nose. His gaze was not comforting—it darted about restlessly from one object to another and quickly averted as soon as it met another's gaze. Their conversation was lively, nevertheless. Mr. Pitwell had seen a lot, experienced a lot, understood, so it seemed, the cotton trade from the ground up, and himself owned, according to his own statement, a substantial plantation in Alabama.

Thus dinnertime drew near. The sun had not yet gone down, and the table was set up on the piazza because of the cool breeze and the pleasant view over the fields and the neighboring plantations. The hammock was drawn back on one of the posts, but Gabriele leaned pensively next to it and looked out onto the road that led to the Mississippi and on which she expected the messenger to return. Saise sat at her feet, caressing her hand and leaning her hot cheek against it, and—followed the glances of her mistress and friend.

The men's steps could now be heard on the stairs.

"He is staying a long time," whispered Gabriele.

"Quite long," said Saise, and suddenly she felt her friend's eyes fixed on her—she did not meet them but, rather, nestled against her more ardently and tightly.

"Saise—are you still not reassured?" asked Gabriele. "Is something else the matter? Just look how fire-red you have become."

"Good evening, ladies," said the voice of the stranger.

"For God's sake, child—what's wrong? All the blood is draining from your cheeks!" cried the Creole woman frightened, noting the change in her friend's expression.

"Good evening, children," repeated Mr. Beaufort. "Mr. Pitwell, my daughter and her friend, a young Indian.—Now, Gabriele—is Saise ill? What is the matter with the girl?"

"I really do not know, Father—she just turned pale, and now her whole body is trembling violently—Saise?"

"Yes," whispered the beautiful girl, straightened up, turned toward the stranger, stared at him for a moment, and then fell unconscious to the floor with a scream that cut to the quick.

Gabriele, whom the truth struck like lightning, threw her shawl over her friend's face—but it was too late.—Pitwell, alerted by the odd behavior, jumped toward her, hardly aware of what he was doing, pulled down the shawl, and cried out with the greatest fright and astonishment, "By thunder—my drowned slave!"

"Your—what?" cried Beaufort, taking a wild leap toward him. "Your *slave?* Man, are you crazy? That is an Indian, and they are not sold."

"It is false!" moaned Gabriele in horrible anguish, supporting the unfortunate girl's lifeless body. "It is a wicked lie—this girl has been abducted from her people—a low piece of villainy has been committed—Saise is as free as I—you may not lay violent hands on her."

"I demand back my property," the stranger said darkly and simultaneously reached into his pocket and took out a packet of tied-together papers—"Here is her bill of sale," he then continued, turning toward the planter. "Her father was an Indian, her mother was a mulatto—just look at her hair. And if her present fright does not vouch that she is the right one, then the mark on her left shoulder documented here does."

Beaufort silently perused the paper and then stepped toward Saise.

"Back, Father, for God's sake, back!" cried Gabriele in utmost fear. "You must not believe that man's words—they are false, by the eternal God above!"

"Gabriele," said her father in a friendly but also very serious tone. "This is a matter in which you have no further voice. If the mark is *not* there, as I hope—for the creature deserves the *gallows* if she has nigger blood in her veins and dares to eat at the same table with white people—then the accusation is unfounded. But if it is there, then the person will not stay another five minutes under my roof, or I shall not rest—you know that I keep my word."

"Father—I swear to you by all the saints—this bill of sale is counterfeit—

Saise has told me everything—she has been shamefully abducted from her people—her father slain, she herself dragged away."

"Fairy tales," smiled Pitwell, shaking his head. "Have you ever seen a runaway nigger, Miss, who would not have made up such a credible story?"

"Father—Father!" Gabriele pleaded and tried to hold him back. But now, exasperated, he pushed her aside and shouted, "Now you've gone too far—I am not hurting the creature. If she is an Indian, then she is as free as we ourselves, but if—ha!—by Jove—there it is—Mr. Pitwell—"

"Stop!" cried Gabriele, whose glance often and anxiously roved toward the nearby street—"stop! There comes Mr. St. Clyde—wait for his arrival, he can, he *must* not allow it."

"Mr. St. Clyde should go to the devil!" the old planter said angrily. "Can he interfere with the rights of a strange man? Mr. Pitwell, the girl is yours, and she has my daughter to thank that she won't get a suitable number of lashes beforehand. Damn! A nigger who is impudent enough to deny her hide!"

"We can put her in one of the Negro cabins until tomorrow morning," said Pitwell, approaching and extending his hand to the still unconscious girl. "Tomorrow morning—"

A man's hurried steps became audible on the stairs.

"Mr. St. Clyde—help!" cried Gabriele with the greatest urgency. At the same moment, however, that the Creole woman uttered this name and the young man appeared in the door, Saise opened her eyes again. A single glance told her everything—for a few seconds she hid her face in her friend's bosom, but then she got up, supported by Gabriele and, quivering softly, looked around with her large, dark eyes wide open.

"For God's sake—what has happened here?" cried St. Clyde, jumping toward the trembling girl and supporting her. "What has happened, Miss Beaufort?"

"Save Saise," the maiden called out—"save Saise from that scoundrel!"
The stranger turned pale as a ghost and looked around wildly.

"Gabriele," called the father, "now I've had enough!—Mr. St. Clyde, leave the *nigger* alone—it does not suit a white man—"

"Mr. Beaufort!"

"That's right—the girl is a slave who has escaped from this gentleman."

"That is a lie," said Saise suddenly, raising herself up high and proudly. The word *nigger* had given her back all her strength and power—she felt that the moment she had long feared had arrived. But in that it had come, it had also lost all its terror. All her composure had returned, and the Indian, the free daughter of the forests, had awakened in her.—In vain, however, she now re-counted with clear, convincing words the whole villainy of that scoundrel who stood next to her, smiling and shrugging his shoulders. In vain she called God as her witness—she was in *Louisiana*—a *white man* had reclaimed her as his escaped slave—the frizzy hair spoke for his claim, even more so, and almost in-disputably, the *bill of sale* with her sketch. Had not a short time ago a white girl with blonde hair and blue eyes even been sold at auction as the daughter of a mestiza, and if she herself was almost white, she remained a slave. How much more so, then, an Indian whose brown skin color the American considered to be inferior to his and esteemed only a bit higher than that of the Ethiopian race.

When all pleas went unheeded, Gabriele wanted to *buy* her friend from the stranger. But St. Clyde protested against this and, indeed, with a warmth that, even if it derived from purely humane motives, did him honor.

"No!" he cried, "no—that would be to admit that she belongs to that de-spised race! She should stand clear and free, even if I should prove it with my own blood. Mr. Pitwell, you will not leave this parish before you have cleared yourself of the charge against you."

"Who accuses him?" Beaufort flared up—"Who accuses him, sir? A *nig-ger*—his own slave? Are you foolish enough to believe that the court would consider such an accusation? You ought to know the laws of the state better."

"I myself accuse this man," cried St. Clyde, "I myself—not this unfortunate woman who must not be handed over to him until then."

"That might be difficult for you to accomplish," said Pitwell, scornfully. "Fortunately, I am familiar enough with the local customs. You can accuse me, but you may not withhold my property."

"Sir, first you must prove that Saise is your property!" cried St. Clyde.

"That has been proven, Mr. St. Clyde!" replied Beaufort coldly—"and now I would be much obliged if you did not cause any further disturbance.—Mr. Duxon," he then turned to the overseer who at this moment appeared in the door, "be so kind to put this runaway slave"—and he pointed to Saise—"into one of the Negro cabins. But you must guarantee me her security."

"Saise—" cried Duxon astonished, hardly believing his eyes and ears— "Saise—a nigger?—Aye, the dev——"

"Sir!" cried St. Clyde indignantly.

"For God's sake," pleaded Saise, grasping his arm, "do not fight against su-perior strength now—turn to the courts—they must help me. I am under the protection of the United States. My father ceded his land to them, and they promised to stand by him. You may only hold me until I can send a messenger to my tribe. They all will come here and bear witness that I am the daughter of their chieftain. Oh, if only my brother knew—"

"No Indians are necessary for that," smiled Pitwell. "I can attest that myself. But who was your mother? A mestiza[12]—is it written otherwise here? This mestiza belonged to my friend from whom I bought you, and if he left you in your father's care for so many years, then it was only so that he should raise you. But you still remain his slave."

"My mother was the daughter of a Sioux chieftain," cried Saise, raising herself up proudly, "and whoever claims differently *is lying!*"

Old Beaufort's fist struck the unfortunate woman to the ground with one blow.

"What?" he shouted, "is the nigger animal trying to call a white man a liar in my presence? Is it not enough that she first had to lie to me and make a fool of me?"

He would hardly have ended his words without a challenge because St. Clyde sprang toward him with a cry of revenge on his lips. But Gabriele threw herself at him and implored him by all that was holy to him, by all that he loved, to spare her father.—Now the overseer stepped between them and called to the young man defiantly, "Mr. St. Clyde, I give you fair warning not to utter any more superfluous words. From this moment on the mamselle is under *my* watch, and I will run a foot of cold steel into the body of anyone who wants to protect my *niggers* from me!" And as he said these words he pulled his heavy bowie knife out from under his vest.

Clyde was unarmed and also knew that the laws protect an overseer or slave owner when a stranger interferes in their affairs without invitation. Only a short time ago an abolitionist from Ohio was shot without the murderer having had more inconvenience than a quarter-hour hearing. For now he had to yield to raw force, but he swore to himself to save Saise even if it cost him his own life.

"Mr. Beaufort," he cried, turning to the planter once again, "you will be answerable to me for the mistreatment of this unfortunate girl. I have no power to counter your atrocity. Do with the poor girl what your conscience allows, but the eternal God up above is my witness that from now on I declare myself to be Saise's protector, and the laws of the state must and will aid me. Farewell, Miss Beaufort, and oh!—do not abandon the poor girl—at least grant her the consolation of feeling that she is not all alone in the world."

The overseer, meanwhile, had beckoned two Negroes who were just bringing tools to the house to come up and called to them, "Bring the girl there down to Mother Betty's cabin, and you, Ben, stand guard next to it—your black hide will serve as security. I will skin you alive if you let her escape."

"No fear, Massa," said the Negro, grinning, "but what girl, de Lor' bless you, I don't see any girl to take along, Missus Saise?"—

St. Clyde jumped down the stairs, swung himself onto his horse, and bounded toward the Mississippi. Gabriele bent down sobbing over the poor child and tied her own shawl around her bleeding forehead, but the two Negroes stared from one to the other with mouths wide open and could not comprehend what had happened until their superior's renewed call and the threatening wave of the whip reminded them to carry out the order. They lifted the Indian girl from the floor and soon thereafter disappeared with her into one of the low, uniform Negro cabins that surrounded the master's house in long, regular rows, similar to a little town. Gabriele retired to her room. The men, however—the overseer was invited by his employer to stay for dinner today as well—sat down at the table, and Beaufort appeared to try to wash down all aggravation and ill humor with the icy claret. Before he went to bed, he thanked the stranger once again for freeing himself and his house from the shame of sheltering "damned nigger blood" next to white people.

Mr. Pitwell had been shown his night's lodgings. Since the air was cool, as he said, he preferred to walk along the river with the overseer for a quarter of an hour, went down with him, and strolled between an allée of chinaberry and tulip trees to the plantation entrance, which was shaded by a thick fig and orange hedge.

"Listen, Pitwell"—said Duxon, standing still—"were you up to one of your old tricks again, eh? Is the girl a nigger or not?"

"What is it to you?" grumbled Pitwell, looking around anxiously. "No one can overhear us here?"

"Not a soul—but come—you must tell me about it. I'll be damned if things are on the up and up. Oh, what the deuce, man, don't be so secretive! Of the two of *us* surely one will not betray the other?"

"Well, then, I'll tell you everything, but come away from here out into the open," whispered Pitwell. "I'm too uneasy here under the trees."

The two respectable people strode together to the bank of the Fausse Rivière and walked up and down arm in arm. Pitwell now candidly told his friend and statesman the whole story but also explained to him that he, despite being safe, did not want to wait until the young fool—St. Clyde—could make his threats come true but, rather, would set out as early as possible in the morning.

"That's a splendid coincidence!" said the overseer, "I am just in the process of settling accounts with Beaufort and can perhaps accompany you if you stay one or two days longer. We can easily come to an agreement about the present second picking. I don't like it here on the river anymore; I want to go to Texas and buy my own plantation."

"What? Earned so much already? That went quickly," laughed the stranger.

"One would have to be a tremendous fool," the overseer opined smiling, "if on *such* a plantation one could not amass a little fortune in three years."

"It would be all right with me to wait that long," said Pitwell, "but I cannot; I have to see that I sell the creature. First, I do not feel quite safe here, and then— I've got other work. Meeting you, by the way, could not have come at a better time. The devil only knows how the little creature avoided drowning. I saw her go under with my own eyes and with bound hands on top of that!"

"The Indians can swim and dive like fish," laughed Duxon. "But do you know what, Pitwell, I'll buy the little thing from you!"

"What—you?—Buy the Creole?"

"Can go to the devil—I'll assume all responsibility."

"And will you buy her the way I can sell her?" the Yankee asked cautiously. "Are you prepared to absorb the loss if the Indians come and reclaim her as the daughter of their chieftain?"

"Yes, certainly," the overseer cried scornfully, "but in turn I must have her cheaply—I will give you two hundred dollars."

"Hello—that is too little—remember, the girl is worth eight hundred."

"If I leave you in the lurch, not even fifty cents," sneered Duxon.

"No, man, two hundred is too little, by God, then I would rather leave things to chance. Give me *three,* and she is yours!"

"Done—come along to my house, sign the bill of sale over to me, and get the money."

"And do you think that I can stay here a few hours without any danger?"

"A few years, if you want. Once I have the girl, then all of Louisiana won't tear her from me. The laws in all slave states are on my side, and nothing in the world will be more dangerous than to try to defy them. Come, Pitwell, in ten minutes the beautiful Indian girl must be mine, and tomorrow I will claim my entitlement. Afterward her whole tribe can come and swear—all the same to me."

The two men strode hastily back to the overseer's house, which stood between the Negro cabins and was distinguished from them only by a higher roof and a gallery, and concluded the agreed-upon deal. Pitwell got the money, and Saise was signed over to the overseer as solely his legal property. Beaufort himself was to undersign as a witness the following morning.

St. Clyde, meanwhile, had so driven his horse on with spurs and whip that when he stopped in front of the judge's door in Pointe Coupée, it swayed back and forth for a few seconds and then, weak and exhausted, collapsed. But without even glancing at it, St. Clyde flew up the stairs, barged into the judge's room, and, telling him of the outrage in a few words, called upon him for support.— The judge was also an honorable man, strictly just and humane in the execution of his duties. But he shook his head doubtfully when he heard of the bill of sale that appeared to have been issued legally. He knew the power of such a document.

"Young man," he said after a long pause, while looking up at the young Creole thoughtfully, his hand propping up his head, "this is a wicked matter. First, it, of course, seems to me that you are viewing the whole thing a bit too romantically. But then, if everything were as you describe it, I cannot see how it could be settled. We may not act *against* the laws, even if we really believe the poor girl is being wronged."

"But you surely would not allow a free Indian girl to be captured and sold?" cried St. Clyde angrily. "The same could happen to every white person if two scoundrels agree to write a bill of sale for him and to swear that his mother was a mestiza."

"That is not likely," smiled the judge. "Before a white person were sold, there would have to be powerful proof that he really descended from Negro blood— but you must not believe all such stories of runaway Negroes. Great God! they sometimes lie a blue streak."

"Wouldn't it be possible to remove the Indian girl from the hands of that man until one could produce the witnesses from her tribe?"

"Good friend, the tribe lives about seven to eight hundred miles away from here. Mr. Beaufort himself brought her more than four hundred miles down the river. No, then all such Indians like, for example, mulattoes and mestizos could claim pure Indian blood flowed through their veins and then petition to go up to the Eskimos and fetch witnesses. No, that won't work. Even if we really had the witnesses here, they still are—Indians. The smartest thing would be for you to *buy* the girl if it is as important to you as it seems to me."

"*Buy?*" cried St. Clyde, his voice quivering with pain, "*buy?*—and then she really is a slave? Is there no way to save the poor girl from this disgrace?"

"I am afraid—not—in any case this would be the surest way to detain her for the moment. Perhaps that stranger can be persuaded to take only a partial payment, and then one can see what else can be done in this matter. What do you say to that?"

"Oh, good judge," sighed the young Creole sadly, "you know very well that I am *poor*. My only horse has just collapsed, and I hardly have enough left to buy a new one. How can I scare up the amount that that scoundrel will demand for Saise?"

"Listen, St. Clyde, I want to suggest something to you. I myself will buy the girl and keep her at my house. When you have earned the money—then—I will leave her to you."

"*Buying*, always *buying!*" moaned the Creole.

"Accept my suggestion," said the judge sincerely, "she will be treated like a daughter in my home."

"Fine, then, so be it," cried St. Clyde. "I must acquiesce. At least it will save her for the moment, but then I will fetch the witnesses of her free birth, even if I have to bring them down from the ice regions of the North."

"It won't help you much. By the way, if you absolutely must have a messenger to that tribe, then I can, by chance, advise you on how to find one. This morning seven or eight Indians from West Feliciana Parish, from across the Mississippi, were here in Pointe Coupée. They sold venison and in exchange took back powder, lead, and whiskey."

"From what tribe were they?"

"Probably Choctaws, some of them always dwell here in the vicinity.[13] But first get the deal in order. For if things really are as you think and the good man does not have a clear conscience, he will hardly stay long in this area but, rather, will want to bring his spoils to safety.—So—give this paper here only to Mr. Beaufort; he can conclude the purchase for me. My wife is all alone now and already knows the Indian girl. The two certainly will get along very well."

"Yet, good judge, I must have a different horse. Can you sell me one?"

"How much do you want to spend?" he asked, for an American never lets pass an opportunity for a horse trade.

"I've got forty dollars left, making allowance for the necessities."

"Good—I'll get you a horse, but it is impossible for you to still leave tonight."

"Immediately!—"

"Nonsense, don't let your fervor spoil your game. Evenings at eight, old Beaufort has had his fill of claret and goes to bed. First of all, it is impossible to rouse him after that, and if you really were to succeed, I would like to see the mood he is in. He is indisposed until nine o'clock tomorrow morning, and if you ride off from here at eight, you will find him having breakfast—that is the best time. By the way I have entreated Beaufort to delay the payment for three days and to take Saise in during that time. Perhaps I will still succeed in rescuing her. Tomorrow I want to speak with Beatty,[14] one of our best lawyers here. If there is a way for us to prove the identity of the chieftain's daughter, he certainly will find it."

Filled with new hopes, St. Clyde finally was persuaded by the judge's arguments to agree to his suggestions and to spend the night at his home. But on the next morning, as he was galloping along the broad street with the letter that was supposed to rescue Saise from the rogue's clutches, he realized clearly for the first time that he loved this unfortunate girl, and there would be no further tranquillity for him in this world than that he could find at her side. To be sure, he was poor and had nothing but his strength and perseverance. The daughter of the forests, however, accustomed to privation from childhood on, would hardly long to return to the more civilized life of the settlements if, as he hoped and believed, he really were not indifferent to her. But first she had to be free, free again, like the bird of the air and the deer of the prairie, and this fear taken from her. He spurred his gallant horse on to a faster trot when he thought of the poor girl, and under the high, shady magnolias he flew quickly and happily along. Finally, he reached the settlements of the Fausse Rivière. He burst through the little town at full gallop—rushing past plantation after plantation—he had already passed "Poydras College,"[15] and there—there the high, splendid roof gleamed at him through the lush, green leaves. He reached the hedge of oranges, sprang from his horse, hanged its reins across an old, half-withered fig tree, and flew up the steps, where he knew that Mr. Beaufort had his breakfast every morning.

"Hello, St. Clyde," Beaufort called to him in a friendly tone. "It is nice of you to come back. I was a bit grumpy last evening, but the damned nigger vexed me so. Now, come here—there's another chair back there—Scipio, you rascal, can't you pay attention when a gentleman is looking for a chair?" he paused to direct this friendly reminder toward a little Negro boy waiting on the table.

St. Clyde glanced anxiously around the room in which Gabriele and Saise otherwise never were absent at this hour.

"You are looking for my daughter?" asked Beaufort, noticing the glance— "not very well this morning, asks to be excused."

"And—and Saise?"

"Listen, St. Clyde," old Beaufort said, laying down his knife, "if we are to remain good friends, then don't spoil my breakfast and leave the old story be. The matter is settled."

"Settled? By God, how? Is Saise gone?"

"Not yet, but now be so kind to sit down. The claret is excellent and the beefsteak superb."

"Mr. Beaufort, I am to deliver this letter from the judge to you; he beseeches you to comply with his wish."

"Fine," said Beaufort, shoving the letter under his plate without looking at it, "will try to do that afterward."

"It is urgent, Mr. Beaufort, the fate of a life depends on it," Mr. St. Clyde bade.

"Now I've had about enough," Mr. Beaufort cried, half-laughing, half-annoyed. "Do you think I would do the whole world the favor of letting my beefsteak get cold and my claret warm? What cannot wait until after breakfast will not be attended to at all. That is *my* motto, and now sit down; otherwise, I will get really angry."

St. Clyde saw that it would not help to raise any further objections. Therefore, he sat down next to the planter, but it was not possible for him to take even a bite. He drank a few glasses of wine to cool his boiling blood and then paced restlessly back and forth in the gallery scented with blooms and blossoms. Meanwhile, Mr. Beaufort finished his leisurely breakfast, slowly sipped the last drop of wine, then wiped his mouth, leaned back a bit in his chair, and said, drawing a deep breath, "So—now we will go down a bit and watch, how—"

"But the letter—"

Oh yes, so—I almost forgot it. Now, what does the judge write?—Dear Friend—am interested—since I urgently need—wife alone—request sincerely, me—Saise—by heaven, the damned nigger again!—to buy—nonsense, comes too late—important reasons—to delay the delivery—nonsense, comes too late, I say—uncommon pledge—utmost respect and friendship—yes, sorry—comes too late—"

"But you said just a few seconds ago that Saise was not gone yet? How is this possible?"

"My overseer bought her," responded Beaufort, picking at his teeth. "Now turn to him and leave me out of the matter—I'm fed up with being bothered about the creature."

"But Mr. Beaufort, what in the savior's name could have made you so hard toward the poor girl? Up to now you always treated her more like a daughter than a stranger."

That's just it, sir!" cried the old planter indignantly, "that's just it—to be disgraced in front of all my Negroes. Don't you think that the blackguards are almost dying of laughter because their master sat at a table so long with one of their race?"

"But if Saise were really of pure Indian blood and you, without knowing it, had abetted a piece of villainy?" asked St. Clyde, looking the old man straight into the eye. "If that stranger had *fabricated* this bill of sale with base companions and the help of a judge and through you, an unfortunate girl, who, up until now, considered you to be her second father, were pushed into unspeakable misery?"

Beaufort stared at the young man for a moment, but then he shook his head in annoyance and cried: "Foolishness—nonsense—you come with a whole package full of ifs and buts, and—by thunder, sir!—leave me in peace with your lamentations. The wench is sold—I signed the bill of sale myself, and now enough! Go to the overseer if it is so important to you, with fifty dollars profit he will let her go again—or—it is better that you go on down to the field and send him up to me, I have something to discuss with him."

The old man strode into the next room and slammed the door behind him in vexation. But he was no longer angry with the young Creole but, rather, with himself. For the first time the thought dawned on him that he had probably acted too hastily and had allowed his violent temper to get the better of him. He could, of course, not undo what had already been done, but now he wanted to try and see if he could not at least make it better. He intended to buy Saise and then investigate whether black blood really flowed through her veins. Until then she could move into a small house by herself and would not need to come into contact with him or his daughter.

One hour later Duxon stood again with Pitwell at the bank of the river.

"Pitwell," said the former, "I do think it would be better for us to leave tomorrow already; the matter seems to eat at old Beaufort—he's having second thoughts."

"Do you think he noticed something?" asked Pitwell anxiously.

"It wouldn't surprise me," Duxon muttered through clenched teeth. "The dandy was here again and probably put an idea into his head. Just imagine—he wanted to buy the wench off me."

"Who? Mr. Beaufort?"

"Yes—both—first the greenhorn and then, when I went to the master, he himself.—He had, while I was speaking with him, a letter in his hand, and I would bet my neck that it was from the judge. Since I have some trifles chalked up to me here, I don't see why we should delay any longer. When I did not want to sell the Indian to him, he began to spew bile, as usual, and said I should come to him in an hour and settle accounts. I want to take advantage of this opportunity; such a quick settlement will avoid many an unpleasantry. I can put all my other affairs in order by morning; you be ready by then, too. In four days we must be in Texas."

"Good," said Pitwell pensively, "but, Duxon, we're going to have company— I—I have a few friends who are waiting for me behind Fischer's landing. You— you won't mind traveling a bit quickly?"

Duxon looked at him sharply from the side and after a brief pause inquired, "But then may I also know why?"

"And will you give me your word of honor that you will keep silent?" whispered Pitwell, looking around carefully.

"Do you need my *word of honor* for that?" the overseer smiled.

"Now, I see that you understand me, Duxon," the Yankee continued softly. "I have a little bit of business going again, just like we did before. A rich planter from the other bank of the Mississippi wants to transport his slaves to Texas because in Louisiana they are worth too much to other people, and he will pay me one hundred dollars per head. We were set across below Waterloo yesterday morning, and with the help of two partners I brought all the Negroes, a hundred and fifteen men, into the swamp between Fischer's landing and the cutoff—did you see the three who passed by this morning? Those were the last. Every one of them has a false pass. Now you know everything, and if you are smart, then you will not only join us but also take along a few—companions. Doesn't Beaufort have any Negroes who don't like life in Louisiana anymore? You could tell them they were going to a better climate."

"That's true," muttered Duxon, gazing down in deep thought. "But Pitwell, the matter has another, indeed quite wicked, catch. I don't doubt for a moment that we will succeed in getting away, and you already have seen to the weapons. However—if Texas were to join the United States, like everyone is saying, what then? Then the government will hand us over."

"Good God," laughed Pitwell, "if the government intended to start handing over everyone who has committed some kind of crime, then who would cultivate the land, breed cattle, or fight against the Mexicans and Comanches? No, Duxon, don't get any gray hairs over that; we are safe. Those fine fellows know that quite well, too; otherwise, they never would have voted for joining the Union."

"I think you are right," said Duxon. "In any case, it would not be difficult to move farther west, where neither Texas nor Uncle Sam can do anything to us.[16] Many a man will stand by us if it should get to that point."

"Seven-eighths of Texas," laughed Pitwell.

"Well then, so be it. If that is the case, it would be better to leave tomorrow morning before daybreak so that we are all together around ten or eleven o'clock. We need not be afraid of being followed from here because Beaufort does not get up so early, and I will see to it that he thinks the missing slaves are occupied somewhere.—Will Saise go with us willingly?"

"Is that the question of an overseer? Don't you have a whip?"

Duxon smiled and said scornfully, "You don't seem to understand how to treat *ladies*. But I have another way—I'll take our little gig and drive.[17] As an excuse, those who stay behind can tell the boss afterward—of course, not until he inquires about it—I'd brought my things to Fischer's landing, where boats dock constantly. But, pox and poison! today I wanted to stay with my little—*woman*, and now I will have to run around until tomorrow morning, so that I don't know which way to turn. Well, what the deuce! I can catch up with that in Texas, ha ha ha! She won't get upset."

"Hardly," said Pitwell dryly, "let's get going—do you have weapons?"

"Two rifles, a bowie knife, and three pairs of pistols. You know, an overseer must always be able to build a small fortress around his house."

"Good, if you take a wagon, then you can bring everything along—such things are always useful. But there down the allée comes the young dandy who is making such a fuss about the Indian. The lady of the house is with him; what is her name?"

"Gabriele—a splendid girl. Too bad that you can't fabricate a bill of sale for *her*—I'd take her, too!"

The Yankee cast a warning glance at him, and, in order not to be seen together with the overseer any further, went up along the river. Meanwhile, the overseer had his horse saddled and rode out to the field, picked out a certain number of Negroes, and ordered them to get their axes to chop down some trees in a somewhat more remote part of the woods that he would point out to them. Soon thereafter he disappeared with them into the marshland that bordered the plantation.

St. Clyde and Gabriele walked side by side toward the river.

"My heavens, sir," said the maiden, as they approached the outer enclosure—"what is the matter? You seem to be terribly agitated; I have never seen
you like this."

"I have to go," whispered the young man, his pale hand pressed firmly to his
hot, feverish brow—"I have to go—must get help. Not until this terrible catas-
trophe did I realize that I—" He was silent and turned away.

"That you love Saise," whispered Gabriele in a soft monotone and stared up
at the Creole.—"Isn't it true, St. Clyde, you—love the Indian woman?"

"Yes, Miss Beaufort—yes—why should I keep it from you," St. Clyde said
suddenly, standing still and looking fixedly into the young maiden's eyes. "Why
should I hesitate to admit it to you? You were the unfortunate woman's friend
as long as she was in your protection.—Even toward me, the poor, homeless,
foreign wanderer, you have always been good and kind.—I want to confide in
you, and insofar as it lies in your power, you will support me."

"For sure—for sure," said Gabriele in a barely audible voice.—"But—if
Saise—really were—a Negro? If—oh God!—do not be angry with me, I do
not know what I am saying. No, no—Saise is free—must get *free* and—happy!"

She buried her face in her hands, and the light, clear teardrops welled
through her delicate fingers.

"Oh, Miss Beaufort!" cried St. Clyde, moved. "You are so kind to the unfortunate girl; how can I ever thank you?"

Gabriele forcibly pulled herself together. "What do you want to do? What is
your plan?" she inquired quickly. "How do you think you can save Saise, since
you yourself told me that scoundrel had sold her to Duxon, who had a falling
out with my father? What can you do about those wretched creatures if the law
is on their side?"

"Nothing more *through* the law," said St. Clyde in a stifled voice—"everything *without* it. The judge told me yesterday that a band of Choctaw hunters
was camped at the Mississippi; they must help me. If I cannot convince them
to save a daughter of their own race from slavery, if they are so dissolute that
even *that* makes no impression on them, then I have another, more powerful
means at my disposal—*whiskey*. Whiskey can move a border Indian to all sorts
of wickedness; why not to a good deed for a change?—it is the *last* resort."

"But the danger to which you will be exposed?"

"Danger? Is there danger, when the worst thing that could happen to me is
to die? No, Miss Beaufort—I could have lived *without* Saise, if I knew her to be
happy, but to sense that she has been handed over to the most dreadful ruin,

languishing in humiliating bondage, the free daughter of the forest a slave—
no—no—life would then be madness.—But I must go—precious time is flying.—Duxon had an argument with your father and wants to leave. The whole
settlement is talking about how he deceived him and made a fortune in the few
years that he has been here. Therefore, he will not delay in bringing it to safety,
and if he goes by boat, perhaps to New Orleans, then it would be impossible to
track down an individual in that enormous city. But now my request—will you
look after Saise?"

"How can I?" responded Gabriele, with anxiously clasped hands. "She is
Duxon's property."

"I know, but you have a lot of influence on your father, even on that knave.
It is the power that virtue always has over vice, the awe that evil cannot overcome when confronted by good. Insist that Saise not yet be relinquished to him
today, or, if you cannot prevent that, that she spend this night with you or at
least under the protection of the old Negro woman."

"You intend to abduct her?" asked Gabriele, dismayed.

"No," said St. Clyde, darkly, "her bill of sale would remain in the hands of
that scoundrel, and Saise would always be miserable thinking about it. No—I
have to get hold of that *bill*. The laws won't help me. May God help me. Promise
to protect Saise in the meantime?"

"Yes," whispered Gabriele and, turning her face away, gave him her hand—
"and you want?"

"To save Saise or—die," answered the young Creole firmly.

"And then—if you—if Saise is yours?"

"I will look for a faraway land, where people are not sold and mistreated like
animals. I come from France—my family is said to be among the noblest in the
country. I will return there."

"With Saise?"

"With my wife."

"Then fare thee well, St. Clyde, fare thee well; may God protect and defend
you!"

She called this out and with quick steps hurried back to the house. But on
the spot where she had stood lay the white rose that had just rested on her
breast. St. Clyde picked it up, kissed it, sheltered it at his heart, then hastened
to his horse, mounted, and galloped up the road along the river. Arriving there,
he took no longer than was necessary to get the flatboat ferry ready to take him
and his steed to the other bank, and soon the little boat, propelled by four

sturdy arms, was swimming on the broad surface of the mighty stream toward the eastern bank.

"Were Indians brought across on this ferry yesterday?" he inquired after a while of the elder of the two, who seemed to be the owner of the vessel.

He looked at St. Clyde and laughed.

"No," he said, "have you ever heard of an Indian having himself carried across on a ferry? Not I—they can use *that* money better for something else. For that there's whiskey, and wherever the red people can save a cent for *that* purpose, they would rather toil away for days in their own fashion—that is, not with something like work."[18]

"So, they did not cross here?" asked St. Clyde, alarmed.

"Oh yes, of course," responded the younger, "but not on the ferry. They all sat in two little canoes that they'd brought over from there and had their horses on reins or ropes swim behind them."

"And do you think that I will find them?"

"I don't think that it will be difficult. Ben, who came down from there, told me they had a large number of whiskey bottles with them, and so they probably did not go hunting today. They landed a little ways farther up, and if you want to trouble yourself to go to the house that you see shimmering through the willows and cottonwood trees, then, I think, they will set you on the right track."

At this moment the boat docked at the bank. St. Clyde led away his horse, which was seeking firm ground with its hooves, and pressed the fare in the hands of the younger man, who had sprung onto land to hold the ferry with the rope. He jumped into the saddle and trotted rapidly toward the low residence standing close to the shore. For the moment it still was surrounded by high, lush forest growth from which the new settler intended to hew the future means of his existence, cordwood for steamboats.

The backwoodsman stood in the doorway.

"Good day, sir," St. Clyde called to him, "have you seen anything of the Indians who landed not far from here yesterday?"

The man cocked his ear in the direction of the woods, without responding to the question at all, and stayed in this position for several minutes. St. Clyde, however, who perhaps thought that he had not even heard the question, repeated it and asked for a reply. As if carved out of stone, the man remained standing until the young man could no longer repress an impatient "But, sir!"

"Can you find a man if he is sitting in the woods screaming his lungs out?" he countered, the pretty sure sign of a New Englander.

"If I am close enough to hear it, why not?" cried the Creole crossly. "But I asked you whether you had heard—"

"You can hear them yelling over there in the woods," said the American dryly and pointed his short pipe cut out of cane toward a narrow cow path that ran straight into the thicket.

"The Indians?" asked St. Clyde, astonished.

"Ahem!" the other nodded and continued to smoke without paying any attention to the stranger. The Creole, however, who had listened in the direction of the woods for a moment, also thought he heard wild, confused sounds in the still forest, called out a brief thanks to the man, and galloped as fast as the rather thick underbrush allowed toward the commotion that resounded ever louder and clearer. After a short ride he reached a forest glade close to the edge of a small lake-like swamp that had remained after the Mississippi flooding and not yet dried up fully. Here he saw a drama that was as picturesque as it was strange.

Stretched out on the luxuriant floor of grass, surrounded by a semicircle of glowing, puffing fire, lay seven red-skinned hunters under the enormous cottonwood trees that reached toward heaven. The smoke drew over them and was supposed to ward off the attacking mosquitoes. Some with, others without their hunting shirts but each one holding an almost empty whiskey bottle, they rejoiced and shouted, howling more than singing old battle cries and war songs and newly learned French and English melodies. One, who seemed to be the leader of the band and was still the soberest, had taken his pointed scalping knife as a baton and at quite regular intervals jabbed it into the green grass on which he lay, his face turned toward the airy treetops, while the others, all in about the same position or place, accompanied him not just with their voices but also with heels and fists, each one, of course, according to his own eardrum-bursting melody.

The leader of the band seemed to be the first to notice the stranger. Without stirring more than necessary to measure him from top to bottom with a quick glance, while a faint, drunken smile crossed his face, he held the bottle out to him and stammered, "Here—stranger—here—dri—take a drink!"

"Great God!" moaned St. Clyde, looking at the half-conscious savage figures, "great, almighty God—are these the people I hoped would help me?—lost—lost—all—all lost!"

He covered his face with his hands and for several seconds sat sunk in still, mute pain.

"Drink—damn it," the leader cried again—"you think you're too good to drink out of the bottle with Indian, eh? Poor Indian is son of great Indian chief—go to hell!" He sank back against the tree roots and began his song anew.

The Creole sprang from his horse and paced back and forth next to the drunken hunters, arms crossed and eyes fastened to the ground, while the savage leader looked up to the green forest cathedral with glazed, fixed eyes and sang the verses of an Indian battle or victory song:

> I slay the chieftain of the Muskogee;[19]
> His wife—there on the trunk burned she,
> And by the hind legs above,
> I hung the favorite dog, his love.
> Huh—huh—huh from the Muskogee,
> Wah—wah—wah—the scalp here see!

At the Muskogee's name St. Clyde stood still and listened.—He knew that the Riccarees, even recently, had fought some bloody battles with this tribe, but the Choctaws and Muskogees also fought each other—it must be their battle song. Nevertheless, he turned to the young chief and asked, "To what tribe do you belong—are you a Choctaw?"

Ignoring the question, the Indian continued singing:

> I peeled his skull quite naked and bare,
> And here is his scalp, with the scalplock hair,
> His flesh is in the panther's jaw,
> On his bloody bones the wolves do gnaw,
> Huh—huh—huh—from the Muskogee,
> Wah—wah—wah, the scalp here see!

"Are you a Choctaw, Indian?" The Creole now asked more insistently, bending down to him and placing a hand on his shoulder. "Speak—are you a Choctaw?"

The savage mumbled a half-audible curse and continued:

> His sinew I need to span the bow,
> When I follow the traces of each foe,
> And now tremble the women Muskogee,
> Like straws in the storm before the Riccaree,
> Huh—huh—huh, of the Musko—

"What the devil is the matter with you?" he stopped suddenly, as St. Clyde let out a joyful cry of astonishment when he heard the name of this tribe.

"Ha, Riccaree!—You are a Riccaree?" "You are a Riccaree?" he repeated after a brief pause.

"Well, then—what about it?" was the Indian's short answer, trying to find
the melody he lost in the interruption, while he absentmindedly tapped his feet
on the grassy ground.

"Then you must come with me and save a child of your tribe who is in imminent danger."

"My tribe is in Missouri," muttered the red son of the forests, humming
softly to himself:

> His sinews I need to span the bow,
> When I follow the tracks of the fleeing foe—

"But they have abducted her!" cried St. Clyde in despair. "Man, has this devilish whiskey burned all your senses that you have no sympathy, no feelings anymore?"

"Have no more whiskey?" the hunter repeated with a thick tongue—"no—
no more, only a bit—give some."

"Ha!" exclaimed the Creole, seized by a good idea. "You shall have whiskey,
a whole barrel full, but come with me now and help me."

"Barrel full whiskey?" mumbled the Indian, raising himself halfway—
"whole barrel full?" The thought was too magnificent for him; he could not
even grasp it. His companions' chorus broke out again into such a bellowing
battle cry, whereby they flailed their arms wildly in the air, that an alligator, who
was sunning himself on a log floating in the water not a hundred feet away,
looked up startled and then silently slid into the quieter element.

"Barrel full whiskey?" the Indian repeated after a long pause. "Much whiskey that—come!" and, in vain, he tried to get up again.

The Creole supported him now and with great effort brought him to an upright position. But what did that help? What could he do with this unconscious
mass of raw, craving sensuality? Was this the man who could help him free his
beloved? He let him go, and the young chief reeled against the next tree, his jaw
sunk to his breast.

"Poor Saise!" sighed St. Clyde.

"Ais?" the Indian stammered with a heavy tongue—"Ais? Who is speaking
of Nedaunis-Ais?—She is dead—I want whiskey—whiskey!"

"Whiskey!" the band rejoiced, who took in the last loudly uttered word—
"Whiskey, yippee!"

"*Nedaunis-Ais?* You know her?" the Creole cried and sprang toward the reeling man.

"Leave me alone, or I will thrust steel into your body," the savage growled.—"Damn you!"

"Nedaunis-Ais *is alive!*" the other thundered, ignoring the threat.—"She *is alive,* and you must help me to *save* her—"

"Alive? save? where?" cried the drunken man, now trying to grasp the clear meaning of the words, while his eyes stared fixedly at the stranger.

In a few words St. Clyde now told his attentive listener the story of the Indian girl, while the Indian stood there with hands pressed firmly against his temples and inhaled every syllable from his lips. But, finally, as he began to comprehend what it was about, and as the unfortunate girl's fate appeared before him in clear, sharp colors, then, inflamed by anger and rage, he grasped the bottle lying next to him that was still a third full and with a wild throw smashed it against the next tree trunk.

"Poison—poison—poison!" he cried at the same time.—"My sister sold and I drunk—poison—poison, the white man's firewater—poison—whiskey!"

"Whiskey! yippee" rejoiced those who still had enough senses left to understand the last words.

"But stop—stop!" cried the young Indian suddenly, brushing his long, black hair from his brow, "it is still not too late—there is still time!"—and pulling off his hunting shirt and his leggings, with one leap he jumped into the water from this spot on the shore, which was several feet high, dove down a few times, and swam toward land. Without troubling to put on his clothes again, he ran into the woods, from which, barely half an hour later, he returned on the back of a small, snorting pony. His clothes and weapons were soon gathered together, and almost before the Creole could mount his horse, he signaled to him to follow.

"But your companions," said St. Clyde now—"what can we two accomplish alone?"

"Come," said the son of the forest, "come. Do you want to stay until tomorrow, to hear them speak with thick tongues: more *whiskey*—more *whiskey?* They are Choctaws—I must go—you come along—we two enough."

He did not wait for any further reply from his companion but, rather, with reins flying galloped toward the Mississippi, threw himself into the current once more to extinguish the effect of the firewater, and then, after donning his few articles of clothing, pulled out a canoe hidden in the bushes. St. Clyde had to sit down in the middle of it and guide one horse on each side by the reins, while the Indian himself paddled the boat quickly and skillfully across the broad, strong current.

But St. Clyde had been held up first by the Indian, then by the crossing, long enough that the sun was already setting when they reached the western bank. The Creole now had to take charge and led Saise's brother, whom he had found by such chance, to the judge. Along the way Wetako—as the Riccaree was called—told him that he had pursued his abducted sister and had even caught and slain the vile abductors. But his months-long wanderings to find a trace of the abducted girl, who had been pulled from his rescuing arms through the scoundrel's devilish ruse, had been in vain. Despairing over that, he finally had joined a band of Choctaws who hunted in Louisiana's forests and sold the felled game in the neighboring little towns. Sick of life and in pain, made indifferent to everything that he had otherwise esteemed and cherished, he yielded to drink and therewith followed the example of his entire unfortunate tribe.

The twofold bath and the sudden shock of the partly good, partly bad news that his sister was alive and in distress had expelled any trace of intoxication. The Indian, the cold, calculating savage, had reawakened in him, and with a rapid glance he surveyed the dangers that threatened the being that he loved most on earth. To be sure, he did not know the white people's laws, but he knew how difficult, how almost impossible, it was for an Indian to get back from them anything the whites lay a hand on. From the start he seemed to have no other thought than to save Saise by means of cunning or force. Either means was all the same to him as long as he achieved his goal.

It was dark night when they finally reached the judge's home, but important changes seemed to have transpired in those few hours. Individual constables who were pursuing a planter and his accomplice had come over from the borders of the state of Mississippi, which lay to the north. The fugitives must have stayed together as far as Waterloo, but from there they seemed to have separated. Two of the pursuers raced down along the riverbank to make all arrangements to stop further flight, while the rest followed the stronger trail upriver to prevent, insofar as possible, the fugitives from turning to the interior of the land and reaching the Texas border.

The judge, who had also been notified, immediately suspected the stranger. Late in the afternoon he had already sent messengers to the Fausse Rivière to have him arrested, not because of the Indian girl but to question him with respect to the suspicion that he was in league with those thieves who had stolen the Negroes. At the same time he hoped to determine whether Saise was a slave or whether she had been shamefully abducted from her tribe.

Now St. Clyde insisted on obtaining a delay in Saise's delivery. The judge was amenable to this, but they had to await the deputy sheriff's return because the chief sheriff was busy upstream and the two constables downstream. Much to his consternation the Creole was forced to wait for his arrival. Of course, he offered to take the letter over himself, but that would not have been legal. The judge consoled him by saying that a few hours surely would not make a difference since, in any case, he would be at the Fausse Rivière by daybreak and could spare the poor girl from being dragged away into captivity. But the deputy sheriff did not come. Hour after hour they waited anxiously, and the judge finally cried in vexation, "A pox on the fellow!—I soon shall be forced to demand that the sheriff let go this wretched Fritz Haydt.[20] There's no doing anything with him: he gets loaded, lets the mulatto women on the Fausse Rivière make a fool of him, and then fails to carry out his duties."

"I will go meet him," St. Clyde offered, "perhaps he is lingering along the way—"

"That would not help you much," the judge opined. "For if he is dallying, you will not find him. He is pretty secretive about his amusement spots. But if he does not come by tomorrow morning, then I myself will ride over with you, and we will settle the matter together."

They spent the night in fear and agonized anticipation. The Riccaree could not understand why they were waiting and kept on insisting that they set out to free and avenge his sister.

There was a loud pounding at the door—it was past two o'clock, and the frogs' silence indicated that morning was nigh—and the slave standing guard opened it. Up the stairs bounded not the deputy sheriff but, rather, the constable, announcing in a few words that, according to a reliable source, Pitwell was the paid abductor of all the plantation Negroes and could no longer be found on the Fausse Rivière either. But Beaufort's overseer must also be in league with him because he, too, most likely having been alarmed, had taken off in the middle of the night with the Indian girl he had just bought. She, however, had not followed him willingly but had to be transported in ordinary slave chains.

"Wah!"—cried Wetako, jumping up from the ground where he had been crouching—"away—away—we must away!"

St. Clyde, too, grabbed his hat and wanted to follow him. The judge, however, stepped in their path and asked them to wait a moment. Then he made clear to them that they could accomplish little or nothing until a sufficient number of planters had gathered who could then follow them in concert. But that would not be until tomorrow noon, and therefore he also wanted to ask them to join forces with the constables to notify all the planters about the incident as quickly as possible. Even if the rescue were delayed by a few hours, it could be accomplished with greater certainty. Neither the Creole nor the Indian wanted to hear anything about this.

"No!" cried the latter—"Nedaunis-Ais in chains, and Wetako with knife and rifle on her trail—we want to leave!"

"For God's sake—do not commit murder!" the judge called after them, frightened.—"You do not know our laws—a life sentence would be the consequence!"

The Indian smiled grimly to himself when he heard these words.

"Why do you not lock up the panther that steals your young horses in the night?" he said scornfully. "Wetako is a man, and his footprints are deep. Follow him if you can!"

He jumped quickly into the saddle, the Creole as well. The latter gave a final wave to the judge who had anxiously warned him, too, and they flew along the road at an attenuated gallop to the spot from where the overseer had started out in order to pick up his tracks.

The first rays of the sun had already reddened the dark-green leaves of the rustling cypresses when the riders reached Beaufort's plantation. Here there was a big uproar. The planters from almost all the neighboring settlements had arrived with double-barreled shotguns, knives, and harpoons. One group, St. Clyde heard, had already taken off to at least detain the fugitives. The two men stayed only long enough to get the most essential information, inquired quickly which way the overseer's gig had gone, and then stormed after him like dark gods of vengeance.

This very gig was the reason that they became suspicious on the plantation sooner than Duxon had hoped, since on that same day he had sent his things on a steamboat to Houston under the address of a Texas trading firm. Some of the Negroes, whom he always had treated cruelly and inhumanely, told their master about their suspicions as well as that a certain number of their fellow slaves, most of whom were the overseer's spies, also were missing and in all likelihood had escaped.

Duxon, moreover, was obliged to leave his newly purchased slave in the care of the old Negro woman on the previous day, since Gabriele had insisted on it, and he feared arousing suspicion if he resisted too obstinately. This delayed his escape in the night, which he needed to expedite after a messenger from Pitwell had warned him. Thus, it came about that he heard his well-mounted pursuers behind him at full heat. As soon as he heard the echoing thunder of the hooves on the hard-trodden road, he turned off the path onto a small, dry stream. The Negroes had already rushed toward the designated area on horses they had stolen from their master or his neighbors, and Duxon had hoped to catch up with them quickly enough. For the moment this stratagem was completely successful, for the planters, unfamiliar with following tracks, did not notice that the wagon wheel ruts had turned off until it was too late. Thus, they went in the direction that the Negroes themselves had divulged because they did not want to turn back and lose time. Later they would be able to get hold of all of them at the meeting place.

Now Duxon, familiar with every square foot of land in these woods and swamps, knew that if he were to follow the edge of a little thicket, he would find a rather open copse and would be impeded only by cypress knees. Hardly a quarter-mile from there another road crossed the marsh that led up to the cut-off,[21] and as soon as he reached it, all pursuers would be thrown off the track.

But he had not reckoned with *one* factor, *Saise's* resistance. As long as he stayed on the road, the poor girl did not give up hope that her beloved—for she, too, was deeply attached to the young Creole—would catch up with them. But now, surrounded only by the rustling trees of the forest, she found herself completely in the power of the person whom she had feared and despised from the first moment she saw him. Believing her fate was sealed, she tried desperately to tear off her chains and free herself.

"Sit still, damn it!" grumbled the overseer, who was not in the best mood in any case, "or I'll hit you on the skull with the whip handle to make you be quiet—do you hear?"

Saise desisted for a moment in exhaustion, but then, trying her last strength anew, she succeeded in tearing off the ropes that held her hands down, if not her chains. At the same time she freed herself of the gag that the scoundrel had used as a precaution and now, driven by fear and despair, let out a cry for help that resounded so loudly and suddenly in the ears of the pony harnessed to the gig that, frightened, it recoiled sideways and ran into the woods. Duxon, also startled by Saise's cry for help, could not rein in the pony quickly enough. Indeed, he lost hold of the reins, and at the next moment the light vehicle hit up against a cypress knee with one wheel and overturned, throwing the master as well as his slave into a nearby thicket.

With an expression of anger and vengeance the scoundrel jumped up, but first the pony required his undivided attention—the gig was carrying his entire fortune, and if the horse ran away, he was lost. So, he quickly grabbed the reins of the wildly stomping pony, pulled it back onto its hind legs such that white foam mixed with the blood from its torn mouth. While the frightened horse stood trembling, Duxon righted the gig with an enormous effort.

Then he vented his full rage on the cause of this accident, for Saise, at first almost stunned by the fall, had collected herself and let out a renewed cry for help.

"Death and damnation!" he cried, flew toward the retreating girl, and with the lead-filled whip handle aimed a blow that would have smashed her head had it hit her. But raising her bound arms, she deflected the blow with the links of the chain.

Duxon wanted to strike again when, still at a great distance, but clearly and distinctly, a sharp, savage cry resounded through the still forest. He stopped to listen, and at this moment Saise seemed to be carved of stone, so fixed and motionless did she look toward the area from which the cry had come.

"Hah! There come several of them, but they are on the street," the overseer muttered to himself. "Pox and poison, it's getting dangerous. Come, my little dove, be sensible now. The first cry that you let out will be your death!" With these words he bent down, grabbed the statue-like girl, and was about to carry her back to the uprighted vehicle. When he touched her, however, her blood, which almost was benumbed by the sound of that call, stirred. She lifted the light chain binding her wrists and struck it down against her abductor's head with all her might, so that he let go and reeled back, half-unconscious. Again the unfortunate girl's cry for help resounded, louder and more urgently than before. Duxon, driven to the brink by pain and rage, hardly heard the responding signal that was coming nearer when he pulled his broad knife from its sheath, sprang at the girl, who recoiled in horror, and, teeth clenched firmly, thrust the sharp steel into her breast.

Mortally wounded, Saise staggered into the yellow foliage. Duxon flew to the wagon in wild bounds, pulled out a large briefcase and hid it under his vest, cut through the pony's traces, hoisted the double-barreled shotgun over his shoulder, leaped onto the horse, and in the next moment disappeared into the thicket.

The bushes on one side of the small clearing had hardly closed behind him, when from the other side two riders on foaming steeds burst onto the scene. But here, as if struck by lightning, they grasped their reins in horror. They stood still for several seconds. While the one then jumped from the saddle with a wild cry of pain and threw himself down next to the dear, poor girl, the other rose to his full height on his animal's back and listened in the direction of the woods with wildly fixed, dull eyes. Suddenly he must have heard a far-off sound, for without deigning the murdered girl a second glance, he spurred on the animal, which was cringing with fear at the smell of blood, jumped with it over the gig that stood in their way, and followed the fleeing murderer, silently, to be sure, but with an expression that flashed death and destruction.

Not a word crossed his lips, no glance turned away from the trail in the soft earth. Swiftly, the horse's reins in one hand, the rifle in the other, he flew through the dense forest and had galloped barely five hundred feet when he caught sight of his enemy, who was busy hacking loose the traces that had become entangled in the thicket, momentarily delaying his flight.

Duxon looked around and recognized that the figure approaching was an Indian. For a moment, however, he really was unsure whether he should fear him as an enemy, for he himself had never had dealings with descendants of those savage tribes and knew that they seldom are a party to fighting quarrels among whites. But when the thought of the murdered maiden who also was one of those unfortunate people flashed through his head, he saw that the young Indian was putting an end to his doubts, for he suddenly stopped his horse, raised his rifle, and the red flash of fire coursed through the eerie darkness of the primeval forest.

The overseer felt he was wounded, but he had no time to reflect—the avenger was rushing toward him. He lifted the double-barreled shotgun to shoot the Indian down, but the hurled tomahawk hit his left elbow, deflecting his shot. Only a few buckshots grazed Wetako's shoulder, and before the murderer, conscious of his guilt, could cock his gun, the avenger flew toward him. The Riccaree's war cry echoed piercingly through the forest, and the miserable creature collapsed with a howl.

Meanwhile, the young Creole kneeled next to the bleeding body of the beautiful, unfortunate girl, his beloved's pale face against his shoulder. He had, indeed, bandaged the wide, gaping wound quickly and carefully, but it was too late—the death blow had penetrated deep into her life. He heard the pursuers, who streamed in from all parts of the area, as they stormed past to prevent the Negroes' abduction. He perceived the Riccaree's war cry but paid no attention. His gaze remained fixed on the red stream of life flowing from the girl he loved so passionately, and night, darkest night, finally fell before his eyes.

When he came to again, the Riccaree was standing at his side. He had wrapped his sister's body in his blanket, and seeing the white man had awakened, lifted it onto his horse.

"Wetako—what are you going to do?" cried the Creole, rising with a start—"where are you going?"

"Want to take the remains of the chieftain's daughter to the Riccaree tribe," said the young Indian with a sad smile. "I want to say it is the peace offering that the white men send them.—They have stolen our old land from us; here is blood to fertilize the new—fare thee well!"

"And the abductor?" inquired St. Clyde, still looking half-stunned at the bloody body.

"The abductor?" the Riccaree replied scornfully, throwing open his deerskin wrap—"he belongs to *me!*" The Creole recognized in horror the bloody scalp attached to the savage's belt. Before St. Clyde could utter another word, the Indian jumped into the saddle behind the corpse, spurred on the snorting animal, and in the next moment disappeared from the white man's view.

In the meantime the planters in pursuit had caught up with the villainous slave thief, Pitwell, and, with the customary haste in which all similar crimes are punished, had hung him on the nearest tree. In his wallet they found sufficient proof that he deserved this death tenfold, for his accomplices' letter proved the pure ancestry of the Indian girl beyond all doubt. Later, when they followed the wagon's trail in order to pursue the overseer, too, they found the signs of the struggle as well as the small wagon itself. Not far from there, leaning pale and rigid against the trunk of a young tree, lay the Creole's body, a spent pistol in his right hand.

From *Stories from Home and Abroad* (1862)

IN THE RED RIVER

The Rio Rojo, or Red River, is one of those mighty tributaries of the Mississippi whose waters roll down from the Rocky Mountains through the vast plains to the Mississippi Delta and—after forming the border between Louisiana and Texas for a stretch—join "the father of waters" in the state of Louisiana. When it has reached the forest land, the river runs for hundreds of miles through low-lying, often swampy banks. The area is, for the most part, still a wilderness where the bear and the panther leave their paw prints, and to date only those higher sections of the river bank that are not exposed to the floods can be cultivated.

The human being, however, is a stubborn creature, and the American is the stubbornest and toughest of all, especially when it comes to earning *money*. He does not acknowledge the difficulties that the terrain throws in his way. Even the bleak swamp, its airs pregnant with fever; the wild current, which marks on the trees along the banks the height at which it has often flooded the lowland; the wilderness, through which there is not even a path leading to other human dwellings—all that can not frighten him or prevent him from building his house in such places to wrest his existence from the forest.

As long as no steamboats navigated the Red River, that wilderness remained unmolested. To be sure, plantations and small towns, which shipped their products to the south on flatboats and keelboats, arose on the high-lying land. But the swamp was left to the wild animals, alligators, and mosquitoes.

The appearance of the first steamboat, however, caused a rapid change. The steamboats needed wood for fuel and preferred to pay quite a high price for it, rather than lying to and losing an enormous amount of time by having their own crew cut it. Soon the backwoodsmen could no longer resist such an enticement. Everywhere at the low banks they landed in boats, and with axes they forced entry into the canebrakes and thickets of thorns. They felled the ancient forest giants, which then—cut and split—were stacked along the riverbank.

The woodcutter's dwelling was soon set up—a low log cabin built in a few days. As far as the river was concerned—aye!—the woodcutter had his boat right in front of his door. If the river ever rose too high, which might not happen again for many years, then he would simply get into his boat and go down-stream to the nearest higher piece of land.

Single people were not the only ones to settle in the wilderness in this fash-ion. Some of these tough fellows, accustomed to such a life, were foolhardy enough to bring their families along. Poor, pale women and skinny, hollow-cheeked children were forced to live in a place that they truly often shared only with the alligators, water snakes, and countless swarms of insects. But what did it matter that they lay prostrate with severe fever for three-fourths of the year and medical aid was out of the question in that wilderness? The man was earn-ing money—a lot of money, often five to six dollars a day. Once they had ac-quired a little capital, they would move to a healthier, better land and settle there forever. They consoled themselves with this thought, and whoever died in the meantime was buried in the swamp to dream of a better world.

Thus there lived in just such a hut a farmer who had moved down from Ken-tucky to "get rich quicker." With the eye of a connoisseur he had selected a somewhat elevated piece of sandy soil—the swollen stream had, in any event, touched at its base—and he built his cabin on it. To be sure, the land sur-rounding it was all the lower, but in exchange there, too, stood a superabun-dance of wood. In the following two years the diligent man who settled here had already earned many a dollar of hard currency, which he kept safe in a box. One more year, and he would be able to leave the swamp and move up north to the mountainous part of Arkansas.

The woodcutter's family consisted of a wife, four children—the eldest boy was already fourteen years old and lent a stalwart hand—and a young Negro boy sixteen years in age, whom he had purchased in the previous year from a steamboat captain. He was totally dependent on the steamboats, not only for the sale of his wood but also for everything that he needed to survive because he had not cleared the land where he was situated. He could make better use of his time, and if another year were to pass, he still would not have lifted his axe to it. Then he would sell whatever wood happened to be lying there, and the boat that took his final load was to lead him away from there, too.

In the last two years the Red River had risen regularly in June and, now and then, had overflowed the riverbank as well. But it had never reached his house, nor had it swept away a single cord of wood. What did he need to worry about the future?

Moreover, in order to be prepared for the worst, he had placed a sturdy boat, which could easily carry them all, fastened to a strong vine, right in front of his house. Before the time came when the waters usually rose, he was careful not to split any more wood than was absolutely necessary to satisfy the next boats. But he did not remain idle, for he felled all the more trees in the forest, leaving them only split in half. If the floods were higher than usual this time, the trees still could not be swept away, and when the water subsided, it would be easy for him to renew a good supply.

This year was namely a leap year, and the people along the Mississippi, and the western rivers in general, claim that in every leap year the waters come down much higher and with much greater turbulence than in other years. I hardly believe this happens *every* leap year. But the fact is that the greatest floods of the Mississippi always occur during a leap year.

Thus June approached, and day after day passed without the river rising noticeably. Perhaps the late spring was to blame for holding back the snow up in the Rocky Mountains. In May it had turned all the warmer, and when the news came downriver of unusually heavy and sustained rains that were supposed to have fallen in the northern part of the country, many an isolated and scattered woodcutter awaited the rising of the river with an anxiously beating heart. Despite this, almost the entire month of June passed without the water level of the Red River changing by more than ten or twelve inches. The steep clay banks of the wide river still stood twenty feet above the river.

On June 29 the first red water came down, and the river began to rise rapidly. Stormy rains set in at the same time, and early on July 1 the river filled its banks up to the edge and beyond. But now the water also spread through the countless bayous or canals into the swamps, and for the moment it seemed to have come to a standstill. Nevertheless, the current was so rapid that the small steamboats traveling on the Red River could not bear up against it. Only two had passed going upstream a while ago and could, perhaps, land here on the way back—if they happened to need wood.

Henderson, as the woodcutter was named, observed the wild current rush by with some equanimity. First of all, he did not even believe that it would rise high enough to harm him, and then his boat ensured him complete safety. His wife, however, looked all the more anxiously at the raging elements, and a strange fear, which could scarcely be allayed, overcame her when she thought of her own and her children's desolate situation.

In the night from July 1 to July 2 it rained in torrents, and the water began to rise again, even though it filled the swamp for many long miles. In the evening it had almost reached the threshold of the house, and the ten or twelve cords of wood that were stacked up behind the house threatened to be lifted and float away.

Henderson, along with his son and the Negro, set to it and threw one half of the wood on top of the other. This pushed down the logs that were already underwater so that they would not float away. Toward evening they finished their work and had to wade through waist-deep water to reach the house again. So, they pulled the boat up to the door and fastened it to the door frame, ate their supper, and went to bed.

But even if the men, tired by their work, soon fell asleep, the woman did not sleep a wink. She heard the water constantly washing and splashing under the rough-hewn planks that served as the floor of the little dwelling. Only toward morning did it become somewhat quieter. She shut her eyes in exhaustion, but it was not long before there was a violent thud against the house.

Startled, the wife rose up in her bed, put down her feet, and screamed out loud, for she stepped into the ice-cold water that was already standing in the house. In an instant the men were at hand, and Henderson, who now understood that they would not have very much time, jumped to secure his boat, but—it was gone!

Pale with horror, in the faint light of dawn, he quickly ran his hands up and down along the door frame to which he himself had fastened the boat the previous evening. His trembling hand felt only the vine to which it had been tied, and for the first time he comprehended the terrible danger in which he and his family found themselves.

His call quickly brought the Negro boy to the spot, for Henderson still hoped that the boat could have washed up and become stuck somewhere down below—but in vain. The cordwood had washed loose and was drifting past the house with the wild current that seemed to seethe from within. Whole logs and gigantic trees, torn loose farther upriver by the dreadful rising current, were drifting and even threatened to destroy the little house. Now and then, when one of the branches jutting out from a mighty timber hit against it and then, turned by the current, shot past, the house shook to its foundation. If the river were to rise by one more foot, then the cabin *could* no longer hold.

And the water rose—rose slowly, but terribly and surely. In the doorway of the hut, looking fixedly at the clay-red river roaring past, the man stood and reflected upon salvation for his own. He himself did not even know how to swim. With the help of one of the timbers floating past, he could keep his head above water and *perhaps* find help farther down. But what would become of his family—of his wife—of the children?

"If only we could hew out a canoe, Massa," whispered the Negro boy at his side.—The American turned around toward him quickly.—That was a prospect of salvation, but did they have enough time to do it?—Even on dry land the three of them would need a full day to make a canoe large enough to carry all of them. Now the water was already going into their house, which stood on the highest spot; it was halfway up their calves and *was rising* every moment. Nevertheless, it occurred to the unfortunate man that even if they could not make a canoe, they at least could build a raft on which they all might be saved.

Masses of wood were drifting past. The Negro, who could swim like a fish, was sent out to hack off vines to tie together single logs, and with calm courage the American set to work.

The woman suggested that they use the upper beams of the house for the raft, but they dared not do that. As soon as they took away the weight that still held the *lower* logs to the ground, the water would lift them, and then they surely would be lost, for the current had already sought its main course right in the direction of the little cabin and from there was rolling into the forest in stormy fury. So powerful was the force and speed with which the current shot past, about one German mile per hour,[1] that the Negro did not dare go far from the house—otherwise, he would not be able to return. In the vicinity of the house, however, all the trees had been felled, and few or no vines could be found.

Now they used everything they could find to tie the timber, and toward noon a number of logs were put together. Meanwhile, the river had risen again by nine inches, and in the cabin the water already was above the beds. The children sat crying on the crude plank table in the middle of the room. The pale, trembling woman hovered next to them to protect her dear ones.

The raft now was about half-finished. However, the current, thrown by a bend in the river across almost the entire river's width, shot toward their side. It was carrying the heaviest logs and driving them with a terrible force against the raft, which was tied to a tree stump standing near the house. John, Henderson's eldest boy, was posted here with a pole in order to push the ends of the logs on the diagonal as they came to break their force. But one of the logs was too heavy, and the boy could not resist its momentum. He managed to secure his pole, but his feet slid out from under him on the slippery wood. As the ancient log seized the raft, tore it in half, and swept away the one part, the boy hardly had enough time to save himself on the other.

In mute despair Henderson saw their last resort destroyed. Even if everyone set about reconstructing the raft with the strength of desperation, the river would not allow it. More and more wood came down. The river had not reached this height in many years, and in violent rage it now lifted up and swept down into its bed the fallen and felled logs that, until now, had lain beyond its grasp. They had hardly managed to add on to the raft again when fresh logs coming down struck against it and completely tore it apart.

The river was still rising—in the last hours the men had stood up to their armpits in water. The table inside the cabin was covered with water and wife and children had to be brought up to the roof. The whole house trembled when single pieces of heavy wood banged against it. How long could it withstand the awful power of the waters? And what should become of them during the night—the terrible, long night?

The sun was already setting, and the unfortunates looked in despair out onto the wild current—their grave perhaps as soon as the next hour! A wilderness swollen with water surrounded them on *all* sides. Help was days away, and only one single canoe had come downstream at midday. But it kept to the other bank, did not heed their cries for help, and was so loaded with people that one could hardly see its rim above the water.

When that glided by, everything returned to mute silence.—Water fowl whirred past or drifted by in large flocks playing and dipping in the flood.— Those were the only living creatures they saw, and their demise seemed inevitable.

"Listen!" the woman suddenly cried and rose up halfway from her precarious seat. "What was that?"

"A steamer!" cried the man, who had listened to the sound for a moment in tormented suspense, "a steamer coming from up above! Thank God, eternal praise and thanks to God—it is our salvation!" Tears burst from the strong man's eyes.

The sound of puffing steam came nearer and nearer. One of the two boats really was coming down rapidly with the current, and now—now it shot out from the bend in the river up above. But it kept to the other side in order to stay away from the drifting wood as much as possible. In anxious haste the unfortunates, who all had taken refuge on the roof, waved cloths and everything else that they could quickly tear off their bodies, while Henderson pulled the shingles from the roof over the door and lifted out his rifle, which was still dry. The shot resounded across the fomenting river, and the imperiled family rejoiced: "Praise God! They've seen us!" The bow of the steamer turned toward them just as it reached the point opposite the cabin. The bell was sounded to signal that the steamer wanted to land, and the imperiled saw help before them in their direst need.

The steamer, which the Negro had recognized to be the *Blackhawk* just as soon as he heard it puffing,[2] crossed over sharply through the current toward them. But its larboard wheel was badly damaged by all the wood drifting in the river; moreover, the engine was not powerful enough to match the current. As the boat managed to make its way, keeping toward the left bank, the current suddenly pulled it a considerable distance downriver, so that farther below it had to swing its bow and stop.

Meanwhile, the unfortunates watched with painful anticipation the movements of the steamer rushing to their rescue. It had now, indeed, reached their bank, as much as the drifting wood allowed. As soon as it tried to push into this wood, however, it put its wheels in jeopardy to such an extent that the engine had to stop running again—and the boat drifted farther and farther downriver.

Now the boat captain tried to run his steamer along the outer side of the drifting logs, which formed a regular path about fifty feet wide. While the bow held sharply against the current, the captain called out something to the unfortunates from the hurricane deck—but they could not understand. Again, an ancient timber hit the log cabin with full force, and even if the cabin still held, the poor people could already sense by its slowly swaying movement that the water had begun to lift the rooms below.

Tirelessly and with all the steam it could muster, the valiant little boat worked against the current. If it succeeded in holding its own, it would only need to travel a piece up past the endangered house and could then easily reach the unfortunates. The steamer's wheels were rattling. The crew on board lugged wood as well as grease in order to create as much heat as possible, and they did everything they could to stem the current. The *Blackhawk* was able to accomplish that, but not an inch more. The boat kept in place for a whole hour, now gaining a few feet, only to be pushed back in the next minute by some piece of wood that got under a wheel.

Henderson, who was watching the boat's success with fevered anxiety, could, in the end, no longer delude himself about their fate. With iron calm he called his eldest boy over to him, gave him his money, which he had shoved into a water-tight powder horn, hung it around his neck, and ordered him to try to swim over to the steamer—in order to call the captain's attention to the terrible danger in which they found themselves. The boy could swim, and the Negro, who was at home in the water, was to accompany him. The woman did not want to let go of her child, but the boy, who hoped to bring swift aid to his parents, pleaded with her himself.

Thus, after a brief farewell the two young fellows started out on their dangerous route. First they jumped across the timber drifting closely together as well as they could. John was the first to lose his footing and disappeared under one of the slippery logs, but Jim, the Negro, was at his side in an instant, and both reemerged farther on out.

The people on board had seen the daring deed, and up front at the bow stood crewmen with ropes to throw to the swimmers. Ten minutes later both boys were on board—they were saved. But now the steamer had done all it could. The wood supply was almost used up, night stood at the door, and the spot where they could expect a safe landing place was still far away. The boy cried and implored that he could not allow his parents' demise; even the rough crewmen had tears in their eyes. But they could not do the impossible.

The boat kept farther out in the river, and the bell rang again—the funeral bell of the poor people waving their cloths in wild desperation from the house half-lifted by the flood. The captain turned away, and the pilot had already received the signal. The bow of the boat turned slowly from the shore, keeping downstream again. A few minutes later the steamer disappeared behind a bend in the river, puffing in the descending night.

That night the boat reached the little town of Natchitoches and here found another, more powerful steamer, the *Roaring River,* which had docked there until the first rush of the flood passed. But the captain of the *Blackhawk* did not rest until he had persuaded the captain of the *Roaring River* to bring about the rescue of the unfortunates, whom he had tried to save in vain.

The *Roaring River* immediately heated its boilers, took a fresh supply of wood, called its crew aboard, and left its secure landing place before daylight. John Henderson, quickened by renewed hope, was on board to point out precisely where their cabin stood. But only very slowly could the stalwart boat stem the dreadful current, and soon it was evening again before they reached the river bend that lay just below their house and that John knew exactly. The house had to be over there—they should have already been able to see it from where they were located. Farther and farther, the stalwart boat struggled upriver— now they could distinctly see the little clearing where the Hendersons lived— the pilot knew the place, too.

John already spied an old, half-dead sycamore from which he once had shot down a wild turkey. The cabin could not be more than twenty feet away from there.—The boy stared until his eyes filled and he began to get dizzy.—On the spot where his cabin had stood the red flood raged and fomented and forced its way into the anxiously swaying cane.

The captain stood next to him, and the boy, who now was pointing toward the spot with outstretched arms, sank to his knees and cried.

Slowly, the boat turned and headed back toward Natchitoches.

From *To America! A Book for the People* (1855)

THE MOUTH OF THE MISSISSIPPI

[Gerstäcker devotes two-thirds of the first volume of his novel of immigration to describing a diverse group of characters from different German states and illustrating the various reasons they leave their homeland and emigrate to America. At the end of a long voyage on the *Haidschnucke*, which is particularly arduous for the passengers in steerage, a young woman dies of fever just as land is finally in sight. All the passengers are sobered when the woman is buried at sea.][1]

The breeze became stronger, and soon the passengers had forgotten about everything else in anticipation of landing. The low riverbank, where still no mountains could be discovered, as much as people were on the lookout for them with eyes aided and unaided by telescopes, became ever more prominent. There the passengers could discern the entrance itself, where the mighty Mississippi flows into the Gulf of Mexico, and "sweet water" came toward them from the land they had longed for.—It was a river that soon would lovingly embrace them with both arms, and the sea, the wide, tedious sea, lay behind them like a heavy dream.

Even the cabin passengers now set out in earnest to pack their things and prepare for an imminent landing. The sailors, under the direction of the second mate, were busily clearing the two anchors that lay on the forecastle and lifting out the large, powerful chain from its dark bed link by link and laying it out on the deck.

"There comes our pilot!" the captain cried at this moment. He had taken the glass and for a few seconds looked over toward the land that still stretched out before them, not revealing a single hill or country house. Flat and bleak, the narrow strip extended along the horizon. Only in the direction toward which the captain was pointing could a small cloud of light smoke be detected. It first seemed to lie over the flat land, and then, when the passengers' gaze was more firmly fixed on it, it began to move and appeared to come nearer.

Meanwhile, Herr von Hopfgarten had quickly gone down to the cabin to tell the ladies that the pilot boat, for which they usually use steamer tugs in the mouths of the Mississippi, was in sight. The steerage passengers, who could tell by the activity on the quarterdeck that something unusual was happening, even if they could not make out *what*—climbed into the shrouds again and onto any high spots on board, following the direction of the captain's and all the cabin passengers' telescopes, hoping to discover whatever might come in sight.

But they were not to remain in doubt for long about the steamer, whose smoke they soon detected with the naked eye, for it was coming markedly closer. The outlines of the upper deck were clearly discernible, and soon individual figures on board could be distinguished. No sooner had the pilot greeted the Bremen flag waving from the *Haidschnucke*'s gaff with the American Stars and Stripes than shouts of joy broke out aboard the emigrants' ship.[2] A thundering "hurrah" resounded over and over again at the colors of the newly gained fatherland.

From now on they forgot everything else as they were swept up in the emotion of finally having reached their goal, which the American pilot steamer fully guaranteed. Everyone had eyes and thoughts only for the steamer rushing up. They already could hear the steamer's wheels churning their way across the Gulf's still water, and they could make out the individual sailors on board. The steamer finally reached them, circled tightly around them, and headed toward their side. When the American captain, who stood on his vessel's wheel case with the megaphone in his hand, shouted his call at them, the rejoicing broke out anew. The American, who put down his megaphone in astonishment, calmly looked at the screaming passengers for a few seconds then turned toward his helmsman and laughed. While both vessels ran alongside each other about one hundred feet apart, the sailors aboard the tug steamer felt obligated to respond to the greeting and answered with a mighty "hip hip hip hurray!" which, in turn, found its echo on the *Haidschnucke*.

No mutual understanding was remotely possible until the screaming subsided. Making use of the first pause, the American raised his megaphone to his lips again. The sea call, which certainly is incomprehensible to the layman at first and which becomes even more unclear by the peculiar, droning echo of the metal megaphone, resounded, "Where do you hail from?"[3]

"Where do you hail from!" the American's call resounded again. . . . Captain Siebelt managed to give the requisite answers to this as well as to subsequent questions, "How long the trip?"—"All well aboard?"

The puffing steamer now kept close to them, and sailors jumped aboard the *Haidschnucke* holding ropes ready to sling on board the tugboat, where they quickly were caught and fastened. The steerage passengers, who, of course, were standing in the way everywhere, were quickly pushed aside here and there. But today they did not care. They had survived ship life, and they easily could put up with a small bit of discomfort for which in a few hours—they no longer had to count the days—the entire American realm would compensate them.

The sailing ship lay tied fast to the much lower little steamer. It had never seemed so large to the passengers as at this moment. But all sails, their sheets loosened, beat against the spars, and the sailors hung from the ropes in order to tie them. Some sailors already climbed the steep rigging like cats and ran out on the spars in order to pull in the sails completely and fasten them to their timbers.

Meanwhile, the wind had gone to sleep completely, as seamen say, and the heat was humid and oppressive. Nonetheless, with the help of the steamer the ship continued its journey far more swiftly than it had sailed in the last few days. The coast, or at least what they had taken for solid land up to now, quickly came closer. But what had appeared to them to be a wide green meadow, on which they had looked—in vain, to be sure—for grazing herds, now turned out to be a wide, sorry marsh. The dirty yellow waters of the mighty Mississippi welled toward them, and the dark-green, slender reeds stood swaying in the strong current and formed the river's only bank below.

"That's America?" cried one of the women, who was standing up front on the forecastle along with the others. Up to that moment her glance was fixed anxiously and expectantly on the land that was coming nearer and nearer.— "Dear God, one can't even go to the shore." With expressions that were not as confident as they had been that morning, some of the other passengers now also gazed upon the desolate expanse of reed and water that surrounded them left and right. A confining, oppressive feeling seized them—the *first* dashed hope in the new land, that they had secretly, but all too eagerly, adorned with all the charms of the southern zones and that now opened before their eyes like an endless standing morass.

"But where, for heaven's sake, do the people live?" the others cried out— "One can't live here in water and reeds?"

Hesitant voices called and whispered in confusion, "There are houses— back there—where?—there, up along the dark-green strip where the sun is flashing on the water, up front to the right. Yes, indeed—there are houses— that's New Orleans!" Even Steinert suddenly had became unusually meek and sat on the bowsprit with his hands folded on his knees to observe the surrounding scenery in silence.

"That New Orleans?—nonsense," some of the sailors laughed. They had visited "the queen of the South"—as the Americans called New Orleans—once before. "This here is just one of the mouths of the Mississippi, and the houses there are the Balize. The high land lies farther up."

"*Farther up*"—that was a new ray of hope in the night of despair that threatened to seize the poor emigrants, "farther up." But they could still not see any mountains. The barren surface seemed to stretch out for many, many miles, and the muddy, grasping river rolled turbidly past them.

"There's a ship—there's another," was the call around the deck. Some pointed out their discovery to the others. "Ha, a whole lot are coming from up there—I can see the masts." The ships were coming from *up there*. Yes, *they* knew what it looked like up there. With a certain reverence the passengers' gaze hung on the faraway vessels, whose outlines they could not yet even distinguish clearly.

Some of the steerage passengers wanted the sailors, who had explained that they had been to New Orleans, to tell them more about the city and its surroundings before they reached the houses, which were becoming ever more distinct.[4] But the sailors were much too busy to be able to respond to their questions, and in the end the passengers had to be content with waiting to see the city for themselves. The wait could not last forever.

They were moving against the strong current rather slowly, leaving behind, now to the left, now to the right, in the bends of the river, the buildings that had already come in sight. Finally, they reached the spot where a number of wooden buildings stood on piles in the middle of this dreadful morass, connected by planks that had been placed high up and surrounded only by reeds and oozy water.

This pilot's village, the so-called Balize, was a sorry sight, and they could not understand how human beings could even exist here. In comparison with the bleak marsh that extended to the north, the east, and the west, the wide expanse of the sea itself soothed the eye. The passengers were alarmed when the bell of the steamboat rang, for now they feared what they had so ardently yearned for that morning—being set on shore. But the signal was intended for a sailing ship lying a bit farther up, which now hoisted its flag and, much to the delight of the emigrants, showed the colors of Hamburg.[5] There lay comrades—partially in travel and completely in sorrow. When the *Haidschnucke*, still waving the flag of Bremen, came closer to the Hamburg ship, it was greeted by the same thundering "hurrah" with which its passengers had just welcomed the American ship. To be sure, they answered the greeting but not nearly as robustly as they had in the morning.

The passengers also learned now that the steamer would tow the other German ship, too. They were not especially happy about that, for they feared, not without reason, that they would move away from this place more slowly. This hardly concerned the American boat, for, of course, it would not let the opportunity to earn twice as much for the same trip slip by. The steamer had indeed first brought the Hamburg ship, the *Orinoco,* here and put it to anchor to fetch a second ship from the Gulf before going up to New Orleans.

Meanwhile, the sailors of the Hamburg ship, singing a loud, rhythmic chant, had hauled up the anchor. The steamer ran up to the ship and took it on its other bow. The ropes were fastened, as they had previously been fastened to the *Haidschnucke,* and a few minutes later the small but powerful steamer puffed up the mighty river with its double burden, not much more slowly than before.

Now the steerage passengers of the *Haidschnucke* had nothing better to do than to hastily try to climb down from their ship, cross over the steamer, and climb aboard their compatriots' ship to meet its passengers. But their hopes were dashed, for not only did the helmsmen strictly forbid them from doing this; the watchmen on the steamer also had strict orders not to let anyone on deck or cross over, and neither pleas nor protests helped persuade the captains to change these regulations. The reason given was not only to prevent disorder but also to obey navigation laws, according to which there could be no communication with foreign ships before they had reached the harbor.

For quite some time now some of the passengers had discovered *trees,* real trees, ahead. For the only vegetation—aside from reeds and old waterlogged and sunken tree trunks—that they could see up to that point had been low willow shrubs. When they reached the trees, they also saw the first firm land projecting from the yellow water.

"There is land—there is land!" the people on the deck rejoiced, as if they had actually believed that America lay in water. "There are trees; there is grass. Hurray for America!" "Hurray for America!" the other ship responded, and the sailors on the steam tug had no objection to joining in the shouts of joy directed at their homeland.

It had become rather late in the day. Whereas both banks of the river had become firmer—they were covered with high trees and there were only occasional reedy patches—no human dwellings could be seen, with the exception of an unsightly little hut here and there. The land appeared to be an uninhabited wilderness that the passengers had populated with bears, panthers, and buffalo, and, in any case, the cultivated land lay still *farther up*. But now they encountered individual ships and twice even a regular little fleet being towed downstream by a single steamer, which was guiding a large ship on each side and towing three small ones attached by long lines behind. Small coastal vessels were also sailing and rowing on the river. Some small, brightly painted boats were manned by colored people and crossed back and forth over the "father of the waters."[6]

The sun was setting, and the briefness of the dusk that some passengers had already noticed at sea was even more noticeable here, where the shady foliage of the high trees was on their side. The sun had hardly disappeared behind the dark strip of forest that covered the opposite, rather far bank, when night fell with unexpected speed. They kept to the left bank of the river in order to load wood for the steamer, and the passengers already looked forward to stepping ashore and examining the marvelous vegetation of the new land. But they still had a long way to go before reaching the land when it already grew dark under the trees, and the light of the individual cabins that appeared hidden there sent their reddish glow across the river. Loading wood also proved difficult, since the steamer could not go very close to land with the deep ships, and the captains did not want to cast anchor. The owner of the wood was prepared for that and had already stacked up a number of cords in a low and very wide flat-bottomed boat. At the captain's call he traveled out a distance into the river and placed the boat straight across the steamer's bow. From here the firewood was quickly thrown aboard, while the engine began to work again and at least braced all four boats against the current. Then the *Haidschnucke*'s ropes were loosened so that the unloaded firewood boat could drift back between them with the current. The steamer tug slowly resumed its journey, keeping close to the middle of the river during the night.

It was a wonderful evening. When the passengers had traveled barely an hour, the moon rose over the trees and poured its silvery light onto the broad river. The passengers from the two ships had gathered at the front of the decks and alternately sang the songs of their homelands in full-toned, harmonic choruses. The songs' serious, melancholy themes resounding over the still river were wondrously moving.

Frau von Kaulitz had tried to get her usual game of whist together, but this evening she could not persuade even Herr von Benkendroff to participate. So, she was sitting alone in her cabin playing patience.[7] To her an evening without a card game was a lost evening. The rest of the passengers sat or stood around the quarterdeck in silent groups, or they whispered to one another in low voices. They were oddly stirred by the familiar sounds of their homeland, to which the heart is never closed—no matter how long ago it left the fatherland, even if it has almost forgotten it. The sounds that we knew and loved as children, that often took root in our infancy, have a unique magic. When we hear them again, they awaken old thoughts, lovely and sad memories, and even if the ear wished to shut out the sounds, the heart would still listen to them.

[Two young sisters discuss the power of these familiar songs and remember the people back home whom they associate with the melodies.]

The passengers of the *Haidschnucke* responded to the Hamburg passengers' last song with the song "Swiss Homesickness." Whereas up to that time the passengers of each ship had formed a kind of alternating chorus, with one group striking up only after the other had finished—and the tugboat crew listened to these songs in silence—the first tones of this dear old native song had hardly sounded when the ship from Hamburg also chimed in, and the full chorus softly and plaintively penetrated the night:

> Heart, my heart, why so sad,
> Why so many sighs of woe,
> Tis so lovely in the foreign land,
> Heart, my heart, why wish for more.

Hushed and still, the girls listened to the lovely, melancholy tones. Softly, softly, hardly moving their lips, they finally joined in with the melody, until they mustered up more courage and still with ardent feeling sang out loud. When the final line, "But it will never be a homeland," sounded, both choirs fell silent—a stillness came over the deck. After these verses no one had the heart to begin another, perhaps trivial song. Today they had greeted the new fatherland with a thunderous "hurrah" when they saw its flag waving in the breeze for the first time. To the old homeland they offered this song with many a covertly suppressed tear, with many a sigh held back forcibly in the breast.

NEW ORLEANS

The passengers of the *Haidschnucke* had been up early on the previous day to discover land.[8] Today they appeared on deck even more punctually, for what they had seen of the land yesterday evening had aroused their curiosity even more powerfully. Most of them climbed out of their hatch at daybreak, much to the seamen's annoyance, who had to swab down the deck especially clean and now found the passengers in the way everywhere. The sailors distributed many a pail of seawater among them with a well-aimed throw, wherever an excuse such as "didn't see" or "couldn't have known" made this possible. Many passengers were already in their best clothes, and some indeed regretted not having saved their "Sunday best" until the decisive moment, having sacrificed them a good twenty-four or more hours too early.

A thin, light fog lay on the water. It filled the riverbanks with a fine haze almost up to the treetops, thus demanding the pilots' undivided attention. As the sun rose higher and higher, however, the white vapors sank to the water like a veil. The poor sea-weary emigrants could hardly suppress a shout of joy when the most splendid, lovely landscape that they had ever imagined, adorned by strange vegetation, magically lay before their eyes.

The dark forest with its waving moss had disappeared or had at least been pushed back, way back, to a low strip on the horizon, to frame the picture that unrolled before their eyes and appeared to have suddenly emerged from the ground. Charming country houses with marvelously branched-out trees, with their dark roofs and white walls, with airy verandas and windows kept cool, peered through dense boskets of tulip trees and orange groves laden with fruit. Wide, regularly arranged rows of low but neat and entirely evenly built houses —the Negro houses belonging to the plantation—adjoined the country houses and separated them from wide, billowing fields of sugarcane and cotton. Gangs of busy Negroes in white outfits worked in the fields. Light, comfortable chaises clattered, and stately riders with broad-rimmed straw hats and thin, light summer clothes galloped up and down the broad street, which seemed to closely follow the riverbank.

The river was as animated as its banks. Masses of small sailboats glided back and forth to the sunny banks. Wide steamers puffed upriver, hauling the products of faraway regions' abundant land. Mighty sea ships lay anchored here and there along the banks. Often they were tied with ropes to some tree in order to take on board cotton bales stacked up high on the land and long, dark rows of sugar and syrup barrels and then to carry them up to the colder parts of the earth.

The brave little steamer chugged on past, towing the two colossuses against the mighty river. Often they brushed so closely against the bank that the passengers could hear the Negroes singing in the fields, and they made out the white women in airy dresses sitting on their flower-adorned verandas, looking at the river and the brisk life and activity around them.

The *Haidschnucke* passengers were beside themselves. As dejected as they had become at the monotonous sight of the flat stretch of marsh at the river's mouth, they now veered to the other extreme just as sharply. The people sang and danced and shouted and laughed and rejoiced like inmates just released from the insane asylum. One yelled to the other that over there lay the farms that they would move into now; there was the land that cost only one and a half dollars an acre. Some even spoke of having paper, pen, and ink brought to them right away to write home so that their entire village would cross the water immediately and take part in the splendor.

The Oldenburg farmers were the most high-spirited. Up front on the forecastle, where they were seated on the starboard anchor and repeatedly calling each other's attention to newly discovered splendors, their rejoicing finally broke out into a song that they had already sung on the Weser River on the first day then seemed to have forgotten completely. Its final verse, sung by the whole crowd as a chorus, was as follows:

> In America the peasants can ride in coa . . . ches,
> In coa . . . ches with silk and vel . . . vet.
> They eat meat three times a day with wine,
> And that is a splendid joy!⁹

They pronounced the word *coa . . . ches* so that the *oa* was completely separate from the *ch*, while they screamed the final word, *joy*, with all their might, perhaps thus to suggest the degree of bliss they felt.

The closer they approached the capital of Louisiana, New Orleans, the more lively the river became. The vessels that connected the individual small towns and plantations with the city became more numerous. Steam ferries crossed back and forth; a number of small sailboats brought the products from the country to the city. Everywhere along the riverbanks, on which lay charming plantation dwellings hidden amid blooming bushes and fruit trees, full ships, brigs, *barques*, and schooners lay anchored, the colorful flags fluttering in the wind. The last were manned mostly by Negroes and mulattoes.

But the boat chugged farther, ever farther. Here and there white masses of houses appeared through dark strips of evergreen magnolias and mighty cottonwood trees that extended to the riverbank. But that was still a long way from New Orleans. The villas grew into towns, and still they kept foaming past—up, up, the vast river. The river's currents carried powerful, bare tree trunks that it had torn from their beds up north and now brought down toward the Gulf stream, for thousands of miles, so that the Gulf would roll them over to the ocean and toward another part of the earth.

Thus, noon came and passed, while the passengers, who had been fully prepared for more than twenty-four hours, impatiently paced back and forth on the deck. They could hardly wait for the time when they would be allowed to step onto this wonderful land.

"There is New Orleans!" said the helmsman, who came toward the forecastle that was crowded with passengers to check the anchor and its fastening. He pointed to the right, where a wide, thin, almost spiderweb-like lattice of masts bordered the horizon.

"Where?—where?" called a jumbled mass of voices, and one voice inquired, "Over there, by the long palisade?"

The helmsman cast a pitying glance at him. Believing that he had given more than enough information, he stepped back down onto the deck to return to his post without answering any more of the thousands of questions directed his way. But the passengers needed no further instruction. As soon as their eyes became accustomed to distinguishing and recognizing faraway objects in their individual outlines, they themselves clearly and plainly made out the masts of countless ships and church towers and domes that stood out sharply against the pure blue horizon. Soon any remaining doubt that they were approaching their destination city dissipated.

From that moment on, however, all restraints were undone, and New Orleans—as well as the bustling, colorful life surrounding it—on which just a few minutes ago their gaze was fixed in mute astonishment, was forgotten. *To land*—every other thought died in that one overpowering feeling. Each individual steerage passenger now seemed especially and single-mindedly determined to block everyone else's way thoroughly by pulling ahead his trunks and other baggage, his crates and hat boxes, baskets and bedding, and to exacerbate the confusion that generally prevailed in steerage in any case. All the pilot's scolding and orders were in vain. In vain were the oaths and curses of the sailors, who bumped into and stumbled over the crates and chests that had been dragged on deck. The passengers acted as if they were afraid they would not be allowed to leave ship when they landed and were preparing everything for the most hasty flight. Finally, the captain went over to them, which he had not done even once during the entire trip, and explained that their being able to go ashore this night was very much in question. The public health officers in New Orleans would first visit the ship and then determine whether the passengers would be allowed to land immediately. He asked them not to block space and passageways everywhere, for the chances were ten to one that they would need both before they left the ship. No one believed him.

Meanwhile, the little steamer had valiantly stood firm against the current and brought its two ships noticeably closer to the appointed landing place. Higher and higher the masts projected out from the flat land and stretched out along the left bank in an immeasurable row. Huge blocks of houses that surrounded the forest of masts in closed rows came into sight. When the passengers looked up the river, the lower city limits were already directly opposite them, surrounded by ships anchored there as by a firm embankment.

Wild, brisk activity prevailed on the ship. Small groups had formed everywhere. They were astounded by and marveled at all the new things around them and with voice and gesture called each other's attention to every new curiosity that appeared. Like children, they laughed and rejoiced and stretched out their arms, as if they could hardly wait for the moment that would finally, finally, bring them in possession of all this splendor. Suddenly the steamer signaled with its bell. The ropes were thrown loose from both ships, and in the next moment the little black vessel, its waves foaming against its bow, slid ahead between the two colossuses it was guiding. Almost simultaneously, the sailors of the two German emigrant ships jumped forward to their anchors.

"Keep clear of the chain—get back—get out of the way!" the seamen yelled confusedly and rudely pushed aside those passengers who did not quite seem to understand that they were in the way or what they were supposed to do. "All clear—let go!" a voice shouted. Everyone else scattered when the anchor hit the water, and the chain rattled terribly as it raced after the anchor through the hawsehole. The chain, which immediately thereafter was wound around the capstan, shook the ship right down into its keel and—held.

The captain informed the restless passengers that the ship had to remain here until the health officers and police had been on board, which most likely would happen soon, and had granted them full freedom to go on land as quickly as they wished. There was nothing they could do about this, and at least the people now had time to observe their surroundings—which proved varied and colorful enough.

On the street that ran closely along the riverbank there was a swarm of people and wagons. Draymen brought down wares in two-wheeled carts, each pulled by one strong horse, in an almost continuous train. Large omnibuses drove up and down, setting off and taking in passengers on all corners. Negroes with heavy burdens on their shoulders hurried past or stood on the wharfs in laughing groups. Riders galloped down the street; small chaises and wagons crisscrossed back and forth. Negro women with baskets or large tin cans on their shoulders plied their wares from house to house, from ship to ship. And what about the loud, rhythmic chants over there? A gang of half-naked Negroes was loading a French ship with large barrels of sugar. A lead singer gave the beat and the rhythm. Six strong fellows ran with the gigantic rolling barrel down the high levee enclosing the riverbank to catch the barrel's momentum at the plank inclined up toward the ship. The Negroes danced and jumped around the barrel—keeping close to it, however, so that they could steer it back in place at the least deviation—and then threw their shoulders against it to roll it up the plank as quickly as it had gone down the levee by itself. The whole time they kept the beat of their melody and did not break it for a moment. The men were so nimble and the huge barrel appeared to move under their hands so easily that the work looked like play.

The river was crowded with vessels. Wherever the eye looked, there was a lively pushing and shoving of steamboats and sailboats and clumsy, wide rowboats and rafts that floated with the current toward plantations or towns situated farther downriver. What colossuses the river carried! The Germans had good reason to be astonished when wide steamboats came down the river. They looked like swimming mountains of piled-up cotton bales that reached from directly above the water's surface to where only two black, puffing smokestacks peeped out. Bales were stacked on bales as regularly as bricks in a wall. They extended from the edge of the lower deck so straight and steep that even the little pilot house that stood at the front of the highest deck just had a small opening to peer through. Cabins as well as steerage remained surrounded by an impenetrable wall of cotton. The harvest brought the bales down from the rich plantations of the southern states, from Tennessee and Arkansas, Mississippi and Louisiana, to be stowed into ships and sent around the world. After only a few days the huge boats would begin their return trip to the northern states, loaded with sea salt, rice, coffee, and the products from tropical lands, their salons and steerage filled with passengers.

But that was not the only thing. Directly toward them came a small, sharply built steamer, its lower deck loaded with cattle and sheep destined to supply the New Orleans market with fresh meat for a day. The steamer had set out last week from Pennsylvania, two thousand English miles away. The passengers of the *Haidschnucke* were at leisure to observe this boat, which ran past them closely. After a short distance it made for the land, set out its boat with four sailors and the helmsman in it, and then suddenly released the planks in the back part, or steerage deck, that had prevented the animals from jumping overboard. It did not take long before the agitated cattle began to shove and come closer and closer to the opening, or board, which still lay ten feet above the river's surface. Then a steer butted his horns against a comrade but was pressed back by him toward the edge of the boat. He slid over it with his back legs, and, bawling with fear, held on for a moment with his front legs before plunging headfirst down into the river. As he bobbed up and was blocked from going up-river by the boat that had been set out, he quickly headed for a piece of land between two ships anchored there. That was exactly the point where the fellows wanted him and where the buyers had already erected a small enclosure to receive the animals swimming to shore. Those who did not go willingly were thrown overboard one by one. When the last one had reached safety, the sheep herd followed en masse. The men only needed to throw the lead wether into the water, and the rest of the herd plunged head over heels after him.

This extraordinary show had so caught the passengers' attention that at first they did not even notice that a few fruit boats had come up to the ship and encircled it with their delicious load. Quite close to the front of one boat sat a sun-bronzed figure with a broad-brimmed straw hat, dressed only in shirt and pants, with a brightly colored silk handkerchief wrapped around his neck. In each hand he held a short, light oar with which he quickly and agilely propelled the tiny, slender vessel forward and guided it back and forth with only the slightest motion. From the middle of the boat back to its square stern the treasures of the tropics, as well as of this sunny land, lay piled up in charming abundance, ready to be enjoyed. A small capuchin monkey in the stern of one boat, a multicolored parrot in the stern of the other, appeared to serve as the backdrop to the enchanting scene. Fragrant pineapples with jagged green crowns, red-cheeked pomegranates, golden oranges, juicy peaches, coconuts in their brown shell, mealy bananas, along with northern apples and pears and plump grapes, covered with pomegranate and orange blossoms, were arranged in colorful, chaotic, but judicious confusion. The emigrants from steerage, accustomed to and tortured by salty fare, stretched their hands toward the treasures on display with all the more longing, since most of them did not have the wherewithal to take possession of them.

Small change!—Oh, whoever had small American or English coins to appropriate part of the riches below!—Just one single piece to refresh their parched gums! How they ran about pell-mell and searched in their pockets and wanted to borrow from each other, and no one had the common coin, as probably also had often happened in the old homeland! Here and there a Spanish dollar appeared. They *had* to buy fruit to properly celebrate their first landing. The steward was also sent down to buy an opulent and welcome desert for the cabin passengers' evening meal. The two Spaniards in the fruit boats did splendid business with the two German ships.

Finally, the public health boat arrived. After a very cursory inspection the ship was declared to be healthy, and in the name of the authorities the passengers were now permitted to go on land as soon as they wished or could. Meanwhile, evening had almost come, and the captain told the cabin passengers that he himself had to go ashore and would gladly take along those who wished to go. But he advised them to spend the night on board and then to disembark tomorrow in leisure and calm. Less fuss was made about the steerage passengers. They were simply informed that for today it was too late to put them ashore, and if they wished, they would be transported tomorrow morning at daybreak. Moreover, they could expect supper again this evening and breakfast tomorrow—and be guided by that.

ASHORE

It was still very early in the morning. Nevertheless the levee was swarming with busy people[10]—since in that warm climate almost all business is concluded in the morning. They were bustling about in great haste and paid scant attention to the new arrivals. Heavily laden two-wheeled and oddly built carts, each drawn by *one* strong horse, moved in an almost unbroken line toward the various ships or into the city. Unloaded carts, with their driver standing up front, quickly trotted back to fetch a new load. Small, one-horse milk carts, packed with a lot of tin cans, rattled over the pavement. Lovely mulatto and quadroon girls, slender and full-bodied, with elastic gaits, brightly colored cloths wrapped coquettishly around their hair, offered fruits and flowers. Men and boys carrying baskets and small glass cases strapped to them, in which a number of notions were on display, stood on the corners or wandered along the ships, offering their wares for sale with uncommon volubility, mostly in a horrid mixture of English-French or Jewish-German.

Then the stores; the oddly large signs with gigantic letters; the herds of cattle here on the outskirts of the city pushing their way through the hordes of people or were being pushed toward their destination—the slaughterhouse; numerous Negroes and mulattoes, mestizos, quadroons, with all imaginable shades from white and yellow to black and brown; the elegant cabriolets next to the dirty market wagons, which bring fruits and vegetables from the interior to the city. It was a confusion of things that the immigrants . . . had not enough eyes to see nor enough ears to hear. At first they went up the levee toward the actual city as if they were caught up in a wild, distorted dream. Pushed back and forth—for today they seemed to get in *everyone's* way—they finally remained standing where a number of men and women sat quietly next to stacked up crates and trunks,[11] hands in their lap, and let the hustle and bustle of the metropolis roll by.

THE RECONSTRUCTION PERIOD
Travel Sketches

When Gerstäcker returned to the United States in 1867 for the third time after an interval of seventeen years, it was part of a more extended journey through North America and the northern part of South America that he describes in the 1868 volume *New Travels through the United States, Mexico, Ecuador, the West Indies and Venezuela*. The highlights of the U.S. portion of the trip were his journey in William Tecumseh Sherman's private railway car to a council with the Indians in North Platte, where Gerstäcker observed negotiations concerning the construction of the North-Pacific railroad, and his final journey down the Mississippi on a steamboat to revisit familiar and well-loved places. As he headed deeper and deeper south, the effects of the Civil War and Reconstruction became ever more apparent.

Disappointment is not unexpected when a traveler returns to a previously cherished site, but Gerstäcker views change in the extreme. When he reaches Louisiana, Gerstäcker's dismay at the ravages of war and the Mississippi River on his beautiful plantation country is palpable. He finds it just that cruel slavery has been abolished and the arrogant planters punished, yet he is saddened by the disarray and devastation. Moreover, he is conflicted about the status of newly liberated blacks, worrying about their survival but alarmed that they were immediately granted privileges and responsibilities of [male] citizenship. Because one objective of Gerstäcker's travels was to assess and report on potential locations for German settlers, he adopts the perspective of the immigrant. Realizing that this will be his final trip to the United States, the country other than Germany in which he feels most at home, Gerstäcker ends his account of the U.S. portion of the trip by reflecting on the prospects of the United States and its people, including the German immigrants, and comparing them with the prospects of Germany and its people.[1]

From *New Travels through the United States, Mexico, Ecuador, the West Indies, and Venezuela* (1868)

TO LOUISIANA

[We pick up Gerstäcker's account of his travels in the United States as he lands in Bayou Sara to spend a few days in the area, where he had resided from 1842 to 1843.]

If you are familiar with the previous conditions of this area, you only need to set foot on land to get a true picture of the entire present-day state of affairs in the South in their necessarily harsh colors.

Pointe Coupée, that old French settlement situated on one of the most fertile and favored stretches of land, used to be a truly magical, beautiful place. The little town of Bayou Sara, which lies across from it, sustained such a lively traffic with the numerous plantations on the opposite bank that a steam ferry ran back and forth continuously.

We landed at the little town in the middle of the night by full moonlight. I remembered it as faithfully as if I had left it barely a week ago—but I did not recognize it. Isolated houses stood scattered about, and even if a bayou that resembled Bayou Sara flowed closely above it, I did not believe this could be the place.

"That's not Bayou Sara?" I said to the helmsman standing next to me. "I don't even want to go ashore here!"

"That's Bayou Sara," he replied dryly, "at least to the extent that they have reconstructed it. The whole town was burned down during the war."

"Set afire?"

"No—fired at. They wreaked havoc here. Well, you'll see for yourself."

There was no more time for conversation, for the steamer was approaching a little dock boat, from which a voice warned not to come too close because an ·old wreck lay below, and with the low river stage now, it could be dangerous for larger boats. So, our boat did not even dock. A small plank was shoved toward us, and as it continued swaying, we few remaining passengers had to get onto the dock boat as best we could.

We accomplished this, but up above I could no longer find my way around between the unfamiliar, newly built houses and the old ruins of single collapsed brick buildings. First of all, I inquired about a hotel where I could find lodging for the night. That turned out to be the Henrietta Hotel—a small wooden shack kept by a "colored lady"—where, despite the late hour, I at least found a decent bed.

The next morning I embarked on my excursion, first of all to look up a few old acquaintances from earlier times and to learn more about current conditions from them. The latter was hardly necessary, for the current conditions were everywhere apparent. Wherever you looked, you saw whites busy with some kind of work or standing behind their store counters, while the "colored gentlemen" appeared to look for and find their occupation in *dolce far niente* in front of the brandy stalls and on the street corner.

The entire little town appeared desolate and disorderly and made a sorry impression. The few people from the old days whom I managed to find matched the ruins around them in every respect. America—how I had looked forward to seeing this land again after such a long, long absence, to revel with old friends in old joys, in old memories—and now?

In the North, yes, there I actually succeeded. There they also had kept pace with the times, and the years of hard work did not remain unrewarded. Their circumstances improved, and they could look back on their careers with satisfaction. But that was not the case in the South, and I found Bayou Sara was really the saddest place of all. After a few hours there I already felt uncomfortable and went up to St. Francisville, where other acquaintances were still living.

There was at least one person who was really happy to see me again, even if the years had not passed without leaving a trace on his brow. He was the justice of the peace in St. Francisville, and we used to live together in Pointe Coupée.[2]

And where were the old friends up there?—dead and buried—died, either peacefully from yellow fever or ruined, gone insane, shot—who knows! Even the house in which I used to live was no longer standing and had been leveled to the ground.

Now I had the urge to go over to Pointe Coupée to visit the places where I had spent so many, many happy days. The residence had, to be sure, burned down, as I had already heard, but at least the garden was still standing and the old tree in which I had dreamed away many a wonderful night in my hammock.

I landed opposite Bayou Sara with the skiff, since the steam ferry now ran only once or twice a day at irregular times, but never for *one* miserable passenger. I landed at what used to be the Taylor plantation, one of the best kept along the entire Mississippi.[3] It had enormous sugarcane and cotton fields and large, serviceable, brick sugar houses. The place was now a wilderness.

The main house was dilapidated, the garden neglected and overgrown, the sugar buildings lay in ruins. The Union troops had burned them down, as the young boatman told me. Only half of the Negro cabins—which used to be painted white, each with a little garden—seemed habitable, and some of them were torn up to supply dry firewood for the rest.

A few dozen terribly dirty Negro men, women, and children of all colors lolled about their old dwellings, but one told me that the new owner had given them notice because he wanted to bring in his own workers, and they only were staying here until they found a new place. Almost all the Negroes had been born on this spot.

"And did they not plant any crops at all on the plantation this year?"

"Plant?" the Negro laughed. "There aren't ten fence posts left on the whole place, and they aren't even needed, for the pigs and cows won't eat the burdocks, the only crop that will grow now."

"No more fences?"

"Not a trace. They were used for firewood during the war, and whatever was not burned then was swept away by the flood afterward, when the Union troops broke through the levee above and released the Mississippi over us. Those were hard times, and we believed that we would all be swept away!"

I strode through the fallow, desolate fields up toward the levee, to the place where the Ferry Hotel used to stand. The old man was right. The fences that had surrounded the abundant sugarcane and cotton fields were gone. Burdocks were growing in the fields themselves, and coco grass, cultivation's wickedest enemy, was eating into them farther and farther. The entire plantation was a terribly sad sight, and I was happy when I finally recognized the high bushes that, as I knew from earlier days, enclosed the garden and grounds of the Ferry Hotel. I wasn't happy for long.

There I stood on the levee, opposite the Ferry Hotel—there was the garden railing and here was the path that went between it and the levee—but on the street itself lay a pile of burned bricks and a few other hewn stones that, as I well knew, used to hold the fireplace of the front parlor. No door led into the former garden, now a desolate place with only a few chinaberry trees that had grown wild,[4] and the one side gate was locked. Close by lived a Frenchman who kept a sorry-looking hotel. It was a gray board cabin with a few wooden partitions in which visitors could find lodging. I asked him to unlock the old place for me, and I must admit that I needed a good quarter of an hour to orient myself—no wonder!

The wild current of the Mississippi had torn into about one hundred feet of the riverbank. First it penetrated the levee and washed it away, and then it inundated half of the garden. My dear old tree had floated away years ago. They had to move the levee, which protected the land from floods, up into the garden, as well as the road, which now ran past the spot where the house used to stand. The house and its back buildings had disappeared. Only the old kitchen remained standing, but it appeared barely held together. The chimney must have been reconstructed somewhat later.

And all the pomegranate, orange, fig, and peach trees, the lovely tulip bushes that used to adorn the road? Fire had eaten away what the water left behind. I could not even see any stumps.

Slowly I walked out through the fields toward my old hunting grounds, where I so often hunted alligator and, in the spring and fall, snipe. The unmowed meadows were overgrown with high, yellow grass; the marshes were dried up by the long drought, so that the alligators had probably retreated to the Mississippi.

And farther up?

All the land lay fallow, for who would go to the trouble of cultivating it as long as the levees, which the Unionists had broken into and later were further destroyed by the floods, were not restored? The next high water would have destroyed any effort wasted on it.

The sun had already set before I traveled from Pointe Coupée back over to Bayou Sara. I was no longer surprised that the beautiful, open river on which the steamers always ran close by Pointe Coupée now formed a single, desolate, and washed-out-looking sandbank that extended halfway to Bayou Sara. It fitted into the entire picture and could not have been otherwise.

And is this the end of the beautiful southern land, the pride of the Union?

When I returned to America and in the northern states often heard some southern planters traveling through state, "We are completely ruined—the whole South is systematically broken and destroyed," I must admit that I took such talk to be gross exaggeration, or at least for the outbursts of utterly despondent hearts. I trusted in the tough American character that, knocked down ten times, always rises to the top again. I certainly believed that the South, no matter how hard and harshly it had been hit, surely would work its way back up in a few years and would get over its old wounds and turn them into scars.

This conviction already began to waver when I met many southern planters on the Mississippi and frequently, yes daily, heard them talk with each other. Now, with the Negro mess prevailing here, with the destroyed plantations, with the owners' broken hearts, I almost fear that the damage will be more difficult to repair than I myself believed.

Had the North been vanquished by the South—and the Union can thank God that this did not happen—then even if the northern farmers had lost everything in the war, they soon would have recuperated and been reinvigorated. They would still have their land—the enemy could not destroy that—and they had always relied on their own strength. But it is different with the South, which had depended not on its own but on the blacks' strength—and now, with one stroke, it stands with the ground torn from under its feet.

The southern "barons," as we may appropriately call them, used to form a very special class of the American population and were the true aristocracy of the entire country. The difference between them and the northern farmers is obvious in the inevitable effect the blow that destroyed all their property had on them.

Take the same case in Europe, or, even better, in Germany—a high, noble estate owner with great wealth and a banker who worked his way up from nothing to millions, for example. Let both become impoverished, and the former is completely and irretrievably ruined, for he has learned nothing but to live according to his estate and to consume that which he earned through the labor of others. He was generous and liberal and despised every petty advantage he might have gained. But that which otherwise constituted the noble aspect of his character now is his curse, for it prevents him, indeed makes it impossible for him, to begin anew by starting out small.

On the other hand, as soon as the banker has discovered his losses and seen the inevitable befall him, he does not lay his hands in his lap in despair but, rather, starts out again small, just as he had before. He knows quite well that his progress will be slow, but he does advance, and after many arduous years he regains an honorable position, while the nobleman is ruined.

The southern planter cannot work himself. He never learned to. Moreover, he held work itself to be something shameful for a white man—therefore his opposition to immigration. He did not want to tolerate any white workers around him; he was ashamed for them in front of his Negroes and prevented small farmers from settling in the southern states as much as it lay in his power. In fact, he achieved his goal for the most part, but this became his curse, since the black workers were taken away from him, and the only ones who could save his property from ruination, German settlers and tenant farmers, are nowhere to be found.

Instead, thousands of idle blacks are hanging around the plantations and the smaller and larger cities and are not yet ready for regular, steady work because it reminds them too much of the slavery that they barely have cast off. They no longer address each other with the familiar "boys" but, rather, with "gentlemen," for which even the crudest Negro now takes himself. They do not even notice that they share the same fate as their former masters—even if it is for quite different reasons.[5]

It is an undisputed fact recognized by all that the mortality rate among the Negroes has increased frightfully since their freedom. If nothing changes, the United States government will not have to worry about its "black brethren" before too many years pass. The cause is obvious. The Negroes were driven to hard work but were not exploited beyond their capacity in order to protect and maintain them for their masters. They got their regular meals and clothing and had no worries. For if they became ill, they had to be nursed, and when they got old, they also had to be fed until they died.

But now things are different, and God forbid that someone should think that I am speaking on behalf of slavery and defending it. It was the scourge and disgrace of the land. The trade in blacks alone was an atrocity that civilized nations ought not to have tolerated. But the abolition of slavery should have transpired in a different, more gradual fashion. The way it happened has not just ruined the former slaveholders and thousands of others, but, supported by the senseless legislation of the radicals, it also has led to the Negroes' destruction. Many, very many, will perish.

One cannot deny that the intellectual capacities of the black race are inferior to those of the whites. Time will tell what effect a proper education will have on the Negroes. Their character is by nature carefree, and this was reinforced by all the previous conditions. Then suddenly these words resounded in their ears: "You are free! You can no longer be separated from your family, never be sold and traded, and you have the same rights that the white race claims— but also the same duties. From now on you must fend for yourself and yours, and if you get old or sick or if you lack food and clothing, then no white person is bound to provide for you anymore."

The Negro does not understand that yet. He does work, but he squanders most of his earnings on the very same day, even if it is only to obtain a few superfluous pleasures of which he used to be deprived. The consequences were and are unavoidable. The past year was not particularly favorable for the cotton crop, the government's heavy tax still kept the impecunious blacks way down, and the little that they really earned was quickly scattered to the winds; indeed, most of them got into pressing debt.

What is going to happen in winter? The plantations are devastated. They don't need very many workers in the towns because everyone is economizing in these hard times and anxiously avoids having any unnecessary work done. Many Negroes lack the bare essentials and, of course, now resort to theft.

Many residents of Bayou Sara assured me that they did not lose one single animal during the entire war. Now there's always a cow missing, and they have to be careful to drive them from the marshes back into town if they do not wish to lose them all. It is the same with chickens and pigs, and it will get worse as soon as the blacks' need increases. That such laziness would set in for a few years was predictable and unavoidable, since a leap from slavery to the most complete freedom was bound to affect these people. That would have evened out after a short time, for even if they were free, the Negroes would have felt they were in an inferior position until they had worked their way out of it through education and intelligence.

In the last election in West Feliciana Parish forty-four of the forty-eight jurymen elected were colored—that is, only four whites out of forty-eight.[6] Apart from the fact that even a white who had never kept slaves and had agitated against slavery his entire life would find it unbearable to appear before a court constituted almost entirely of Negroes without the least education, what are the consequences for the Negroes themselves? Jurymen are never paid. It is an honorary position—one cannot, of course, make any exceptions for the Negroes. On what should the blacks and their families live if the man is carrying out his duty for weeks on end, that is, if he sits in the jury box racking his brains over things he does not understand?

They are going to elect judges who do not understand any more about the law than does a cow. Indeed, in the South they are even talking about putting up a Negro as vice presidential candidate during the next presidential election. Just imagine if the president were to die and a black moved into the White House! One of the most terrible revolutions that the world has ever seen would be the inevitable and immediate result of such an unheard-of case.

Over on Taylor's plantation, and probably on a thousand others like it, are the Negroes, who have been told to leave their old houses, since their labor is no longer needed and the property has now been transferred to other hands. They are without work, without money, and do not know what to do. Winter is at the door, they have conscientiously consumed whatever they earned—

perhaps even more—and they lack the independent character with which the backwoodsman, for example, can settle in the forest with only an axe and a rifle and forge a passable living from the wilderness.

In Bayou Sara itself—as small as the town is—you can see whole troops of blacks loitering in the streets and in front of the bars. What is to become of them?

In the beginning the Freedmen's Bureau supported even idle characters who for the moment could not or would not help themselves, but, of course, that had to come to an end. Here and there a single individual might swindle his way through by playing sick, but that will not work in the long run, since the people are already complaining about the enormous sums that this bureau costs (with a great deal of fraud, of course, on the part of individual civil servants).

The Negroes must soon learn to help themselves, and if they are not able to do that, they will perish. With the bitterness prevailing in the South they truly cannot hope that the whites will take pity on them. And if a different political party takes the helm, no one can predict the consequences.

But the southern planters have no more hope for themselves. They are completely broken in spirit and means, and it is up to a future generation to pull together the little that remains and to begin a new life with it. Yet how clearly everything is pointing to the only path they can take to become self-supporting again.

Up in St. Francisville I was speaking with an old southerner who also had lost almost everything in the war and had to struggle to start over little by little. He had a considerable business and recently started a small retail store and was grumbling bitterly about the Yankees. Then I pointed to the wares that filled his entire store from A to Z: iron and tin wares, wooden pails and brooms, onions and corn, smoked ham and tinned vegetables, trunks and boxes, guns and tools, medicines and patent elixirs, coffee mills and iron pots, calicos and woolen shirts, buttons and braces, shirting and silk, axes and saws. In short, everything that lay on the shelves, hung on the walls, or was strewn about the shop and everything that he himself had sold came from the northern, Yankee states, since the South had, up to now, produced nothing, absolutely nothing, but cotton, sugar, and rice. For everything else the cash traveled up North—it still travels there and makes the "enemies" wealthy.

I asked him whether it would not be better now to take up the battle with the North in an honorable and peaceful way and to try to live life differently. If, because of the lack of Negro labor, it was no longer feasible to plant large cotton crops, what would prevent the planters from growing their own grain and orchard fruits, to fatten their own pigs, and to become as independent as the northern farmer? Factories could be built everywhere; the forests were filled with splendid lumber; many southern states had iron ore—Arkansas, for example, has great quantities—and why could they themselves not process the cotton that they still grew and thus get a better price for it?

At first the old man appeared to be somewhat stunned and looked around his own store with astonishment. It had probably never occurred to him that he really had nothing in his establishment—except perhaps for the *sardines à l'huile*—that did not come from the states of the hated Yankees. Nevertheless, he shook his head and opined that it would not work. No southerner was suited for that, and they would rather begin a new life in an altogether different country that to continue the old life here under the laws of the hated Yankees, who had become absolutely arrogant.

He also confirmed what I had already heard from many others. An extensive emigration society had been founded to look for a different homeland, wherever that might be. They would even rather work under a monarchy than *this* republic. He spoke quite frankly about the new hope that had been awakened in the South after Maximilian's death, namely that France and Germany would take up the cause, while the northern states, of course, would have resisted such an intervention.[7] But then a war would be unavoidable, and I am firmly convinced that in this case the southern states would have joined forces with France against the North, even at the risk of being incorporated into the French Empire, along with Mexico.

Those were only dreams of mad politicians, though, but from the mouths of many planters themselves I know that such dreams existed. Just as I know that in Saxony there are a small number of crazy or at least short-sighted people who still would rather become French than "German" and stubbornly deny that Prussia is part of Germany, too.[8]

No one can tell, of course, what will happen here between now and the next presidential election, for the radicals are really going to extremes. But the South's strength is completely broken. No one thinks of resistance anymore, not even the young, otherwise hotheaded folk. With the military and the Negroes against them, they must acquiesce, and only in isolated cases does the bitterness vent in violence.

Thus, here in St. Francisville one of the most respected and wealthiest planters from Pointe Coupée, named Morgan, is sitting in jail. He shot a Negro in a rage and will probably have to face a jury of nothing but Negroes; it won't be possible to obtain a balanced mix. For that one would need six whites, and only four of the forty-eight jurors are of the Caucasian race. You can imagine that everyone is in a state of suspense about the result.

Nothing in Bayou Sara itself captivated me. With the exception of a brave old shoemaker by the name of Wölfling, the few Germans residing there—living cut off and isolated among Americans—had in those long years become completely ossified and did not want to know anything about Germany anymore. What did they care about Germany—what had Germany cared about them! New immigrants had joined them—a doctor, a pharmacist, a few Jewish peddlers—but they also looked new and lived in new houses, and I did not feel like making their acquaintance. So, I embarked on the first steamer, the *Abeona*,⁹ that docked there and went downstream toward New Orleans. On this horribly slow boat I at least had the opportunity to observe the banks on both sides of the river. They offered little consolation.

What a splendid view the charming plantations used to be, situated in the shade of chinaberry and orange trees, with ladies in their finery sitting on the verandas, half-concealed by flowers, with swinging hammocks and riders galloping down along the levee!

That is all past.

The slaves are, to be sure, free. The speculating Yankees—for they alone used to be the actual slave traders—can no longer stop at a plantation and fill the Negroes' hearts with fear and horror that the traders might buy a family and then separate its individual members and tear them apart. No cruel nigger driver's whip will splay the poor devils' backs, and the "southern lady" also has lost the power to pinch and tread on her female slaves. But all the poetry of this beautiful country has been annihilated along with it, and even if one could console oneself about it, one instinctively is sorry to see these destroyed sites, if only while traveling past.

The splendid plantation houses no longer seem to be inhabited; all the shutters are closed. Nowhere do the fields have fences, and the dark-brown burdock growth with which they are laden can be seen everywhere.

But the punishment for the arrogant cotton barons is perhaps all too just. They did not want to listen, and because they had complete power over their slaves, they thought they were almighty. That is past and the whip taken from their hand. But along with that not only their prosperity but also their self-confidence were destroyed. Whereas they previously did not want to permit any immigrant to settle among them, now they themselves are contemplating turning the rest of their property into cash and looking for a new fatherland.

Baton Rouge,[10] which we passed this morning, seems on the surface at least to have suffered little from the war. Only the large, splendid state house constructed of white stone was burned out in the interior and is still standing, as a ruin, of course. Who would have the money to restore it?[11]

The only thing that looks better is the Mississippi itself, whose water usually rolls toward the Gulf murky and yellow. The fantastically low water level of all the American rivers is the cause. It looks downright clear now, and the waters spraying up front on the bow are transparent. But it is still as wicked and treacherous as ever, washing under the banks and often tearing away entire acres of land at once. In exchange it deposits a sandbank on the opposite side, blocking the door of people who otherwise had a quite good river landing. Some layers of the flooded soil consist of sand, and it almost seems as if the river is secretly licking away at them under water until it washes out considerable terrain. Thus, below Plaquemine we found a spot where along four acres of land a hundred-foot-wide strip suddenly had fallen into the river in one fell swoop. The spot was uniformly deeper than the rest of the land, so that I could see quite well that the surface had collapsed into a complete void.[12]

Such landslides are extremely dangerous when they occur during a period of unusually high water and then take a piece of the levee with them. Now, with the weak labor force, it would not even be possible to repair the damage quickly, and the result would be the flooding of the interior land.

NEW ORLEANS

For my trip, by the way, I seemed to have chosen the most miserable steamboat that traveled the river. Moreover, the crate was towing a keelboat—it had lost another one along the way—and it almost crept behind the current. There was hardly anything to eat and nothing to drink on board, and it was dirtier than I had ever experienced on a Mississippi steamer.

I was quite happy when we finally reached New Orleans, even if it was a Sunday morning, since for an American Sunday is in and of itself boring. Besides, no store is open, and usually travelers do not even know where the private residences of the people whom they would like to visit are.

Even though I had been to New Orleans often during my previous stay, I did not recognize the city now and could not recall a single one of the brand-new houses on the landing. This was quite natural, as I learned later, for not only the houses on the present landing but also two streets behind it were entirely new and stood on land where steamers still docked in my day.

The city of New Orleans has remained only a little behind its northern sisters in growth and, at least until the war broke out, expanded enormously, even if now, of course, this has come to a standstill. But not just human strength and entrepreneurship played a role in this; nature and the never-resting Mississippi helped it along. The "father of waters" constantly changes its banks by washing under and tearing away one side and in return piling up a wide sandbank on the other. That was the case in New Orleans as well. The land was washed away from the opposite town of Algiers and thrown against the levee here—a fortunate circumstance that the city, of course, immediately exploited. It secured everything that it had received from the river with palisades and a strong dam, which simultaneously formed a comfortable wharf. There are enough examples that the old, fickle river sometimes simply demands such gifts back, and therefore it was quite advisable to put a check on such whims.

This created room along the river for several entirely new streets. At the same time, in the back of the city the swamp was drained and the remaining primeval forest uprooted, the soil excavated, and street after street built. Shortly before the war they even began to construct splendid, large houses, such as stand in large number in New York. But the war interrupted all this work, and now there is neither capital nor courage to execute more than is absolutely necessary. That remains for a more tranquil time.

Despite all that, New Orleans has improved in appearance. It used to consist almost exclusively of low houses, and if you stood on the levee, which protected the city from river floods, you could see the old St. Charles Hotel standing above all other buildings. The St. Charles Hotel later burned down and was rebuilt, probably just as high, but now it completely disappears among the neighboring buildings and no longer is a prominent point.[13]

The vegetation of New Orleans is almost tropical. Charming gardens surround nearly all the houses that are not in the immediate core of the city and its business district, for business does not combine well with pleasure. Everywhere, however, even close to Canal Street, where the most beautiful houses stand, the broad leaves of the bananas jut out over the garden walls or the dark, lovely magnolia foliage shades the houses. Indeed, here and there the feathered top of a rather high date palm rises over the roofs, and if you go to the edge of the suburbs, the eye is enchanted by whole groups of fruit-laden orange trees, which, along with the magnolias and bananas as well as the deciduous trees covered with the long, swaying gray moss make a truly charming picture. The summer is so warm and long that in protected areas even the bananas ripen but without producing a significant yield, for they require a more southern degree of latitude and can only reach complete maturation in the tropics.

That the main streets are replete with beautiful and opulent shops goes without saying, and streetcars run through the widespread city in all directions for the unusually moderate price of five cents per person.

New Orleans also has various theaters in the winter season—an English theater, a French opera, and a German theater. I often visited the last, which is under the direction of Ostermann.[14] It is serviceably built, and its interior is very charmingly as well as elegantly furnished. For America it could boast of a quite capable ensemble, and I saw several very successful productions of comedy and opera—especially of *Der Freischütz*[15]—with an overflowing house.

There is no lack of entertainment in New Orleans, for beside the theaters there are also Japanese acrobats, a circus, menageries, and various other spectacles. Here they are beyond the silly Sunday madness that haunts the more northern states under the bigots and can only be upheld in New England with force. According to the Sunday laws there, nothing but "pious" music may be played. How do they circumvent that? In St. Louis, for example, they perform every day. On the two Sundays I was there *Der Freischütz* was performed on one day and on the second the rather insipid Berlin farce *A Poor Devil*. Both times "sacred music" was printed in Latin letters above the usual German script, and that totally sufficed to assuage all doubts. Not a soul had "spiritual music" in mind; it also would not have been suitable to begin a Berlin farce with a chorale.

The Negroes now play a rather prominent role in New Orleans, and on Sunday evenings you notice the "colored ladies" especially promenading in the greatest pomp and finery. What enormous profits the crinoline factories must have gained through the freeing of the blacks, for who among the workers on a plantation would have thought about wearing a crinoline—and who does not wear one now!

The Negro men also are beginning to wear modern dress, but it does not suit them. The black coats fit them only up at the shoulders and hang down as if on a coat rack. The trousers are normally too long—which perhaps is intended to indicate sufficient means—and the white shirt collars and the ties clash. But those who are applying for a position must adopt the costume of the whites, and, of course, they look exactly as if in our country a peasant had been put into ball clothes. Thousands of such black idlers, however, loiter about the city and can only sustain themselves by exploiting the charity of the wealthy members of their race. The Negro is in fact kind toward people of his color and will not easily leave a needy person in the lurch.

You often find artisans among the blacks, especially smiths and carpenters, although they are actually more suited for the occupation of waiter and barber. Strangely enough, I, at least, have never encountered a black merchant or peddler. Trade seems to be their weak side, and perhaps they will work their way into it in the future.

There are lots of Germans in New Orleans, more than I had thought.[16] The most respected firms of the city are owned by Germans. The signs of German artisans and clothing stores run from one end to the other, and there are beer halls on every street. Even if they may have remained German in other respects, the German craftsmen have adopted American prices admirably. My bullet bag had been stolen from my berth on the steamboat to New Orleans, and I had to replace the items here. An upstanding German metalworker charged me 1½ dollars for an old bullet mold that he just bored out a little, 2½ for a screwdriver, 1½ for a scraper, 20 cents for a shutter—a bent little piece of lead—and 2½ dollars for cleaning and polishing the two barrels.

On top of that, the currency situation of New Orleans is the worst in the entire United States. The magistrate felt compelled to print banknotes of the city of New Orleans that only have their full value in single as well as in two- and three-dollar bills. The five- and ten-dollar notes are no longer accepted, or only with the surcharge of an enormous percentage, which, before I left, climbed to 20 percent for a twenty-dollar note. Nevertheless, the city pays all of its employees only in these notes, and recently a mass meeting—supervised by the military, of course—was held to force the magistrate to withdraw this money, which impedes more than promotes trade. That will be very difficult to carry out, for the "city fathers" enjoy considerable advantages through this manipulation, and why should they not steal, when everybody else is doing it?

On the whole, the prices for everything in the United States have risen madly—with the exception perhaps of the usual necessities like meat, flour, and potatoes. People can hardly afford luxury items anymore. The import taxes are enormously high, and, accordingly, the merchants also raise the prices for all domestic goods.

Alcoholic beverages and cigars especially are heavily taxed, so that a halfway decent cigar costs at least 140 thalers per thousand,[17] while a bottle of the vilest whiskey costs one dollar and a quite ordinary Pfalz wine two. Only very inferior French wine is rather inexpensive.

Normal life did not yet prevail in New Orleans, for this year the yellow fever had assumed a very malicious character and had intervened painfully in many—all too many—families. They weren't prepared for this at all, for there had been little of it since the war. It is possible that the city sanitation measures ordered by General Butler, which were carried out thoroughly, and the installation of new canals contributed much to eliminating the epidemic's greatest severity.[18] But if it had been mild since then, so that they hardly feared it, this time it bared its teeth all the more fiercely and also lasted for an unusually long time, into the month of November. Then it subsided. From the tenth to the twentieth of November you heard little about sick people, and mortality assumed its normal rate until suddenly—about the twenty-second—cholera appeared on the scene and replaced the yellow fever. Oddly, the colored people had suffered little or not at all from the yellow fever, but they were to pay for that now, and this awful epidemic of cholera swept through them wickedly.[19]

New Orleans is an unhealthy and dangerous hole, and even if it is surrounded by charming vegetation, I truly would not like to reside there. By the way this year various illnesses are more virulent everywhere. It is probably correct to attribute this severity to the unusually dry and barren season. The water level of the Mississippi this fall has not been as low since 1854. In the West all the mountain streams have dried up; in some places even the springs do not yield water; and wherever they install cisterns, these too are exhausted. This drought has completely dried out the Mississippi swamps as well as other western swamps. Even the alligators in many places have had to retreat to the father of waters, the Mississippi, to find the moisture they need. The vapors of these millions of acres from which the standing water gradually evaporated explains why even in the western forests the cold fever appeared with unusual fierceness and spared almost no cabin.[20]

With each year, by the way, yellow fever seems to take hold increasingly, even in the interior of the country. Who would have believed in earlier times that it could even go up as far as Vicksburg? This year it not only reached Memphis, Tennessee; in Louisiana it even penetrated the interior of the land and was truly virulent in some places.[21]

The world is getting better and better. Who used to know about yellow fever or cholera, of potato and grape blight, of trichinosis and other monstrosities! It really seems as if nature, angered that humans have penetrated so many of her secrets, throws ever newer difficulties in that race's path, to test its strength. If this continues, in one hundred years you will hardly be able to stand being on this earth!

While I was in New Orleans, the *Bavaria* lay down at the wharf—the first German steamship that started a new connection between Germany (Hamburg) and this southern city of the Union. Even the Americans were happy about this beautiful vessel, which ensures a rapid new trade route between Louisiana and Europe while at the same time eliminating a northern connection.[22] Shortly before the departure of the *Bavaria,* its captain and officers received me most cordially, and we spent a pleasurable evening on board. Representatives of the American and German press in New Orleans, as well as many of the city's merchants, also had been invited.

While putting to sea, the *Bavaria* sat on the bar of the Mississippi for several days. It was an ugly spot for sea traffic, for the channel was only eighteen feet deep, and the *Bavaria* drew a bit over nineteen feet at the stern. But the steamship did start to float again, and the shipping companies, which, like all of us, have to pay an apprentice fee for everything learned, now know that in future it will be more advantageous to load the ships with full cargo and only the minimum amount of coal, then take aboard more coal later in Key West or Havana, where the draught can no longer hurt them.

Steam! Everything is driven by steam nowadays, and you can see this most clearly on the Mississippi. Where are those peculiar crates, the flatboats—also called arks—that used to take up a considerable stretch along the landing of New Orleans? The steam on boats and railways has displaced them. Especially at low water levels, you do not see a single flatboat on the entire river. And yet I remember quite well the time when from aboard a Mississippi steamer I could count twenty and more at once, while at landings like Natchez, Vicksburg, and, in particular, New Orleans often lay hundreds in a row.

Now steam rules the world. A bit more or less freight no longer makes a difference—the cargo just must be transported rapidly. The flatboats, which went downstream slowly with the current and often had to lie to for days because of unfavorable winds, could not meet these demands, of course.

Adieu, then, New Orleans, with your sunny, fruit-laden gardens, your rows of stately ships and steamers, your splendid streets and stores and all of your population's striving and thriving! Adieu to you as well, great, lovely, and yet in some spots still bleeding land—adieu, for I probably will not set foot on you again. It almost pains me that I must take leave of you, for I have always cherished you in my heart fully and will truly never forget you.

The United States is, indeed, one of the most beautiful countries of the earth and is destined by nature to become the home of a great and mighty people. For a long time I had carried in my heart a yearning not only for my old friends but almost as much for the magnificent forests and rivers. After a long, long separation—the interval of a generation—this yearning pulled me back there, and I truly do not regret having visited and seen this beautiful country again. And did it correspond to the picture I had pieced together at home from memory?—Yes and no.

If I want to be honest, I must admit that when I was in Germany I believed that among these energetic people, the traces of the American Civil War would have been completely erased after four years, and hardly a sign of the terrible and violent upheaval would remain. As long as I was traveling in the North, this opinion was nowhere refuted. Everywhere the different cities' increasing prosperity and rapid growth revealed the mighty republic's wealth and enormous resources. Splendid new buildings surprised me wherever I went. Enormous undertakings like the Pacific railways, the Michigan Lake tunnel near Chicago, the Cincinnati bridge, testified to the people's unbroken entrepreneurial spirit, and new plans emerged everywhere.

But when I entered the South it was different—far different. All at once the conditions diverged so much—and the South compared so unfavorably to the North—that I could hardly conceive it to be one single country.

Missouri, which also used to be a slave state, could scarcely be counted as part of the South. Its climate also made it more a part of the North, for the most part. Because it was occupied by the northern troops right at the outset and was prevented from waging any war, it avoided the sad fate of its sister states. The decisive difference, in contrast, was already visible in Tennessee and Arkansas. The Negroes were vigorously protected by Freedmen's Bureaus, and troops of soldiers were everywhere. In Tennessee especially, I encountered tent encampments in many places. The horses were tethered next to them as if they were kept at the ready for service. Moreover, a rebellious, defiant spirit prevailed in the population, which often was vented against the hated "Yankees" in contemptuous satirical songs from the war.

And what was the government doing to soothe this spirit and to bring about a reconciliation between the two hostile brother lands? It pinched the South, which already tangibly was suffering competition from other parts of the world, with the most unjust of all taxes—the tax on a raw product, cotton. Besides that, by granting the Negroes the unconditional right to vote, the government subjected the South to the majority of the most despised of all races.

I myself would not object to the Negroes' right to vote. If they are supposed to become citizens of the United States, they must assume their rights. But it is completely unjust to suddenly grant more rights to these people, who have been raised in total ignorance, than are even granted to the free and educated immigrant. The immigrant is required to be in the country for five years before he can participate in the elections. In contrast, suffrage is thrown into the lap of the plantation Negro, who has been raised like a draft animal. This provokes not only the southerner to the most extreme resistance but also most grossly insults and injures the free immigrant.[23]

According to the present laws, the Negro sees himself suddenly placed far higher and more favorably than all the immigrants, even those who have been raised in this country but not born here. For as a native the Negro can be elected president, which, according to the Constitution, is impossible for the foreigner not born here.

The right to vote must be granted to the Negro in the future. But could this not take place in a rational and gradual fashion, so that the blacks are subject to a census that makes their intellectual capacity, as well as certain means, the indispensable stipulation for voting? Through this one would achieve a twofold goal. First of all, it would ensure that only people who really understand what rights and duties they are carrying out would be allowed to vote. Second, the Negro would be forced in a reasonable and intelligent way to work, to strive for a position that is both independent and free of worry.[24]

What is the result of these violent measures now? The Negroes are driven to vote by ambitious, or, rather, victory-seeking agents and office chasers. They do not regard the act of voting to be an honorable admission of their human rights—no, only a defiant demonstration against the whites. They did not need to earn the right for themselves; it was given them. The Freedmen's Bureaus supported their old people and orphans, and now they have complete license to laze about in front of the bars in the cities and to steal the day from the good Lord. They never learned to worry about the future; they do not even know what such worry is, for in the old days their masters were obligated to assume it for them. Should they now begin, when they do not have the least goal in life except for filling their bellies? They don't even think about it, and the result is that many who really are in need prefer stealing over work and become vagabonds. One cannot think ill of them for that because they never knew the concept of property. They did not even own themselves, their wives, or their children. While a price could be put on the slaves, their owners intentionally or thoughtlessly neglected the opportunity to teach them to appreciate the value of property and thus took more away from them than they gave—all higher striving to become true human beings.

And can you blame the Negro for stealing?—He is not so stupid that he does not see what is going on around him. Where the whites give him such a good example, you can hardly reproach him for following it.

The difference between the North and the South with respect to progress in recent years may be great, but the businesses that have been ruined in the North as well as in the South are similar. The stores in the city are almost empty. The numerous cotton presses that are dispersed along the entire levee stand idle, with a few exceptions. Even the steam tugs complain that they have no business. Only the beer halls and bars are flourishing, for in bad times these are frequented the most.

Who can say how long this condition will last? For now there appear to be few prospects for change, and young tradesmen should think twice before emigrating here, for at present it is especially difficult for them to acquire a position. But the Negroes are thriving, and it is really comical to observe the dignity with which the fat old Negro women rustle about in the streets and treat each other with the greatest respect. You really hear only the most high-flown expressions: "Gentlemen . . . ladies . . . Miss Lucy, how are you? . . . How do you feel, Mr. Jefferson?" They also have gained social equality or have pushed their way into it. The most raggedy, repulsive Negro, with an odor that could pollute an entire neighborhood, sits in the streetcars for his five cents next to the finest, most dressed-up lady. Even the youth have risen to become newspaper boys, among whom Negroes never were tolerated before. On the whole you cannot avoid them. According to a silent agreement, they are put into the first car of the railroad trains. Despite their right to vote, they are not tolerated in the cabins of the steamboats, and even the white firemen and deckhands on board the Mississippi steamers eat their noonday meal on separate cotton bales.

On the whole the Negroes deserve credit for conducting themselves modestly vis-à-vis the whites. There are, to be sure, exceptions. For example, on a steamboat a pair of "Colored Ladies" wanted to force their way into the cabin and pressed suit when the captain turned them back. But the court rejected their suit, since the judge decided that every citizen was free to deny another entry into his house or his boat.[25] The same thing happened in a coffeehouse in New Orleans. But these are isolated cases, and almost everywhere the Negroes frequent their own places.

The southern states are still under military occupation. But you must not imagine it to be like in Europe, where the country is flooded with military personnel. Only here and there small troops are posted in different stations or under tents, thus intentionally avoiding every unnecessary demonstration. What purpose would that serve? The people know that Uncle Sam is in charge, and disobeying his orders would not help them. But the South is not thinking of a new war because it senses well enough that its strength is completely broken, its means are exhausted, and such an undertaking would be hopeless. To be sure, the South hopes that the time for revenge will come and for now only bows its head to power under duress. But it does not believe that time is near.

In conclusion, I would also like to refute an idea that I have heard expressed over and over again in Germany, which nevertheless is as erroneous as can be. There are people there who maintain that as a result of the enormous emigration from Germany, the German element in America already has achieved dominance or with time must and will reach it. That is pure fantasy.

It is true that the German is now respected more in America than before, and various powerful factors have worked together toward this. First of all, the year 1848 drove a good bit of intellectual power over to America. What was taken away from *us* at home was to the good of this country. Then in the last American war the Germans remained faithful to the Union, and German blood fertilized the soil next to American blood. Recently, Bismarck's politics and the bravery of the Prussian troops also have contributed to increasing respect for the Germans—no, actually to creating it. It is an old story that a people can only make a claim on respect if they not only show the power that resides in them but also know how to use it.[26] Since this time the American papers are beginning to take notice of Germany. Where they used to make fun of the "Bund,"[27] which had become ridiculous, they are beginning to see that Germany has a voice, and not the most insignificant one, in the European concert and has completely ceased dancing to the French fife.

All that, however, is still far from helping the Germans achieve predominance in America, and just one glance at the country—if we want to see— quickly teaches us otherwise.

In South America, among the enervated Spanish and Portuguese population, especially, such a mass German immigration as there has been to North America could have a noticeable influence and even a positive effect on Germany, if German governments would relinquish the petty opinion that every emigration is a personal insult. They break with every emigrant completely; indeed, they force emigrants to renounce their old fatherland and to become citizens of the foreign land. The German remains a German amid the Romanic race, and in Brazil the grandchildren of the German immigrants still cling to their mother tongue. Even the German peasant feels superior to the native, not only in his capacity for work but also in intelligence, and Germany need not fear any competition from there for centuries to come.

This is different, far different, in North America.

As strange as it may sound, it is actually the street youth who nip in the bud the German element, indeed every foreign element, because they tolerate no other language but the American. At home the parents may speak as much German with their children as they wish, but as soon as the children associate with American children outside of the home, they are ridiculed and laughed at. The natural consequence of this is that the children refrain from speaking German and try in every way possible to look like true Americans. The children soon succeed, and the boy born there is completely and inescapably absorbed into American life. Many, all too many, of the parents try to do the same—of course, not with the same success. We can only hope now that with the changed political conditions at home, they will also cease to be ashamed of their old fatherland, as they all too frequently used to be, unfortunately often with good reason.

But that is the most that we can expect. Their fatherland views them as foreigners, as deserters, and therefore you can hardly expect them to cherish a special affection for the governments there. If they still regard themselves as Germans, then that is only in memory of the homeland—not of the conditions there. They have ceased being Germans in the political sense. Now, having been almost forcibly chased out of their homeland, they use the strength that would have been a blessing and an advantage for the homeland to help lift their new fatherland and make it great. But they are not even thinking of a German oligarchy, which, in fact, exists only in the heads of a few dreamers.

Therefore, we should not view this enormous emigration to North America with indifferent glances, for besides depriving Germany of the most industrious workers, we Germans are not just making America more powerful with every year, but in the course of time we are creating significant competition for ourselves at home.

No one in the world surpasses the American in entrepreneurial spirit; it can only be approximated. The country's resources and wealth are inexhaustible, and the only thing the American lacks in his constant striving is the steady, patient diligence that the German possesses to a high degree. The American could not have wished for a better population for farming and crafts. That this need was met gave him a free hand for everything else. The American has demonstrated and continues to demonstrate whatever else he is able to accomplish with the help of German intellectual vigor. The consequences are inevitable, and the time will come when German industry will lose the American market entirely because, in America, German industriousness found a completely free and unrestricted field for its activity and could develop its abilities there. But the German will never achieve true supremacy in America and, as stated, is not even striving for that.

But my time here is over—down below on the river lies the little vessel that will take me over to Mexico, which has achieved such sad fame. In a few days I will be rocking out there on the lovely blue Gulf to a new world that is still completely foreign to me.

THE RECONSTRUCTION PERIOD
Fiction

Postwar New Orleans is again a site in Gerstäcker's novel *In America: A Picture of American Life in Recent Times* (1872), the sequel to his novel of immigration *To America! A Book for the People* (1855). This novel traces the fate of the German immigrants who, in the first book, landed at the port of New Orleans. It opens at the very end of the Civil War, as Sherman's troops invade Georgia just in time to save a black preacher from being lynched.

In the following chapters, set in New Orleans, Gerstäcker treats Reconstruction from the points of view of a German traveler, the white planters, and the newly liberated blacks. The traveler who comes to young Hebe's rescue will, at the end of the novel, become engaged to this former slave with the intention of taking her back to Germany. The angry planters gathered in the St. Charles Hotel, where they used to reside in luxury while their slaves were auctioned off in the rotunda, are at odds about their future. The older generation wants to export their former way of life to a new country, while the younger generation plans to avenge their losses by forming the Ku Klux Klan. Clearly, the antebellum period is over. Perhaps this is why Gerstäcker shifts from the plantation setting of his earlier fiction to the urban setting when he treats issues concerning the former slaves. His portrayal of the newly liberated blacks' insistence on their right to public accommodations—to ride in streetcars and be served in pubs—is based on actual demonstrations. Indeed, these protests foreshadow the continuing struggle of the Civil Rights movement in the twentieth century.

From *In America*

A Picture of American Life in Recent Times
(The Sequel to *To America!*) (1872)

NEW ORLEANS

In the St. Charles Hotel, in the wide, airy restaurant of the ground-floor rooms, were assembled not only a large number of planters from the *area* but also many from the neighboring states, from Mississippi and Alabama as well as Arkansas, to deliberate what measures should be taken after their defeat by the North. Only when several *unknown* guests entered the establishment, whom they did not wish to have as an audience, did they retire to one of the upper salons, which the hotelkeeper gladly put at their disposal. The majority of the gentlemen were good and old clients, who used to come down to New Orleans frequently during the year. Their peak season, however, was when they sold their cotton, when they not only received considerable sums of money for the cotton delivered but also purchased their yearly supplies and sundries for themselves and for the Negroes. Then, of course, they ran up a considerable bill in the hotel. At that time the champagne flowed as freely as did their slaves' sweat outside under the glowing rays of the sun, and for eight to fourteen days the "gentlemen" led a life of complete license.

Today a more serious purpose called them to the main city of the state. They had not gathered for their annual celebration but to discuss their misfortune, their decline. Moreover, they wanted to consider measures they could take to escape the unbearable pressure of the northern states and to found a free realm for themselves. Freedom—to be sure—only in *their* sense of the word: to keep the slaves in their bondage and to feed solely on their labor.

Speculative heads had devised a plan to buy a stretch of land in the Yucatan from the Mexican government, which also could grant them sovereign rights. They hoped at least that the Mexican government would enter into such an agreement. They wanted to elect delegates who would inspect the land there and determine the place for the colony.

It was a very select gathering that had come together in the St. Charles Hotel today, but the almost wanton gaiety that usually characterized gatherings similar to this one in the cotton season was absent. The gentlemen felt the seriousness of their situation. With the ground pulled out from under their feet, they seemed to have an iron-fisted determination to establish a new livelihood all over again. The luxurious life of power that they had indulged in to excess had ended in horror. Now they stood there like a carpenter without tools, like a banker without capital, left to their own resources and the little that remained. Many of them had so lost their heads that they already saw themselves starving to death.

Not only the elder planters had come to this meeting; their sons were also present and seemed almost more interested than their fathers. They, in particular, had been completely cut off from the future. They had painted such a rosy picture of it, and now a life of hard work lay ahead, whereas they had dreamed only of pleasure and profusion.—Emigrate? To a country where there were no slaves?—To them it was a terrible thought. And what were they supposed to do there? Till the fields themselves? Ridiculous—for those who had kept their own valets, who did not even all know how to saddle their own horses. But they had to and wanted to know at least what the "old men" intended so that they could take steps accordingly. They did not even believe in the possibility of a law that would take away their property, the slaves, with one blow. Yes, the Yankees had decreed that, and for the moment they had the upper hand. But would they be able to carry it out? Never! And equality of the niggers with the whites—nonsense! What judge in all of Louisiana or one of the other southern states would ever have permitted one of them to testify against a white person.

They all felt subjected to the weapons of the North, but they also felt obstinate and defiant. The young folk especially were bent but not broken. Instead of considering acquiescence in the new circumstances, where open resistance would have been foolhardy, they racked their brains about new ways and means to work against the most recent legislation and—even if they had no power over the niggers—at least not concede to them even an inch of rights that the favored white caste might claim.

The old planters, who knew the country better than their sons and understood that a further struggle was useless and hopeless, shook their heads about this and only let the young folk go on because they themselves had enough to think about. They were pretty much in agreement *that* they wanted to emigrate, but *where to* still remained an open question. While some suggested the Yucatan and others preferred northern Brazil, a not insignificant number declared they wanted to go to Havana, where, first of all, there were slaves and then, with a good new supply of compatriots, they perhaps could win the whole island for themselves. They finally decided to send two delegates to the Yucatan as well as to Havana, for in both countries they would be closer to the States than in faraway Brazil, where there was almost no contact. They also would be able to return more easily should more favorable conditions set in again.

"Damned if I'll leave the country!" a young man whispered to one of his friends. "How the Yankees would laugh if we all were to leave like cowards and afterward they could do what they wished with our estates."

"But what other choice do we have?"

"To make life sour for them wherever we have a chance," the first hissed through his teeth. "At least in Tennessee we are determined to yield to force only one step at a time. We are sure that our judges will support us."[1]

"But how?"

"You know the old fraternity of the Ku Klux Klan, don't you?"

"Bah! That's had its day," said his friend. "We have to bring something similar but *new* into being."

"The old will do, if we can revive it. Today I received letters. In Mississippi, South Carolina, yes, even in Georgia, they're seething and boiling. It goes without saying that the Louisiana boys won't be left behind. I myself have already joined, and when the old men are finished later and have gone, then *we* will take charge of the negotiations."

"And are you thoroughly familiar with the Ku Klux Klan statutes?"

"Not exactly, but we are going to establish a fraternity that will draft its own constitution and laws and uphold it with life and limb. No one can testify against an ally in court, or he will be outlawed and fall under his brethren's knives or revolvers. Every oath that he swears is justified if it is done to protect our alliance or to overtake traitors."

"And what will we accomplish with this?"

"Within a short time the entire South will join this alliance, and then just let the North try to enforce its mad laws here."

"They will set new armies on us."

"Against whom? Is there an army they can fight? Not a single soldier. They will not find a visible enemy anywhere, while they know what convictions each citizen cherishes. But we must be united, and then let the niggers dare to cast a vote, or to run for public office. We'll pursue them on the open street with dogs. As for those white people who are not on our side, it would be better for them if they had never even seen *our* states."

"But that is foolhardy, Red," his friend said. "Surely you know that many planters have not offered their plantations for sale—for who buys such large tracts of land now?—but, rather, they want to divide them up in order to attract northern settlers down here."

"And *who* among us is doing that?" Ned cried vehemently. "Only cowards and deserters of the cause. What do *they* care about the land, if only they can bring their own hide to safety? Are we supposed to make allowances for *them*?

And if some damned abolitionist buys *our* land here and wants to move onto it, he'll find out soon enough that he's made a bad mistake. If we're not supposed to keep the Negroes as our property anymore, why, then, we'll make it so hot for them here in the South that they'll thank their God if they escape alive."

"That's always dangerous," his friend said, shaking his head. "It *can* go well, but it can also take a bad turn, and then we'll really pull the shorter straw."

"Bah, humbug!" laughed the young man. "We'll grind them down until they are happy if we come to an agreement with them. Put on the same level as a *nigger?* Damned if I'll ever bow down to one!"

The older gentlemen regarded the matter more calmly. They understood that they could not continue to live in the States as they had before. But they also knew, with better insight than the young folk, that they never could recapture their lost position with force. Since they did not believe that they would ever come to terms with the new conditions, they saw emigration to a neighboring country to be their only salvation. From there they intended to pave the way for better days by becoming firmly established and gradually winning the upper hand. If they succeeded in adopting slavery there, they would receive ample reinforcement from the southern states. Just as they were feeling the abolitionists' pressure bearing down on them from the North, they could then exert a powerful counterforce from the South.

Down the wide, magnificent Canal Street, which had a double track in the middle for the streetcar, a rather sparsely populated car was rolling out in the direction of Lake Ponchartrain. Just four young men, belonging to the upper classes, and an elderly lady were sitting in it. Three of the men were Americans, and acquaintances as well, for they conversed with one another in hushed tones. The fourth was a foreigner. He did not associate with the others and was sitting by himself in one corner of the car.

The driver outside reigned in the horses. In the allée next to the tracks stood a young girl, hardly past childhood but of wondrous beauty—slender, with blonde hair and blue eyes. She wanted to board the streetcar with the old Negro who accompanied her.

The car stopped. "By thunder, that is a marvelously pretty girl!" one of the Americans whispered to his friends.

"But a nigger,"[2] the second man said, so loudly that the young child must have heard it. "I know her. She belonged to Owen Carr and now wants to play the lady."[3]

"Hold on there, my fellow!" called one American, who had let the girl pass but stepped toward the old Negro, who was about to follow her. "See that you get out right now, or I'll throw you out head first. Stop, driver! A nigger wants to ride along. Damned if that will do!"

"But, Massa," the old man cried in fright, "I belong to Miss there."

"You may belong to whomever you wish but not together in a car with white people." With that he seized the old fellow and was about to push him out of the car without any further ado.

"Oh, let's get out again, Uncle Pitt!" pleaded the young girl, who was hardly more than fifteen, at most sixteen, years old, pushing her way back toward the exit.

"Stay here, pretty child," the two other Americans laughed, holding her by the arms. "Just leave the old nigger. We'll see that you get home safely."

"Please, let me out.—Oh, please, let me out!"

"Massa!" the old Negro shouted, resisting the young man's grasp. The young man's arms seemed to be made of iron. "I now have the same right to be here as you do.—I am a free man and no nigger."

"Animal!" the American shouted at him. "You dare lay a hand on a white man?" And he threw himself at him with full force.

The old man was not standing firmly on the threshold of the car. As he took half a step back, he slipped and lost his footing. But he held on all the more tightly to his attacker's collar. As he fell, he pulled the man around, bringing him under him, so that the attacker hit the track first and broke the old man's fall. The young man hit his head against the iron rail. Crazed with pain and rage, he pulled himself up—for the Negro now let go of him as well—and pulled out a revolver from under his vest. In the next moment—the whole thing hardly took a few seconds—the shot resounded through the street.
"Let me out!" the girl cried, deathly afraid.

"You can't do anything about it—forward, driver!" shouted one American.

"Gentlemen, with your permission," said the young foreigner, who had stood up and gone toward the back. "Allow me, Miss, to accompany you out." Calmly but very firmly releasing the young man's arm, with a look that indicated clearly enough that he meant business, he led the child out.

"Go ahead!" called the conductor, who was standing out back and gave the signal to continue. He had seen the shot that caused the Negro to collapse and fall on his face and did not want anything further to do with the matter. The murderer, in fear of being called to account, forcefully threw himself back into the car, as the driver urged on his horses. But before they could get the car going, the young foreigner succeeded in taking his charge to the side steps. Jumping down, he took hold of the girl and lifted her down to the tracks, while the vehicle began to move forward. Thus, a few seconds later the streetcar was already rolling rapidly down the street, and the young man was standing with the girl next to the old Negro's body in the midst of a crowd of people pressing toward them. They had heard the shot and had probably seen the struggle as well and now would gladly witness the outcome.

"Oh my God! Oh my God!" cried the poor young girl, throwing herself upon the old Negro's corpse.—"Uncle Pitt! Uncle Pitt, did you leave me? Dear, good man, have they shot you dead? Oh, and only for my sake, because I became weak and could walk no farther.—Oh, Uncle Pitt, Uncle Pitt, don't be angry with me—I would rather have died for you myself—what in the world should I do *now*? Oh, take your Hebe with you!"

Meanwhile, the young foreigner had examined the man who had been shot, but there was no need for a long investigation. The bullet must have gone straight through his heart, for his pulse had stopped beating immediately.

"Where is your home, Miss?"

The young girl did not even hear the question, and he had to repeat it two or three times. Finally, she said softly and sadly: "*My* home? It was with the old man—now I no longer have a home except for the grave."

The young foreigner looked around.—A cab was just coming along on the nearby carriage road, and he waved at the driver to stop.

"I have a murdered man here and a young girl who wants to go home."

"Aye, sir!" said the man. "Need to call the police first—always want to have the first word."

"The police won't care much about the man," said the foreigner. "He's a Negro."

"A nigger?" cried the cab driver and threw his nose in the air in disdain. "Drive neither dead nor live niggers, sir," and, giving his horse a lash, he drove it up the street.

The young foreigner followed him with his eyes, cursing under his breath—but what could he do? He could call five or six cabs and would receive the same reply from all of them! *Nigger!* The most wretched Irishman, who had sunk far below the animals through booze,[4] would consider himself too good to take a "Negro" home on his wagon, and his only hope now was to find a few colored people who would get the murdered man off the street.

A large crowd of people had gathered around the corpse, which had to be taken off the tracks, since another streetcar was rolling along the same route again, and the connection could not be interrupted. The people stood around the corpse timidly, whispering to each other about what it meant that a *white* lady was grieving over a *nigger*. The way she lay bent over the murdered man made it impossible to recognize her for a former slave.

Meanwhile, the police from a nearby station had noticed the situation. Several constables approached, turned to the foreigner, who had just returned and was trying to persuade the young girl to get up and not attract any more attention.

"Who killed the Negro?"

"An American whom I do not know. He escaped in the streetcar that passed by before this one. There were three men in the car and an old lady."

"Were you a witness?"

"Yes—I was in the car and jumped out to help the unfortunate girl here, who came accompanied by the dead man and wanted to board."

"Does she belong to him?"

"It appears so. You see her sorrow."

"You don't know her?"

"No."

"You will have to come along to the police station to give your statement for the record."

"If you require it, with pleasure. But what is to become of the young lady?"

"We will request that she come along."

The policeman seemed experienced in such matters. He quickly spied a few Negroes, whom he probably knew, and assigned them the task of taking the murdered man's corpse to the nearest police station. Then he hailed a cab. Even though it took some effort to get the young girl to separate herself from the dead man, the friendly words of the foreigner, who called the girl's attention to how many people already had gathered around, finally persuaded her. He told her the policeman required this, in any case, and she could not disobey him.

The second policeman had already taken a different cab in order to pursue the identified streetcar as quickly as possible and find the actual murderer. Of course, much time had already passed, and the criminal had enough time to get off at some street and disappear into the maze of country homes and gardens there.

Having arrived at the police station, where soon afterward the two bearers entered with "Uncle Pitt's" body, Hebe—as the unfortunate young girl was called—she had no other name—had to make a statement for the record and thereby tell her life story.

It was a simple but gripping picture of the conditions that the curse of slavery had created. Thousand and thousands of unfortunate beings had perished or, kept down spiritually as well as physically, spent their lives in servitude.

Hebe did not even know *where* she had been born and only vaguely remembered a woman who had taken care of her and probably was her mother. Then suddenly this woman no longer came to her, and an old Negro woman took over her care. She died as well, but by now Hebe herself was grown up enough to take on light household duties. That was in the house of a rich planter—Mr. Owen Carr—on Lake Ponchartrain. Blushing blood red, the poor child related that, as she grew up, her stay in that house was a torment, until suddenly the news came that *all* slaves were free and could not be detained by their masters. She fled the house, and an old free Negro whom she knew, that unfortunate Uncle Pitt, took her into his home. He lived on a side street a short distance from here. Today she had been in the city with him to be registered under a specific name, according to the new law. Along the way the heat had made her weak and half-faint. They had wanted to take the horse-pulled streetcar, and then the terrible thing happened. The kind old man, who had taken her in like a child—with whom alone she had sought refuge and found protection—was murdered.

"Did you know the man who did it?"

"No.—He simply could not tolerate a Negro boarding the streetcar."

"Would you recognize him again?"

She did not know. His back was turned to her.

"It wasn't *this* gentleman?"

"Oh, no. Truly not." This gentleman had just helped her to leave the streetcar after the shot had already been fired, while the others had wanted to hold her back.

"Did the dead man have a family?"

"Yes—his wife is still alive, and even her old mother lived with him." The old woman had also been freed, for when she became too old to work, Uncle Pitt asked to take her in and care for her if her previous owner would write her a letter of manumission, which he did gladly. Then the owner would no longer have to provide for her. That was all he gave her for lifelong faithful service.

At that time the courts in the southern states were in a difficult position. The sudden change from slavery to freedom for the colored race had happened too quickly to familiarize them with their rights as well as their duties. But their former masters also could not or would not yet comprehend that they had to relinquish the privileges they had inherited from their forefathers and comply

with the new laws. In a word, everything still was too new—nothing was reg-
ulated yet, and it was difficult always to intervene at the right time and in the
right way. Moreover, many of the northern civil servants still sympathized with
the South. Even in the northern states people had been taught from their youth
on that the Negroes, or *niggers* as they generally were called with contempt,
were an utterly inferior human race—indeed, they were closer to animals than
to humans. Not only the planters, who were motivated by-self interest, no, even
some blockheaded German "scholars," denied that the Negroes had human
emotions. And the southern clergymen used the Bible—from which, as we all
know, *everything* can be proven—to demonstrate that God himself had instituted and approved of slavery.

According to the men's opinion, then, nothing could be done in this case,
especially since the guilty party could not even be found afterward. In order to
avoid unpleasant discussions the three young men had left the streetcar along
the way. How would it be possible to find them again in the immense city, especially since there was no certain plaintiff? A Negro was shot dead in the
street—that was a fact. The coroner confirmed that the "Negro's" cause of
death was a shot in the chest—that was all. Then the Negro was taken out and
buried—not for his sake but for the sake of the local authorities. The murderer
could not be found, and the matter was settled.

And Hebe? The court had heard everything from her that she knew—she
was free to go. But when she stumbled out of the police station the young foreigner followed her, took her arm without any further ado, although at first she
shyly pulled away, and said sincerely, "Don't be afraid, Miss, I am not a southerner, not even an American. I come from far across the sea, where we have condemned slavery for a long time and even fought bravely to banish it from this
beautiful and otherwise free country. You can trust me to accompany you
home."

"I am a nigger, sir," said the poor creature in a severely bitter tone. "Leave
me. From now on I *must* find my way alone, in any case."

"You won't impress me whether you call yourself a nigger or not," the foreigner said good-naturedly. "I won't leave you now until I know that you are
back home safely—where is it?"

"*My* home?" the poor child said sadly. "When Uncle Pitt was still alive, it was
with him, but his wife is old and poor.—He could earn money, but she can't
anymore, and I must see where I can find shelter now—preferably out in potter's field, next to Uncle Pitt," she added softly and shyly.

"And would you be willing to take a position with a *foreign* family?" When he saw her look up at him timidly and almost fearfully, he quickly added, "With people who don't share the local prejudices and will treat you well?"

Hebe slowly turned away as if she were thinking over his suggestion. Then in a timorous, soft voice she finally said, "Who would have me? But—I'll help myself. Even if I am not accustomed to hard work, I still can do it. I'll find work in the city—I don't want anything for nothing, for free."

"That would not be the case," said the young foreigner. "But don't you have any possessions? No clothes or linens?"

"Possessions!" the girl sighed bitterly. "A few weeks ago I myself was a possession and could call nothing my own. What could I have taken along when I left my former master's house? Uncle Pitt borrowed whatever I needed from the poor woman."

"Poor child," said the young man. "Absolutely cast out into the world in such young years! But I do want to see whether some good people might not take you in. Let me go to your house with you now, to the unfortunate old man's house. You still have the difficult task of telling the poor woman the sad news and of comforting her."

The girl still gazed up at him shyly.

"You are not an American?" she finally asked. "Your accent sounds different."

"No. I am a German."

"Uncle Pitt always told me that the Germans treated the Negroes much better than did the Americans. Oh, if you are not afraid of Negroes and would come along to the poor old woman's house! I am so frightened of going to her by myself and telling her the terrible news."

"I will go with you, dear child."

"And Uncle Pitt? What will become of the poor old man!"

"The police knew him and will take care of everything. I promise you that he will have a proper burial. Did the murdered man live far from here?"

"No, not far. But will nothing at all happen to the murderer? Will he go unpunished for taking a human life?"

The young German shrugged his shoulders. "I almost fear that the police will not go to any great pains to find him," he replied. "Unruly conditions still prevail here, my poor child. But a better day is dawning for all of you. Just as the North has won and secured your freedom, you all must continue to build upon it. The children of your race are now allowed to attend schools and develop into capable people. In time the curse of your race will die out, and a new life will begin."

"When we are lying in the grave—" the young girl said gloomily. "But we're here at Uncle Pitt's house. Would that the next hour were over!"

THE MEETING

Meanwhile, there was a wild scene out on Canal Street and at the streetcar, for news of the vile murder had spread like wildfire among the colored population, who were enraged by the cause of this bloody dispute.[5]

They had shot a Negro because he had dared to board a streetcar.—Had not the laws of the United States made them equal to the whites in every respect? Did the whites want to begin oppressing them again?

The Negroes—strong, dark figures—gathered on all the public squares. Many of them still kept their weapons hidden under their jackets; others wore their revolvers and knives boldly and openly in their belts. Threatening words were spoken, and the whites, who had already heard about the cause of these gatherings, timidly retreated into the side streets.

Various old Negroes took the greatest pains to calm the rising storm. They saw that nothing good could come of it. They just should be patient for a little while. The elders warned that one first should know exactly who began the quarrel, how it had been conducted, and who was at fault. But Uncle Pitt was too well known in New Orleans and was such a well-respected person among the Negroes for those who were already stirred up to have any doubt that the old man had been shamefully and wantonly murdered. As the throng grew, they rolled down toward the streetcar tracks, with only the vague feeling for the present that they no longer would tolerate any oppression and were ready to confront it.

Having arrived there, however, they decided to take the various streetcars to show the whites that no one had the right to make them get out as long as they had paid the fare. They quickly filled and overfilled the two streetcars coming from different directions. The few unfortunate white passengers who happened to be inside thanked God when they finally worked their way to the door and could get out. Of course, no one thought of resisting the dark, threatening band.

At first things went no further than this demonstration. The people merely had wanted to prove that they were allowed to ride in the streetcars as much as the "buckras" and had made their point. Heated by this sense of victory, however, they decided to have a drink and chose for this purpose a very large café on the street that was mostly frequented by planters. The innkeeper, a Frenchman, was foolish enough to deny them entry.

"Boys!" he shouted at them, when he saw them approaching his establishment, and stepped into the doorway with his waiters. "Not in here. Over there you will find refreshment—not here for colored people."

"What is he saying?" called those who came after and had not understood the words but probably noticed that he did not want to let them in. "Whack the damn Frenchman on the head!"

But those up front were less embittered by the denial of entry than by the way he addressed them. "Boys"—that's what they used to be called when they stood under the overseer's whip. Now they had become gentlemen, as the old colored ladies reminded them over and over again every day. A white person had just as little right to call them "boys" as to whip them. Moreover, this was a public establishment where one could get food and drink in exchange for money. Why did the foreigner, the Frenchman, want to turn away those who had been born in this country?

"Hello, gentlemen!" cried the group's spokesman, a tall, big-boned, full-blooded Negro. "Are there any boys here? Here all are gentlemen—colored gentlemen—understood?" With that he pushed just a bit against the Frenchman's chest, so that the man reeled back a few steps.

"Shentelmen!" the Frenchman cried, somewhat intimidated by the fellows' decisive appearance. Up until now he had been accustomed to them obeying his every word, and woe to anyone who had not done that.—"This is no place for colored shentelmen, this—."

"Oh, bite the dust!" cried another, broad-shouldered mulatto. He threw the Frenchmen to the ground like a sack and, followed by the others, pushed his way into the hall. Now the waiters, mostly mulattoes, wanted to turn the intruders out. Most of them had been free Negroes. They were annoyed that these people of their own race—"plantation Negroes" to boot, as they called the lowest class of colored and whom they themselves probably called "niggers"—behaved so impudently. It would have been better had the waiters refrained from doing so, for this aggravated the confrontation, and things now turned nasty. Had they let them have their way, the Negroes would in any case have streamed in, spread themselves out at the tables imperiously—as did the *white* gentlemen—and would have paid for their drinks. They wanted nothing more than to secure their rights and their equality with the whites. But now the affair assumed a different character. Blood had flowed, the crowd was agitated and excited, and the subservient spirits inside the café all too soon regretted not having received their fellow men in a more friendly manner.

As the crowd pressed through the doorway, they sent those few who still tried to block their way flying into the corners. All the chairs were smashed in no time, and the chair legs made excellent weapons. The throng's loud, neighing "ha ha ha" reverberated through the room. Then one of them propped his arm up on the bar and flew over it in one leap. Imitating a waiter—he himself had been one before—he said with the friendliest expression in the world, "Gentlemen, what will it be? Bordeaux, champagne, brandy, whiskey, cocktail, mint julep?"

"Champagne," the crowd roared. "Champagne and brandy! Hurray for Endymion!"

Their comrade's name was indeed Endymion, and there was, perhaps, no more dissolute face in all of the southern states of America, even if his thick, nappy wool was trimmed almost foppishly. Because he was drinking quite consciously, he could not serve the rest fast enough, and soon others assisted him The *white* guests quickly left the café through the back door to avoid any clash with the "niggers." In less than ten minutes the whole splendid café was swarming with jubilant Negroes, who plundered the supplies and smashed bottles and glasses in mad high spirits. They knew their host to be a resolute foe of the Negroes and had long planned on paying his establishment a call because he allowed no colored people to enter his place as guests.

Outside the noise in the streets continued. A dangerous element had been stirred up. The "niggers" who were not working at all in this first period of Reconstruction camped in and in front of the bars of the city. As long as the little bit of money they had managed to save earlier under the most unfavorable circumstances lasted, they led a completely disorderly life before they began thinking of new resources. But they still had no taste for work—they had had too much of that—and burglaries were an everyday occurrence, especially in those times. At every moment all the idle people were ready to rush any place where something out of the ordinary was going on—thus, the long days passed pleasantly for them. In barely an hour thousands had gathered in that district, initiating ever greater mischief and threatening civil unrest.

Meanwhile—and it had taken long enough—the police were summoned and the military called in. Up the wide Canal Street the troops were gathering to advance slowly from there and clear the way. The nearest Negroes yielded willingly. They had not come here with any particular purpose in mind and had no thought of defying the authorities. They just wanted to preserve their rights, and the most sober among them believed they had achieved their goal and offered no resistance. Matters were different as the police advanced toward the coffeehouse, from which the Frenchman rushed toward them and announced with the most furious gestures that the Negroes had plundered his whole establishment. That was not the case, but the swarm of men had seized the drinks and treated themselves better than most likely was good for them. Nevertheless, the matter would have run its course without any further bloodshed had there been a calm request to leave. But the whites, too, were now provoked, and the police boldly apprehended a few of the loudest fellows in the crowd to arrest them and make them responsible for the damage.

Of course, Endymion was among them, but he had no intention of surrendering of his own free will. The Negro possessed truly enormous strength. Two fellows seized him simultaneously, and quick as lightning he took them by the throats with both hands and, despite their resistance, banged their heads together with such force that they collapsed unconscious and lay on the floor as if they were dead.

That was the signal to attack.—Shots fell, knives were pulled, and angular chair legs were smashed down on unfortunate heads. Since the Negroes themselves pushed their way out into the open, the battle moved to the street and lasted until a larger military force moved in and the "colored people" took flight in all directions. It was high time that this happened, for in the more remote parts of the city the rumor was already spreading that a battle between the black and white races had broken out. Negroes as well as mulattoes—armed for the most part—flocked around to join members of their race. Then God have mercy on New Orleans should the "niggers" win! But now the reinforcements came too late: the actual battlefield was already cleared. Yet it had still cost enough blood, and the better-armed white troops especially, supported by citizens, had killed a considerable number of "niggers." The white population was so agitated that they saw the specter of a Negro revolution before their eyes. On this evening no colored person could have let himself be seen on the street, for without a doubt he would have been slaughtered.

Notes

Introduction

1. Peter J. Brenner observes that the political oppression and the social upheaval and impoverishment caused by the industrial revolution that Gerstäcker registers precisely in his works were not the motivating factors behind his own flight from Germany. Rather, he resisted the quotidian relationships of ordinary bourgeois life. *Reisen in die neue Welt: Die Erfahrung Nordamerikas in deutschen Reise- und Auswandererberichten des 19. Jahrhunderts* (Tübingen: Niemeyer, 1991), 162.

2. Gerstäcker sometimes adds a consonant to the proper noun. For example, in letters to Adolph Hermann Schulz he addresses his friend as Herrmann. Friedrich Gerstäcker, *Mein lieber Herzensfreund! Briefe an seinen Freund Adolph Hermann Schultz, 1835–1854,* ed. Thomas Ostwald (Braunschweig: Friedrich-Gerstäcker-Gesellschaft e. V., 1982). The documents concerning the purchase and sale of the property on which the Ferry Hotel was located are signed "Charles Roetken." Conveyance Records, Pointe Coupée Parish Clerk of Court (1839, entry no. 2043; 1841, entry no. 2455). I will retain Gerstäcker's spelling, "Roettken," in his own writings.

3. I have been unable to establish Korn's first name. Gerstäcker usually refers to men by their surnames only.

4. Scholars have not been able to locate any excerpts in *Rosen,* for copies of the issues of this period are not extant. Thomas Ostwald, chairman of the Friedrich Gerstäcker Society and Gerstäcker's biographer, bibliographer, and editor of republished volumes, told me that he considers this story to be apocryphal. Jeffery L. Sammons believes there is no reason to doubt this claim, in *Ideology, Mimesis, Fantasy: Charles Sealsfield, Friedrich Gerstäcker, Karl May, and Other German Novelists of America* (Chapel Hill: University of North Carolina Press, 1998), 115. Because of Gerstäcker's customary veracity, I would agree.

5. *Streif- und Jagdzüge durch die Vereinigten Staaten Nordamerikas,* 2 vols. (Dresden: Arnold, 1944). The first edition of this travel book was translated anonymously as *Wild Sports in the Far West* (London: Routledge, 1854). It was reprinted with introduction and notes by Edna L. Steeves and Harrison R. Steeves (Durham, N.C.: Duke University Press, 1968). James William Miller has edited and translated Gerstäcker's account of his experiences in Arkansas in *In the Arkansas Backwoods: Tales and Sketches by Friedrich Gerstäcker* (Columbia: University of Missouri Press, 1991).

6. *Die Regulatoren in Arkansas: Aus dem Waldleben Amerikas,* 3 vols. (Leipzig: Otto Wigand, 1846). "Regulators" were vigilantes.

7. *Die Flußpiraten des Mississippi* (Leipzig: Costenoble, 1848).

8. For example, in his introduction to a collection of Gerstäcker's short stories entitled *Amerikanisches Sklavenleben* (Slave Life in America) H. M. states that Gerstäcker's stories were popular in the nineteenth century because they satisfied the cosmopolitan tendencies of the Germans and their preference for the strange and exotic (Berlin: Hermann Hilger, 1930).

9. Letter from Capt. D. Haye to Friedrich Gerstäcker, written in 1857. GII 23, no. 61, Stadtarchiv Braunschweig.

10. *Friedrich Gerstäcker der Weitgereiste. Ein Lebensbild.* Introduced to the German youth by August Carl (Gera, Ger.: Issleiss und Rietzschel, 1873). Travel books for juveniles were popular pedagogical material in the last quarter of the nineteenth century.

11. Friedrich Gerstäcker, typescript copy of "Tagebuch 2," GIX 23:19a, transcribed by Herr Poetsch, sen., Gerstäcker Papers, Stadtarchiv Braunschweig.

12. Friedrich Gerstäcker, typescript copy of "Tagebuch 3," GIX 23:20a, transcribed by Herr Poetsch, sen., Gerstäcker Papers, Stadtarchiv Braunschweig. My translation.

13. *Mein lieber Herzensfreund!* 194.

14. Letter headed "Cincinnati, 16th November, 1838, State of Ohio," *Mein lieber Herzensfreund!* 199–213.

15. *Mein lieber Herzensfreund!* 226–29.

16. Cited in Thomas Ostwald, *Friedrich Gerstäcker: Leben und Werk,* with a bibliographical appendix by Armin Stöckert (Braunschweig: A. Graff, 1976), 21.

17. Friedrich Gerstäcker, *Neue Reisen durch die Vereinigten Staaten, Mexiko, Ecuador, Westindien und Venezuela,* vol. 13, 2d ser., of *Gesammelte Schriften von Friedrich Gerstäcker* (Jena: Costenoble, 1872), 162.

18. Vol. 18 of *Gesammelte Schriften.*

19. *Mississippi-Bilder: Licht- und Schattenseiten transatlantischen Lebens,* vol. 10 of *Gesammelte Schriften.*

20. *Nach Amerika! Ein Volksbuch,* vols. 11–12 of *Gesammelte Schriften. In Amerika: Amerikanisches Lebensbild aus neuer Zeit,* vol. 19, 2d ser., of *Gesammelte Schriften.*

21. See, for example, the nineteenth-century historian Charles Gayarré's romantic descriptions of the early expeditions. *History of Louisiana,* vol. 1: *The French Domination,* 4th ed. (1903; rpt., New Orleans: Pelican, 1965); Álvar Núñez Cabeza de Vaga's account of the futile struggle to enter the Mississippi mouth in 1528, in *Louisiana Sojourns: Traveler's Tales and Literary Journeys,* ed. Frank de Caro, with Rosan Jordan (Baton Rouge: Louisiana State University Press, 1998), 14–15; *Iberville's Gulf Journals,* ed. and trans. Richebourg Gaillard McWilliams, intro. Tennant S. Mc Williams (University: University of Alabama Press, 1981); Pierre H. Boulle, "Some Eighteenth-Century French Views on Louisiana," in *French Louisiana: A Commemoration of the French Revolution Bicentennial,* ed. Robert B. Holtman and Glenn R. Conrad (Lafayette: Center for Louisiana Studies, 1989).

22. See, for example, *A Bibliography of Fiction by Louisianians and on Louisiana Subjects,* ed. Lizzie Carter McVoy and Ruth Bates Campbell (Baton Rouge: Louisiana State University Press, 1935); and Suzanne Disheroon-Green, "Romanticizing a Different Lost Cause: Regional Identities in Louisiana and the Bayou Country," in *A Companion to the Regional Literatures of America,* ed. Charles L. Crow (Malden, Mass.: Blackwell, 2003), 306–23.

23. Travel literature was one of the most popular genres in German literature among writers, publishers, and readers during the period 1815–48. Beyond its general function to teach, to inform, and to acculturate, it served specific political and social purposes in a transitional period marked in German lands by the struggle between reactionary, conservative forces and liberal, progressive forces. Wulf Wülfing, "Reiseliteratur und Realitäten im Vormärz," in *Reise und soziale Realität am Endes des 18. Jahrhunderts,"* ed. Wolfgang Griep and Hans-Wolf Jäger (Hei-

delberg: Carl Winter, 1983), 371; "Reiseliteratur," in *Vormärz: Biedermeier, Junges Deutschland, Demokraten, 1815–1848*, ed. Bernd Witte, vol. 6 of *Deutsche Literatur: Eine Sozialgeschichte*, ed. Horst Albert Glaser (Reinbek bei Hamburg: Rowohlt, 1980), 180–94. Recent scholarship emphasizes that the mentalities shaping travel literature, and specifically literature on North America, may be regressive (the search for a prelapsarian paradise) or progressive (the desire to confront the political, social, economic, and material dimensions of modernization). Peter J. Brenner, *Reisen in die Neue Welt: Die Erfahrung Nordamerikas in deutschen Reise- und Auswandererberichten des 19. Jahrhunderts* (Tübingen: Niemeyer, 1991). Wynfried Kriegleder is persuaded by this argument, although he faults Brenner for not clearly distinguishing that the requirements of genre—"fiction" or "texts laying claim to authenticity"—shape the image of the United States. *Vorwärts in die Vergangenheit: Das Bild der USA im deutschsprachigen Roman von 1776 bis 1855* (Tübingen: Stauffenberg Verlag, 1999), 26.

24. "Pages from a Journal of a Voyage Down the Mississippi to New Orleans in 1817," ed. Felix Flugel, *Louisiana Historical Quarterly* 7, no. 3 (1924): 414–40. I thank Brian J. Costello for this reference.

25. Ed. Savoie Lottinville and trans. W. Robert Nitske (Norman: University of Oklahoma Press, 1973), 32–35, 85–130.

26. Ed. Heinrich Luden (Weimar: Hoffmann, 1828), 70–110.

27. Carl Postl, whose primary pseudonym was Charles Sealsfield, took his vows at the Order of the Holy Cross with the Red Star in 1814 and in the following year became secretary to the grandmaster. For reasons still not clear to scholars he became disaffected—perhaps rebelling against the repressive Austrian police state guided by Metternich—and in 1823 escaped to the United States, winding up in New Orleans. For the next three years he lived in New York and Pennsylvania, spending the winter months in Louisiana. Sealsfield may have purchased a plantation somewhere along the Red River, but no one has been able to verify this. He returned to Europe, successfully avoiding recognition, and visited the United States three more times. Only the letters *C.P.* on his headstone in Solothurn, Switzerland, where he spent his final years, and his last will and testament were clues that revealed this man was Carl Postl. Sammons, *Ideology, Mimesis, Fantasy*, 3–12.

28. Vol. 2 (Stuttgart: Cotta, 1827), 166–247. The abridged English version has been reprinted as *The United States of North America as They Are*, new intro. William E. Wright (1828; rpt., New York: Johnson Rpt., 1970), 144–218.

29. Karl J. R. Arndt gained access to some of Sealsfield's correspondence, including a letter to a prospective publisher in which above the signature is written, "Below St. Francisville, Louisiana, the 28 of March 1829." "Recent Sealsfield Discoveries," *Journal of English and Germanic Philology* 53, no. 3 (1954): 166. Citing this letter, Eduard Castle speculates that this might be the place where Sealsfield owned a plantation. *Der Große Unbekannte*, 264.

30. *A Lady's Second Journey Round the World* (New York: Harper and Brothers, 1856), 398–415. I thank Brigitta Bader-Zaar for this reference. In her paper at a conference at Louisiana State University in March 2005, Bader-Zaar made similar observations on the text.

31. Ernst von Hesse-Wartegg, *Travels on the Lower Mississippi, 1879–1880: A Memoir*, ed. and trans. Frederic Trautmann (Columbia: University of Missouri Press, 1990), 121–239.

32. [Pictures of Life in the Western Hemisphere], in *Sämtliche Werke*, ed. Karl J. R. Arndt, vols. 11–15 (Hildesheim: Olms, 1976–77).

33. New Feliciana is called West Feliciana today.

34. *Vorwärts in die Vergangenheit*, 321–46, 409–17.

35. *Ideology, Mimesis, Fantasy*, 70.

36. Ludwig Freiherr von Reizenstein, *Die Geheimnisse von New-Orleans*, ed. Steven Rowan (Shreveport: Éditions Tintamarre, 2004); *The Mysteries of New Orleans*, ed. and trans. Steven Rowan (Baltimore: Johns Hopkins University Press, 2002). See also Patricia Herminghouse, "The German Secrets of New Orleans," *German Studies Review* 27, no. 1 (2004): 1–16.

37. *Das Landhaus am Rhein* (Stuttgart: Cotta, 1869); *The Villa on the Rhine*, biographical sketch by Bayard Taylor, 2 vols. (New York: Leypoldt and Holt, 1869). See Irene Stocksieker Di Maio, "Das Republikanische, das Demokratische, das Pantheistische: Jewish Identity in Berthold Auerbach's Novels," in *A Companion to German Realism, 1848–1900*, ed. Todd Kontje (Rochester, N.Y.: Camden House, 2002), 223–57.

38. Natchez, Miss.: Natchez Printing and Stationary Co., 1897.

39. Earl F. Bargainnier examines late-nineteenth- and early-twentieth-century literature that romanticizes the antebellum period in "The Myth of Moonlight and Magnolias," *Louisiana Studies* 15, no. 1 (1976): 5–20.

40. Trans. of *Louisiane* by June P. Wilson (New York: William Morrow, 1978). Hans Jürgen Lüsebrink sees social merit in this novel because it condemns the southern planters' egotism in enslaving people with black skin. "Prise de possession littéraire et nostalgie exotique—la Louisiane dans la littérature française (17e–20e siècle)," in *Creoles and Cajuns: French Louisiana— La Louisiane française*, ed. Wolfgang Binder (Frankfurt am Main: Lang, 1998), 267–85. But this comes very late in the game, and any social merit is severely compromised, in my view, by the exclusive focus on the planter class and a plot line in which the heroine saves the plantation through a sexual encounter with the Yankee general Benjamin Butler and then provides similar comfort to the Confederate general Richard Taylor.

41. Ernest J. Gaines, "Bloodline," *Bloodline* (1968; rpt., New York: Vintage Contemporaries, 1997), 157–217; *The Autobiography of Miss Jane Pittman* (1971; rpt., New York: Bantam, 1972).

42. N.p., n.d.

43. (New York: Nan A. Talese / Doubleday, 2003), 182.

44. See Caryn Cossé Bell, "'Une Chimère': The Freedmen's Bureau in Creole New Orleans," in *The Freedmen's Bureau and Reconstruction: Reconsiderations*, ed. Paul A. Cimbala and Randall M. Miller (New York: Fordham University Press, 1999), 140–60; and John C. Rodrigue, "The Freedmen's Bureau and Wage Labor in the Louisiana Sugar Region," in Cimbala and Miller, *Freedmen's Bureau and Reconstruction*, 193–218.

45. See, for example, Lorenzo Dow Turner, *Anti-Slavery Sentiment in American Literature prior to 1865* (Washington, D.C.: Association for the Study of Negro Life and History, 1929).

46. Anton Zangerl maintains that certain stylistic devices undermine the suspense in Gerstäcker's narratives. He also, however, cites a letter from Gerstäcker to his publisher, Costenoble, expressing the wish to make a novel interesting and suspenseful. *Friedrich Gerstäcker (1816–1872) Romane und Erzählungen: Struktur und Gehalt* (Bern: Lang, 1999), 196–201. Despite transparencies of plot, Gerstäcker's stories are suspenseful, even though his conscious effort was, more likely, motivated by commerce rather than ideology.

47. See Sammons, *Ideology, Mimesis, Fantasy*, 153–54.

48. The first edition is *Neue Reisen durch die Vereinigten Staaten, Mexiko, Ecuador, Westindien und Venezuela*, 3 vols. (Jena: Costenoble, 1868). Vol. 1 is *Nord-Amerika*.

49. *Wie ist es denn nun eigentlich in Amerika? Eine kurze Schilderung dessen, was der Auswanderer zu thun und dafür zu hoffen und erwarten hat* (Leipzig: Wigand, 1849).

50. *Der deutschen Auswanderer Fahrten und Schicksale* (Leipzig: Brockhaus, 1847).

51. Vol. 19, no. 3, of *Gesammelte Schriften*, 87–88.

About the Translation

1. *Dictionary of Literary Biography*, vol. 129: *Nineteenth-Century German Writers, 1841–1900*, ed. James Hardin and Siegfried Mews (Detroit: Gale Research, 1993), 110–19; *Gerstäcker-Verzeichnis*, ed. Manfred R. W. Garzmann, Thomas Ostwald, and Wolf-Dieter Schuegraf (Braunschweig: [Stadtarchiv u. Städt. Bibl.], 1986).

2. *In the Arkansas Backwoods*, 27.

3. *Der Flatbootmann: Amerikanische Erzählung* (Prague: Kober, 1858).

"Roving Expedition" and "Louisiana Sojourn"

Streif- und Jagdzüge durch die Vereinigten Staaten Nord-Amerikas, vol. 18 of *Gesammelte Schriften*, 149–75, 485–518.

1. In Gerstäcker's description of his journey from Arkansas through the disputed border territory between the United States and Texas into Texas and back, the notation of dates in both the first (1844) and second (1856) published editions is careless and confusing. The Steeves found a ten-month gap in the narrative and speculated whether Gerstäcker was involved in some adventures requiring discretion. *Wild Sports in the Far West*, xviii. The Steeves' contention, however, throws off the entire chronology of the travel narrative. Like James William Miller, who has compared Gerstäcker's diaries and correspondence to the travel books, *In the Arkansas Backwoods, xiii–xviii*, I consider this is sloppiness on Gerstäcker's part and believe he was in Louisiana in the second half of March to the beginning of April.

2. The Great Raft was the most extensive logjam in any of the American rivers. It actually consisted of a series of small rafts that filled in with debris. Lamar Clayton Curry, "Economic Implications of the Red River Raft" (master's thesis, Louisiana State University, 1939), 18. According to John Edward Guardia, it can be traced in Western historical time to De Soto (sixteenth century). "Successive Human Adjustments to Raft Conditions in Lower Red River Valley" (master's thesis, University of Chicago, 1927), 6. Estimates of the length of the raft vary from 60 to 150 miles; it was about 20 miles wide. As the matter on the lower end decayed and additional debris accumulated at the top, the location of the raft shifted northward. Curry cites an 1805 report on the conditions of the Red River by the Indian agent Dr. John Sibley to the secretary of war, recommending removal of the raft for the sake of land reclamation, the prevention of further destruction of property, and the settlement of fertile land to the east (55–56). In his letter of August 1, 1828, to the Hon. A. H. Sevier, delegate to Congress, from the Territory of Arkansas, Dr. Joseph Paxton surmised that the raft was at least three hundred years old. He recommended the construction of an artificial raft at the backline to dispose of the driftwood in order to prevent destruction of U.S. property, to make fertile land more desirable, to gain access to valuable woods, and to strengthen the U.S. frontier strategically. Typescript copy of March 7, 1969, Louisiana Special Collections, Hill Memorial Library, Louisiana State University.

Capt. William Henry Shreve insisted that it would be cheaper and more effective to remove the raft completely than to circumvent it by excavating canals and deepening bayous. Grace Elizabeth Dyer, "The Removal of the Great Raft in Red River" (master's thesis, Louisiana State University, 1948), 19. The raft was removed in four stages: (1) 1828–33, preliminary studies with the aim of making passage around the raft safe; (2) 1833–39, Capt. Shreve's removal of the logjams with steamer snag boats he had invented and an excavation crew; (3) 1839–71, the formation of new rafts because removal of the driftwood had ceased; and (4) 1872, Lt. E. A. Woodruff's final removal of the raft with nitroglycerin. Curry, "Economic Implications of the Red River Raft," 59–60.

3. All italics in the primary texts are Gerstäcker's.

4. This lake has variant spellings: Sodo Lake, Soto Lake. Jacques D. Bagur states that Soda Lake and Clear Lake came into existence in recent, rather than geologic, times, hypothesizing this occurred in 1800 through a break in the first large bend of the Red River above Shreveport. *A History of Navigation on Cypress Bayou and the Lakes* (Denton: University of North Texas Press, 2001), 5–14. With the removal of the Great Raft, it has virtually disappeared. J. E. Guardia, "Results of Log Jams in Red River," *Bulletin of the Geographical Society of Philadelphia.* 31, no. 3 (1933): 104. J. Fair Hardin states it has been drained and cultivated. "An Outline of Shreveport and Caddo Parish History." Rpt. from *Louisiana Historical Quarterly* 18, no. 4 (1936): 14.

5. Spanish moss (*Tillandsia usneoides*) is an air-feeding plant, or epiphyte, found mainly upon cypress, gum, oak, and pecan trees. Contrary to popular belief, it is not a parasite. It was used as mattress stuffing and upholstery. Raymond J. Martinez, *The Story of Spanish Moss: What It Is and How It Grows* (New Orleans: Hope, n.d. [1969]).

6. Flatboats were used to transport both goods and passengers, in particular settlers, downriver on the Mississippi and its lower tributaries. Essentially rectangular boxes with living quarters in the stern, they varied in length from twenty to sixty feet and in width from ten to twenty-five feet, with sides about five feet high. Because they could not move against the current, they were broken up for lumber used to build sidewalks and houses at their destination. Frank Donovan, *River Boats of America* (New York: Crowell, 1966), 22–23.

7. Cotton was better suited to many more areas of Louisiana than was sugar. With the exception of the pine hills and pine flats, which were too infertile for farming, it was grown in northern Louisiana and the Florida parishes. Joe Gray Taylor, *Louisiana: A History* (1976; rpt., New York: Norton, 1984), 65.

8. Judith Kelleher Schafer confirms Gerstäcker's assertion, stating that despite ample evidence of excessive violence and cruelty to slaves, whites seldom were convicted of this criminal behavior. Even though the 1806 Louisiana Black Code protected the slave from the harshest of treatments, slaves could not testify against whites, as the author notes. Furthermore, whites could evade a protection afforded slaves when no witnesses were present. This protection required the accused to produce evidence that they did not treat the slave cruelly, but a loophole allowed the accused to clear themselves by their own oath. Finally, other whites were loath to interfere in matters involving master and slave. *Slavery, the Civil Law, and the Supreme Court of Louisiana* (Baton Rouge: Louisiana State University Press), 1–57.

9. A Terzerol was a pocket pistol (from the Italian).

10. Shreveport was named in honor of Capt. William Henry Shreve, who cleared the Red River with his snag boats and excavation crews, thus making the river navigable past Shreveport.

The land around Shreveport had belonged to the Caddo Indians, forest dwellers who lived in permanent villages. As displaced Indian tribes and white settlers moved down the Red River Valley from Arkansas, however, and the Caddo tribes felt pressure from the Spaniards to the west and the French to the south, the Caddos' conditions deteriorated, and they decided to sell their land to the United States. In the Caddo Indian Cession Treaty of July 1, 1835, the Indians reserved 640 acres to their friend and interpreter Larkin Edwards. Edwards sold his land to the speculator Angus McNeill on February 3, 1836, after which the land was divided into seven shares—one owned by Shreve—and the Shreve Town Company was formed. Captain Shreve had a map drawn up for the layout of the city on the Upper Bluffs. In the second agreement, signed on February 7, 1837, outlining the duties of the shareholders, the name was changed from Shreve Town to Shreveport. Captain Shreve never resided in Shreveport. The organization of the town was coincident with the Republic of Texas, and wagon trails converged on Shreveport. The thousands of new settlers looked to Shreveport for their supplies and for a market for their cotton. Curry, "Economic Implications of the Red River Raft," 68–88; J. Fair Hardin, "An Outline of Shreveport and Caddo Parish History," *Louisiana Historical Quarterly* 18, no. 4 (1936): 759–871; Holice Henrici, *Shreveport: The Beginnings* (Lafayette: Center for Louisiana Studies, 1985), 16–37.

11. J. Fair Hardin notes that rough men predominated in this typical frontier river town, "a haven for all the vices inherent in such places," until the arrival of the Episcopal missionary bishop Leonidas Polk in 1839. "An Outline of Shreveport and Caddo Parish History," 74.

12. Natchitoches is the oldest town in Louisiana and is named after one of the Louisiana Caddo-speaking tribes that was present fifteen hundred years ago. In 1711 Father Hidalgo wrote to Le Mothe de Cadillac, the governor of the Louisiana territory of New France, "to come and trade at Hidalgo's mission" because the Spanish government would not fund his intended mission on the eastern border of Texas territory. Dates vary, but sometime between 1712 and 1714 Louis Juchereau de St. Denis led a party of twenty-four to thirty Frenchmen and a few Tunica Indian guides up the Mississippi and Red rivers to Natchitoches. He established an outpost with two houses, one for lodgings and one for merchandise, before continuing westward to find the Spanish and Father Hidalgo's mission. This journey created the Camino Real. The Spanish initially took St. Denis captive, but St. Denis's diplomatic skills were so great that he married the Spanish commandant's step-granddaughter, forming an alliance with the Spanish. In 1716 he led a Spanish expedition back east to the French colony. The Spanish established settlements along the way, ending with the Mission of San Miguel de los Adaes, twelve miles west of Natchitoches. Under St. Denis's control Natchitoches became a successful center of illegal trade between the French, the Spanish, and the Indians. It was an important port city because the Great Raft blocked further travel up the Red River. But the raft was removed in the late 1830s, and by 1840 the Red River completely bypassed its historic Cane River channel. Natchitoches shifted from a trade economy to an economy based on the surrounding cotton plantations. Curry, "Economic Implications of the Red River Raft"; Daniel Graves, *Profiles of Natchitoches History* (Natchitoches: Museum of Natchitoches and Its Supporters, 1996); Richard Seale, "The Town of Natchitoches," in *Natchitoches and Louisiana's Timeless Cane River* (Baton Rouge: Louisiana State University Press, 2002), 6–28; Germaine Portré-Bobinski and Clara Mildred Smith, *Natchitoches: The Up-to-Date Oldest Town in Louisiana* (New Orleans: Dameron-Pierson, 1936).

13. The name *Blackhawk* reappears in the short story "In the Red River." A number of steamboats with this name are listed. The only one with a date early enough for Gerstäcker to have

encountered it is noted in *Merchant Steam Vessels of the United States, 1807–1868, "The Lytle List,"* comp. William H. Lytle, ed. and intro. Forrest R. Holdcamper (Mystic, Conn.: Steamship Historical Society of America, 1952), 20. It was built in 1833 in Cincinnati, Ohio, where it had its home port. We cannot be sure whether this was the same vessel.

14. Old River connects the Mississippi and Red rivers in central Louisiana at about the 31st parallel. At this narrow confluence, where the waters shed from a large part of the American continent, the deltaic plain begins, with the Red River tributary entering and the Atchafalaya River distributary leaving the Mississippi River. Because the Mississippi attempted to send more water down the Atchafalaya, in 1954 the Old River control structure was constructed at Simmesport to prevent this change in the Mississippi's channel. Albert C. Cowdrey, "Land's End," in *Agriculture and Economic Development in Louisiana*, ed. Thomas A. Becnel, vol. 16 of *The Louisiana Purchase Bicentennial Series in Louisiana History* (Lafayette: Center for Louisiana Studies, 1976), 24; Sue Lyles Eakins, "The Atchafalaya," in *The Rivers and Bayous of Louisiana*, ed. Edwin Adams Davis (Baton Rouge: Louisiana Education Research Association, 1968), 114; Fred B. Kniffen and Sam Bowers Hilliard, *Louisiana: Its Land and People*, rev. ed. (1968; rpt., Baton Rouge: Louisiana State University Press, 1988); Charles Robert Goins and Jon Michael Caldwell, *Historical Atlas of Louisiana* (Norman: University of Oklahoma Press, 1995), 6.

15. The first European reference to this area is found in the journal of Pierre le Moyne, sieur d'Iberville, who, along with his brother, Jean Baptiste le Moyne, sieur de Bienville, explored the Mississippi River Valley to secure France's claim to the heartland of North America. In 1699 the two brothers came upon what was then a twenty-two-mile-long oxbow curve in the Mississippi River and took a shortcut through a partially carved channel approximately four miles in length. Iberville called this place "la Pointe Coupée," or the cut point. The cutoff is commonly believed to have been completed by 1722, but historical writings suggest that the Mississippi may have taken its new course through the channel as early as 1713.

The original dwellers in this area were nomadic Paleo-Indians. The precontact Indians of Pointe Coupée were displaced by the Okelousa, who, in turn, were displaced by the Pascagoula, from the Mississippi Gulf, and the Ofo and Tunica, from between the Yazoo and Pearl rivers in central Mississippi. According to an 1803 account, fifty or sixty remaining Tunica Indians lived on the west bank of the Mississippi near Pointe Coupée.

French and French-Canadian wood runners were the earliest white settlers at Pointe Coupée, established around 1708. By the mid-eighteenth century Anglo-American and Spanish (from Spain and the Canary Islands) names appear in local records. Even under Spanish rule (1762–1800), however, the officers of the post at Pointe Coupée, established perhaps as early as 1718, were of French origin. Blacks, mostly slaves but also some free blacks, formed a large part of the population from early times. Judy Riffel, "Early History"; W. R. Bailey, "Parish Boundaries and Geography"; and Rosemary Rougon Rummler, "Indians," in *Pointe Coupee Parish History and Its Families*, ed. Judy Riffel (Baton Rouge: Le Comité des Archives de la Louisiane, 1983), 3–19; Hilgard O'Reilly Sternberg, "The Pointe Coupée Cut-Off in Historical Writings," *Louisiana Historical Quarterly* 28, no. 1 (1945): 69–84.

Of eighteenth-century Pointe Coupée, with its extensively mixed-race population, Gwendolyn Midlo Hall maintains, "It is here that one can closely observe the incubation of new, hybrid cultural forms in response to the human and ecological environment. Red, white, and black met under crisis conditions. The insecurity of this frontier world created a society in which the three races were deeply dependent upon each other and physical survival was often more important than accumulation of wealth. Racial lines were blurred, and intimate relations among peoples of all three races flourished." *Africans in Colonial Louisiana: The Development of Afro-Creole Culture in the Eighteenth Century* (Baton Rouge: Louisiana State University Press, 1992), 238. Following Louisiana statehood in 1812, Anglo-Americans settled in the northern part of what then became one of the twelve original parishes of the state. During the antebellum period Pointe Coupée enjoyed a thriving plantation economy based on sugar, cotton, and slave labor. Brian J. Costello, *New Roads: A Community in Retrospect* (New Roads, La.: Cajun Electric, 1993), 5–7.

In current usage *Pointe Coupée* is spelled without the acute accent. Because Gerstäcker used the accent, I retain it in this text in both the main body and the annotations, except in citations in which it is not used.

16. According to Louis C. Hunter, the common practice was to take on wood twice daily. In the early days the crew cut and gathered the wood for fuel. As steamboats grew more numerous and their operations more extensive, "the preparation of steamboat fuel became an important backwoods industry." Wood became the principal cash crop for farmers living along the waterways and the sole source of income for the backwoodsmen. *Steamboats on the Western Rivers: An Economic and Technological History* (Cambridge, Mass.: Harvard University Press, 1949), 264–64. Louisiana legislation protected the wood yard owners with respect to payment. *Acts Passed at the Second Session of the Fifteenth Legislature of the State of Louisiana* (New Orleans: J. C. de St. Romes, 1842), 280–81. I thank Carl A. Brasseaux for these sources.

17. Gerstäcker had traveled to South America twice before revising and expanding this second edition account of his first sojourn in the United States.

18. The *Chillicothe* was a 253-ton side-wheel steamer built in Pittsburgh, Pennsylvania, its first home port, in 1837.

19. A German mile is about five English statute miles.

20. Bayou Sara and the adjacent town of St. Francisville are in present-day West Feliciana Parish on the east bank of the Mississippi River. Although Hernando de Soto, who died in his camp at the mouth of the Red River, claimed all of what is the United States for Spain in 1542, his claims were not established. The first white man known to have set foot on the soil of West Feliciana was the Chevalier de Tonti, companion to René Robert Cavelier, sieur de La Salle, who claimed the territory for France in 1642. Tonti dwelled among the Houma Indians, who at that time had a large village opposite the mouth of the Red River. In 1706 the Tunica took refuge with the Houma but then turned on their hosts and nearly exterminated them. Ironically, geographic sites of the area are named after the treacherous Tunica.

Rule over this area was as complicated as it gets in the history of Louisiana. It was Spanish, French, English, Spanish again, then independent as part of West Florida, taken possession by the United States in 1810, joined to the state of Louisiana de facto in 1819, and divided into West and East Feliciana parishes in 1824. The earliest European sojourners were missionaries of the Catholic Church, and the village of St. Francisville retained the name of a monastery built by French Capuchin monks about 1785 that burned down shortly thereafter. Even though the Company of the Indies had a concession in the Tunicas, the Felicianas remained sparsely populated until they passed into the hands of the British (1763), and Americans of Irish, Scotch, English, and, occasionally, Huguenot descent moved there after the American Revolution. Therefore, the early white population was predominately Anglo. The area had a relatively healthy climate, rich soil of loam and fine clay, and a great variety of flora and fauna. During the 1830s West Feliciana developed into one of the richest economic sections of the South. It was the site of prosperous cotton and sugar plantations during the antebellum period. In the 1840 census the ratio of slave to white population was nine to two.

St. Francisville, the parish seat, sat on a two-mile-long ridge overlooking Bayou Sara and the Mississippi River. The precise date of its founding is unclear. It may have been slightly earlier than the establishment of Bayou Sara, in 1790. Originally named Clay's Bayou, Bayou Sara was renamed after an old woman who lived on the banks of the bayou. A prosperous port town in antebellum days, it was one of the largest shipping ports between Natchez and New Orleans. But the town began to decline with the advent of the railroad and was disenfranchised in 1926. The flood of 1927 washed away all that remained. Louise Butler, "West Feliciana: A Glimpse of Its History," *Louisiana Historical Quarterly* 7, no. 1 (1924): 90–120; *Louisiana: A Guide to the State*, comp. Workers of the Writers' Program of the Work Projects Administration in the State of Louisiana (New York: Hastings House, 1940), 463–65; Edwin Adams Davis, *Plantation Life in the Florida Parishes of Louisiana, 1836–1846: As Reflected in the Diary of Bennet H. Barrow* (New York: AMS Press, 1967), 3–10.

21. Elliot Ashkenazi contends "that the American South in antebellum days and in the decade or so after the war offered Jewish immigrants an agrarian economic and social structure similar to that of France and southwestern Germany, the area of emigration." After 1840 there were a surprising number of Jewish merchants in East and West Feliciana parishes who lived mostly in Bayou Sara, Clinton, and Jackson. *The Business of Jews in Louisiana, 1840–1875* (Tuscaloosa: University of Alabama Press, 1988), 3, 70. Samuel C. Hyde Jr. notes that "religious tolerance, which typically existed between Catholics and Protestants in the Florida parishes, was extended to Jews in the Felicianas, where small but influential Jewish communities developed at St. Francisville and Clinton." *Pistols and Politics: The Dilemma of Democracy in Louisiana's Florida Parishes, 1810–1899* (Baton Rouge: Louisiana State University Press, 1996), 6.

22. Surveying Gerstäcker's representations of Jews, Sammons observes that, with a few exceptions, they "recurrently exhibit elements of the traditional anti-Semitic discourse." *Ideology, Mimesis, Fantasy*, 160.

23. Gerstäcker is not exact here. He describes his operation of this hotel further in "Louisiana Sketches: The Ferry Hotel in Point Coupée," in this volume. According to the Conveyance Records, Point Coupée Parish Clerk of Court, New Roads, La., Frances N. Ogden sold the property and its improvements to Charles Roetken on June 4, 1839 (1839, entry no. 2043). The land was bounded on the lower side by the property of William Taylor, a name that appears in Gerstäcker's short stories. Charles Roetken, in turn, sold the lot and improvements to Frederick Fischer on February 27, 1841. In accordance with Louisiana law, Roetken's wife Leopoldine, née Welker, signed an attached document approving the sale and relinquishing any matrimonial or dotal rights to the property (1841, entry no. 2455). According to Harriet Spiller Daggett, the community arises by virtue of the marriage itself and comes into the law of Louisiana as article 63, title 5, book 3, of the Code of 1808. In 1825 the code was modified slightly and became article 2369. *The Community Property System of Louisiana* (1931; rpt. with addenda, Baton Rouge: Louisiana State University Press, 1944), 8. Nowhere does Gerstäcker mention that Charles Roet-

ken had a wife, although the character Roettken in the story "The Purchased Hangman" has a wife named Emilie.

The clerk of court Anglicized the purchaser's name as Fisher, but the signature reads "Frederick Fischer." It was Fischer's brother Charles who mismanaged the hotel because he suffered from alcoholism. In conjunction with the sale of the property, Roetken also sold to Frederick Fischer a fifty-one-year-old male slave named Figaro (1841, entry no. 2456). The first time the Ferry Hotel is actually named in a conveyance document is when Frederick Fischer sold the property to Savinien Pourciau in 1852 (entry no. 2393). I am grateful to Brian J. Costello, who furnished these and other documents and information concerning the history of Pointe Coupée.

24. *Author:* Pointe Coupée is actually the name of an entire French settlement in Louisiana that extends along the west bank of the Mississippi for about twenty miles.

25. St. Francis Church. Brian J. Costello, *A History of Pointe Coupée Parish, Louisiana* (New Roads, La.: by the author, 1999), 68.

26. Coco grass is the popular misnomer for the purple nutsedge (*Cyperus rotundus*). According to James L. Griffin of the Department of Agronomy at Louisiana State University, the nutsedge is the number-one weed problem worldwide.

27. In a note to a subsequent travel entry Gerstäcker states that *Creole* means a person born in Louisiana. The definition of *Creole* has changed over time and varies among different groups, but in explaining the historical reasons for such change, Joseph G. Tregle Jr. posits the consensus in early-nineteenth-century New Orleans concerning the meaning of the term *Creole*: "To state simply that a person was a 'creole' meant that he was native to the state, whether white or black, free or slave, Gallic or Yankee. Reference to 'the creoles' implied equation with the *ancienne population,* the indigenous Latin inhabitants. The simple plural form of the term might embrace all native-born . . . unless the context of the comment obviously ruled out slaves or free persons of color." "Creoles and Americans," in *Creole New Orleans: Race and Americanization,* ed. Arnold R. Hirsch and Joseph Logsdon (Baton Rouge: Louisiana State University Press, 1992), 141. See also Tregle's earlier articles "Early New Orleans Society: A Reappraisal," *Journal of Southern History* 18, no. 1 (1952): 20–36; and "On That Word 'Creole' Again: A Note," *Louisiana History* 23, no. 2 (1982): 193–98.

Viewing the term from a non-Eurocentric position, Gwendolyn Midlo-Hall explains that the term *Creole* derives from the Portuguese word *crioulo,* meaning a slave of African descent born in the New World. Later the term included Europeans born in the New World. Although, according to Hall, "the most precise current definition of a creole is a person of non-American ancestry, whether African or European, who was born in the Americas . . . creole has come to mean the language and folk culture that was native to the southern part of Louisiana where African, French, and Spanish influence was most deeply rooted historically and culturally." Like Tregle, Hall discusses the racial, social, and cultural reasons why in the late nineteenth century Louisiana whites of French or Spanish descent redefined *Creole* to mean exclusively white, and Hall also notes that mixed-race Creoles took greatest pride in their French ancestry. *Africans in Colonial Louisiana,* 157–58.

Recently, Carl A. Brasseaux has surveyed each group that identifies with the term *Creole,* explaining the different understandings of that term and discussing how various ethnic groups use Creole identification to retain or advance their standing in Louisiana's social hierarchy.

Brasseaux distinguishes between *Creole* as a noun or an adjective that refers to people and *creole* to refer to products native to Louisiana. "Creoles: A Family Portrait in Black and White," *French, Cajun, Creole, Houma: A Primer on Francophone Louisiana* (Baton Rouge: Louisiana State University Press, 2005), 85–115.

28. The majority of white settlers at Pointe Coupée were of French descent. Pointe Coupée was also more densely populated by black slaves than any other place in Louisiana. Riffel, *History of Pointe Coupee and Its Families*, 4. According to Brian J. Costello, the educated Pointe Coupée Creoles used standard French in speech and writing to keep a distance between themselves and their Anglo neighbors and the lesser-educated Creoles as well. Standard French predominated legal documents until the mid-nineteenth century. *History of Pointe Coupée Parish, Louisiana*, 91. Joseph G. Tregle Jr. describes the social and political ethnic rivalry between the Creoles of Latin origin, known as the *ancienne population,* and the more recently arrived French immigrants, on the one hand, and the Anglo-Americans who poured into Louisiana after the Purchase, on the other: *Louisiana in the Age of Jackson: A Clash of Cultures and Personalities* (Baton Rouge: Louisiana State University Press, 1999). Although the Constitution of Louisiana of 1812, a condition for statehood, made English the language of record in judicial and legislative proceedings, it was copied in both English and French. Warren M. Billings, "From This Seed: The Constitution of 1812," in *In Search of Fundamental Law: Louisiana's Constitutions, 1812–1974,* ed. Warren M. Billings and Edward F. Haas (Lafayette: Center for Louisiana Studies, 1993), 6–7, 19. Because of continuing protests by the French-speaking population, in 1822, legislation was enacted permitting the use of French in most legal business. Tregle, *Louisiana in the Age of Jackson,* 84–85. See also Mark F. Fernandez, *From Chaos to Continuity: The Evolution of Louisiana's Judicial System, 1712–1862* (Baton Rouge: Louisiana State University Press, 2001), on the clash of the diverse cultures.

29. Fritz Haydt appears as a character in Gerstäcker's short story "The Purchased Hangman."

30. The argument that the slave is better off than the German peasant is intended to underscore the dire circumstances of the peasant, not to defend slavery. Ida Pfeiffer believed Russian serfage to be far more severe than American slavery with respect to basic needs, *A Lady's Second Journey Round the World,* 405–6. In a similar vein Mayne Reid's first-person British narrator in the novel *The Quadroon; or, A Lover's Adventures in Louisiana* (London: George W. Hyde, 1856), protesting against excessive taxation, exclaims, "On my soul, I hold that the slavery of the Louisiana black is less degrading than that of the white plebian of England" (1:57). The black abolitionist William Wells Brown, however, gives such views short shrift: "Some American writers have tried to make the world believe that the condition of the laboring classes of England is as bad as the slaves of the United States. . . . The English labourer may be oppressed, he may be cheated, defrauded, swindled, and even starved; but it is not slavery under which he groans. He cannot be sold; in point of law he is equal to the prime minister." *Clotel; or, The President's Daughter,* in *The Norton Anthology of African American Literature,* ed. Henry Louis Gates Jr. and Nellie Y. McKay (New York: Norton, 1997), 268.

The proper feeding, clothing, and housing of slaves was a concern among planters, for they needed to keep their investments healthy and efficient. The tone of the literature on the care of slaves resembles that of studies on animal husbandry in an age that was becoming increasingly scientific. See *Advice among Masters: The Ideal in Slave Management in the Old South,* ed. James O. Breeden (Westport, Conn.: Greenwood, 1980).

31. The U.S. Congress banned the importation of African slaves in 1804, but the smuggling of slaves continued on a fairly large scale for the next twenty years and never ceased completely in the antebellum period. Joe Gray Taylor, *Louisiana: A History* (1976; rpt., New York: Norton, 1984), 72. See also Taylor, "The Foreign Slave Trade in Louisiana after 1808," *Louisiana History* 1, no. 1 (1960): 36–43.

32. In her studies on slavery and Afro-Creole culture in Louisiana, Gwendolyn Midlo Hall explains that two-thirds of the slaves brought to Louisiana by the French slave trade came from Senegambia. The Senegal concession of the Company of the Indies included Upper Guinea, and some of the slaves destined for Louisiana were brought from a *captiverie* on the Upper Guinea coast. *Africans in Colonial Louisiana: The Development of Afro-Creole Culture in the Eighteenth Century* (Baton Rouge: Louisiana State University Press, 1992), 29–34. The chapter "Senegambia during the French Slave Trade" is reprinted in *A Refuge for All Ages: Immigration in Louisiana History*, ed. Carl A. Brasseaux (Lafayette: Center for Louisiana Studies, 1996). Hall's study of the documents listing the origin of African slaves in eighteenth-century Pointe Coupée notes the use of the vague term *Guinea* in some instances, a term that applies to a general region rather than to specific tribes (283, 287). The Upper Guinea connection of slaves in Pointe Coupée (and elsewhere) may be the reason for the continuing use of the term *Guinea Negro*. This term, however, appears to have had early and widespread use. For example, Tregle notes the use of the general term *Guinea Negro* for blacks of African descent in an early-seventeenth-century Spanish document. "Creoles and Americans," 13; and William L. Van Deburg notes the term being used in another state. *The Slave Drivers: Black Agricultural Labor Supervisors in the Antebellum South* (Westport, Conn.: Greenwood, 1979), 9.

Focusing on the slave trade in New Orleans during the French and Spanish colonial periods, and briefly on the period after the Louisiana Purchase, Thomas Ingersoll maintains that the Louisiana slave population was far more ethnically diverse than Hall's studies would indicate. "The Slave Trade and the Ethnic Diversity of Louisiana's Slave Community," *Louisiana History* 37, no. 2 (1996): 133–61. Yet, as Ingersoll himself acknowledges, much of Hall's study focuses on the area around Pointe Coupée. It is quite likely that this historical term continued to be used in Louisiana, and elsewhere, regardless of the fact that slaves of other ethnicities were being introduced through the illegal slave trade from Africa and the legal trade of slaves from the more northerly states.

33. Gerstäcker had no sympathy for Methodist ministers, whom he characterized as foolish or nefarious. Himself a deist at most, he was basically uninterested in religious practice and gave it short shrift in his writings, except that he abhorred the destruction of indigenous cultures brought about by missionaries. While Gerstäcker's perception that the master might introduce Christianity to the slave quarters as a controlling device was correct, he did not appreciate the positive role religion could play in Afro-American communal life. Nor does he here seem to recognize the degree to which the slaves drew on their African heritage by dancing and shouting, thus shaping their own worship rituals. See, for example, John W. Blassingame, *The Slave Community: Plantation Life in the Antebellum South* (New York: Oxford University Press, 1972), 59–75; and Eric J. Sundquist, *To Wake the Nations: Race in the Making of American Literature* (Cambridge, Mass.: Belknap Press, 1993), 60. Discussing the three things that characterized the religion of the slave, "the Preacher, the Music, and the Frenzy," W. E. B. Du Bois claims that the shouting when the Spirit of the Lord passed by was the component "more devoutly believed in

than all the rest." *The Souls of Black Folk,* ed. Henry Louis Gates Jr. and Terri Hume Oliver (1903; rpt., New York: Norton, 1999), 120. For some diverse views on religious instruction held by planters, see Breeden, *Advice among Masters,* 224–38. Eugene D. Genovese examines both the strengths and the weaknesses Christianity afforded its enslaved people. *Roll Jordan, Roll: The World the Slaves Made* (1972; rpt., New York: Vintage, 1976), 159–284. Albert J. Raboteau, too, claims "the effect of religion upon the attitudes, motivation, and action of slaves was complex." *Slave Religion: The "Invisible Institution" in the Antebellum South* (Oxford: Oxford University Press, 1980), 304. Religion could nurture docility, foster rebellion, or promote reciprocity. Slaves often cherished religious notions that ran counter to the teachings of the masters. *Slave Religion,* 289–319. Focusing on Louisiana, Joe Gray Taylor and Ann Patton Malone provide a differentiated picture of the relationship between masters and slaves with respect to religious training and practice, depending on the time period, the denomination, and the proclivities of individual slaveholders. Taylor, *Negro Slavery in Louisiana* (Lafayette: Louisiana Historical Association, 1963), 133–52; and Malone, *Sweet Chariot: Slave Family and Household Structure in Nineteenth-Century Louisiana* (Chapel Hill, N.C.: University of North Carolina Press, 1992), 241–50.

34. Gerstäcker means that he will dispense with a scientific description of the woodcock. In the German original the word for the bird is *Schnepfe,* which may be translated as *snipe* or *woodcock.* Louisiana was home to both long-billed shorebirds. The common snipe (*Capella gallinago*) is slimmer and has a smaller head than the American woodcock (*Philohela minor*). George H. Lowery Jr., *Louisiana Birds,* 3d. ed. (Baton Rouge: published for the Louisiana Wildlife and Fisheries Commission by Louisiana State University Press, 1974), 303–6. I believe Gerstäcker means the woodcock because his American, indeed Louisiana, contemporary in composing sketches in the sporting genre is Thomas Bangs Thorpe, who describes hunting this nocturnal bird as "a sport *entirely local* in its character . . . confined to a narrow strip of country running from the mouth of the Mississippi, up the river about three hundred miles." "Woodcock Fire Hunting," in *A New Collection of Thomas Bangs Thorpe's Sketches of the Old Southwest,* ed. David C. Estes (Baton Rouge: Louisiana State University Press, 1989), 123–26. The sketch first appeared in the *Spirit of the Times,* 9, May 1, 1841, 103. Estes, "Textual Notes," in *New Collection,* 327.

35. Mary Queen of Scots (Mary Stuart), 1542–87, was suspected of being involved in the murder of her second husband and in a plot against Elizabeth I, queen of England, 1533–1603. She was beheaded in 1587, but her conduct at the trial and execution gained her admiration. The highlights of Friedrich Schiller's five-act tragedy, *Maria Stuart* (1801), are the confrontation between the two queens and Maria Stuart's execution, when she accepts her death as penance for earlier crimes.

36. Duke Paul Wilhelm, Gerstäcker's predecessor in Pointe Coupée, provides a more logical and far less racist explanation for why blacks might have been the alligator's victims. He notes, "Negro women who have to do their washing on the edge of the water often have accidents because an alligator approaches very slowly under the water, seizes its prey quickly by the feet and draws it into the water to drown." *Travels in North America, 1822–24,* 117. Given the overwhelming ratio of blacks to whites in the parish and the fact that far more blacks would be working along riverbanks and in swamps, they naturally would more readily have fallen prey to the alligator than would have whites.

37. At a somewhat later time than Gerstäcker's presence in Pointe Coupée, the diary of Au-

rora Margueritte Morgan of Morganza Plantation in northern Point Coupée notes on several occasions that Mr. William Harbour and/or his sister Sue dined at the plantation (June and July 1854). Morgan Family Papers. William A. Harbour was a planter and sheriff of Point Coupée Parish during 1853–54 and married into the Morgan family. Brian J. Costello, pers. comm., January 2005.

38. Here Gerstäcker's recollection is incorrect. There was no newspaper called the *Pointe Coupée Chronicle*. The paper to which he refers is the *Louisiana Chronicle*, a weekly published simultaneously in St. Francisville and Bayou Sara from January 20, 1838, to February 11, 1854 [?]. Its editor and printer was J. A. Kelly (see n. 39). The Louisiana Newspaper Project Printout, October 1991 (Baton Rouge: Louisiana State University Libraries, 1992), 145.

39. Using Louisiana census indices of the period, I have not been able to locate any Kellys in Pointe Coupée Parish. This does not mean, however, they were not present. Several Kellys (J. Kelly, L. Kelly, and S. Kelly in East Feliciana Parish; and Jas. A. Kelly in West Feliciana Parish) are listed in *1840 Louisiana State Wide Census Index*, ed. Frances T. Ingmire (Signal Mountain, Tenn.: Mountain Press, 1997). James A. Kelly, as noted earlier, was the editor and printer of the *Louisiana Chronicle*. He also was initially selected to be the official printer for the proceedings of the 1844–45 constitutional convention, which convened in Jackson, Louisiana, in East Feliciana Parish, until the convention moved to New Orleans. Because Florence M. Jumonville states that Kelly set up shop in Jackson, and he was selected over a New Orleans printer who had submitted a lower bid, we may conclude that he is the Jas. A. Kelly of West Feliciana. Jumonville, "'The People's Friend—The Tyrant's Foe': Law-Related New Orleans Imprints, 1803–1860," *A Law unto Itself? Essays in the New Louisiana Legal History*, ed. Warren M. Billings and Mark F. Fernandez (Baton Rouge: Louisiana State University Press, 2001), 50–51. See also Judith K. Schafer, "Reform or Experiment? The Louisiana Constitution of 1845," in *In Search of Fundamental Law: Louisiana's Constitutions, 1812–1974*, ed. Warren M. Billings and Edward F. Haas (Lafayette: Center for Louisiana Studies, 1993), 23.

40. One of the early mentions of William A. Beatty is a sheriff's deed in his favor dated December 15, 1845. Conveyance Records, Point Coupée Parish Clerk of Court (1845, entry no. 3990). Beatty and his wife owned property in the parish. According to Brian J. Costello, Beatty's descendants remain in Point Coupée Parish today (pers. comm., January 2005). Aurora Margueritte Morgan's diary also notes the presence of a Mr. Beatty at Morganza Plantation on several occasions in 1854.

41. St. Francis Church was the oldest church in Point Coupée. Brian J. Costello, *The Catholic Church of Pointe Coupée: A Faith Journey* (Marksville, La.: Randy DeCuir, 1996), 3. Roger Baudier explains this clash between the parishioners and the priest, Father Martin, in its broader context. Under American law the Catholic Church was not recognized as a legal entity; hence, it could not acquire or hold real property. To give the individual parishes of the diocese a legal entity, corporations were formed, composed of trustees elected by the parishioners. There were conflicts between the board of wardens, comprising the trustees, and Church officials over the authority to appoint priests and to manage Church affairs throughout the United States. The most infamous clashes in Louisiana had been transpiring in St. Louis Cathedral since 1805. When Father Antoine Blanc, who had served as priest for St. Francis Church in Pointe Coupée (1820–26), accepted the appointment as bishop of New Orleans in 1835, he sought to regain control of the Cathedral. In turn, its trustees declared Bishop Blanc's appointment of Father Eti-

enne Rousselon as priest in 1842 as null and void. Although Father Rousselon withdrew, conflicts escalated. The bishop condemned the wardens as schismatics and refused to appoint a new priest; the wardens, in turn, sought damages in the parish court. When Judge Maurian threw out the case, they turned to the state supreme court. But before the court ruled, the wardens also sought to enact legislation severely limiting Church authority in all aspects of Church affairs. Finally, in June 1844 the Supreme Court ruled that it could not authorize the wardens to intervene in matters of spiritual authority. Baudier, *The Catholic Church in Louisiana* (1939; rpt., New Orleans, 1979), 335–51. See also Charles E. Nolan, *A History of the Archdiocese of New Orleans* (Strasbourg: Éditions du Signe, 2002), 29–31. Bishop Blanc, however, did not wish to take the supreme court decision as the basis for agreement with the wardens. Such an admission would imply that the court had authority in matters concerning religious discipline. The court, too, recognized this would violate the spirit of the Constitution. Thus, the bishop and the wardens came to an independent agreement in October 1844. Brother Alfonso Comeau, C.S.C., "A Study of the Trustee Problem in the St. Louis Cathedral Church of New Orleans, Louisiana, 1842–1844," *Louisiana Historical Quarterly* 31, no. 4 (1948): 960–63.

Gerstäcker, a nominal Lutheran, would likely have sided with the wardens, finding that authority resting in the hands of the wardens, hence the parishioners, to be more democratic.

42. D. Philip Bourquin is listed as a foreign and domestic exchange broker residing on the corner of Royal and Customhouse streets. *New Orleans Directory for 1841; Made by the United States Deputy Marshals* (New Orleans: Michel and Co., 1840). By 1846 he was located at Esplanade between Derbigny and Roman streets and was listed as a trader and speculator. *New Orleans Annual and Commercial Register for 1846* (New Orleans: E. A. Michel, 1846). Korn is not listed in the city directories of the period.

43. This was mostly likely the side-wheel steamer built in Louisville, Kentucky, in 1842. Its first home port was St. Louis, Missouri. *Merchant Steam Vessels of the United States.*

44. This suburb is not to be confused with the city of Lafayette in south-central Louisiana. On April 1, 1833, the faubourgs (suburbs) of Nuns, Lafayette, and Livaudais were incorporated into the city of Lafayette. The faubourg Delassize was subsequently incorporated on March 21, 1844. Lafayette and New Orleans were consolidated on February 22, 1854, Lafayette becoming the fourth district of New Orleans. Kathryn C. Briede, "A History of the City of Lafayette," *Louisiana Historical Quarterly* 20, no. 4 (1937): 894–964. Current sections of the area that was Lafayette are the Lower Garden District and parts of the Garden District and the Irish Channel. Richard Campanella, *Time and Place in New Orleans: Past Geographies in the Present Day* (Gretna, La.: Pelican, 2002), 182.

45. German ship registers (Lloyd's Register, Germanischer Lloyd, House) do not go back as far as 1843. The names "Johann Friedrich" and "Olbers," however, appear frequently at later dates. Volker Reissmann, Staatsarchiv Hamburg, per email, 8 November 2005.

46. The historian Joseph Logsdon observes that coffee still is an important component of New Orleans' shared, public culture. The port received its first shipment of green coffee beans in the eighteenth century. By 1846 New Orleans was the second busiest port in the world, and more than eight million dollars was generated by the importation of coffee from proximate Latin American countries that year. Coffee stalls were scattered throughout New Orleans, and coffeehouses were the sites of business transactions. "Freshly Brewed: New Orleans' Coffee

Legacy," *Louisiana Cultural Vistas* 8, no. 1 (1997): 4; Louise McKinney, "House of Brews: New Orleans' Coffee Culture," *New Orleans* 29, no. 12 (1995): 69–72.

47. The *Porpoise* was a 320-ton side-wheel towboat with a wooden hull. Designed to push barges, it was in operation from 1828 to 1855. Captain Wood offered towage out of New Orleans, to and from the Gulf of Mexico. Way surmises it was used also as a tug for sailing vessels, which this journal confirms. *Way's Steam Towboat Directory,* comp. Frederick Way Jr., with Joseph W. Rutter (Athens, Ohio: Ohio University Press, 1990), 184.

48. The settlement described here is Balize, located at one of several passes leading into the Gulf. Tom Weil explains, "over the years, five Balizes—or settlements at the Mississippi's mouth—served guarding and guiding functions. The first two lasted for a total of 130 years, until the passes they served grew too shallow for ships. The third occupied a sliver of ground by Southeast Pass during the Civil War era." *The Mississippi River: Nature, Culture and Travel Sites along the "Mighty Mississip"* (New York: Hippocrene Books, 1992), 489. The current version of Balize is Pilottown, built in the 1890s. Stephen E. Ambrose and Douglas G. Brinkley, *The Mississippi and the Making of a Nation: From the Louisiana Purchase to Today* (Washington, D.C.: National Geographic Society, 2002), 16–17.

49. Stephen E. Ambrose and Douglas G. Brinkley explain that by the early nineteenth century the sandbar that built up at the mouth of the river was often too high for the larger ships to pass, and they had to wait for a rise in the river. In 1875 construction began on a system of jetties from the termination of the riverbanks that would use the force of the river's current to scour out the sandbar at the mouth. *Mississippi and the Making of a Nation,* 16–22.

"New Orleans"

Mississippi-Bilder: Licht- und Schattenseiten transatlantischen Lebens, vol. 10 of *Gesammelte Schriften,* 617–31.

1. *Author:* Every mall in Spanish cities is named after the Prado in Madrid. In New Orleans it is the bank of the Mississippi, or the "levee."

2. From Friedrich Schiller's ballad "Die Kraniche des Ibykus."

3. Jean-Baptiste Le Moyne, sieur de Bienville, served as governor of the Louisiana colony from 1701 to 1712.

4. This date is erroneous. On November 3, 1762, the Bourbon king of France, Louis XV, signed the Treaty of Fountainebleau, ceding Louisiana to Bourbon Spain in order to keep that territory out of the hands of the British. John Wilds, Charles L. Dufour, and Walter G. Cowan, *Louisiana Yesterday and Today: A Historical Guide to the State* (Baton Rouge: Louisiana State University Press, 1996), 11.

5. Don Antonio de Ulloa, the Spanish governor of Louisiana, arrived in New Orleans in March 1766, four years after France had ceded the Louisiana colony to Spain. He met with resistance.

6. At the beginning of the twentieth century Walter Reed and his team of researchers proved that yellow fever is an acute viral infection endemic of West Africa that was carried as part of a monkey to mosquito cycle. It is transmitted in the Americas by the *Aedes aegypti* mosquito, which breeds in containers of water (on ships and in urban areas primarily). Mosquitoes

ingest the virus when they draw blood from an infected human and then expel the virus into the blood of a new victim by biting. Michael B. A. Oldstone, *Viruses, Plagues, and History* (New York: Oxford University Press, 1998), 45–72; Jo Ann Carrigan, *The Saffron Scourge: A History of Yellow Fever in Louisiana, 1796–1905* (Lafayette: Center for Louisiana Studies, 1994). At the time Gerstäcker first published this sketch of New Orleans, the most devastating outbreak of yellow fever had occurred in 1833, when it, combined with a cholera epidemic, claimed ten thousand out of a population of fifty-five thousand. Grace King, *New Orleans: The Place and the People* (New York: Macmillan, 1915), 285.

7. During Gerstäcker's time it was believed that yellow fever was caused by unhealthy vapors or miasmas.

8. Because blacks had built up greater resistance to yellow fever than whites and Native Americans, they were considered useful for transporting the corpses of those who had succumbed to the viral infection. With so many dying, the large coffin contained several corpses.

9. Scipio is a stereotypical slave name, not the name of a particular individual.

10. *Author:* These are the nicknames for the inhabitants of Ohio, Indiana, and Kentucky.

11. The bitter ethnic strife between the Creole- and foreign French and the Anglo-Americans after the Louisiana Purchase resulted in the division of New Orleans into three semiautonomous municipalities in 1836. Two downtown municipalities were dominated by French-Creoles and the uptown municipality by Americans. The ethnic makeup of each municipality was never as sharply drawn as the geopolitical lines would indicate, and concentrations of commercial activity actually distinguished the three sections. New Orleans was reconsolidated in 1852. Arnold R. Hirsch and Joseph Logsdon, eds., "Introduction to Part II: The American Challenge," *Creole New Orleans: Race and Americanization* (Baton Rouge: Louisiana State University Press, 1992), 92–93; Tregle, "Creoles and Americans," *Creole New Orleans: Race and Americanization*, 131–85; Richard Campanella, *Time and Place in New Orleans: Past Geographies in the Present Day* (Gretna, La.: Pelican, 2002), 119.

12. The term *calaboose* is derived from Creole French or Spanish *calabozo*, meaning "dungeon." *The Random House Dictionary of the English Language.* Because the first prison in New Orleans, situated on St. Peter and Chartres streets, was built during the Spanish regime, its name probably originated during that period. The term *calaboose* is used, however, in other parts of the United States. When this edifice was destroyed, secret rooms, instruments of torture, and an underground passageway were discovered, suggesting that the Capuchin monks may have carried out inquisitions forbidden by Governor Miro. The prison to which Gerstäcker refers was completed in 1834 upon a parallelogram bounded by Marais, Trémé, St. Anne, and Orleans streets. Henry C. Castellanos, *New Orleans as It Was* (1895; rpt., Baton Rouge: Louisiana State University Press, 1978), 102–4; Lyle Saxon, *Fabulous New Orleans* (1928; rpt., New Orleans: Robert L. Crager, 1947), 151–52.

13. The first Irish policeman joined the force in New Orleans around 1830. By 1850 the Irish were the most overrepresented ethnic group. This was attributable in part to the great number of Irish immigrants during that period. But in-group solidarity (in contrast to the Germans) that facilitated access to this plum patronage job, the lack of education for other kinds of occupations, and the Irish cultural penchant for fighting were also factors in the strong Irish presence on the police force. Dennis C. Rousey, "'Hibernian Leatherheads': Irish Cops in New Orleans, 1830–1880," *Journal of Urban History* 10, no. 1 (1983): 61–84.

14. *Author: Arrah* is an Irish epithet.

15. Gerstäcker is correct about contemporary usage of the term *Creole* in Louisiana. See note 27 to "Louisiana Sojourn," in this volume. See also Donald H. Usner on the application of the term to plants and animals and on the creolization of agricultural practices. "'The Facility Offered by the Country': The Creolization of Agriculture in the Lower Mississippi Valley," in *Creolization in the Americas,* ed. David Buisseret and Steven G. Reinhardt (College Station: Texas A&M University Press, for the University of Texas at Arlington, 2000), 35–62.

Ice produced in Louisiana in the 1840s was indeed a novelty. Although commercial ice plants existed in the state during the antebellum period, ice usually was shipped to the New Orleans area from New England by ocean vessels or from the upper Mississippi and Ohio rivers on barges during the winter months. Edwin Adams Davis, *Louisiana: A Narrative History,* 3d ed. (1961; rpt., Baton Rouge: Claitor's, 1971), 322.

During his 1826 visit to New Orleans, Bernhard, duke of Saxony-Weimar-Eisenach, noted the arrival on March 14 of the brig *Arcturus* carrying ice. He explains that ice was stored in brick houses, covered with planks and sawdust, because ice pits could not be dug in New Orleans ground. The ice lasted until August. Griep and Jäger, *Reise und soziale Realität,* 2:99.

16. Although the etiology of yellow fever had not yet been established, Gerstäcker correctly describes its symptoms and course in the footnote: "Yellow fever usually begins with shivering that lasts about half an hour, during which there are rarely any other symptoms. This is followed by high fever with pain in the eye sockets and throbbing temples. The eyes become inflamed in a peculiar manner and the body is seized by weakness and exhaustion. A pulse of 120 degrees, a burning thirst, a desire for cold liquids, occasional vomiting, pain and heat in the stomach, a white-coated tongue with red edges. According to how the patient behaves and is treated, this condition lasts with more or less intensity from twenty-four to twenty-eight hours, after which the symptoms all cease and the patient feels quite well and relieved, except that at certain moments his features betray fear and great unrest. That lasts from twelve to twenty-four hours, and if the fever does not lift entirely, it returns with vomiting and hallucinations. In addition there is a headache, difficulty in urination, violent hemorrhaging, black vomiting and—death." The hemorrhaging and vomiting results from liver injury associated with infection. Oldstone, *Viruses, Plagues, and History,* 46.

"In Bayou Sara" and "The Houseboy and the Cow"

"In Bayou Sarah" and "Der Hausknecht und die Kuh," *Aus meinem Tagebuch,* vol. 15 of *Gesammelte Schriften,* 467–70, 453–57.

1. Jeffrey L. Sammons observes that such remarks belong to "the familiar topos of German and, no doubt, generally European anti-Americanism" criticizing "the pervasive commercial atmosphere, the subordination of all values to moneymaking." *Ideology, Mimesis, Fantasy: Charles Sealsfield, Friedrich Gerstäcker, Karl May, and Other German Novelists of America* (Chapel Hill: University of North Carolina Press, 1998), 174.

2. The *Ricinus communis* is commonly known as the castor bean plant. It is a native of the tropics and once was relatively common in the South. It has palmately divided leaves and grows to an average height of ten feet and width of six feet. Neil Odenwald and James Turner, *Identi-*

fication, Selection, and Use of Southern Plants for Landscape Design, 3d ed. (Baton Rouge: Claitor's, 1996), 527.

3. William A. Beatty.

"A Drill" and "The Ferry Hotel in Pointe Coupée"

"Louisiana Skizzen," *Wilde Welt*, vol. 4, 2d ser., of *Gesammelte Schriften*, 449–67.

1. Gerstäcker is referring to the Civil War.

2. The names John Riley and James Riley, both of West Feliciana Parish, appear in the *1840 Louisiana State Wide Census Index.*

3. Gerstäcker uses this English phrase in the German original.

4. This is Frederick Fischer, whose purchase and sale of the Ferry Hotel property was noted earlier. Fischer is listed in the *1840 Louisiana State Wide Census Index*. In *Feliciana Confederates: A Compilation of the Soldiers of East and West Feliciana Parishes 1861–1865* is the following entry:

"FISHER FREDERICK (F.) . . . . 20th La. Infantry, Co. I

49 year old Justice of the Peace in 1860, post office: St. Francisville, La., born in Wittenberg, Germany; enlisted at Camp Lewis 12–21–61; present on rolls to Apr 62; roll for May–Jun 62, absent sick since 2–27–62; roll from 7–1–62 to 10–31–62, dropped, left the ranks on march through Tennessee 8–28–62.

5. A modern steam ferry still transports passengers between the foot of St. Francisville and the landing near New Roads.

6. Charles Fischer.

7. St. Charles Borromeo Church, located twenty-five miles upriver from New Orleans on the east bank, was established around 1740. When it was replaced in 1806 by a frame church, painted red, it became known as the "Little Red Church." The site was a riverboat landmark where captains on downriver voyages paid off their crews. Mary Ann Sternberg, *Along the River Road: Past and Present on Louisiana's Historic Byway* (Baton Rouge: Louisiana State University Press, 1996), 110. The bluffs actually end just below Baton Rouge.

8. Here the term means "bachelor."

"Mr. Mix"

"Mr. Mix," *Buntes Treiben*, vol. 16, 2d ser., of *Gesammelte Schriften*, 575–80. Although this anecdote was written after Gerstäcker's second visit to Louisiana, it is included in this section because it concerns an antebellum experience.

1. There are no Mixes in the early records of West Feliciana Parish. In the early nineteenth century Charles Alsandor (aka Alexander) Mix came to Pointe Coupée Parish from Philadelphia. He and his descendants operated cotton gins up until 1970. Brian J. Costello, pers. comm., January 2005. Also Riffel, "Early History," 29. There is no town of Portland. Present-day Clinton lies about twenty miles east of St. Francisville.

"The Slave," "The Purchased Hangman," "The Planter," and "Jazede"

Mississippi-Bilder: Licht- und Schattenseiten transatlantischen Lebens, vol. 10 of *Gesammelte Schriften,* 5–43, 93–119, 169–93, 433–76. The story "The Planter" was previously translated anonymously in *Western Lands and Western Waters* by Frederick Gerstäcker (London: S. O. Beeton, 1864), 331–52; I have consulted this translation.

1. *Author:* a jesting name for the United States, based on the initial letters: *United States, Uncle Sam.*

2. The *Great Western* was the earliest regular transatlantic steamer, sailing between Bristol (Avonmouth) and New York. It made its maiden voyage in 1838. *Passenger Liners of the Western Ocean: A Record of the North Atlantic Steam and Motor Passenger Vessels from 1838 to the Present Day,* 2d rev. ed. (London: Staples Press, [1957]), 41–42.

3. I could not find a Seal listed in Pointe Coupée Parish. The *1840 Louisiana State Wide Census Index* lists a James Seals and an L. J. Seals in East Feliciana Parish.

4. *Author:* Mustangs are small Indian horses.

Baton Rouge is a French settlement on the Mississippi. [It is true that the French claimed Louisiana in the late seventeenth century, and Iberville's expedition sighted the bluffs of Baton Rouge in March 1699. But the French concession established at Baton Rouge in 1718 was abandoned by 1727. Continuous development of the town began after 1763, when Great Britain acquired the territory of East and West Florida from Spain and that portion of Louisiana north of the Isle of Orleans and east of the Mississippi. Therefore, Baton Rouge, like the Felicianas, had more of an Anglo than French character. Rose Meyers, *A History of Baton Rouge, 1699–1812* (Baton Rouge: Louisiana State University Press, 1976), 1–41.]

5. *Author:* a contemptuous term for *Negro.*

6. It was illegal for whites to game with blacks, even free blacks. This most likely exacerbated the white men's rage at Alfons's audacity.

7. *Author:* the offspring of a white man and a mulatto woman. [For all practical purposes this definition is accurate for the antebellum South, although the common definition is simply that a quadroon has one-quarter "Negro blood."]

8. The Taylor plantation was situated on the lower side of the property on which stood the Ferry Hotel in Pointe Coupée. Its owner, William Taylor, was the nephew of President Zachary Taylor.

9. *Author:* a water turkey, a kind of diver that is found in great numbers in the southern waters of North America, especially on the Mississippi.

The *Gavia immer* is a migratory bird found in Louisiana from November to mid-April. Lowery, *Louisiana Birds,* 101–2.

10. Waterloo was a busy shipping port located about five miles south of Pointe Coupée, the parish seat until 1846. Waterloo was abandoned after heavy flooding in 1882 and again in 1884. Ann DeVillier Riffel and Judy Riffel, *A History of Pointe Coupee Parish and Its Families* (Baton Rouge: Le Comité des Archives de la Louisiane, 1983), 32, 38.

11. *Author:* This is the Creole's favorite dish.

12. *Author:* Flatboats are large boats used to transport commodities that float down with the river's current.

13. Lydia Maria Child's short story "The Quadroons" has a similar ending. When the octoroon Xarifa's beloved George, her white music master, is fatally shot in a failed attempt to rescue her from the highest bidder, a "wealthy profligate," Xarifa sinks into intense melancholy and fractures her head against the wall in a frenzy of despair. *An Anthology of Interracial Literature: Black-White Contacts in the Old World and the New,* ed. Werner Sollors (New York: New York University Press, 2004), 232–39.

14. An unpublished history, "Old Families of Louisiana," states: "The Morgan family whose plantation on the Mississippi was well known in connection with the Morganza levee, which yearly was the cause of so much solitude to the people of the interior back of it, are of descent from Colonel Charles Morgan, the original, or one of the original proprietors of 'Morganza.' He was a prominent planter of his day, and a member of the first legislature convened in the territory of the newly formed state of Louisiana." Charles Morgan, whose family traces its ancestry back to Irish nobility, went South at an early date, around 1800, and married Hiacenthe (variant spellings: *Hycient,* anglicized *Hyacinth*) Allain at Pointe Coupée. Morgan Family Papers, 5, 18. According to Ann Patton Malone, Charles Morgan and his brother-in-law, Judge Jacob Charles Van Wickle, were notorious for removing slaves from the state of New Jersey, circumventing an 1812 law requiring consent before removal. Just before the implementation of an 1818 law prohibiting the exportation of slaves, they removed at least sixty slaves not just for their own use but for speculation. *Sweet Chariot: Slave Family and Household Structure in Nineteenth-Century Louisiana* (Chapel Hill: University of North Carolina Press), 101–2.

15. I have not been able to find a case in which a French Creole murdered his wife. Included, however, in a letter dated August 2, 1839, from Father Jean Martin of Pointe Coupée to Bishop Antoine Blanc of New Orleans is news that they hanged an American who had killed two children with an axe. http:/archives.nd.edu/calendar/cal1839.htm.

16. Beauvais were among the earliest settlers in Pointe Coupée. Riffel, *History of Pointe Coupee Parish and Its Settlers,* 4. *Louisiana Census Records II, Iberville, Natchitoches, Pointe Coupée and Rapides Parishes, 1810 and 1820* indicates that Armand [*sic*] Beauvais owned twenty-one slaves and John B. Beauvais owned twenty-three slaves in 1810. Arnaud Beauvais was acting governor of Louisiana from October 6, 1829. His property was sold at a sheriff's auction in 1837. *A Dictionary of Louisiana Biography,* ed. Glenn R. Conrad (Lafayette: Louisiana Historical Association, 1988), 1:55.

17. Conveyance records show that Roetken owned a slave named Figaro. Although records of slave sales in Pointe Coupée Parish indicate that French planters owned slaves with classical names, I have not found one slave named "Scipio." For example, the succession inventory of Vincent Ternant, builder of Parlange plantation home, lists slaves with a variety of classical, Anglo, and French names, with a few African and Native American names as well (1842, entry no. 2931). The type of name might depend, in part, on whether the slaves were born on the plantation or purchased. I suspect Gerstäcker resorted to a literary convention in naming the slave Scipio here and in other stories. Prominent slave characters named Scipio appear, for example, in John Pendleton Kennedy's *Swallow Barn; or, A Sojourn in the Old Dominion,* originally published in 1832, and in William Gilmore Simms's short story "The Lazy Crow: A Story of the Cornfield," in *The Wigwam and the Cabin, or Tales of the South* (1845) (Charleston, S.C.: Walker, Richards and Co., 1856), 2:99–126. Gerstäcker translated Simms's work; he was most likely familiar with the latter.

18. *Author:* the dam built at the Mississippi.

19. Fritz Haydt is the jailer Gerstäcker mentions in the account of his first Louisiana sojourn.

20. A piastre is the former peso or dollar of Spain and Spanish America.

21. In his lurid description of various executions that transpired in the New Orleans parish prison, Henry C. Castellanos remarks that in the earlier part of the nineteenth century, the prison had no official executioner. "Sheriffs were frequently nonplussed in the performance of this revolting duty, and were at times compelled to solicit the pardon of such minor criminals as were willing, for that consideration, to undertake the job." *New Orleans as It Was,* 127.

22. The premise of the following plot is the age-old stereotype of the venal Jew. The ambiguous nickname Gold-Wolfie appears to be an endearment but actually suggests the stereotype that Jews have an undue interest in acquiring money.

23. The town of False River (Fausse Rivière) was located along Bayou Fordoche, southeast of the present town of Fordoche. *History of Pointe Coupée Parish and Its Settlers,* 24–25.

24. Although elsewhere, in the short stories set in the Pointe Coupée and Bayou Sara—St. Francisville areas, Gerstäcker correctly defines a Creole as anyone native to Louisiana, it is also correct to understand a Creole to be a native of Louisiana of French descent; he speaks Creole French. The American, having moved down from the North, is understood to be of Anglo descent, and a French person has come directly from France. See note 27 to "Louisiana Sojourn," in this volume, pp. 287–88.

25. The building that served as the courthouse until it burned down in 1846 had been the post at Pointe Coupée. The citizens of the parish purchased the building and property from the U.S. government after it was vacated in 1806. The courthouse and the adjacent jail were located at the Bayou Sara ferry landing on the Mississippi River near present-day Pointe Coupée.

26. The *1840 Louisiana State Wide Census Index* lists a Geo. Long of West Feliciana Parish and a Lola George of Pointe Coupée.

27. Creoles of French ancestry tended to live in the southern half of Pointe Coupée parish and Americans to the north.

28. The "great bend" was that point near Charles Morgan's plantation, Morganza, where the Mississippi River changed its course by an almost ninety-degree angle.

29. The town of False River is synonymous with the town of New Roads on False River. Costello, pers. comm., January 2005.

30. This character's name may be based on Daniel Turnbull (1799–1861), who founded Rosedown Plantation in West Feliciana Parish in 1835. He also operated Styopa, Catalpa, Middleplace, Hazelwood, Grove, Inheritance, Woodlawn, and De Soto plantations. LSU Special Collections database: Turnbull-Bowman-Lyons Family Papers (MS 4026), 2. Rosedown Plantation was purchased by the state of Louisiana in 2000.

31. The *1840 Louisiana State Wide Census Index* lists a Chas. Hawthorne in East Feliciana Parish.

32. Charles E. Rosenberg characterizes cholera as the classic epidemic disease of the nineteenth century. In 1883 Robert Koch isolated the bacterium, *Vibrio comma,* that causes cholera. The disease thrives in unsanitary conditions, often related to poverty, and spreads along any pathway leading to the human digestive tract. Cholera is marked by diarrhea, acute spasmodic vomiting, and painful cramps, followed by dehydration. *The Cholera Years: The United States in 1832, 1849, and 1864,* with a new afterword (1962; rpt., Chicago: University of Chicago Press, 1987), 1–4.

33. According to Page Smith, one of the most sensational events of 1841 was the failure of the Bank of the United States because its president had misused bank funds. *The Nation Comes of Age: A People's History of the Ante-Bellum Years,* vol. 4 (New York: Penguin, 1984), 196. Perhaps Gerstäcker fictionalizes this event.

34. The *1840 Louisiana State Wide Census Index* lists a B. F. Wharton in East Feliciana Parish.

35. Texas had the reputation as being a haven for absconders, ne'er-do-wells, and criminals far out of proportion to their actual numbers. *Encyclopedia of Southern History,* 1215.

36. Randolph B. Campbell discusses the rapid expansion of slavery in Texas after independence in 1836. Most slaves migrated with their southern-born masters. *An Empire for Slavery: The Peculiar Institution in Texas, 1821–1865* (Baton Rouge: Louisiana State University Press, 1989).

37. *Author:* the American nightingale. [The northern mockingbird (*Mimus polyglottos*) sings day and night. Its reputation stems from its ability to imitate many other birds. Lowery, *Louisiana Birds,* 466–69.]

38. *Author:* a kind of diver, also called water turkey.

39. The Quapaw tribe was concentrated in southern Arkansas by the time of the first European encounter. In the period between 1820 and 1830 they settled among the Caddo in northwestern Louisiana, but floods and disease drove them back to Arkansas. Fred B. Kniffen, Hiram F. Gregory, and George A. Stokes, *The Historic Indian Tribes of Louisiana: From 1542 to the Present* (Baton Rouge: Louisiana State University Press, 1987), 87, 91–92. The Quapaws are kin to the Osages, who along with the other Dhegiha Sioux peoples—the Omahas, Kansas, and Poncas—lived in the Ohio Valley before migrating west and southwest sometime prior to 1673. W. David Baird, *The Quapaw Indians: A History of the Downstream People* (Norman: University of Oklahoma Press, 1980), 3–5.

40. Jeffrey L. Sammons observes that Quapas's "comic, ingratiating manner masks a rage against white oppressors." "Nineteenth-Century German Representations of Indians," in *Germans and Indians: Fantasies, Encounters, Projections,* ed. Colin G. Calloway, Gerd Gemünden, and Susanne Zantop (Lincoln: University of Nebraska Press, 2002), 189.

41. According to Stanley Faye, "the schooner small or large was always the typical privateer craft of Northerly American waters." "Types of Privateer Vessels, Their Armament and Flags in the Gulf of Mexico," *Louisiana Historical Quarterly* 23, no. 1 (1940): 118–30. For a detailed but nonanalytical account of privateers and their activities in the Gulf of Mexico during the peak years 1800–1820, see Faye, "Privateersmen of the Gulf and Their Prizes," *Louisiana Historical Quarterly* 22, no. 4 (1939): 1012–94.

42. The beautiful quadroon is a stock figure in literature treating the antebellum South. According to Eve Allegra Raimon, the trope of the "tragic mulatta" (which includes the mixed-race mulatta, quadroon, and octoroon) "operates as a vehicle for exploring the complexities surrounding the interrelated identifications of race and national allegiance." *The "Tragic Mulatta" Revisited: Race and Nationalism in Nineteenth-Century Antislavery Fiction* (New Brunswick, N.J.: Rutgers University Press, 2004), 4. Gerstäcker here also captures the dynamics of race relations among French or French Creoles and Africans in the French-dominated parishes, Pointe Coupée in particular. Beginning with the colonial period, interracial liaisons—regardless of the extent to which they were consensual on the part of the black women—were not uncommon. In his study of Creole Pointe Coupée, Brian J. Costello maintains that many prominent early

families have white and colored branches. Planters usually freed the mother of their offspring and recognized their children, and some Creoles of color held plantations in the antebellum period. *Creole Pointe Coupée: A Sociological Analysis* (New Roads, La.: John and Noelie Laurent Ewing, 2002).

43. The "Lytle List" documents ten merchant steam vessels named *Cuba.* The steam ship *Cuba,* which traveled between Galveston and New Orleans, is recorded as having arrived at least nine times in New Orleans. *Passenger Lists Taken from Manifests of the Customs Service Port of New Orleans, 1839–1849. Including Names of Sloops, Brigs, Schooners, Sailing Ships, and Steamboats, as Well as Passenger Embarkation Ports and Destinations,* Work Projects Administration of Louisiana, 1941.

44. Daniel H. Usner Jr. remarks that present-day historians are "finally scrutinizing the initiatives taken by Indians themselves to maintain desirable forms of subsistence and exchange on their own terms," thus replacing "the stereotype of passive victims of dependency with a more accurate picture of resourceful participants in economic change." *American Indians in the Lower Mississippi Valley: Social and Economic Histories* (Lincoln: University of Nebraska Press, 1998), 95.

45. Kniffen, Gregory, and Stokes state that Indians have long been marginal to the plantation areas of Louisiana. "If Indians lived near a plantation, the owner became their patron, offering them credit and protection from exploitation, at least by others. In exchange, they were required to hunt, entertain guests with ball games and dances, make baskets, tan hides, and perform other services that might, on occasion, include the recovery of runaway slaves." *Historic Indian Tribes of Louisiana,* 93.

46. Richard G. Follett discusses the ambiguous role that alcohol played in master-slave relations. Slaves trafficked in pilfered goods, including whiskey, with river traders. Whiskey provided a psychic escape from bondage, but planters also controlled their slaves by using whiskey as a reward for hard labor. *The Sugar Masters: Planters and Slaves in Louisiana's Cane World, 1820–1826* (Baton Rouge: Louisiana State University Press, 2005), 166–71.

47. The whip, the slave driver's symbol of authority, varied in its construction from plantation to plantation. William L. Van Deburg, *The Slave Drivers: Black Agricultural Labor Supervisors in the Antebellum South* (Westport, Conn.: Greenwood, 1979), 11.

48. Loo is a game of cards in which forfeits are paid into a pool: euchre is a fast, trick-based game.

49. Congress passed the Indian Removal Act in 1830, authorizing the United States president to arrange by treaty the exchange of western lands for the holdings of all Native American nations east of the Mississippi. President Andrew Jackson was interested primarily in the removal of the five large southern nations—Choctaws, Chickasaws, Creeks, Cherokees, and Seminoles. In 1836, following a few scattered Creek attacks in Alabama, Jackson sent in troops. The Second Seminole War in Florida, lasting from 1836 to 1842, took a far greater toll on both sides. Michael D. Green, "The Expansion of European Colonization to the Mississippi Valley, 1780–1880," in *The Cambridge History of the Native Peoples of the Americas,* vol. 1, pt. 2: *North America,* ed. Bruce G. Trigger and Wilcomb E. Washburn (Cambridge: Cambridge University Press, 1996), 516–25.

50. When all are restored to hope.

51. I saw the fields of . . .

52. Young girl with black eyes

You reign over my soul
Here, behold the rings
The crosses of gold—.

53. Slave insurrection and deeply ingrained fear of it in whites was a factor almost from the beginning. Joe Gray Taylor notes a conspiracy discovered as early as 1730. *Louisiana: A History* (1976; rpt., New York: Norton, 1984), 12. In 1795 a conspiracy organized from the estate of Julien Poydras in Pointe Coupée was uncovered. Gwendolyn Midlo Hall characterizes the conspiracy as "part of a multiracial abolitionist movement supported by a large segment of the dispossessed of all races in Louisiana and throughout the Caribbean: a manifestation of the most radical phase of the French Revolution." *Africans in Colonial Louisiana,* 344–45. The Deslondes Slave Revolt of 1811 was the largest in United States history in terms of slave participation. Charles Deslondes, a mulatto from Saint-Domingue (present-day Haiti) and a slave driver on the plantation of Col. Manuel Andry near Norco, about thirty-one miles upriver from New Orleans, organized 150 to 500 slaves. As the insurgents, armed with whatever they could find, marched on to New Orleans, white inhabitants fled before them. This revolt had national reverberations. Instilling fear in slave owners in other states, it led to the enactment of stricter slave control measures in the South. But the severity of the suppression—the heads of executed slaves were mounted on poles—was also a factor in forming abolitionist sentiment. James H. Dormon, "The Persistent Specter: Slave Rebellions in Territorial Louisiana," *Louisiana History* 18, no. 4 (1977): 389–404, rpt. in *Carnivals and Conflicts: A Louisiana History Reader,* ed. Samuel C. Hyde Jr., C. Howard Nichols, and Charles N. Elliot (Fort Worth: Harcourt College Publishers, 2000), 191–99; and Thomas Marshall Thompson, "National Newspaper and Legislative Reactions to Louisiana's Deslondes Slave Revolt," *Louisiana Historical Quarterly* 33, no. 1 (1992): 5–29. Pointing out the difficulties of establishing why slaves did or did not participate in the 1811 rebellion— the participants being relatively few—Daniel C. Littlefield notes a few instances of great hostility between slave and master. "Slavery in French Louisiana: From Gallic Colony to American Territory," in *Creoles and Cajuns,* 91–93. By the 1830s and 1840s southern slaveholders perceived an increased ideological threat from the abolitionists. Fear of insurrection, agitated by a regular progression of slave plots discovered, led to a vicious cycle of repression. Junius Peter Rodriguez, "Ripe for Revolt: Louisiana and the Tradition of Slave Insurrection, 1803–1865" (Ph.D. diss., Auburn University, 1992), 170–220.

54. The characters cut from the landing on the Mississippi River through a canal to Lake Pontchartrain. The lake connected to Lake Borgne and thus to the Gulf. Tregle, *Louisiana in the Age of Jackson,* 6.

"The Daughter of the Riccarees"

"Die Tochter der Riccarees: Lebensbild aus Louisiana," *Aus zwei Welttheilen: Gesammelte Erzählungen,* vol. 13 of *Gesammelte Schriften,* 391–446.

1. *Author:* overseer, the chief overseers of the Negroes, mostly whites, that is, Americans, also often Creoles. The overseers subordinate to them, usually Negroes themselves, are just called "nigger drivers," as, in general, *nigger* is the contemptuous and frequently used expression for *Negro.*

2. False River. The twenty-two-mile-long oxbow lake created when the main channel of the

Mississippi shifted, separating the bend from the river except in times of flood. Not to be confused with the former town of False River, now New Roads, named after this lake. Brian J. Costello, *A History of Pointe Coupee Parish, Louisiana* (New Roads, La.: by the author, 1999), 14.

3. *Author:* an African expression, usually used for everything that is small and cute. [*Pickaninny* may be derived from the Portuguese *pequenino,* meaning "very little one." *The Random House Dictionary of the English Language* (New York: Random House, 1967). In the story's context it is an affectionate term for a Negro child, but now it would be offensive.]

4. The more common name for Riccaree is Arikara. The northernmost Caddoan tribe, the agricultural Arikara probably originated somewhere in the Southwest; they began moving northward along the Missouri River during the seventeenth century. The Arikara suffered a smallpox epidemic in the 1780s, and this disease severely reduced their number again in 1837. In the early 1820s they were at war with the U.S. Army in the Dakotas and briefly retreated to Nebraska, settling among their relatives, the Pawnee. *A Concise Dictionary of Indian Tribes of North America,* ed. Barbara A. Leitch (Algonac, Mich.: Reference Publications, 1979), 49–51.

5. The position taken by Saise's father resembles that taken by the chiefs of the Cherokee Nation. The Cherokees were the most acculturated of all the native peoples, but this did not prevent their ultimate removal from already shrinking tribal lands in 1838–39. Russell Thornton estimates that population loss on the journey west of the Mississippi, the bitter Trail of Tears, may have been double the commonly held estimate of four thousand. "The Demography of the Trail of Tears Period: A New Estimate of Cherokee Population Losses," in *Cherokee Removal: Before and After,* ed. William L. Anderson (Athens: University of Georgia Press, 1991), 75–95.

6. According to William G. McLoughlin, there is conflicting evidence about the nature of black-Indian relations, in part because not all Indian tribes treated blacks the same. Nevertheless, one can assume a general trend of relationships worsening after the colonial period as a result of increased pressure on the Indian by the white man, as McLoughlin traces in his study of southeastern Indian tribes. *The Cherokee Ghost Dance: Essays on the Southeastern Indians, 1789–1861* (Mercer, Ga.: Mercer University Press, 1984). In the case of Louisiana, Gwendolyn Mido Hall emphasizes cooperation between blacks and Indians in the colonial period, although various native tribes allied themselves differently. *Africans in Colonial Louisiana,* 97–118. Kniffen, Gregory, and Stokes state that Indians had been tolerant of blacks in the early colonial period, but soon "white instigation of racially linked conflict forstalled union of the two races." Indians came to scorn both blacks and the institution of slavery. *Historic Indian Tribes of Louisiana,* 93–94. Gerstäcker's story illustrates Native American hierarchical notions of race resulting from the confrontation with white racism and domination.

7. *Author:* the Mississippi.

8. *Author:* the Indian term for "wife."

9. Here Gerstäcker uses *manitou* in the singular sense, defined by David Leeming and Jake Page to mean "great spirit" or "all-encompassing power." *The Mythology of Native North America* (Norman: University of Oklahoma Press, 1998) 70–71. According to Werner Müller, this understanding of the term is abstract and Europeanized, even the *manitou* of the sky is a sensate being, as are all the *manitous* (in the plural) that pervade the universe. *Die Religionen der Waldlandindianer Nordamerikas* (Berlin: Dietrich Reimer, 1956), 238–53.

10. *Author:* A loafer is a vagabond, and calaboose the jail in New Orleans.

11. *Author:* a common question in Louisiana, which always refers to cotton, since the owner's wealth is estimated according to that.

12. A mestizo, or the feminine mestiza, is a person of mixed race. Here it means a mix of Indian and black.

13. The Choctaw were migrants to Louisiana from east of the Mississippi and became the most widespread Indian tribe in Louisiana. They so prospered in the years from 1780 to 1830 that they refused to leave Louisiana under the Treaty of Choctaw Removal, in effect from 1828 to 1835. They traded and sold game, furs, baskets, wild honey, and medicinal herbs. Kniffen, Gregory, and Stokes, *Historic Indian Tribes of Louisiana*, 74, 94–97.

14. Beatty was an Irish lawyer who resided at the Ferry Hotel in Pointe Coupée when Gerstäcker managed it.

15. Founded in 1829 through the last will and testament of the local planter, merchant, statesman, and philanthropist Julien Poydras (1740–1824), Poydras College, a boys' academy, was the first endowed college in Louisiana. It closed during the Civil War and reopened only briefly. Riffel, *Pointe Coupee Parish History*, 56; and Brian J. Costello, pers. comm., January 2005.

16. *Author:* Uncle Sam is the nickname of the United States, after the initial letters of *United States*.

17. A gig is a light, two-wheeled, one-horse carriage.

18. Kniffen, Gregory, and Stokes maintain that the Choctaw "rejected the white man's wages, identifying them with institutionalized slavery." *Historic Indian Tribes of Louisiana*, 96–97.

19. Anglo-Americans called the Indians of Alabama and Georgia who had a Muskogean tribal affiliation "Creeks." Joel W. Martin, *Sacred Revolt: The Muskogees' Struggle for a New World* (Boston: Beacon Press, 1991), 6–13. Note that Gerstäcker's Indian character uses the name Muskogee (*mosko:kalki*) that native peoples used to designate their cultural identity or tribal affiliation.

20. The character is fashioned after the actual deputy sheriff, Fritz Haydt, who also figures in "The Purchased Hangman."

21. *Author:* the name for a bend in the Mississippi where the current has made a new, closer path.

"In the Red River"

"Im Red River," *Heimliche und Unheimliche Geschichten,* vol. 20 of *Gesammelte Schriften,* 376–87. Originally published as *Heimliche und unheimliche Geschichten: Gesammelte Erzählungen,* 2 vols. (Leipzig: Arnold, 1862). The word *unheimlich* means "uncanny," but here, juxtaposed with the word *heimlich,* it is a play on words, implying the notions of both "eerie" and "foreign."

1. Rounded off, a German mile equals 7.42 kilometers.

2. There was a 137-ton side-wheeler named the *Blackhawk* built in 1833. Since it was built in and had its home port in Cincinnati, I am uncertain whether this vessel was later on the Red River. *Merchant Steam Vessels of the United States, 1807–1868,* 20.

"The Mouth of the Mississippi," "New Orleans," and "Ashore"

Nach Amerika! Ein Volksbuch, vols. 11–12 of *Gesammelte Schriften.* The translation consists of excerpts from these chapters. Originally published as *Nach Amerika! Ein Volksbuch,* 3 vols. (Leipzig: Costenoble, 1855).

1. Louis Voss discusses the same difficulties—especially for the passengers in steerage—that Gerstäcker describes in his novel: a journey of 70 to 120 days, insufficient ventilation, poor sanitation, bad or insufficient food, lack of water, and diseases. The German Society of New Orleans was founded in May 1847 to assist the immigrants with difficulties that continued once they had landed. *Louisiana's German Heritage: Louis Voss' Introductory History,* ed. Don Heinrich Tolzmann (Bowie, Md.: Heritage, 1994), 74–76.

2. The colors of the Bremen flag correspond to the coat of arms of Bremen: white key on red ground (http://www.flaggenlexikon.de).
Author: The American flag has red and white stripes with a blue square containing white stars in the upper corner at the flagstaff. In the beginning of the Union there were thirteen stars, according to the number of states, but with each new state a new star was added.

3. This question is put in English in the original.

4. According to Alan Conway, before the Civil War, New Orleans was second only to New York in the number of passengers who made that port their destination. Poorer immigrants from Ireland and Germany could travel to New Orleans cheaply because they served as ballast for ships carrying cotton back to Europe. From New Orleans immigrants moved up the Mississippi Valley and toward the West. "New Orleans as a Port of Immigration, 1820–1860." *Louisiana Studies* 1, no. 3 (1962): 1–22.

5. The flag of Hamburg corresponds in design and colors to the coat of arms of Hamburg: white castle on red ground (http://www.flaggenlexikon.de).

6. *Author:* In the metaphoric language of the Indians the Mississippi is called "father of waters."

7. Solitaire.

8. New Orleans was one of four major ports of entry, along with New York, Philadelphia, and Baltimore. Immigrants bound for the Midwest could more easily make their way up the Mississippi than cross-country. *Louisiana's German Heritage,* xi.

9. Dorothy Anne Dondore cites this doggerel verse in the original as an example of verses extolling the riches of new territory in *Prairie and the Making of Middle America,* 241.

10. *Author:* One cannot separate the New Orleans levee from New Orleans itself, for it comprises most of the city and is the city's sole protection against the river, which often rises twelve to fifteen feet higher than the bank. Because the entire bank of the Mississippi is so low and was so exposed to the powerful river's annual floods, the settlers, in order to preserve the valuable arable land, had to construct a high dam along the entire riverbank. This dam was laid out when the French ruled the land, and they called it a "levée," a name that the Americans later adopted. The New Orleans levee, which runs down along the entire city for more than eight English miles, has an average width of 150 feet and is 15 feet above the low-water level. It is an equally long landing place and depository, where the enormous amount of wares that come from the interior and are bound for the interior arrive and are shipped out. On the side facing the city, it rolls down in a gentle decline, whereas on the side facing the river, which has washed up a considerable amount of alluvial soil, wooden wharfs had to be erected here and there so that the goods could be put ashore easily and dry.

11. Louis Voss notes that the immigrants brought all their household effects in wooden boxes, which were sometimes as large as a one-story house. *Louisiana's German Heritage,* 77. In both fiction and nonfiction Gerstäcker cautions immigrants not to make this costly and cumbersome mistake.

"To Louisiana" and "New Orleans"

"Nach Louisiana" and "New Orleans," *Neue Reisen durch die Vereinigten Staaten, Mexiko, Ecuador, Westindien und Venezuela*, vol. 13, 2d ser., of *Gesammelte Schriften*, 161–200. Originally published in *Nord-Amerika*, vol. 1 of *Neue Reisen durch die Vereinigten Staaten, Mexiko, Ecuador, Westindien und Venezuela* (Jena: Costenoble, 1868).

1. Compared with the antebellum period, there were far fewer German travelers to Louisiana during Reconstruction. The reader might wish to compare Baron Ernst von Hesse-Wartegg's slightly later description of the effects of the Civil War and Reconstruction on race relations, commerce, and plantation culture and economy in Louisiana. *Travels on the Lower Mississippi, 1879–1880*, ed. and trans. Frederic Trautmann (Columbia: University of Missouri Press, 1990), 123–234.

2. This is the lawyer Beatty.

3. The *1840 Louisiana State Wide Census Index* lists a Wm. Taylor residing in East Feliciana Parish and a Wm. Taylor in Pointe Coupée. The index tells us nothing save the names of the residents. Compare p. 286, n. 23, and p. 297, n. 8.

4. The chinaberry, a deciduous tree native to Asia and Australia, was introduced to the United States in the eighteenth century. In early spring it flowers in graceful, lilac-colored panicles. Neil Odenwald and James Turner, *Identification, Selection, and Use of Southern Plants for Landscape Design*, 3d ed. (Baton Rouge: Claitor's, 1996), 384. Many literary travelers through Louisiana have commented on the blooms' sweet scent.

5. According to C. Peter Ripley, blacks showed initiative independent of the federal government's "free labor" system under General Banks, a system they regarded as paternalistic. They engaged in individual sharecropping and established agricultural collectives. *Slaves and Freedmen in Civil War Louisiana* (Baton Rouge: Louisiana State University Press, 1976), 69–89. But no matter what the arrangement was between the former slave owners and the freedmen, the planters rarely were satisfied with their former slaves' exertions. William Kaufman Scarborough, *Masters of the Big House: Elite Slaveholders of the Mid-Nineteenth-Century South* (Baton Rouge: Louisiana State University Press, 2003), 373–405.

6. Because the ratio of black slaves to whites in parishes with large plantations was sometimes more than ten to one (Joe Gray Taylor, *Louisiana: A History* [1976; rpt., New York: Norton, 1984], 75), the resulting ratio of former slaves on the jury was not as inequitable as Gerstäcker believed.

7. Maximilian, brother of the Hapsburg emperor, had but a brief reign in the short-lived Mexican Empire (1864–67). His tenure relied on the presence of French troops. When Napoléon III was compelled to withdraw them, Maximilian took command of his forces and was captured and shot, whereupon the empire dissolved.

8. Prussia and Saxony were rival German states since the War of the Austrian Succession (1740–48) and the Seven Years War (1756–63). Although the last phrase of the analogy is somewhat unclear, it refers to the fact that Saxony was loathe to the prospect of becoming part of a German empire under Prussian hegemony.

9. The *Abeona*, a 151-ton side-wheel steamer, was built in Pittsburgh, Pennsylvania, in 1831. Its first home port was New Orleans. *Merchant Steam Vessels of the United States, 1807–1868.*

10. The ship's carpenter, M. Jean Penicaut, traveling with Pierre Le Moyne, Sieur d'Iberville, recorded in his diary the location the French explorers named Baton Rouge after its Choctaw-language Indian name, Istrouma, meaning "red stick." It was most likely located on Scott's Bluff, the present-day site of Southern University. The thirty-foot-high painted red pole, to which fish bones were attached, may have served as the Houma Indians' totemic symbol of tribal unity. The pole occupied a marginal position between the Houma and the Bayougoula tribes. Andrew C. Albrecht, "The Origin and Early Settlement of Baton Rouge, Louisiana," *Louisiana Historical Quarterly* 28, no. 1 (1945): 5–68.

11. In 1846 the state legislature designated Baton Rouge to replace "sinful" New Orleans as the state capital. Construction of the new statehouse, designed by James Dakin in the neo-Gothic style, began in late 1847. In April 1862 the state government moved first to Opelousas, then to Shreveport. The statehouse was gutted by a fire on December 28, 1862, during Union occupation. Throughout the Reconstruction period New Orleans again served as the capital, but in 1879 the legislature voted to move the capital back to Baton Rouge. After the statehouse was repaired, the legislature and the executive branches returned to Baton Rouge in 1882. Baton Rouge suffered more physical damage than Gerstäcker observed. Mark T. Carleton, *River Capital: An Illustrated History of Baton Rouge* (Woodland Hills, Calif.: Windsor Publications, 1981), 2–3, 34, 64–65, 85–93, 114.

12. The town of Plaquemine, incorporated in 1838, takes its name from the bayou that once flowed from the Mississippi River on the west bank. It was a regular stop for packet boats in the antebellum period. Because portions of the town were repeatedly destroyed by flooding, levee construction began in 1866. The levee, however, cut off access to the bayou, and construction of the Plaquemine Lock began in 1895 and was completed in 1909. The lock was decommissioned in 1961. Mary Ann Sternberg, *Along the River Road: Past and Present on Louisiana's Historical Byway* (Baton Rouge: Louisiana State University Press, 1996), 210–12.

13. The original St. Charles Exchange hotel between Common and Gravier streets, completed in 1837, was nationally known for its luxury and became the model for large-scale hotels in the United States. Designed by Gallier and Dakin, the building had a columned facade and an octagon dome with views of the city and river. It boasted 350 rooms and a gentlemen's dining room that could accommodate five hundred people. Slaves were brought from nearby pens and auctioned at the exchange. The building was destroyed by fire in 1851 and was immediately rebuilt. Joe Gray Taylor, *Louisiana: A History* (1976; rpt., New York: Norton, 1984), 63; Nathaniel Cortlandt Curtis, *New Orleans: Its Old Houses, Shops and Public Buildings* (Philadelphia: J. B. Lippincott, 1933), 186–88; *New Orleans City Guide,* 313.

14. Gustav Ostermann began in 1865 by renting the French Opera House, including its scenic facilities, for biweekly productions. Ellen C. Merrill, *Germans of Louisiana,* foreword by Don Heinrich Tolzmann (Gretna, La.: Pelican, 2005), 291.

15. A Romantic opera by Carl Maria von Weber (1821), which draws upon the expressive powers of folk music. *The Larousse Encyclopedia of Music,* ed. Geoffrey Hindley (Secaucus, N.J.: Chartwell Books, 1971), 270.

16. Records from 1870 show that the German immigrant population in New Orleans was the highest of all immigrant groups. There were 15,239 Germans, compared, for example, to 8,845 French and 960 Spaniards. John F. Nau, "The German People of New Orleans, 1850–1900," in *A Refuge for All Ages: Immigration in Louisiana History,* ed. Carl A. Brasseaux, The Louisiana

Purchase Bicentennial Series in Louisiana History, vol. 10 (Lafayette: Center for Louisiana Studies, 1996), 393. First published in the *Louisiana Historical Quarterly* 54 (1991): 30–45.

According to Robert T. Clark Jr., the most important wave of German immigrants to New Orleans (the third) consisted of German liberals, fervid democratic idealists. Before the Revolution of 1848 they sought a better life than that afforded under Metternichian rule; after the revolution was quashed, some were forced to escape German lands. "The German Liberals in New Orleans (1840–1860)," *Louisiana Historical Quarterly* 20, no. 1 (1937): 137–51. During the entire period of the Civil War, German immigration to Louisiana ceased completely. Robert T. Clark Jr., "Reconstruction and the New Orleans German Colony," *Louisiana Historical Quarterly* 23, no. 2 (1940): 501.

17. One thaler was equal to three marks.

18. Maj. Gen. Benjamin F. Butler commanded New Orleans from May 1, 1862, to early 1863. The margin between unionists and secessionists in Louisiana had only been 5 percent, and the citizens of New Orleans felt deceived by their government and abandoned by the military command, thus affording Butler the opportunity to win over the residents of the city. But the general's initial encounter with rabble-rousers and an obdurate mayor and city leaders increased his resolve to enforce his proclamation sustaining martial law. His manner offended people, and antagonisms were exacerbated. Most infamous was the "Woman Order" intended to stop the "ladies" from insulting, spitting at, and emptying slop pots on Union soldiers. A woman showing contempt "shall be regarded and held liable to be treated as a woman of the town plying her avocation." Chester G. Hearn, *When the Devil Came Down to Dixie* (Baton Rouge: Louisiana State University Press, 1997), 76–109. Nevertheless, according to Joe Gray Taylor, Butler had found the filthiest city in the United States and put the unemployed, runaway slaves and his own troops to work cleaning it up. There was no epidemic of yellow fever in New Orleans during the Civil War. *Louisiana Reconstructed, 1863–1877*, 6–7.

19. The state board of health returned to civilian control in 1866. By May 1867 the *Picayune* deplored the unsanitary conditions prevailing in the city. Yellow fever most likely was reintroduced in midsummer of 1867 by a cargo vessel from Havana. No class was exempt from this fever, but the fever took its greatest toll among the poor. Jo Ann Carrigan, *The Saffron Scourge: A History of Yellow Fever in Louisiana, 1796–1905* (Lafayette: Center for Louisiana Studies, 1994), 96–101.

20. In Gerstäcker's day it was still erroneously believed that yellow fever was caused by miasmas.

21. In Louisiana yellow fever appeared as far north as Shreveport and as far west as Lake Charles. It took a particularly severe toll in New Iberia on Bayou Teche, about fifteen miles from the coast, and in Washington, forty miles to the north. Carrigan, *Saffron Scourge*, 101–3.

22. The "Hapag" (Hamburg-America Line) opened a service to New Orleans in the late 1860s, using its oldest steamers. The *Bavaria* (ca. 2100 tons) originally belonged to the Hamburg-Brazilian S.N. Company as the *Petropolis*. *Passenger Liners of the Western Ocean*, 157.

23. According to Robert T. Clark, this resentment was shared by German immigrants residing not only in New Orleans but also throughout the United States. "Reconstruction and the New Orleans German Colony," 505.

24. In his study *Black Legislators in Louisiana during Reconstruction* (Baton Rouge: Louisiana State University Press, 1976) Charles Vincent demonstrates that blacks were prepared for lead-

ership roles during Reconstruction: "Historically New Orleans already had a large, wealthy, well-educated, articulate free black population. . . . In addition, former slaves fought as soldiers and attended regimental night schools in preparation for freedom and leadership. Other elements providing training and aid to the emerging black leaders were the black churches, black family, urban setting, Freedmen's Bureau, jobs in the Customhouse, native shrewdness, and skills and education acquired before emancipation" (xiv). John W. Blassingame also maintains that during the antebellum period blacks had established the institutions and social structures and developed skills and knowledge that would serve the black community during Reconstruction. *Black New Orleans, 1860–1880* (Chicago: University of Chicago Press, 1973), 22.

25. Kathryn Page discusses a later 1872 case in which Madame DeCuir, a *femme de couleur* and widow of a prosperous Pointe Coupée planter, himself a Creole of color, sued the owner of the steamboat *Governor Allen* for having denied her first-class accommodations. Because Louisiana's 1868 constitution prohibited racial discrimination in public conveyances, the Eighth District Court of Orleans Parish awarded her a thousand dollars, but the Louisiana Supreme Court overturned the ruling in 1878, when the era of Reconstruction had died. "Defiant Women and the Supreme Court of Louisiana in the Nineteenth Century," in *A Law unto Itself? Essays in the New Louisiana Legal History,* ed. Warren M. Billings and Mark F. Fernandez (Baton Rouge: Louisiana State University Press, 2001), 184–90. See also Costello, *History of Pointe Coupée Parish, Louisiana,* 129.

26. Gerstäcker refers to the fact that Otto von Bismarck, premier of Prussia at this time, waged two brief wars, against Denmark in 1864 and Austria in 1866, and reorganized Germany under Prussian leadership in the North German Confederation. Although German liberals such as Gerstäcker initially opposed Bismarck, he won them over by promising German unification, which liberals believed was the necessary basis for bringing about reforms.

27. This is the German Confederation founded at the Congress of Vienna (1814–15), which returned power to the old, conservative forces following the defeat of Napoléon.

"New Orleans" and "The Meeting"

"New Orleans" and "Die Begegnung," *In Amerika: Amerikanisches Lebensbild aus neuerer Zeit,* vol. 19, pt. 1, ser. 2, of *Gesammelte Werke,* 129–50.

1. Albion Winegar Tourgée, a reconstructionist, cites the testimony of Confederate general N. B. Forrest that the Klan was first instituted in Tennessee in 1866. Further, "the best and highest classes of the South did participate in, aid, and abet the movement." Tourgée, *The Invisible Empire* (1880; rpt., Baton Rouge: Louisiana State University Press, 1989), 27, 37.

2. As a reversal of the theme of blacks who cannot be distinguished from whites, Gerstäcker states that the skin color of Jacob, the German houseboy in the Ferry Hotel, is no different from that of a mulatto.

3. Gerstäcker explains: "The lightest and last gradation of the Negro race were the quadroons, for the children of these and whites could no longer be distinguished in their mixture from whites, and even according to the laws of the slaveholders they were free. The only recognizable sign of Negro blood in the quadroons were their fingernails, which had a narrow, yellow rim at the root. There also were the whites of the eyes, but their coloration could only be

detected by people who were thoroughly familiar with racial descent in its various forms. Among the quadroons, especially among the women, one very often finds individuals with light blonde silky soft hair and blue as well as brown eyes."

Werner Sollors devotes an entire chapter, "The Bluish Tinge in the Halfmoon; or, Fingernails as a Racial Sign," to the various functions of the motif of the fingernail as a racial identifier prevalent in European and American literature extending from the mid-nineteenth to the mid-twentieth century. This superstition, according to Sollors, is not based on anatomical fact. *Neither Black nor White yet Both: Thematic Explorations of Interracial Literature* (New York: Oxford University Press, 1997), 142–61. See also Jeffrey L. Sammons on Gerstäcker's absorption of this old wives' tale. *Ideology, Mimesis, Fantasy: Charles Sealsfield, Friedrich Gerstäcker, Karl May, and Other German Novelists of America* (Chapel Hill: University of North Carolina Press, 1998), 154. Gerstäcker is also mistaken about quadroons being free, and his own story about Hebe belies this.

4. In his discussion of Irish immigrants in New Orleans, Earl F. Niehaus notes contemporary opinion that the Irish were intemperate. The second wave of Irish immigrants were victims of famine in Ireland and lived in impoverished and squalid conditions in New Orleans. The majority succumbed to malaria, cholera, and yellow fever. "The New Irish, 1830–1862," in *A Refuge for All Ages: Immigration in Louisiana History,* ed. Carl A. Brasseaux, The Louisiana Purchase Bicentennial Series in Louisiana History, vol. 10 (Lafayette: Center for Louisiana Studies, 1996), 378–91.

5. In 1867 there was a protest about streetcar segregation in New Orleans. During the antebellum period the strictly segregated streetcars had been a source of inconvenience and humiliation for the blacks. After the Civil War most lines continued to be segregated, and the cars designated for blacks were clearly marked with stars. While blacks were excluded from two-thirds of the cars in service, impatient whites would ride the "star cars." There were a series of deliberate individual challenges to streetcar segregation in late April and early May. Finally, on the weekend of May 4–5, crowds of blacks jeered and threw projectiles at white streetcars, taking over one streetcar from its driver. Streetcar company officials continued to enforce the policy of passive resistance; drivers were to refuse to continue on their route when blacks boarded a streetcar designated for whites. By Sunday afternoon blacks overtook more streetcars, and Mayor Edward Heath feared rampant violence as gangs of armed blacks roamed the streets and gangs of whites sought them out for confrontation. Reluctant to call out the federal troops, the moderate Republican Heath went to Congo Square to address about five hundred protesters. Promising to reexamine streetcar policies immediately, he urged the protesters to return to their homes before a bloodbath ensued. In the previous year, on July 30, 1866, 34 blacks had been killed and 119 wounded when a race riot erupted over the attempt to reconvene the 1864 constitutional convention in order to disenfranchise former Confederates and to enfranchise blacks.

The protesters disbanded, and on the following morning Heath and Gen. Philip Sheridan, commander of the Fifth Military District, met with streetcar company officials. Fearing loss of property and business with continuing disorder, the officials reluctantly agreed to abandon the "star system." Chief of police Adams warned, "No passenger has the right to eject any other passenger, no matter what his color." With the exception of one incident, when a gang of armed whites ousted the black passengers from a mixed car, New Orleanians adjusted to streetcar desegregation. Roger A. Fischer, "A Pioneer Protest: The New Orleans Street-Car Controversy of

1867," *Journal of Negro History* 53, no. 3 (1968): 219–33; rpt. in *The African American Experience in Louisiana: Part B, from the Civil War to Jim Crow,* ed. Charles Vincent, vol. 11 of The Louisiana Purchase Bicentennial Series in Louisiana History (Lafayette: Center for Louisiana Studies, 2000), 328–38. For the constitutional convention riot, see James G. Hollandsworth Jr., *An Absolute Massacre: The New Orleans Race Riot of July 30, 1866* (Baton Rouge: Louisiana State University Press, 2001).

Selected Bibliography

Primary Sources

GERSTÄCKER'S WORKS

Gerstäcker, Friedrich. *Amerikanisches Sklavenleben.* Intro. H. M. Berlin: Hermann Hilger, 1930.

———. *Gesammelte Schriften von Friedrich Gerstäcker.* Jena: Costenoble, 1872.

———. *In the Arkansas Backwoods: Tales and Sketches by Friedrich Gerstäcker.* Ed. and trans. James William Miller. Columbia: University of Missouri Press, 1991.

———. *Mein guter Herr von Cotta: Friedrich Gerstäckers Briefwechsel mit dem Stuttgarter Cotta Verlag, Eine Briefedition.* Ed. and intro. Karl Jürgen Roth. Braunschweig: Friedrich Gerstäcker-Verlagsgesellschaft, 1992.

———. *Mein lieber Herzensfreund! Briefe an seinen Freund Adolph Hermann Schultz 1835–54. Briefe I.* Ed. Thomas Ostwald. Braunschweig: Friedrich-Gerstäcker-Gesellschaft, 1982.

———. Papers. Stadtarchiv Braunschweig, Germany.

———. *Reisen um die Welt: Ein Familienbuch.* 6 vols. Leipzig: Wigand, 1847. (Not based on own experiences.)

———. *Western Lands and Western Waters.* London: S. O. Beeton, 1864.

———. *Wild Sports in the Far West.* With notes and intro. Edna L. Steeves and Harrison R. Steeves. 1854. Rpt. Durham, N.C.: Duke University Press, 1968.

GERSTÄCKER'S TRANSLATIONS

Carlton, William. *Der schwarze Prophet: aus den Zeiten Irischer Hungersnoth.* 2 vols. Dresden: Arnold, 1848.

China, das Land und seine Bewohner. Ill. Allanson. 1848. Rpt. Braunschweig: Friedrich Gerstäcker Gesellschaft, 1985.

Hoffman, Charles Fenno. *Wilde Szenen im Wald und Prairie mit Skizzen amerikanischen Lebens.* 2. vols. Dresden: Arnold, 1845.

[Ann S. Stephens]. *Jonathan Slick oder Leben und Treiben der vornehmen Welt in New York.* 2. vols. Leipzig: Otto Wigand, 1845.

Melville, Hermann. *Omoo oder Abenteur im stillen Ocean mit einer Einleitung die sich den "Marquesas-Inseln" anschließt und Toby's glückliche Flucht enthält.* 2 pts. Leipzig: Gustav Mayer, 1847.

Rowcroft, Charles. *Die Abenteuer eines Auswanderers: Erzählungen aus den Colonien von Van Diemens-Land.* 3 vols. Leipzig: Otto Wigand, 1845.

Simms, W[illiam] G[ilmore]. *Wigwam und Hütte: Erzählungen aus dem Westen Amerika's.* Dresden: Arnold, 1846.

Smith, Mrs. Seba. *Der Indianer-Häuptling und die Gefangene des Westens.* 2 vols. Grimma: Druck und Verlag des Verlags-Comptoirs, 1847.

EDITION BY GERSTÄCKER

T. F. M. Richter's Reisen zu Wasser und zu Lande. Für die reifere Jugend zur Belehrung und zur Unterhaltung für Jedermann. 4th rev. ed. by Friedrich Gerstäcker. 2 vols. Leipzig: Otto Wigand, 1857.

OTHER WORKS

A Bibliography of Fiction by Louisianians and on Louisiana Subjects. Ed. Lizzie Carter McVoy and Ruth Bates Campbell. Baton Rouge: Louisiana State University Press, 1935.

Acts Passed at the Second Session of the Fifteenth Legislature of the State of Louisiana, 280–81. New Orleans: J. C. de St. Romes, 1842.

Butler, Louise. *Red Heart: A Story of West Feliciana.* Dedicated to Sir Arthur Conan Doyle. N.p.p., 1935.

Child, Lydia Maria. "The Quadroons" (1842). In *An Anthology of Interracial Literature: Black-White Contacts in the Old World and the New.* Ed. Werner Sollors. New York: New York University Press, 2004.

Computer Indexed Marriage Records: Pointe Coupee Parish, Louisiana, 1736–1832. Ed. Nicholas Russell Murray: Hammond, La.: Hunting for Bears, n.d.

Computer Indexed Marriage Records: West Feliciana Parish, 1791–1875. Ed. Nicholas Russell Murray. Hammond, La.: Hunting for Bears, n.d.

Conveyance Records, Point Coupée Parish Clerk of Court, New Roads, La.

1840 Louisiana State Wide Census Index. Ed. Frances T. Ingmire. Signal Mountain, Tenn.: Mountain Press, 1997.

The 1840 Census' of East and West Feliciana Parishes of Louisiana. Transcribed and with notes added by Claude B. Slaton. Shreveport, La.: J. and W. Enterprises, 1986.

Databases for the Study of Afro-Louisiana History and Genealogy, 1699–1860. Ed. Gwendolyn Midlo Hall. CD-ROM. Baton Rouge: Louisiana State University Press, 2000.

Denuzière, Maurice. *Bagatelle.* Trans. (of *Louisiane*) June P. Wilson. New York: William Morrow, 1978.

Feliciana Confederates: A Compilation of the Soldiers of East and West Feliciana Parishes, 1861–65 (Louisiana). Comp. Michael F. Howell. St Francisville, La., 1989.

Flaggenlexikon Web site. http://www.flaggenlexikon.de.

Flügel, J. G. "Pages of a Journal of a Voyage Down the Mississippi to New Orleans in 1817." Ed. Felix Flugel. *Louisiana Historical Quarterly* 7, no. 3 (1924): 415–40.

Gaines, Ernest J. *The Autobiography of Miss Jane Pittman.* 1971. Rpt. New York: Bantam, 1972.

———. *Bloodline.* 1963. Rpt. New York: Vintage Contemporaries, 1997.

Hesse-Wartegg, Ernst von. *Travels on the Lower Mississippi, 1879–1880.* Ed. and trans. Frederic Trautmann. Columbia: University of Missouri Press, 1990.

Iberville's Gulf Journals. Ed. and trans. Richebourg Gaillard McWilliams. Intro. Tennant S. McWilliams. University: University of Alabama Press, 1981.

In the Hands of Strangers: Readings on Foreign and Domestic Slave Trading and the Crisis of the Union. Ed. Robert Edgar Conrad. University Park: Pennsylvania State University Press, 2001.

Kennedy, John Pendelton. *Swallow Barn; or, A Sojourn in the Old Dominion.* Intro. Lucinda H. MacKethan. 1832; rev. 1851. Rpt. Baton Rouge: Louisiana State University Press, 1986.

Louisiana Census Records II, Iberville, Natchitoches, Pointe Coupee and Rapides Parishes, 1810 and 1820. Comp. Bruce L. Ardoin, with a foreword by James L. Forester. Baltimore: Genealogical Publishing Co., 1972.

Louisiana History: An Annotated Bibliography. Comp. Florence M. Jumonville. Westport, Conn.: Greenwood Press, 2002.

Louisiana Newspapers, 1794–1940. Louisiana Historical Survey Division of Community Service Programs, Work Projects Administration, October 1941.

Louisiana Sojourns: Travelers' Tales and Literary Journeys. Ed. Frank De Caro and Rosan Jordan. Baton Rouge: Louisiana State University Press, 1998.

Martin, Valerie. *Property.* New York: Nan A. Talese / Doubleday, 2003.

Morgan Family History—1871, 1938, folders 1–3. Louisiana Special Collections. Hill Memorial Library, Louisiana State University.

New Orleans Annual and Commercial Register for 1846. New Orleans: E. A. Michel, 1846.

New Orleans City Guide. The WPA Guide to New Orleans: The Federal Writers' Project Guide to New Orleans. Intro. Historic New Orleans Collection. 1938. Rpt. New York: Pantheon, 1983.

New Orleans Directory for 1841; Made by the United States Deputy Marshals. New Orleans: Michel and Co., 1840.

The Norton Anthology of African-American Literature. Ed. Henry Louis Gates Jr. New York: Norton, 1997.

Notre Dame Web site http://archives.nd.edu/calendar/cal1839.htm.

Passenger and Immigration Lists Bibliography, 1538–1900. Being a Guide to Published Lists of Arrivals in the United States and Canada. Ed. P. William Filby. Detroit: Gale Research, 1981.

Passenger Liners of the Western Ocean: A Record of the North Atlantic Steam and Motor Passenger Vessels from 1838 to the Present Day. 2d ed. Comp. Cdr. C. R. Vernon Gibbs. London: Staples, 1957.

Paul Wilhelm, duke of Württemberg. *Travels in North America, 1822–1824.* Trans. W. Robert Nitske. Ed. Savoie Lottinville. Norman: University of Oklahoma Press, 1973.

Pfeiffer, Ida. *A Lady's Second Journey Round the World: From London to the Cape of Good Hope, Borneo, Java, Sumatra, Celebes, Ceram, the Moluccas, etc., California, Panama, Peru, Ecuador, and the United States.* Trans. anon. New York: Harper and Brothers, 1856. Original: *Meine zweite Weltreise.* Vienna: Carl Gerold's Sohn, 1856.

Paxton, Joseph. "Letter from Dr. Joseph Paxton, of Hempstead County, to Hon. A. H. Sevier, Delegate to Congress from the Territory of Arkansas, in Relation to the Raft of Red River." February 16, 1829 (dated August 1, 1828). Photocopy. Louisiana Special Collections, Hill Memorial Library, Louisiana State University.

Reid, Capt. Mayne. *The Quadroon; or, A Lover's Adventures in Louisiana.* 3 vols. London: George W. Hyde, 1856.

Reise Sr. Hohheit des Herzogs Bernhard zu Sachsen-Weimar-Eisenach durch Nordamerika in den Jahren 1825 und 1826. Ed. Heinrich Luden. 2 vols. Weimar: Hoffmann, 1828.

Reizenstein, Ludwig Freiherr von. *Die Geheimnisse von New-Orleans.* Ed. Steven Rowan. Shreveport: Éditions Tintamarre, 2004.

———. *The Mysteries of New Orleans.* Ed. and trans. Steven Rowan. Baltimore: Johns Hopkins University Press, 2002.

Sealsfield, Charles. *Sämtliche Werke.* Vols. 11–15. Ed. Karl J. R. Arndt. Hildesheim: Olms, 1976–77.

———. *The United States of North America as They Are.* 1828. Rpt, with new intro. William Wright. New York: Johnson Reprint, 1970.

———. *Die Vereinigten Staaten von Nordamerika, nach ihrem politischen, religiösen und gesellschaftlichen Verhältnisse betrachtet. Mit einer reise durch den westlichen theil von Pennsylvanien, Ohio, Kentucky, Indiana, Illinois, Misuri* [sic], *Tennessee, das Gebiet Arkansas, Mississippi* [sic] *und Louisiana von C. Sidons* [pseud.]. 2 vols. Stuttgart: Cotta, 1827.

Seibert, Mary Frances. *Zulma.* Natchez: Natchez Printing and Stationary Co., 1897.

Ship Registers and Enrollments of New Orleans, Louisiana. Vols. 1–6. Prepared by the Survey of Federal Archives in Louisiana. Service Division, Work Project Administration, University, La. Hill Memorial Library, Louisiana State University, 1941.

Simms, William Gilmore. *The Wigwam and the Cabin, or Tales of the South.* 1845. Rpt. Charleston: Walker, Richards and Co., 1852.

Stowe, Harriet Beecher. *Uncle Tom's Cabin.* 1852. Rpt. New York: Modern Library, 1996.

Thorpe, Thomas Bangs. *The Master's House; or, Scenes Descriptive of Southern Life.* 3d ed. 1854. Rpt. New York: J. C. Derby, 1855.

———. *A New Collection of Thomas Bangs Thorpe's Sketches of the Old Southwest.* Ed. with critical intro. and textual commentary by David C. Estes. Baton Rouge: Louisiana State University Press, 1989.

Turnbull-Bowman-Lyons Family Papers. "Bibliographical/Historical Note." Louisiana Special Collections, Hill Memorial Library, Louisiana State University.

Way's Packet Directory, 1848–1983: Passenger Steamboats of the Mississippi River System since the Advent of Photography in Mid-Continent America. Comp. Frederick Way Jr. Athens: Ohio University Press, 1983.

Way's Steam Towboat Directory. Comp. Frederick Way Jr., with Joseph W. Rutter. Athens: Ohio University Press, 1990.

Secondary Sources

ON GERSTÄCKER AND GERMAN LITERATURE OF NORTH AMERICA

Arndt, Karl J. R. "Recent Sealsfield Discoveries." *Journal of English and Germanic Philology* 53, no. 2 (1954): 160–71.

Brenner, Peter J. *Reisen in die neue Welt: Die Erfahrung Nordamerikas in deutschen Reise- und Auswanderungsberichten des 19. Jahrhunderts.* Tübingen: Niemeyer, 1991.

Castle, Eduard. *Der große Unbekannte: Das Leben von Charles Sealsfield (Karl Postl).* Vienna: Manutius, 1952.

Der exotische Roman: Bürgerliche Gesellschaftsflucht und Gesellschaftskritik zwischen Romantik und Realismus. Intro. and commentary by Anselm Kiefer. Stuttgart: Klett, 1975.

Di Maio, Irene S. "Borders of Culture: The Native American in Friedrich Gerstäcker's North American Narratives." *Yearbook of German-American Studies* 28 (1993): 53–75.

———. "Unity and Diversity in Friedrich Gerstäcker's North American Novels of Immigration." In *German? American? Literature? New Directions in German-American Studies.* Ed. Winfried Fluck and Werner Sollors, 113–33. New York: Lang, 2002.

Durzak, Manfred. "Nach Amerika: Gerstäcker's Wiederlegung der Lenau-Legende." In *Amerika in der deutschen Literatur: Neue Welt-Nordamerika-USA.* Ed. Sigrid Bauschinger, Horst Denkler, and Wilfried Malsch. Stuttgart: Reclam, 1975.

Evans, Clarence. "Gerstäcker and the Konwells of White River Valley." *Arkansas Historical Quarterly* 10, no. 1 (1951): 1–36.

Friedrich Gerstäcker der Weitgereiste. Ein Lebensbild. Introduced to German youth by August Carl. Gera: Issleiss and Rietzschel, 1873.

Galerie der Welt: Ethnographisches Erzählen im 19. Jahrhundert. Ed. Anselm Maler in collaboration with Sabine Scholt. Stuttgart: Belser, 1988.

German? American? Literature? New Directions in German-American Studies. Ed. Winfried Fluck and Werner Sollors. New York: Lang, 2002.

Germans in America: Aspects of German-American Literary Relations in the Nineteenth Century. Ed. E. Allen McCormick. New York: Brooklyn College Press, 1983.

Gerstäcker-Verzeichnis: Erstausgaben, Gesammelte Werke und Sekundärliteratur mit Nachweis im Stadtarchiv, in der Stadtbibliothek Braunschweig, und in der Friedrich-Gerstäcker-gesellschaft-Braunschweig. Ed. Manfred Garzmann, Thomas Ostwald, and Wolf-Dieter Schuegraf. Braunschweig: n.p., 1986.

Herminghouse, Patricia. "The German Secrets of New Orleans." *German Studies Review* 27, no. 1 (2004): 1–16.

Kriegleder, Wynfrid. *Vorwärts in die Vergangenheit: Das Bild der USA im deutschsprachigen Roman von 1776 bis 1845.* Tübingen: Stauffenburg, 1999.

Landa, Bjarne Emil. "The American Scene in Friedrich Gerstäcker's Works of Fiction." Ph.D. diss., University of Minnesota, 1952.

Mikoletzky, Juliane. *Die deutsche Amerika-Auswanderung des 19. Jahrhunderts in der zeit-genössischen fiktionalen Literatur.* Tübingen: Niemeyer, 1988.

Olson, May E. "Louisiana in Imaginative German Literature." Master's thesis, Louisiana State University, 1937.

Ostwald, Thomas. *Friedrich Gerstäcker: Leben und Werk.* Bibliographical appendix by Armin Stöckert. Braunschweig: A. Graff, 1977.

————. "Friedrich Gerstäckers enthnographische Realien." *Galerie der Welt: Ethnograph-isches Erzählen im 19. Jahrhundert.* Ed. Anselm Maler in collaboration with Sabine Scholt.

Pagni, Andrea. "Friedrich Gerstäckers 'Reisen' zwischen Ferne und Heimat: Überlegungen zum Reisebericht im literarischen Feld Deutschlands um 1850." *Studien zur Literatur des Frührealismus.* Ed. Günter Blamberger, Manfred Engel, and Monika Ritzer. Frank-furt: Lang, 1991.

Rosenblatt, Rudolf. "Friedrich Gerstäcker und die amerikanische Kultur." *Friedrich Ger-stäcker und seine Zeit.* 7:3–17. *Mitteilungen der Friedrich-Gerstäcker Gesellschaft.* Braun-schweig, 1981.

Roth, Karl Jürgen. *Die außereuropäische Welt in deutschsprachigen Familienzeitschriften vor der Reichsgründung.* St. Katharinen: Scripta-Mercaturae, 1996.

————. *Die Darstellung der deutschen Auswanderung in den Schriften Friedrich Gerstäck-ers.* Braunschweig: Friedrich-Gerstäcker-Gesellschaft, 1989.

Sammons, Jeffrey L. "Friedrich Gerstäcker: American Realities through German Eyes." In *Germans in America: Aspects of German-American Literary Relations in the Nineteenth Century.* Ed. E. Allen McCormick, 75–90. New York: Brooklyn College Press, 1983.

————. "Friedrich Gerstäcker (1816–1872)." *Dictionary of Literary Biography.* Vol. 129: *Nineteenth-Century German Writers, 1841–1900.* Ed. James Hardin and Siegfried Mews, 110–19. Detroit: Gale Research, 1993.

————. "Friedrich Gerstäcker: German Realist of the American West." *Yale University Li-brary Gazette* 1, no. 2 (1996): 39–46.

————. *Ideology, Mimesis, Fantasy: Charles Sealsfield, Friedrich Gerstäcker, Karl May, and Other German Novelists of America.* Chapel Hill: University of North Carolina Press, 1998.

————. "Nineteenth-Century German Representations of Indians from Experience." In *Germans and Indians: Fantasies, Encounters, Projections.* Ed. Colin G. Calloway, Gerd Gemünden, and Susanne Zantop, 185–93. Lincoln: University of Nebraska Press, 2002.

————. "The Shape of Freedom in Charles Sealsfield's Plantation Novels." *Schatzkammer der deutschen Sprache, Dichtung und Geschichte* 21, nos. 1–2 (1995): 1–20.

Schuchalter, Jerry. *Narratives of America and the Frontier in Nineteenth-Century German Literature.* New York: Lang, 2000.

Schutz, H. "Friedrich Gerstäcker's Image of the German Immigrant in America." In *Deutsch-lands literarisches Amerikabild.* Ed. Alexander Ritter, 319–37. Hildesheim: Georg Olms, 1977.

Seyfarth, Erich. *Friedrich Gerstäcker: ein Beitrag zur Geschichte des exotischen Romans in Deutschland.* Freiburg im Breisgau: Jos. Waibel, 1930.

Van de Luyster, Nelson. "Emigration to America as Reflected in the German Novel of the Nineteenth Century: Especially in the Fiction of Bitzius, Laube, Gutzkow, Auerbach, Freytag, Storm, Keller, Spielhagen, Heyse, Raabe." Ph.D. diss., University of North Carolina, Chapel Hill, 1941.

Weber, Paul C. *America in Imaginative German Literature in the First Half of the Nineteenth Century.* New York: Columbia University Press, 1926.

Zangerl, Anton. *Friedrich Gerstäcker (1816–1872), Romane und Erzählungen: Struktur und Gehalt.* Bern: Lang, 1999.

ON THE HISTORY AND LITERATURE
OF LOUISIANA AND NORTH AMERICA

Advice among Masters: The Ideal in Slave Management in the Old South. Ed. James O. Breeden. Westport, Conn.: Greenwood, 1980.

Albrecht, Albert C. "The Origin and Early Settlement of Baton Rouge, Louisiana." *Louisiana Historical Quarterly* 28, no. 1 (1945): 5–68.

Ambrose, Stephen E. and Douglas G. Brinkley. *The Mississippi and the Making of a Nation: From the Louisiana Purchase to Today.* Washington, D.C.: National Geographic Society, 2002.

Ashkenazi, Elliot. *The Business of Jews in Louisiana, 1840–1875.* Tuscaloosa: University of Alabama Press, 1988.

Bagur, Jacques D. *A History of Navigation on Cypress Bayou and the Lakes.* Denton: University of North Texas Press, 2001.

Baird, W. David. *The Quapaw Indians: A History of the Downstream People.* Norman: Oklahoma University Press, 1980.

Bargainnier, Earl F. "The Myth of Moonlight and Magnolias." *Louisiana Studies* 15, no. 1 (1976): 5–20.

Baudier, Roger. *The Catholic Church in Louisiana.* New Orleans: [A. W. Hyatt Stationery Mfg. Co.], 1939.

Bell, Caryn Cossé. "'*Une Chimère*': The Freedmen's Bureau in Creole New Orleans." In *The Freedmen's Bureau and Reconstruction: Reconsiderations.* Ed. Paula A. Cimbala and Randall M. Miller. New York: Fordham University Press, 1999.

Berzon, Judith R. *Neither Black nor White: The Mulatto Character in American Fiction.* New York: New York University Press, 1978.

Billings, Warren M. "From This Seed: The Constitution of 1812." In *In Search of Fundamental Law: Louisiana's Constitutions, 1812–1974.* Ed. Warren M. Billings and Edward F. Haas, 6–20. Lafayette: Center for Louisiana Studies, 1993.

Blassingame, John W. *Black New Orleans: 1860–1880.* Chicago: University of Chicago Press, 1973.

———. *The Slave Community: Plantation Life in the Antebellum South.* New York: Oxford University Press, 1972.

Boulle, Pierre H. "Some Eighteenth-Century French Views on Louisiana." In *French*

Louisiana: A Commemoration of the French Revolution Bicentennial. Ed. Robert B. Holtman and Glenn R. Conrad. Lafayette: Center for Louisiana Studies, 1989.

Brasseaux, Carl A. *French, Cajun, Creole, Houma: A Primer on Francophone Louisiana.* Baton Rouge: Louisiana State University Press, 2005.

Brasseaux, Carl A., and Keith P. Fontenot. *Steamboats on Louisiana's Bayous: A History and Directory.* Baton Rouge: Louisiana State University Press, 2004.

Briede, Kathryn C. "A History of the City of Lafayette." *Louisiana Historical Quarterly* 20, no. 4 (1937): 894–964.

Brink, Florence Roos. "Literary Travellers in Louisiana between 1803 and 1860." *Louisiana Historical Quarterly* 31, no. 2 (1948): 394–424.

Butler, Louise. "West Feliciana: A Glimpse of Its History." *Louisiana Historical Quarterly* 7, no. 1 (1924): 90–120.

The Cambridge History of the Native Peoples of the Americas. Vol. 1, pt. 2: *North America.* Ed. Bruce G. Trigger and Wilcomb E. Washburn. Cambridge: Cambridge University Press, 1996.

Campanella, Richard. *Time and Place in New Orleans: Past Geographies in the Present Day.* Gretna, La.: Pelican, 2002.

Campbell, Randolph P. *An Empire for Slavery: The Peculiar Institution in Texas, 1821–1865.* Baton Rouge: Louisiana State University Press, 1989.

Carlton, Mark T. *River Capital: An Illustrated History of Baton Rouge.* Woodland Hills, Calif.: Windsor, 1981.

Carrigan, Jo Ann. *The Saffron Scourge: A History of Yellow Fever in Louisiana, 1796–1905.* Lafayette: Center for Louisiana Studies, 1994.

Castellanos, Henry C. *New Orleans as It Was.* 1895. Rpt. Baton Rouge: Louisiana State University Press, 1978.

Clark, Robert T., Jr. "The German Liberals in New Orleans (1840–1860)." *Louisiana Historical Quarterly* 20, no. 1 (1937): 137–51.

———. "Reconstruction and the New Orleans German Colony." *Louisiana Historical Quarterly* 23, no. 2 (1940): 897–972.

Comeau, Brother Alfonso, C.S.C. "A Study of the Trustee Problem in the St. Louis Cathedral Church of New Orleans, Louisiana. 1842–1844." *Louisiana Historical Quarterly* 31, no. 4 (1948): 897–972.

A Companion to the Regional Literatures of America. Ed. Charles L. Crow. Malden, Mass.: Blackwell, 2003.

A Concise Dictionary of Indian Tribes of North America. Ed. Barbara A. Leitch. Algonac, Mich.: Reference Publications, 1979.

Conway, Alan. "New Orleans as a Port of Immigration, 1820–1860." *Louisiana Studies* 1, no. 2 (1962): 1–22.

Costello, Brian J. *The Catholic Church in Pointe Coupee.* Marksville: Randy DeCuir, 1996.

———. *Creole Pointe Coupée: A Sociological Analysis.* New Roads, La.: John and Noelie Laurent Ewing, 2002.

————. *From Porche to Labatut: Two Centuries on the Pointe Coupee Coast.* Baton Rouge: Franklin Press, 2002.

————. *A History of Pointe Coupee Parish, Louisiana.* New Roads, La.: Brian J. Costello, 1999.

————. *The Life, Family, and Legacy of Julien Poydras.* [La.: Brian J. Costello through John and Noelie Laurent Ewing,] 2001.

————. *New Roads: A Community in Retrospect.* New Roads, La.: Brian J. Costello through Cajun Electric, 1993.

————. *Quintessential Creoles. The Tounier Family of Pointe Coupee.* New Roads, La.: Brian J. Costello through John and Noelie Laurent Ewing, 2003.

Cowdry, Albert C. "Land's End." In *Agriculture and Economic Development in Louisiana.* Ed. Thomas A. Becnel. Louisiana Purchase Bicentennial Series in Louisiana History. Lafayette: Center for Louisiana Studies, 1976.

Cox, Rosemary D. "The Old Southwest: Humor, Tall Tales, and the Grotesque." In *A Companion to the Regional Literature of the Americas.* Ed. Charles L. Crow, 247–65. Malden, Mass.: Blackwell, 2003.

Creole New Orleans: Race and Americanization. Ed. Arnold R. Hirsch and Joseph Logsdon. Baton Rouge: Louisiana State University Press, 1992.

Creolization in the Americas. Intro. David Buisseret. Ed. David Buisseret and Steven G. Reinhardt. College Station: Texas A&M University Press, 2000.

Cummins, Light Townsend. "An Enduring Community: Anglo-American Settlers at Colonial Natchez and in the Felicianas, 1774–1810." *Journal of Mississippi History* 55 (1993): 133–54.

Current-Garcia, Eugene. "Thomas Bangs Thorpe and the Literature of the Ante-Bellum Southwestern Frontier." *Louisiana Historical Quarterly* 39, no. 2 (1956): 199–222.

Curry, Lamar Clayton. "Economic Implications of the Red River Raft." Master's thesis, Louisiana State University Press, 1939.

Curtis, Nathaniel Cortlandt. *New Orleans: Its Old Houses, Shops and Public Buildings.* Philadelphia: J. B. Lippincott, 1933.

Daggett, Harriet Spiller. *The Community Property System of Louisiana.* 1931. Rpt. with addenda. Baton Rouge: Louisiana State University Press, 1945.

Davis, Edwin Adams. *Plantation Life in the Florida Parishes of Louisiana, 1836–1846: As Reflected in the Diary of Bennet H. Barrow.* New York: AMS Press, 1967.

————. *Louisiana: A Narrative History.* 3d ed. 1961. Rpt. Baton Rouge: Claitor's, 1971.

A Dictionary of Louisiana Biography. Ed. Glenn R. Conrad. 2 vols. Lafayette: Louisiana Historical Association, 1988.

Disheroon-Green, Suzanne. "Romanticizing a Different Lost Cause: Regional Identities in Louisiana and the Bayou Country." In *A Companion to the Regional Literatures of America.* Ed. Charles L. Crow, 306–23. Malden, Mass.: Blackwell, 2003.

Dondore, Dorothy Anne. *The Prairie and the Making of Middle America: Four Centuries of Description.* Cedar Rapids, Iowa: Torch, 1926.

Donovan, Frank. *River Boats of America.* New York: Thomas Y. Crowell, 1966.

Dormon, James H. "The Persistent Specter: Slave Rebellions in Territorial Louisiana." In *Carnivals and Conflicts: A Louisiana History Reader.* Ed. Samuel C. Hyde Jr., C. Howard Nichols, and Charles N. Elliot. Fort Worth: Harcourt College, 2000. From *Louisiana History* 18, no. 4 (1997): 389–404.

Dorsey, Florence L. *Master of the Mississippi: Henry Shreve and the Conquest of the Mississippi.* Boston: Houghton Mifflin, 1941.

Du Bois, W. E. B. *The Souls of Black Folk.* Ed. Henry Louis Gates Jr. and Terri Hume Oliver. 1913. Rpt. New York: Norton, 1999.

Dyer, Grace Elizabeth. "The Removal of the Great Raft in Red River." Master's thesis, Louisiana State University, 1948.

Erkkila, Betsy. *Mixed Bloods and Other Crosses. Rethinking American Literature from the Revolution to the Culture Wars.* Philadelphia: University of Pennsylvania Press, 2005.

The Encyclopedia of Southern History. Ed. David C. Roller and Robert W. Twyman. Baton Rouge: Louisiana State University Press, 1979.

Faye, Stanley. "Privateersmen of the Gulf and Their Prizes." *Louisiana Historical Quarterly* 22, no. 4 (1939): 1012–94.

———. "Types of Privateer Vessels, Their Armament and Flags in the Gulf of Mexico. *Louisiana Historical Quarterly* 23, no. 1 (1940): 118–30.

Fernandez, Mark F. *From Chaos to Continuity: The Evolution of Louisiana's Judicial System, 1712–1862.* Baton Rouge: Louisiana State University Press, 2001.

Fischer, Roger A. "A Pioneer Protest: The New Orleans Street-Car Controversy of 1867." *Journal of Negro History* 53, no. 3 (1968): 219–33. Rpt. in *The African American Experience in Louisiana: Part B, From the Civil War to Jim Crow.* Ed. Charles Vincent, 328–38. Vol. 11 of the Louisiana Purchase Bicentennial Series in Louisiana History. Lafayette: Center for Louisiana Studies, 2000.

Follett, Richard. *The Sugar Masters: Planters and Slaves in Louisiana's Cane World, 1820–1860.* Baton Rouge: Louisiana State University Press, 2005.

Frederickson, George M. *The Black Image in the White Mind: The Debate on Afro-American Character and Destiny, 1817–1914.* New York: Harper and Row, 1971.

The Freedmen's Bureau and Reconstruction: Reconsiderations. Ed. Paula A. Cimbala and Randall M. Miller. New York: Fordham University Press, 1999.

Gaines, Francis Pendleton. *The Southern Plantation: A Study in the Development and the Accuracy of a Tradition.* Gloucester, Mass.: Peter Smith, 1962.

Gardner, Jared. *Master Plots: Race and the Founding of American Literature, 1787–1845.* Baltimore: Johns Hopkins University Press, 1998.

Gardner, Sarah E. "The Plantation School: Dissenters and Countermyths." In *A Companion to the Regional Literatures of America.* Ed. Charles L. Crow, 266–87. Malden, Mass.: Blackwell, 2003.

Gayarré, Charles. *History of Louisiana.* With a biography of the author by Grace King and bibliography by W. M. Beer. 4th ed. 4 vols. 1903. Rpt. New Orleans: Pelican, 1965.

Genovese, Eugene D. *Roll, Jordan, Roll: The World the Slaves Made.* 1972. Rpt. New York: Vintage, 1976.

Goins, Charles Robert, and Jon Michael Caldwell. *Historical Atlas of Louisiana.* Norman: University of Oklahoma Press, 1995.

Graves, Daniel. *Profiles of Natchitoches History.* Natchitoches, La.: Museum of Natchitoches and Its Supporters, 1996.

Guardia, J[ohn]. E[dward]. "Some Results of the Log Jams in the Red River." *Bulletin of the Geographical Society of Philadelphia* 31, no. 3 (1933): 103–14.

———. "Successive Human Adjustments to Raft Conditions in the Lower Red River Valley." Master's thesis, University of Chicago, 1927.

Hall, Gwendolyn Midlo. *Africans in Colonial Louisiana: The Development of Afro-Creole Culture in the Eighteenth Century.* Baton Rouge: Louisiana State University Press, 1992.

Hardin, J. Fair. "An Outline of Shreveport and Caddo Parish History." *Louisiana Historical Quarterly* 18, no. 4 (1935): 759–871.

Hearn, Chester G. *When the Devil Came Down to Dixie: Ben Butler in New Orleans.* Baton Rouge: Louisiana State University Press, 1997.

Henrici, Holice H. *Shreveport: The Beginnings.* Lafayette: Center for Louisiana Studies, University of Southwestern Louisiana, 1985.

A History of Pointe Coupee Parish and Its Families. Ed. Judy Riffel. Baton Rouge: Le Comité des Archives de la Louisiane, 1983.

Hollandsworth, James G. *An Absolute Massacre: The New Orleans Race Riot of July 30, 1866.* Baton Rouge: Louisiana State University Press, 2001.

Holmes, Jack D. L. "The Abortive Slave Revolt at Pointe Coupée, Louisiana, 1795." *Louisiana History* 11, no. 1 (1970): 341–62.

Hunter, Louis C., with the assistance of Beatrice Johnes Hunter. *Steamboats on the Western Rivers.* Cambridge, Mass.: Harvard University Press, 1949.

Hyde, Samuel C., Jr. *Pistols and Politics: The Dilemma of Democracy in Louisiana's Florida Parishes, 1810–1899.* Baton Rouge: Louisiana State University Press, 1996.

Images of America: Travelers from Abroad in the New World. Comp. Robert B. Downs. Urbana: University of Illinois Press, 1987.

Ingersoll, Thomas N. "The Slave Trade and the Ethnic Diversity of Louisiana's Slave Community." *Louisiana History* 37, no. 3 (1996): 133–61.

John, Juliet. *Dickens's Villains: Melodrama, Character, Popular Culture.* Oxford: Oxford University Press, 2001.

Johnson, Walter. *Soul by Soul: Life Inside the Antebellum Slave Market.* Cambridge, Mass.: Harvard University Press, 1999.

Jumonville, Florence M. "'The People's Friend—The Tyrant's Foe': Law-Related New Orleans Imprints, 1803–1860." In *A Law unto Itself? Essays in the New Louisiana Legal History.* Ed. Warren M. Billings and Mark F. Fernandez. Baton Rouge: Louisiana State University Press, 2001.

King, Grace. *New Orleans: The Place and the People.* New York: Macmillan, 1915.

Kniffen, Fred B., Hiram F. Gregory, and George A. Stokes. *Historic Indian Tribes of Louisiana: From 1542 to the Present.* Baton Rouge: Louisiana State University Press, 1987.

Kniffen, Fred B. and Sam Bowers Hilliard. *Louisiana: Its Land and People.* Rev. ed. 1968. Rpt. Baton Rouge: Louisiana State University Press, 1988.

Larousse Encyclopedia of Music. Ed. Geoffrey Hindley. Intro. Anthony Hopkins. Secaucus, N.J.: Chartwell, 1971.

Leeming, David, and Jake Page. *The Mythology of Native North America.* Norman: University of Oklahoma Press, 1998.

Le Page du Pratz, Antoine Simon. *The History of Louisiana, or of the Western Parts of Virginia and Carolina.* Trans. from the French. Ed. Joseph G. Tregle Jr. 1774. Rpt. Baton Rouge: Louisiana State University Press, 1975.

Littlefield, Daniel C. "Slavery in French Louisiana: From Gallic Colony to American Territory." In *Creoles and Cajuns: French Louisiana—La Louisiane Française,* 91–114. Frankfurt am Main: Lang, 1998.

Logsdon, Joseph. "Freshly Brewed: New Orleans' Coffee Legacy." *Louisiana Cultural Vistas* 8, no. 1 (spring 1997): 4–6.

Louisiana: A Guide to the State. Comp. Workers of the Writers' Program of the Works Projects Administration in the State of Louisiana. New York: Hastings House, 1940.

Louisiana History: An Annotated Bibliography. Comp. Florence M. Jumonville. Westport, Conn.: Greenwood, 2002.

The Louisiana Newspaper Project Printout, October 1991. Baton Rouge: LSU Libraries, 1992.

Louisiana's German Heritage: Louis Voss' Introductory History. Ed. Don Heinrich Tolzmann. Bowie, Md.: Heritage Books, 1994.

Lowery, George H., Jr. *Louisiana Birds.* 3d. ed. Published for the Louisiana Wild Life and Fisheries Commission. [Baton Rouge]: Louisiana State University Press, 1974.

Lüsebrink, Hans-Jürgen. "Prise de possession littéraire et nostalgie exotique—la Louisiane dans la littérature française (17e-20e siècle)." In *Creoles and Cajuns: French Louisiana—La Louisiane française,* 267–85. Ed. Wolfgang Binder. Frankfurt am Main: Lang, 1998.

Malone, Ann Patton. *Sweet Chariot: Slave Family and Household Structure in Nineteenth-Century Louisiana.* Chapel Hill: University of North Carolina Press, 1992.

Martin, Joel W. *Sacred Revolt: The Muskogees' Struggle for a New World.* Boston: Beacon, 1991.

Martinez, Raymond J. *The Story of Spanish Moss: What It Is and How It Grows.* New Orleans: Hope, [1969].

McCall, Edith. *Conquering the Rivers: Henry Miller Shreve and the Navigation of America's Inland Waterways.* Baton Rouge: Louisiana State University Press, 1984.

McGinty, Garnie William. *A History of Louisiana.* 4th ed. New York: Exposition, 1951.

McKinney, Louise. "House of Brews: New Orleans' Coffee Culture." *New Orleans* 29, no. 12 (1995): 69–72.

McLoughlin, William G. *The Cherokee Ghost Dance: Essays on the Southeastern Indians, 1789–1861.* Mercer, Ga.: Mercer University Press, 1984.

Melodrama: The Cultural Emergence of a Genre. Ed. Michael Hays and Anastasia Nikolopoulo. New York: St. Martin's, 1999.

Merrill, Ellen C. *Germans of Louisiana.* Foreword by Don Heinrich Tolzmann. Gretna, La.: Pelican, 2005.

Meyers, Rose. *A History of Baton Rouge, 1699–1812.* Baton Rouge: Louisiana State University Press, 1976.

Moltmann, Günter. "The Pattern of German Emigration to the United States in the Nineteenth Century." In *Immigration, Language, Ethnicity.* Ed. Frank Trommler and Joseph McVeigh, 14–24. Philadelphia: University of Pennsylvania Press, 1985. Vol. 1 of *America and the Germans: An Assessment of a Three-Hundred-Year History.* 2 vols.

Müller, Werner. *Die Religionen der Waldlandindianer Nordamerikas.* Berlin: Dietrich Reimer, 1956.

Multilingual America: Transnationalism, Ethnicity, and the Languages of American Literature. Ed. Werner Sollors. New York: New York University Press, 1988.

Natchitoches and Louisiana's Timeless Cane River. Baton Rouge: Louisiana State University Press, 2002.

Nau, John F. *The German People of New Orleans.* Leiden: Brill, 1958.

———. "The German People of New Orleans, 1850–1900." *Louisiana Historical Quarterly* 54 (1991): 30–45.

Nelson, Dana D. *The Word in Black and White: Reading "Race" in American Literature, 1638–1867.* New York: Oxford University Press, 1992.

Niehaus, Earl F. "The New Irish, 1830–1862." In *A Refuge for All Ages: Immigration in Louisiana History.* Ed. Carl A. Brasseaux, 378–91. Vol. 10 of the Louisiana Purchase Bicentennial Series in Louisiana History. Lafayette: Center for Louisiana Studies.

Odenwald, Neil, and James Turner. *Identification, Selection, and Use of Southern Plants for Landscape Design.* 3d ed. Baton Rouge: Claitor's, 1996.

Oldstone, Michael B. A. *Viruses, Plagues, and History.* New York: Oxford University Press, 1998.

Page, Kathryn. "Defiant Women and the Supreme Court of Louisiana in the Nineteenth Century." In *A Law unto Itself? Essays in the New Louisiana Legal History.* Ed. Warren M. Billings and Mark F. Fernandez, 178–90. Baton Rouge: Louisiana State University Press, 2001.

Portré-Bobinski, Germaine, and Clara Mildred Smith. *Natchitoches: The Up-to-Date Oldest Town in Louisiana.* New Orleans: Dameron-Pierson, 1936.

Raboteau, Albert J. *Slave Religion: The "Invisible Institution" in the Antebellum South.* 1978. Rpt. Oxford: Oxford University Press, 1980.

Raimon, Eva Allegra. *The Tragic "Mulatta" Revisited: Race and Nationalism in Nineteenth-Century Antislavery Fiction.* New Brunswick, N.J.: Rutgers University Press, 2004.

The Random House Dictionary of the English Language. New York: Random House, 1967.

A Refuge for All Ages: Immigration in Louisiana History. Ed. Carl A. Brasseaux. Vol. 10 of the Louisiana Purchase Bicentennial Series in Louisiana History. Lafayette: Center for Louisiana Studies, 1996.

Reichardt, Ulrich. *Alterität und Geschichte: Funktionen der Sklavereidarstellung im amerikanischen Roman.* Heidelberg: C. Winter, 2001.

Richard, C. E. *Louisiana: An Illustrated History.* Baton Rouge: Foundation for Excellence in Louisiana Public Broadcasting, 2003.

Rickels, Milton. *Thomas Bangs Thorpe. Humorist of the Old Southwest.* Baton Rouge: Louisiana State University Press, 1962.

———. "Thomas Bangs Thorpe in the Felicianas, 1836–1842." *Louisiana Historical Quarterly* 39 (1956): 169–97.

Ripley, C. Peter. *Slaves and Freedmen in Civil War Louisiana.* Baton Rouge: Louisiana State University Press, 1976.

The Rivers and Bayous of Louisiana. Ed. Edwin Adams Davis. Baton Rouge: Louisiana Education Association, 1968.

Rodrigue, John C. "The Freedmen's Bureau and Wage Labor in the Louisiana Sugar Region." In *The Freedmen's Bureau and Reconstruction: Reconsiderations.* Ed. Paula A. Cimbala and Randall M. Miller. New York: Fordham University Press, 1999.

Rodriguez, Junius Peter. "Always 'En Garde': The Effects of Slave Insurrection up the Louisiana Mentality, 1811–1815." *Louisiana History* 33, no. 4 (1992): 399–416.

———. "Ripe for Revolt: Louisiana and the Tradition of Slave Insurrection, 1803–1865." Ph.D. diss., Auburn University, 1992.

Rosenberg, Charles E. *The Cholera Years: The United States in 1832, 1849, and 1866.* With a new afterword. 1962. Rpt. Chicago: University of Chicago Press, 1987.

Rousey, Dennis C. "'Hibernian Leatherheads': Irish Cops in New Orleans, 1830–1880." *Journal of Urban History* 10, no. 1 (1983): 61–84.

Roussève, Charles Barthelemy. *The Negro in Louisiana: Aspects of His History and His Literature.* New Orleans: Xavier University Press, 1937.

Sandford, J. I. *Beautiful Pointe Coupee and Her Prominent Citizens.* New Orleans: Press of the American Printing Co., 1906.

Saxon, Lyle. *Fabulous New Orleans.* 1928. Rpt. New Orleans: Robert L. Crager, 1947.

Scarborough, William Kauffman. *Masters of the Big House: Elite Slaveholders of the Mid-Nineteenth-Century South.* Baton Rouge: Louisiana State University Press, 2003.

Schafer, Judith K. "Reform or Experiment? The Louisiana Constitution of 1845." In *In Search of Fundamental Law: Louisiana's Constitutions, 1812–1974.* Ed. Warren M. Billings and Edward F. Haas. Lafayette: Center for Louisiana Studies, 1993.

———. *Slavery, the Civil Law, and the Supreme Court of Louisiana.* Baton Rouge: Louisiana State University Press, 1994.

Seale, Richard. "The Town of Natchitoches." In *Natchitoches and Louisiana's Timeless Cane River.* Baton Rouge: Louisiana State University Press, 2002.

Seebold, Herman de Bachelle. *Old Louisiana Plantation Homes.* 2 vols. Gretna, La.: Pelican, 1971.

Smith, James L. *Melodrama*. London: Methuen, 1973.

Smith, Page. *The Nation Comes of Age: A People's History of the Ante-Bellum Years*. Vol. 4. New York: Viking Penguin, 1981.

Sollors, Werner. *Neither Black nor White yet Both: Thematic Explorations of Interracial Literature*. New York: Oxford University Press, 1997.

Sterkx, H. E. *The Free Negro in Ante-Bellum Louisiana*. Rutherford, N.J.: Fairleigh Dickinson University Press, 1972.

Sternberg, Hildgard O'Reilly. "The Pointe Coupée Cut-Off in Historical Writings." *Louisiana Historical Quarterly* 28, no. 1 (1845): 69–84.

Sternberg, Mary Ann. *Along the River Road: Past and Present on Louisiana's Historic Byway*. Baton Rouge: Louisiana State University Press, 1996.

Sundquist, Eric J. *To Wake the Nations: Race in the Making of American Literature*. Cambridge, Mass.: Belknap Press of Harvard University Press, 1993.

Tadman, Michael. *Speculators and Slaves: Masters, Traders, and Slaves in the Old South*. Madison: University of Wisconsin Press, 1989.

Taylor, Joe Gray. *Eating, Drinking, and Visiting in the South: An Informal History*. Baton Rouge: Louisiana State University Press, 1982.

———. "The Foreign Slave Trade in Louisiana after 1808." *Louisiana History* 1, no. 1 (1960): 36–43.

———. *Louisiana: A History*. New York: Norton, 1976.

———. *Louisiana Reconstructed, 1863–1877*. Baton Rouge: Louisiana State University Press, 1974.

———. *Negro Slavery in Louisiana*. Baton Rouge: Louisiana Historical Association, 1963.

Thornton, Russell. "The Demography of the Trail of Tears Period: A New Estimate of Cherokee Population Losses." In *Cherokee Removal: Before and After*. Ed. William L. Anderson. Athens: Georgia University Press, 1991.

Tourgée, Albion Winegar. *The Original Empire*. Intro. and note by Otto H. Olsen. 1880. Rpt. Baton Rouge: Louisiana State University Press, 1989.

Tregle, Joseph G., Jr. "Creoles and Americans." In *Creole New Orleans: Race and Americanization*. Ed. Arnold R. Hirsch and Joseph Logsdon. Baton Rouge: Louisiana State University Press, 1992.

———. "Early New Orleans Society: A Reappraisal." *Journal of Southern History* 18, no. 1 (1952): 20–36.

———. *Louisiana in the Age of Jackson: A Clash of Cultures and Personalities*. Baton Rouge: Louisiana State University Press, 1999.

———. "On That Word 'Creole' Again: A Note." *Louisiana History* 23, no. 2 (1982): 193–98.

Tunnell, Ted. *Crucible of Reconstruction: War, Radicalism, and Race in Louisiana, 1862–1877*. Baton Rouge: Louisiana State University Press, 1984.

Turner, Lorenzo Dow. *Anti-Slavery Sentiment in American Literature prior to 1865*. Washington, D.C.: Association for the Study of Negro Life and History, 1929.

Usner, Daniel H., Jr. *America Indians in the Lower Mississippi Valley: Social and Economic Histories*. Lincoln: University of Nebraska Press, 1998.

Van Deburg, William L. *The Slave Drivers: Black Agricultural Labor Supervisors in the Antebellum South.* Westport, Conn.: Greenwood, 1979.

Vincent, Charles. *Black Legislators in Louisiana during Reconstruction.* Baton Rouge: Louisiana State University Press, 1976.

Weil, Tom. *The Mississippi River: Nature, Culture and Travel Sites along the "Mighty Mississip."* New York: Hippocrene Books, 1992.

Wilds, John, Charles L. Dufour, and Walter G. Cowan. *Louisiana, Yesterday and Today: A Historical Guide to the State.* Baton Rouge: Louisiana State University Press, 1996.

Wilkie, Laurie. *Creating Freedom: Material Culture and African-American Identity at Oakley Plantation, Louisiana, 1840–1950.* Baton Rouge: Louisiana State University Press, 2000.

Wülfing, Wulf. "Reiseliteratur." In *Vormärz: Biedermeier, Junges Deutschland, Demokraten 1815–1848.* Vol. 6 of *Deutsche Literatur: Eine Sozialgeschichte.* Ed. Horst Albert Glaser, 180–94. Hamburg: Rowohlt, 1980.

———. "Reiseliteratur und Realitäten im Vormärz: Vorüberlegungen zu Schemata und Wirklichkeitsfindung im frühen 19. Jahrhundert." In *Reise und soziale Realität am Ende des 18. Jahrhunderts.* Ed. Wolfgang Griep and Hans-Wolf Jäger. Heidelberg: Winter, 1983.